Physics of Computer
Memory Devices

A

Physics of Computer Memory Devices

S. MIDDELHOEK

Technische Hogeschool Delft,
Afdeling der Electrotechniek,
Delft, The Netherlands

P. K. GEORGE

Rockwell International,
Electronics Research Division,
Anaheim, California, U.S.A.

P. DEKKER

Technische Hogeschool Delft,
Afdeling der Electrotechniek,
Delft, The Netherlands

1976

Academic Press

London . New York . San Francisco

ACADEMIC PRESS INC. (LONDON) LTD.
24/28 Oval Road
London NW1

United States Edition published by
ACADEMIC PRESS INC.
111 Fifth Avenue
New York, New York 10003

Library of Congress Catalog Card Number: 75–4633
ISBN: 0 12 495050-7

Printed in Great Britain by
C. F. Hodgson & Son Ltd., London

PREFACE

At an ever-increasing rate during the past few decades, computers have grown in size, speed, complexity and versatility. This growth was made possible by the rapid development of electronic digital technology, from tubes, *via* transistors and integrated circuits to large scale integration, and the availability of suitable physical effects to enable the construction of relatively inexpensive and efficient computer memories. These memories were usually the result of immense interdisciplinary efforts of physicists and electrical engineers, and it can be said that communication problems often stood in the way of even better memories. This book has been written with the aim of improving the understanding between the different disciplines. The electrical engineer will find a description of the physical principles of the storage elements he is using or is going to use, whereas the physicist can learn which material properties are most relevant to the proper functioning of a memory device. The book is intended only as an introduction to this interesting field. The reader who wants to study the subjects in depth is referred to the original literature as given in the text.

The material of the book is divided mainly, though not dogmatically, in accordance with the practice in computer literature. Chapter 2 deals with delay line memories in which the propagation delay of a signal in a medium is used to store digital information. Chapter 3 is devoted to the large group of matrix memories which are characterized by a matrix array of physical elements which can, in most cases, be activated by the coincidence of a signal on a row and a column conductor. Chapter 4 describes memories in which access to a memory spot is by means of a light or electron beam. In the last chapter (5), the so-called electromechanical surface memories are described in which a storage surface and a transducer are electromechanically brought together for the reading or writing operation.

The present book has arisen from notes used by two of the authors in teaching courses to students in the Department of Electrical Engineering at D.U.T. (Delft University of Technology), Delft, The Netherlands.

The authors are indebted to their colleagues Mr. A. Venema and Miss N. Wiegman for helpful comments and suggestions and to Mrs. S. Haile-Smith who assisted in correcting many linguistic imperfections.

Most of the manuscript typing was done by Mrs. E. Mak and Miss G. Ploeger; their help and perseverance is gratefully acknowledged.

The authors would also like to express their gratitude to Mr. W. Th. J. van Kan and to Mr. G. van Berkel Jr. for converting many scrawls into nice figures.

S. Middelhoek

P. K. George

P. Dekker

Contents

Chapter 1

INTRODUCTION

1.1. COMPUTER ARCHITECTURE

The most important difference between digital computers and desk calculators is that computers can perform long sequences of arithmetic operations without the intervention of an operator [1.1.1–3]. In order to do so computers contain a device called memory, which stores both the instructions and the numerical data needed for the operations [1.1.4–6]. A block diagram of a digital computer is shown in Fig. 1.1.1. The input unit enables the operator to feed in the information to be processed and also the instructions to the computer. Many input devices exist, such as punched tape or card readers, electric typewriters, cathode ray tubes in combination with light pens and magnetic disk or tape stores. The data transfer rate of these devices is very low in comparison to the processing speed of the arithmetic unit, therefore it becomes necessary to hold the data and instructions for immediate use in a memory which allows fast access to the stored information. The transfer from the input device to this memory occurs at the

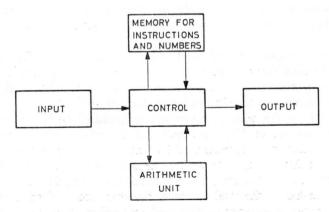

FIG. 1.1.1. Block diagram of a digital computer.

1

direction of a control unit. The control unit is the heart of the computer and is necessary to direct the flow of data and instructions between the different parts of a computer.

The control unit directs which data is to be read from memory and sent to the arithmetic unit. In the arithmetic unit common arithmetic operations such as addition, subtraction, multiplication and division are applied to the information. After processing, the information and the results are returned to memory. The memory, the control and the arithmetic units are usually contained in one large box commonly referred to as the central processing unit (CPU).

The information flow from memory to the output devices is also directed by the control unit. The results can be reported in many ways by using one or a combination of the following devices; paper tape or card punches, electric typewriters, numerical displays, electro-mechanical printers, visual display units, plotters and magnetic tape or disk stores.

The output results which are stored on paper tapes or cards and magnetic tapes or disks can thereafter be used as input information. The input and output devices are not contained in the CPU and are therefore often called peripheral equipment (PE). Information can be stored on the information carriers in the input and output devices as well as in memory which is a part of the CPU.

Due to the physical separation between CPU and PE, the PE information carriers are often called external or off-line memories, whereas the CPU memory is called an internal or on-line memory. For both types of memory the same kind of device can be used. In older machines, for example, a magnetic drum was used as internal memory; today it could be used only as external memory. For external memories the emphasis lies on the realization of large, but inexpensive memories which, consequently, have high access times.

For internal memories, the access time should be low. This makes it necessary to use rather expensive devices, such as cores and transistors which allow random access to each memory element. For economical reasons these internal memories are usually not larger than 10^6–10^7 bits.

During the last few decades the processing speed of the control and arithmetic units has increased by three orders of magnitude. Today's processing units easily allow the processing of 10^6 instructions per second. To take advantage of this speed, large on-line memories are necessary and it is no wonder that the internal memory in modern machines, due to its size, can represent one-half of the total computer hardware cost. When the information in the internal memory is processed, new information from the off-line memory has to be transferred to the on-line memory. The fast processor has to wait for this transfer. Since external memories have high access times, it is evident that the processor is not used very economically. The problem indicated here is known by the name "memory access gap" [1.1.7]. Two methods for solving this gap problem are being probed. The scientists in the laboratories of the computer industries are doing research to find memory technologies which allow larger, faster and yet not more expensive memories. The bubble memory and the magneto-optical memory as described in the following chapters are serious attempts in this direction. We can call it the hardware attack on the memory gap.

The other way to solve this problem is to make more intelligent use of the present hardware, this is the so-called software or firmware attack. One way of doing this is to set up a hierarchy of memories. The gap between slow external and fast internal memory is filled with a memory which is larger than the internal memory and faster than the external one.

Information is transferred first from, for instance, an electromechanical storage device like a disk, to a large but slow ferrite core memory and then to a fast core memory. Such a large but slow memory is called a buffer memory. Another way of solving the problem is by making the CPU a little more intelligent. When the CPU can be told to know in advance what data and information will be processed next, it is possible to transfer this information to the internal memory in time for processing. When this can be realized for the largest part of the program, the computer has an internal memory with the access time of the real internal memory and with the capacity of the external memory. This solution is referred to as virtual memory [1.1.8] and requires a complicated memory control organization for keeping track of what part of a program is in what kind of memory and when it is needed. The most important memory gap exists between the internal and external memory units. However, in the last decade still another gap appeared, namely the one between the arithmetic unit and the internal memory. Transistor circuits can work at much faster speeds than ferrite cores. In large expensive machines therefore a small so-called "cache" memory is added with access times comparable to those of the logic circuits [1.1.9]. The organization of the data flow between this cache memory and the large internal memory is organized by a memory control unit, which has a similar function as that described for the virtual memory.

At present the advancement in storage techniques depends on research in three areas:

a. development of better firmware, such as control microprograms,

b. the improvement of existing technologies in order to make larger, faster and less expensive memories and

c. the investigation of new memory technologies to replace existing technologies or to fill memory gaps.

In the following chapters the physics of the most important memory devices of the past, the present and the near future are described.

1.2. HISTORY OF STORAGE TECHNIQUES

The history of storage techniques for calculators and computers starts around 1833 when the ingenious English scientist Charles Babbage proposed his analytical engine [1.2.1]. He planned to store 1000 numbers each of 50 decimal digits and for the first time indicated the need not only to store numbers, which were needed in the calculations, but also to store the different instructions needed to perform the computations. The actual machine was unfortunately never built because of the limitations of the mechanical engineering of those days. Babbage proposed to use mechanical counting wheels (Fig. 1.2.1) each having 10 positions to store decimal numbers. The instructions were supposed to be stored in punched cards similar to the cards used by the Frenchman Jacquard to control the manufacturing of brocaded material. One of the first computers ever built, the Harvard Mark I which was finished in 1944, was built in the manner of Babbage's machine. The storage counter wheels were electromechanically operated. The storage

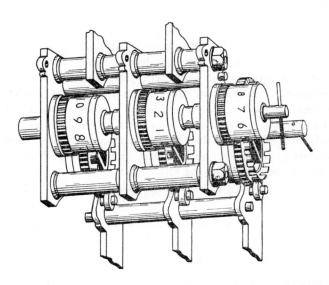

Fig. 1.2.1. Mechanical counting wheels of the analytical engine of C. Babbage.

capacity was 72 numbers, each 23 decimal digits long. Some years earlier in 1941 Atanasoff and Berry at Iowa State University introduced a new kind of storage technique. In the computer they used a rotating drum with 32 tracks each of 51 capacitors. A binary digit was represented by the polarity of the charge on a capacitor [1.2.2]. The Iowa machine is considered to be the first special purpose electronic computer because it used about 300 vacuum tubes for the arithmetic unit.

The first large electronic computer was built at the University of Pennsylvania and contained about 18 000 vacuum tubes. The famous machine called ENIAC (Electronic Numerical Integrator And Calculator) was completed in 1945 and worked for many years despite the large amount of relatively unreliable tubes. The ENIAC had a very small data storage capacity; only 20 decimal numbers could be stored in 10 stage vacuum tube flip-flop shift registers. For the storage of instructions and function tables about 6000 switches could be set by hand. After completion of the ENIAC, a new machine the EDVAC (Electronic Discrete Variable Automatic Computer) was initiated. This machine would have a large memory to store data as well as programs. The storage device proposed for the EDVAC was the mercury delay line invented by J. W. Mauchly and J. P. Eckert of the University of Pennsylvania in 1944 [1.2.3].

A mercury delay line consists of a tube filled with mercury (Fig. 1.2.2) with a piezoelectric quartz transducer at both ends. The velocity of sound in mercury is about 1.5 m ms^{-1} and in a tube 1.5 m long it takes 1 ms for a mechanical vibration set up by one transducer to reach the other end. The binary information was usually modulated on to a carrier of around 10 MHz; about 1000 bits can be stored in a 1.3 m mercury tube. The mercury delay line was used for many early computers and also for the first large commercial computer, the UNIVAC.

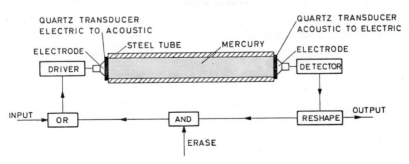

FIG. 1.2.2. Mercury delay line memory.

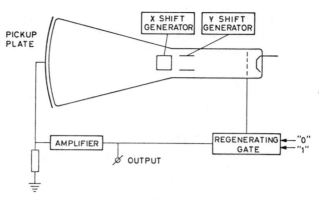

FIG. 1.2.3. Williams-tube store.

Besides the mercury delay line, the EDVAC machine also had a new large auxiliary memory consisting of reels of nickel plated bronze wire on which the digits could be recorded magnetically. The wire storage was typically the predecessor of the magnetic tape storage and was also used as input and output memory.

Around 1948 the development of computers also started in England at the University of Manchester. The memory used in the first Manchester machine was based on the use of conventional cathode-ray tubes. The memory system was invented by Williams and Kilburn [1.2.4] and is known as the Williams-tube memory. This memory consists, in principal, of a cathode ray tube with a pickup plate attached externally to the face of the tube (Fig. 1.2.3). When the electron beam is directed to a spot on the screen and the operating voltage is high enough (1000–2000 V), secondary electrons will leave the spot. Since the number of secondary electrons is larger than the number of primary electrons arriving at the spot, the potential of the spot becomes about 2.5 V positive with respect to the rest of the phosphor screen. Because of the small capacity between the spot and the pickup plate in front of the tube face, a small positive pulse on the pickup plate will occur, which

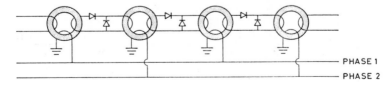

FIG. 1.2.4. First magnetic shift register memory [1.2.5].

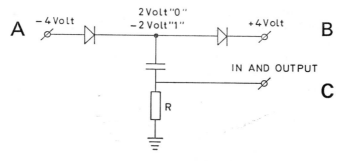

FIG. 1.2.5. Diode-capacitor memory cell.

can be amplified. When the spot is accessed for a second time, no signal is induced. Therefore, by bombarding the screen with electrons one can read the information stored. Because the built-up charges will decay in a few seconds, the information has to be regenerated. It is evident, that the operation of a real Williams tube is much more complicated, but because the tube is not used in any machine today a more detailed description will not be given. Besides the Williams tube, some other electrostatic memory systems were also developed. The first M.I.T. computer called Whirlwind I used cathode ray tubes with a second electron gun, which made regeneration unnecessary. Another electrostatic tube the "Selectron" was developed by Rajchman of RCA. The electrostatic memories were used with great success in early scientific machines. In 1954 IBM announced its new Type 704 machine, which was available with either electrostatic memory or with a magnetic core memory, which was invented a few years earlier. Due to the poor reliability of electrostatic storage not one customer ordered the machine with an electrostatic memory system.

The Manchester machine was also the first machine to apply a magnetic storage drum. The drum used had a nickel surface and was about 10 in in diameter and 12 in high; 256 heads were employed. The drum could contain 1024 words of 40 digits each. Magnetic drums were used in many machines.

The first commercially successful machine, the IBM type 650, contained such a drum as main memory. Today drums are only used as peripheral memory in special purpose machines.

At Harvard the development of computers continued after the successful completion of the Harvard I. In 1950 a machine called Harvard III was completed, which for the first time used magnetic tape for input and output of data. Today this is still a much used technique, although the tape stores have been much improved. Another development going on at this time at

B

Harvard was centred around finding an inexpensive and more reliable replacement for vacuum tube shift registers. An Wang and Way Dong Woo succeeded, under the direction of Aiken [1.2.5], in fabricating registers composed of metallic magnetic cores with square hysteresis loops and diodes (Fig. 1.2.4). By pulsing the cores in the right manner, an output signal from one core could be used to set the next core in the desired information direction. The diodes were necessary to define the information transfer direction. The magnetic shift registers were successfully used in the Harvard IV for high speed data storage. Although a lot of research and development has been spent on core registers, today they are not used, mainly because transistor registers are much faster and less expensive.

Around 1951 two other ways of storing data were developed which are worth mentioning. At Harwell, England a small digital computer was built, which used so-called Dekatrons for storing decimal numbers. Dekatrons are cold-cathode gas discharge tubes with 10 cathodes and a common anode. The discharge takes place between the anode and any one cathode and is stepped from one cathode to the next by applying pulses to the appropriate electrodes. Each tube can store one decimal digit. The Harwell machine contained 320 of these tubes. Speed, necessary high voltage and price prevented large scale use of Dekatrons.

Around 1951 another interesting memory technique was developed at the National Bureau of Standards for its SEAC computer. The basic storage-element consisted of two diodes and a capacitor (Fig. 1.2.5). A "1" was represented by a positive charge, a "0" by a negative charge on the capacitor. During holding, both diodes were reverse biased by applying suitable voltages at A and B. For reading, the points A and B were forced to ground and a positive or negative voltage appeared across the resistor R. In order to write, the point C was held at a positive or negative voltage during which time the points A and B were returned to their normal voltages. Because of some unavoidable leakage, periodic regeneration was necessary. A small memory based on diode-capacitor cells was built and thoroughly tested. It was capable of storing 256 words of eight bits each and operated on a 6 μsec cycle time [1.2.6].

It was also in 1951 that the idea occurred to J. W. Forrester and W. N. Papion [1.2.7] of the Lincoln laboratory of M.I.T. in Boston that the magnetization direction in a magnetic core could be used to store binary information in an economic, coincident-current selection method. The first cores consisted of many turns of nickel-iron tape, but very soon it was recognized by Forrester and Rajchmann of R.C.A. that ferrites were very suitable core materials.

The first computer with a ferrite core memory was the Whirlwind I built at the Lincoln laboratory in 1953. The advantages of the ferrite cores were so convincing, that in a very short time all new machines were built with such core memories and the mercury delay line. The Williams tube and the magnetic drum fell into oblivion. Notwithstanding the many new kinds of memory systems proposed in the years that followed even today the ferrite core dominates the memory market.

One of the first ideas to challenge the ferrite core was based on the hysteretic properties observed in ferroelectric materials [1.2.8]. The "1" and the "0" state can be represented by the two remanent polarization states of a spot in a ferroelectric plate. Ferroelectric materials are afflicted with many unfavourable properties, and a practical memory system made of them has not been introduced so far.

A more serious challenger, namely magnetic film, was proposed by Blois [1.2.9] in 1955. He found that when a planar magnetic film of a Ni–Fe alloy was deposited by evaporation in vacuum on glass in the presence of a magnetic field, such a film exhibited a square hysteresis loop parallel to the field direction during evaporation. This means that a magnetic film can be used as a bistable storage element. The paper Blois nucleated a tremendous world wide effort to understand the physics of magnetic films and to design storage systems with them. Although a few experimental planar thin film memories have been constructed at different places, the ferrite core withstood this attack gloriously.

In 1960 Long [1.2.10] proposed a new kind of thin film storage device consisting of a copper wire that is electroplated with a rather thick magnetic Ni–Fe film. The plated wire memory was less expensive to make than the planar one and had the advantage of producing much higher sense signals than the planar devices.

Plated wire memories were investigated by many computer makers, but only one company, Sperry Rand Corporation, has been using these memories on a large scale, in their UNIVAC 9000 computer series since 1966 [1.2.11]. At the same time that Blois proposed planar magnetic films, the ferrite core got competition from an unexpected camp. In 1956 Buck [1.2.12] proposed using superconductive effects to make flip-flops called cryotrons. The appeal of the proposal was so large that many laboratories even today spend huge amounts of money on these devices, probably, in vain. A much more successful device was developed around 1956, namely the RAMAC disk file [1.2.13]. With respect to the magnetic drum the bit density per cubic centimetre increased dramatically. The acceptance of disk storage by industry was again considerably increased when it became clear that the disk packs could be made exchangeable [1.2.14]. Today disk storage is the most popular external mass storage used and this certainly will be the case in the near future.

A memory element used by Bell in electronic telephone exchange computers was presented in 1957 and was called the twistor [1.2.15]. This device consists mainly of a strip of magnetic material wrapped around a conducting wire. However, in business computers the twistor found no applications.

Around 1960 business as well as scientific computers were widely accepted and customers started formulating their wishes, of which the demand for larger internal and external storage was most heard. Therefore, the computer companies inaugurated intensive drives for physical effects which could be used for storage purposes. A massive amount of literature and a few useful devices were the result. Most devices are still being studied and will be amply treated in the following chapters. The most important developments follow here in bird's eye view.

In 1958 Mayer [1.2.16] suggested storing information in MnBi films by temporarily elevating the temperature of a small spot above the Curie temperature by heating it with an electron beam. This storage method is, therefore, called Curie point writing.

The tunnel diode invented by Esaki in 1957 showed high switching speed and also bistability, and it was natural that around 1960 [1.2.17] the suitability of the tunnel diode as a logic or as a storage element was investigated. Since it is a two-terminal device it proved difficult to make memory matrices with tunnel diodes and today interest in this device is not very large.

A proposal worth mentioning and which was first published in 1962 is known as thermoplastic recording [1.2.18]. In this external mass storage, information is stored by deforming the surface of a thermoplastic tape by means of an electron beam. Reading is done optically.

The manufacture of ferrite cores requires much labour and therefore is expensive. Hence, methods were studied by which a ferrite matrix could be batch fabricated with the drive wires embedded in the ferrite plates [1.2.19]. The problems of producing large homogeneous sheets of ferrites with properties comparable to the discrete ferrite cores has never been solved.

Some magnetic materials like GdI garnets show two sublattices, the magnetizations of which compensate each other at a temperature called the compensation temperature. For GdIG this is around 14°C. At this temperature the coercive force of the material is very high compared to other temperatures. In 1965 Chang et al. [1.2.20] proposed using this effect for mass storage. Writing would be performed in a GdIG plate by the coincidence of a magnetic field and a heating laser beam; reading would be carried out by means of the Kerr or Faraday effect.

During all the years that new memory devices were proposed, it also occurred to many people that a transistor flip-flop would constitute a suitable memory element. However price, size and energy consumption made the transistor much less attractive than the ferrite core.

TABLE 1.2.1. History of storage techniques

Year	Storage device	Inventors	Reference	First large scale commercial use
1833	mechanical counting wheel	C. Babbage	[1.2.1]	
1941	capacitor drum	J. V. Atanasoff and C. Berry	[1.2.2]	
1944	vacuum tube flip-flop			1949 IBM 604
1944	mercury delay line	J. W. Mauchly and J. P. Eckert	[1.2.3]	
1948	nickel plated wire			
1948	Williams tube	F. C. Williams and K. Kilburn	[1.2.4]	1954 IBM 704
1948	magnetic drum			1955 IBM 650
1950	magnetic tape			1951 UNIVAC
1950	core shift register	A. Wang, W. D. Woo	[1.2.5]	
1951	dekatron			
1951	diode capacitor cell		[1.2.6]	
1951	ferrite core matrix	J. Forrester and W. N. Papion	[1.2.7]	1954 IBM 704
1952	ferroelectric cell	J. R. Anderson	[1.2.8]	
1955	magnetic thin film	M. S. Blois	[1.2.9]	
1956	cryotron	D. A. Buck	[1.2.12]	
1956	RAMAC disk file		[1.2.13]	1956 IBM
1957	twistor	A. H. Bobeck	[1.2.15]	Bell telephone exchanges
1958	Curie point writing	L. Mayer	[1.2.16]	
1960	tunnel diode cell		[1.2.17]	
1960	plated wire	T. R. Long	[1.2.10]	1966 UNIVAC 9000
1962	thermoplastic recording		[1.2.18]	
1963	ferrite plate	R. Shahbender et al.	[1.2.19]	
1965	compensation point writing	J. T. Chang et al.	[1.2.20]	
1965	semiconductor memory	J. S. Schmidt	[1.2.21]	1969 IBM 360/85
1967	bubble memory	A. H. Bobeck	[1.2.23]	
1969	charge transfer	F. L. J. Sangster, W. S. Boyle and G. E. Smith	[1.2.24] [1.2.25]	

The first paper on semiconductor memories appeared in 1965 [1.2.21]. Four years later semiconductor memories were first used in a commercial product, the IBM 360/85. Only a part of the main memory was built with semiconductors, the rest still consisted of ferrite core matrices. The first machine to contain an all semiconductor main memory was the IBM 370/145 which was announced in 1970 [1.2.22]. Today many more members of the computer industry are replacing ferrite cores or plated wires with semiconductor memories, and it is certain that the ferrite core will decline in the future.

Computer technology is increasingly being used for applications such as telephone switching, measurement instruments, displays, etc. These applications usually do not require short cycle times and therefore serial rather than random access is satisfactory.

Around 1967 Bobeck of Bell [1.2.23] proposed using magnetic bubble domains for storage of information. When a platelet of a suitable magnetic material with the easy axis normal to the plane is subjected to a bias field also normal to the platelet, small circular domains appear. By means of deposited conductors on the platelet it is possible to shift the bubbles through the platelet. Like magnetic thin films and superconductive films, this idea nucleated a huge research and development effort but it is not impossible that it will experience a similar fate.

More or less as an answer to the bubble memory, or so some people claim, around 1969 a device was proposed which is based on the transfer of charge in a semiconductor wafer by a suitable electrode structure. One such device is called the bucket brigade circuit [1.2.24] and was invented at Philips in the Netherlands, whereas the other device is called the charge-coupled device (CCD) and was invented at Bell (U.S.A.) [1.2.25]. Because these devices can be made by a technology the computer industry is very familiar with, it can be expected that charge transfer devices have a more certain future than their magnetic counterparts.

Although it can be expected that in the future many more devices will be presented based on an inventive use of new or old material properties, it seems probable that the magnetic disk memory as external mass storage and semiconductor flip-flops as internal main memory elements will govern the scene of the next decade.

In table 1.2.1 the most important years, in which inventions and commercial use of these inventions were presented, are indicated. It can easily be seen from the table that very few invented memory devices were really used in commercial machines. This may explain why computer industry management is becoming increasingly reluctant about budgeting new spectacular devices.

REFERENCES

[1.1.1] A. P. Speiser, "Digitale Rechenanlagen", Springer Verlag, Berlin, 1967.
[1.1.2] R. K. Richards, "Electronic Digital Systems", John Wiley and Sons, Inc., New York, 1966.

[1.1.3] S. H. Hollingdale and G. C. Tootill, "Electronic Computers", Penguin Books, Harmondsworth, 1970.

[1.1.4] W. Renwick and A. J. Cole, "Digital Storage Systems", Chapman & Hall Ltd., London, 1971.

[1.1.5] C. J. Dakin and C. E. G. Cooke, "Circuits for Digital Equipment", London Iliffe Books, Ltd., London, 1967.

[1.1.6] R. K. Richards, "Electronic Digital Components and Circuits", D. van Nostrand Company, Inc., Princeton, New Jersey, 1967.

[1.1.7] E. W. Pugh, Storage hierarchies: gaps, cliffs and trends, *IEEE Trans. Mag.*, **MAG-7**, 810–814, 1971.

[1.1.8] R. P. Parmelee, T. I. Peterson, C. C. Tillman and D. J. Hatfield, Virtual storage and virtual machine concepts, *IBM Syst. J.*, **11**, 99–130, 1972.

[1.1.9] C. J. Conti, D. H. Gibson and S. H. Pitkowsky, Structural aspects of the system/360 model 85, *IBM Syst. J.*, **7**, 2–4, 1968.

[1.2.1] B. V. Bowden, "Faster Than Thought", Sir Isaac Pitman and Sons, Ltd., London, 1955.

[1.2.2] R. K. Richards, "Electronic Digital Systems", John Wiley and Sons, Inc., New York, 1966.

[1.2.3] Moore School of Electrical Engineering. The EDVAC; a preliminary report on logic and design, University of Pennsylvania, Philadelphia, 1948.

[1.2.4] F. C. Williams and T. Kilburn, A storage system for use with binary digital computing machines, *Proc. IEE*, **96**, part III, 81–100, 1949.

[1.2.5] A. Wang and W. D. Woo, Static magnetic storage and delay line, *J. Appl. Phys.*, **21**, 49–54, 1950.

[1.2.6] H. D. Huskey and G. A. Korn, "Computer Handbook", McGraw–Hill Book Co., New York, pp. 12/116–12/126, 1962.

[1.2.7] J. W. Forrester, Digital information storage in three dimensions using magnetic cores, *J. Appl. Phys.*, **22**, 44–48, 1951.

[1.2.8] J. R. Anderson, Ferroelectric materials as storage elements for digital computers and switching systems, *J. AIEE*, **71**, 916–922, 1952.

[1.2.9] M. S. Blois, Preparation of thin magnetic films and their properties, *J. Appl. Phys.*, **26**, 975–980, 1955.

[1.2.10] T. R. Long, Electrodeposited memory elements for a nondestructive memory, *J. Appl. Phys.*, **31**, 123s $\simeq$ 124s, 1960.

[1.2.11] G. A. Fedde, Plated-wire memories: Univac's bet to replace toroidal ferrite cores, *Electronics*, **40**, 101–109, May 15, 1967.

[1.2.12] D. A. Buck, The cryotron-A superconductive computer component, *Proc. I.R.E.*, **44**, 482–493, 1956.

[1.2.13] T. Noyes and W. E. Dickinson, Engineering design of a magnetic disc random access memory, *Proc. Western Joint Computer Conf.*, 42–44, 1956.

[1.2.14] J. D. Carothers, R. K. Brunner, J. L. Dawson, M. O. Halfhill and R. E. Kubec, A new high density recording system: the IBM 1311 disk storage drive with interchangeable disk packs, *Proc. Fall JCC*, **24**, 327–340, 1963.

[1.2.15] A. H. Bobeck, A new storage element suitable for large sized memory arrays—the twistor, *Bell Syst. Tech. J.*, **36**, 1319–1340, 1957.

[1.2.16] L. Mayer, Magnetic writing with an electron beam, *J. Appl. Phys.*, **29**, 1454–1456, 1958.

[1.2.17] J. C. Miller, K. Li and A. W. Lo, The tunnel diode as a storage element, *Int. Solid State Circ. Conf. Digest*, 52–53, 1960.

[1.2.18] W. E. Glenn and J. E. Wolfe, Thermoplastic recording, *Int. Science and Techn.*, 28–35, 1962.

[1.2.19] R. Shahbender, C. Wentworth, K. Li, S. Hotchkiss and J. A. Rajchman, Laminated ferrite memory, *RCA Review*, **24**, 705–729, 1963.

[1.2.20] J. T. Chang, J. F. Dillon, Jr., and U. F. Gianola, Magneto-optical variable memory based upon the properties of a transparent ferrimagnetic garnet at its compensation temperature, *J. Appl. Phys.*, **36**, 1110–1111, 1965.

[1.2.21] J. S. Schmidt, Integrated MOS random-access memory, *Solid State Design*, **6**, 21–25, 1965.

[1.2.22] J. K. Ayling and R. D. Moore, Main monolithic memory, *IEEE J. Solid State Circuits*, SC–6, 276–279, 1971.

[1.2.23] A. H. Bobeck, Properties and device applications of magnetic domains in orthoferrites, *Bell Syst. Tech. J.*, **46**, 1901–1925, 1967.

[1.2.24] F. L. J. Sangster and K. Teer, Bucket-Brigade electronics New possibilities for delay, time axis conversion and scanning, *IEEE J. Solid State Circuits*, SC–4, 131–136, 1969.

[1.2.25] W. S. Boyle and G. E. Smith, Charge coupled semiconductor devices, *Bell Syst. Tech. J.*, **49**, 587–593, 1970.

Chapter 2

DELAY LINE MEMORIES AND MATERIALS

2.1. DELAY LINE MEMORIES

2.1.1. INTRODUCTION

The delay line was the earliest invention used for large-scale storage of digital information [2.1.1]. Its application to information storage in computers was an outgrowth of the World War II effort to develop and improve radar systems. Although the first mercury delay lines have long since become obsolete, the solid delay line [2.1.2] still finds continuous use as a memory device in small serial computers and electronic calculators. It is also used in buffers in computer systems and in cathode-ray tube display refreshers as well as in digital integrators, digital differential analysers and serial adders. Renewed interest in serial or sequential storage has been spurred on by the recent appearance of commercially available semiconductor shift registers and the charge-coupled devices which offer an alternative, but fundamentally similar, method of information storage. While the low bit frequency digital delay lines are expected to give way to MOS shift registers as semiconductor prices drop, the high frequency devices are expected to remain competitive. The digital surface wave delay line offers the possibility of large storage capacity with a minimum of surface processing. Since the technology necessary for producing surface wave devices is similar to that used in making semiconductor integrated circuits, they are potentially very attractive from an economic standpoint for special purpose analogue and digital applications. While at present delay line information storage represents a small portion of digital memory technology, the current interest in combining low cost memory units with instrumentation to achieve greater versatility promises increasing applications.

Digital delay lines can be divided into two basic categories depending on the mechanism used to transmit information from the input to the output of the device. In an electromagnetic delay line an electrical signal is fed into the input terminals of a coaxial cable or an appropriately synthesized electrical network and is retrieved at the output at some later time. The signal in this

15

case propagates entirely in the form of electrical energy. In contrast the ultrasonic delay line involves conversion of the electrical energy into mechanical form at the input of a delay medium and subsequent reconversion to the electrical form at the output; the mechanical energy propagates through the delay medium in the form of a sound wave. Physically the ultrasonic line consists of a transmitting transducer, a delay medium and a receiving transducer. Since the delay characteristics of each type of line depend directly upon the velocity of the associated electrical or sound wave, some simple considerations yield insight into the properties of these devices. Electromagnetic energy propagates at the speed of light which is 3×10^8 m s^{-1}, while sound in a solid travels typically at 4×10^3 m s^{-1}. Therefore a factor 10^5 in path length is involved when comparing coaxial to ultrasonic lines at fixed delay. At a bit rate of 100 MHz which represents the upper limit of current technical capabilities, the storage of 100 bits in a delay cable corresponds to a 300 m length which is rather impractical on a volume and cost per bit basis. Accordingly the distributed or quasi-distributed electromagnetic delay line has been relegated to specialized low capacity applications [2.1.3]. Because the speed of sound is much less than that for light the ultrasonic delay line can be constructed more compactly for a given delay than its electromagnetic counterpart and by virtue of its electrical characteristics is capable of storing larger quantities of digital information. Where a typical electromagnetic line might have a capacity of 10 bits, an ultrasonic line might have a capacity of 10^3 bits. A more revealing parameter than capacity is bit density which corresponds to the inverse of the volume of material required to store a single bit. A large bit density implies dense packing of information and is generally considered favourable. The bit density of an ultrasonic delay line is typically 100–1000 times that of an electromagnetic one. It is for this reason, and also because of capacity considerations, that acoustic devices have received significantly more attention. The first generation computers EDVAC and UNIVAC used recirculating delay line memories in which the delay medium was mercury. Acoustic information was inserted and extracted from this medium via quartz piezoelectric transducers. Mercury delay lines have long since become obsolete—the subject of solid delay lines currently reflects the greater interest in the area of delay line information storage and accordingly forms the basis of this chapter. Section 2.1.2 describes, from a system standpoint, how a simple delay line memory works and how delay lines can be organized to form large capacity location—and content—addressable memories. A parallel search technique which allows rapid access to stored data is mentioned as it can be used to advantage in connection with surface wave devices. The basic physical limitations placed upon information capacity are discussed in Section 2.2.1 and this leads directly to bulk wave material considerations which appear in Section 2.2.3. The remainder of the chapter is subdivided between bulk (Section 2.3) and surface wave delay lines (Section 2.4) and represents a transition from devices of the present to those of the future. The perspective of the discussion ranges from applied, in the first few introductory sections, to the more physical, in the latter, in an effort to reveal the basic principles underlying the operation of such devices.

2.1.2. DELAY—A COMPUTER STORAGE MECHANISM

The rate at which information can be transferred from one point in space to another is limited by the propagation velocity of light. An electric or acoustic signal in traversing a finite distance incurs a time delay proportional to the path length. Information may, therefore, temporarily be stored in space in the form of a propagating wave. It is this concept which underlies the operation of a delay line storage unit.

The essential features of a recirculating delay line memory are shown in the block diagram of Fig. 2.1.1. The operational characteristics of this type of memory unit are similar to those of a drum or disk store. Binary digits to be stored are inserted sequentially into the delay line in the form of a series of electrical pulses and are allowed to propagate through the delay medium to the output where they are subsequently regenerated and reinserted into the delay line. The series of bits is continually recirculated until it is required

	READ	WRITE	RECIRCULATE
READ SELECT	1	0 OR 1	0 OR 1
WRITE SELECT	0 OR 1	1	0
DATA INPUT	0 OR 1	0 OR 1	0 OR 1
R/W ENABLE	1	1	0 OR 1

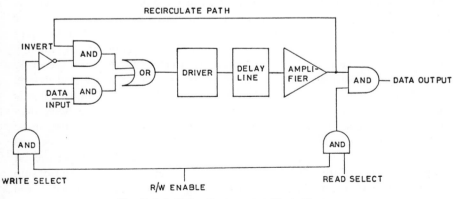

FIG. 2.1.1. Delay line memory block diagram.

externally and is in this sense stored. In Fig. 2.1.1 the write select line allows input pulses to enter the memory loop at appropriate time intervals upon command from the computer and simultaneously controls the recirculation of information. Information may be transferred out of the loop by raising the voltage of the read select line to the equivalent of a 1. If the delay line has a capacity of N bits and a time delay of T_d seconds there will be T_d/N time intervals during which such read-write transfers can take place. For the device to operate, the location and order of these time slots must be known. This timing and counting function is accomplished by introducing an externally generated continuous series of clock pulses which control the gating of new pulses into the delay line and which also drive an address counter. Interruption of the recirculate mode causes the stored data to be lost. This volatility of information in a delay line store represents a serious handicap relative to that of a magnetic store in which loss of power is a less critical factor. On the other hand the delay line store has a redeeming quality and that is its potential high-speed information handling capability. The storage capacity N, the bit rate f_b, and delay time T_d are related by the equation

$$N = f_b \times T_d. \qquad (2.1.1)$$

Since information processing is performed at the output of the delay line, the maximum access time is determined by T_d. The philosophy of high-speed operation is to make the bit rate f_b as large as is practical in view of material considerations and to make the maximum access time T_d small enough so that very simple geometrical shapes can be used. In general this will result in a low capacity system, however, by combining a large number of such modules at the expense of additional regeneration circuitry, a large capacity rapid access system can be constructed which will handle extremely high bit rates. The high bit frequency of operation of these devices limits the choice of suitable delay line materials as will be discussed in Section 2.2.1. For slower systems access time is not such a critical factor and it becomes economically advantageous to think in terms of maximizing capacity thereby eliminating the need for more regeneration circuits. In this case the delay path becomes relatively long and must be folded to yield a compact device. The frequency of operation is low enough, however, so that less exotic materials such as polycrystalline metals may be used. The capacity of a delay line storage unit is determined by how close together the bits can be spaced without overlapping at the output. As will be discussed in Sections 2.2.1 and 2.2.2, the relevant electrical characteristic determining the bit capacity is bandwidth. This is to be expected in view of the close relationship between rise time and bandwidth which applies to electrical transmission systems. The close analogy between a digital delay line and a binary com-

2. DELAY LINE MEMORIES AND MATERIALS 19

munication channel in the information theory sense suggests that the maximum rate of information transmission will be limited by the bandwidth and therefore that the bandwidth-delay product determines the maximum bit capacity. Before going into the details of this result it is worthwhile to consider briefly the organizational aspects of delay line memories.

The format adopted to store data in digital applications involves organizing the memory into words of a fixed bit length. The total capacity of the memory is then equal to the total number of words that can be stored multiplied by the number of bits per word. This information can be stored conveniently in delay lines in two ways. In the serial-by-bit–serial-by-word configuration the bits of each word are fed sequentially into a memory unit such as shown in Fig. 2.1.1. If the total capacity exceeds that of a single delay line, one or more of such units can be placed in cascade. In effect the length of the delay line is simply extended and the block diagram of Fig. 2.1.1 applies, but with the delay line possibly containing regeneration stages. Alternatively, in the serial-by-word–parallel-by-bit scheme the individual delay lines are operated in parallel as shown in Fig. 2.1.2. In this configuration, the bits of a word appear in a single time slot. The addressing and control circuitry can be the same as that used for simple serial organization. Accordingly on a cost per bit basis this system allows more economical use of the addressing, timing and control circuits. Instead of counting bits, the address circuitry counts words which amounts to a factor of M in savings.

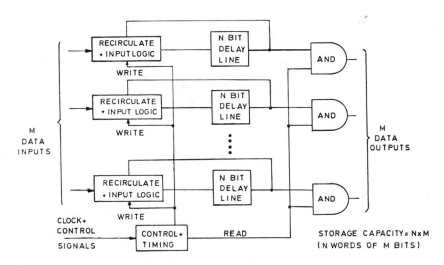

FIG. 2.1.2. Parallel channel operation.

2.2. FUNDAMENTAL CONSIDERATIONS

2.2.1. DISTORTION OF PULSE WAVEFORMS

An acoustic delay line (including transducers) behaves as a linear system so long as the associated input and output electrical signals are not too large [2.2.1]. Such a device can be regarded as a linear, passive, two-port, electrical network [2.2.2] and is for present purposes best regarded simply as an electric filter. When considering the transmission of electrical signals through such a linear network, it is convenient to introduce the Fourier transforms of the input and output waveforms. The Fourier transformation of a time function is defined by

$$E(\omega) = \mathscr{F}\{E(t)\} = \frac{1}{2\pi} \int_{-\infty}^{\infty} E(t)e^{-i\omega t}\,dt, \qquad (2.2.1)$$

and the inverse transform by

$$E(t) = \mathscr{F}^{-1}\{E(\omega)\} = \int_{-\infty}^{\infty} E(\omega)e^{i\omega t}\,d\omega. \qquad (2.2.2)$$

It is then possible to characterize a two-port electrical system such as a delay line by a transfer function $H(\omega)$ which relates the Fourier transform of the input and output signals as shown for the idealized network of Fig. 2.2.1.

The function $A(\omega)$ is referred to as the amplitude characteristic while $B(\omega)$ is known as the phase characteristic. The output signal can be expressed in terms of the Fourier transform of the input signal and the transfer function as follows.

$$E_{\text{OUT}}(t) = \mathscr{F}^{-1}\{E_{\text{OUT}}(\omega)\} = \mathscr{F}^{-1}\{H(\omega)E_{\text{IN}}(\omega)\}. \qquad (2.2.3)$$

Now if it happens that $A(\omega) = A_0$ and $B(\omega) = \omega T_{\text{d}}$, then $H(\omega) = A_0\,e^{i\omega T_{\text{d}}}$ and as can easily be verified

$$E_{\text{OUT}}(t) = A_0\,\mathscr{F}^{-1}\{e^{i\omega T_{\text{d}}}\,E_{\text{IN}}(\omega)\} = A_0\,E_{\text{IN}}(t - T_{\text{d}}). \qquad (2.2.4)$$

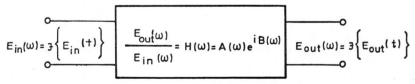

FIG. 2.2.1. Transmission network and frequency transfer function $H(\omega)$.

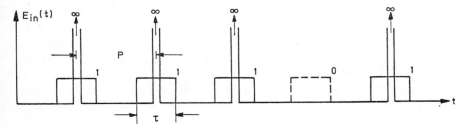

FIG. 2.2.2. Binary pulse sequence.

Hence under the conditions that the amplitude characteristic is a constant and the phase characteristic is linear with frequency, this being true for all frequencies, then the output signal is a replica of the input signal delayed in time by T_d seconds and altered in magnitude by the factor A_0. A distortionless system such as this which does not change the shape of the transmitted signals is to be regarded as the ideal delay line. It is physically impossible to construct a device with these characteristics and it is customary to talk in terms of the deviation of the amplitude characteristic from the constant A_0 as giving rise to amplitude distortion and the deviation of the phase characteristic as giving rise to phase or delay distortion [2.2.3]. In general a signal is degraded by both of these factors thereby limiting the amount of information that can be transferred through the device and hence the storage capacity in memory applications. A somewhat oversimplified argument illustrates this point. Consider a train of digital pulses as shown in Fig. 2.2.2 representing a typical binary number to be stored in a recirculating delay line memory.

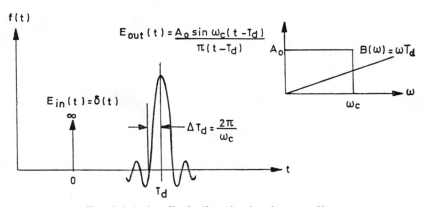

FIG. 2.2.3. Amplitude distortion in a low pass filter.

Since the effect of each pulse in this sequence can be considered separately and the results for all superimposed to give the total output, it is necessary to consider only one pulse which for mathematical simplicity will be taken to have zero width ($\tau = 0$) but infinite height (i.e. is a delta function). If this waveform is fed into a system for which the amplitude characteristic is constant for all frequencies below a cutoff frequency ω_c and zero elsewhere and the phase characteristic is linear over the corresponding frequency range (ideal low-pass filter) then the output waveform will exhibit amplitude distortion and will be of the form shown in Fig. 2.2.3.

While at first it is tempting to place the input pulses immediately next to each other ($P = 0$) in order to achieve maximum storage capacity, it is clear that this will yield overlapping pulses at the output and hence a loss of information. The factor determining the minimum allowable pulse spacing P_{min} is in this case the bandwidth ω_c. The dispersion ΔT_d in time of the output waveform in Fig. 2.2.3 is inversely related to the bandwidth according to $\Delta T_d = 2\pi/\omega_c$. Hence a broader bandwidth implies a narrower output pulse and therefore the possibility of closer pulse spacing and as a consequence increased storage capacity. The optimum spacing corresponds to $P_{min} = \Delta T_d = 2\pi/\omega_c$.

In reality the amplitude characteristic of an ultrasonic delay line is more like that of a bandpass device [2.2.1], [2.2.4], [2.2.5] than that of a low-pass filter as suggested by the earlier discussion. $A(\omega)$ displays a maximum at the midband frequency f_m and falls off approximately symmetrically such

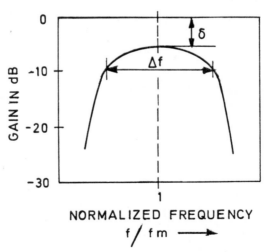

FIG. 2.2.4. Ultrasonic delay line characteristic.

that the amplitude response is zero for very low ($f \approx 0$) and very high frequencies ($f \gtrsim f_{max}$). A typical delay line characteristic in Fig. 2.2.4 illustrates this behaviour. The 3dB bandwidth is indicated by Δf and the midband insertion loss by δ.

The bandpass form of the amplitude characteristic is a consequence of the resonant character of the associated transducers.

In the case of bulk wave devices, folded magnetostrictive delay lines occupy the low frequency range (≈ 1 MHz), glass and fused quartz multiple reflection delay lines the intermediate frequency range (≈ 100 MHz) and straight-through crystalline monolithic and crystalline composite devices the high frequency and microwave ranges (≈ 1 GHz). Surface wave devices have been operated over a broad range of frequencies but are expected to become important at high frequencies (≈ 100 MHz) where large bandwidths are available and small ultrasound components can be fabricated using semiconductor IC technology. In non-magnetostrictive delay lines piezoelectric plate transducers are employed to excite bulk waves at low frequencies while thin-film or diffusion layer counterparts are used at the higher frequencies. Surface waves can be conveniently generated by evaporating an electrode array on the surface of a piezoelectric crystal. The principle of operation is very similar to that of a bulk wave device. Examination of the relationship between mid-band frequency f_m and bandwidth Δf for bulk wave devices indicates generally that the higher the operating frequency the greater the bandwidth. This is in fact predictable for a given piezoelectric transducer on the basis of fractional bandwidth considerations [2.2.6] so long as the delay medium does not significantly influence the overall shape of the frequency characteristic of the delay line. Since for a given access time the maximum storage capacity is expected to be related to the bandwidth of the device, it is evident that high frequency operation has a definite advantage. Unfortunately the acoustic losses increase with frequency for most materials and accordingly for a prescribed mid-band insertion loss δ, fewer and fewer materials can be used as the mid-band frequency f_m is increased. Generally the materials that can be used at high frequencies are rather specialized and cannot be easily synthesized. For this reason other more lossy delay mediums have been used but at lower frequencies. In this regard, for a fixed access the time specification on the insertion loss δ and the choice of a particular delay medium places an upper limit on the frequency, and, by virtue of the fractional bandwidth considerations, on the storage capacity. As the length of the delay line is increased, the losses become more severe and to obtain the same δ it is necessary to decrease f_m. Hence the increase in length of the line at fixed δ is accompanied by a decrease in bandwidth. So long as the added dispersion of the pulse train (measured as a length) due to the reduction in bandwidth is less than the increase in length of the delay line the capacity

c

of the system will increase. At some point, however, the change in dispersion offsets the added length and the capacity of the systems no longer increases. Again in an indirect way the losses of the delay medium determine the capacity of the memory unit. Since the frequency dependence of the acoustic attenuation plays a major role in determining the choice of delay line materials, a discussion of the acoustic properties of solids is given in Section 2.2.3. In the following section the relationship between bandwidth and capacity is made more explicit for a bandpass device.

2.2.2. DELAY LINE INFORMATION CAPACITY

In the previous section a rather idealized model of a digital pulse train (a series of impulses with zero width) was used to introduce the concept of dispersion. In reality it is neither convenient nor economical to use pulses of zero width. It can be shown that the optimum response (defined in terms of

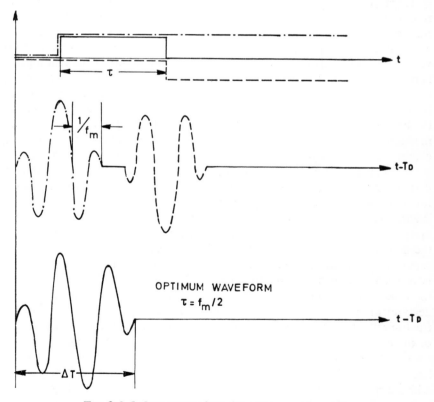

FIG. 2.2.5. Output waveform for optimum pulse width.

maximum amplitude and minimum width) of a bandpass system occurs for the choice τ equals $f_m/2$. This result may be understood by combining the transient responses of a bandpass system to oppositely polarized step functions separated in time by τ. Since the transient oscillations occur at the mid-band frequency f_m, the time equivalent of one half a period of this frequency is required to produce constructive interference displaying the optimum properties between waves 180° out of phase. These ideas are illustrated in Fig. 2.2.5 for an ideal bandpass system.

For a more realistic system the form of the output will depend on the specific frequency characteristic involved and can be quite different from that shown in Fig. 2.2.5 [2.2.4]. However, the essential point to be made here is that the width of the optimum response Δt is governed by the 3-dB bandwidth Δf according to the empirical formula

$$\Delta t \times \Delta f \approx 2. \qquad (2.2.5)$$

Hence if the output pulses are to be completely resolved, the bit rate must not exceed $1/\Delta t$. From eqn (2.1.1) this yields the storage capacity

$$N \approx \Delta f(T_d) \times T_d/2 \qquad (2.2.6)$$

where the implicit dependence of the bandwidth upon the delay time (or delay line length) is exhibited. For the return to zero mode of operation suggested by the previous discussion, N is equal to half the delay time-bandwidth product. This method of coding information is not particularly efficient, however, and it is possible to increase the storage capacity by a factor of two by distinguishing only between changes in the bit sequence [2.2.7]. The return to zero (RZ) and non-return to zero (NRZ) methods of recording information are contrasted in Fig. 2.2.6.

It is easy to see that under worse case conditions (...1111... sequence for RZ and ...0101... sequence for NRZ) just twice as much information can be sorted for a given bandwidth using the non-return to zero mode of operation. The implementation of this form of coding can be obtained by placing flip-flops in cascade with the delay line at the input and output terminals.

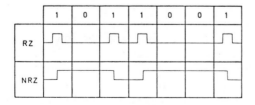

FIG. 2.2.6. RZ and NRZ operation.

The upper limit on the delay-bandwidth product for ultrasonic delay lines is of the order of 10^4. This represents to an order of magnitude the maximum storage capacity attainable for a single such device.

2.2.3. ACOUSTIC PROPERTIES OF MATERIALS

Knowledge of the loss mechanisms responsible for acoustic attenuation is helpful in determining the appropriate materials for ultrasonic device applications. Since such considerations apply not only to delay lines but also to acousto-optical devices (see Chapter 4 for description of an information storage system using the photo-elastic effect for information processing), it is worthwhile to review some of the more important intrinsic and extrinsic damping mechanisms. It is convenient from the device standpoint to focus attention on room temperature ($T \sim 300$ K) and frequencies which span the ultrasonic range (100 kHz–1 GHz). The propagation of an ultrasonic wave through a lossy medium may be characterized by a travelling wave of the form

$$A = A_0 \, e^{-\alpha Z} \cos{(kZ - \omega T)} \qquad (2.2.7)$$

where A is the magnitude of the particle displacement, ω is the angular frequency and k is the propagation constant equal to ω/v with v being the phase velocity. The attenuation constant α describes the rate at which the amplitude of the wave decays and is usually measured in dB per cm or equivalently in dB per μs. In general to specify α it is necessary to know the type of wave motion (i.e. longitudinal, shear) and also the propagation direction. There are two sources of contributions to the attenuation and they arise from what will be called intrinsic mechanisms, which depend only on scattering between the ultrasonic wave and the other fundamental excitations in a crystalline solid (phonons, electrons, magnons, etc.), and extrinsic mechanisms, which depend on the interaction between the ultrasonic wave and imperfections (impurities, dislocations, grain boundaries etc.) and are a strong function of the metallurgical state of the material. For most common materials the extrinsic losses mask the more fundamental behaviour and it is only under very special circumstances that the intrinsic losses become the dominant factor. Unfortunately the latter condition usually corresponds to the most favourable attenuation and at the same time to a rather specialized metallurgical phase (crystalline state) which cannot be produced easily. As will be discussed, for low frequency applications (~ 1 MHz) it is possible to use polycrystalline metals, provided the associated grain size is small and the acoustic path length is not too large. For higher frequency applications (~ 100 MHz) low loss glasses and vitreous silica are useful, while at still higher frequencies (~ 1 GHz) crystalline dielectrics such as sapphire (Al_2O_3), rutile (TiO_2), YIG ($Y_3Fe_5O_{12}$) and quartz (SiO_2)

can be used. When the intrinsic losses become the dominant factor in determining the attenuation, as it is in the case for these crystalline dielectrics, then it is possible to define a figure of acoustic merit from which the properties of similar materials can be predicted.

The problem of acoustic attenuation in solids is complicated by the presence of competing loss mechanisms; fortunately it is possible to single out a few of the more important ones at room temperature. In the following discussion no attempt is made at completeness.

2.2.3.1. Ultrasonic Attenuation by Grain Boundary Scattering

A principal limitation on the use of polycrystalline materials for acoustic applications is set by the attenuation due to grain boundary scattering [2.2.8]. Scattering of ultrasonic waves in solids is brought about by inhomogeneities in the elastic properties of the media. A polycrystalline material consists of crystalline grains of the constituent material with their principle axes oriented randomly throughout the volume of the solid. Since each grain is elastically anisotropic and misoriented with respect to its neighbours, the entire space of the solid is filled with inhomogeneities. Understandably, the theoretical description of ultrasonic attenuation in such a medium is limited to rather idealized situations. As a starting point it is most often assumed that the grains are roughly spherical (equiaxed) and that they are oriented randomly (no preferred orientation). The analysis then involves the solution of an extremely complicated boundary value problem in which mode conversion plays an important role. The earliest attempt to solve this problem relied heavily on generalizations of Rayleigh's work on scattering from an obstacle in a fluid which displays the classical λ^{-4} behaviour or equivalently an f^4 frequency dependence for the wavelength λ much greater than the characteristic dimension of the inhomogeneity. The more exact formulation of the problem is similar in this respect and as might be expected two different solutions emerge depending on the ratio of the acoustic wavelength λ to the average grain diameter $\bar{D}$. The results obtained are given below, and apply to a single phase homogeneous material with no inclusions or voids and the grain anisotropy assumed to be small.

In the Rayleigh limit $(\lambda > 2\pi\bar{D})$ one finds

$$\alpha = Tf^4 S \quad (\lambda > 2\pi\bar{D}) \tag{2.2.8}$$

in which T is a measure of the average grain volume from a grain distribution function appropriately describing the metallurgical state of the material.

As the frequency of ultrasound waves is increased, the wavelength at some point becomes smaller than the average grain diameter $\bar{D}$ and one enters into the intermediate scattering region, where

$$\alpha = \bar{D}f^2 \Sigma \quad (\lambda < 2\pi\bar{D}) \tag{2.2.9}$$

correctly describes the attenuation. Here $\bar{D}$ is defined in terms of the same grain distribution function as is used to compute T. The scattering coefficients S and Σ depend on the density, the wave velocities and the crystalline elastic properties. They are thus intrinsic parameters of the material and vary with the type of wave motion (longitudinal or shear).

Comparing α for different materials, it appears that aluminium and chromium are inherently low loss materials. This fact was recognized and exploited by Meitzler in the construction of polycrystalline aluminium strip delay lines [2.2.9].

The confirmation of the behaviour described by eqns (2.2.8) and (2.2.9) may be obtained experimentally and is shown in Fig. 2.2.7 for longitudinal waves in nickel [2.2.8]. The measured data is in overall quantitative agreement with that predicted on the basis of eqns. (2.2.8) and (2.2.9). The theoretical curves in Fig. 2.2.7 were obtained by calculating points in the f^4 and f^2 regions, drawing lines of slope 4 and 2 respectively through these points, and interpolating between these lines using the arc of a circle. The high frequency theoretical point for longitudinal waves is found to be somewhat low. Exact quantitative agreement here is not so important

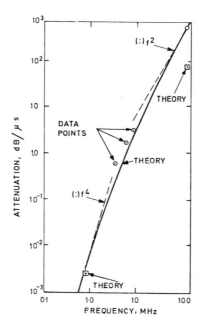

FIG. 2.2.7. Longitudinal wave attenuation in polycrystalline nickel—comparison of experimental data with theoretical predictions [2.2.8].

as the concept that the rapid f^4 dependence of the attenuation limits the usefulness of such materials in ultrasonic applications. From Fig. 2.2.7 it is apparent that for frequencies above 10 MHz the attenuation becomes prohibitive for applications involving propagation over long distances. It is for this reason that delay lines using a polycrystalline metallic delay medium have in the past been operated at low bit rates. At very low frequencies the attenuation due to grain boundary scattering becomes smaller than that due to hysteresis loss [2.2.10] which rises linearly with frequency (not shown). The complete functional dependence of the attenuation for a polycrystalline material is tabulated in Table 2.2.1.

TABLE 2.2.1.

Range	Functional dependence
$\lambda > 2\pi\bar{D}$	$\alpha = B_1 f + A_4 \bar{D}^3 f^4$
$\lambda < 2\pi\bar{D}$	$\alpha = A_2 \bar{D} f^2$
$\lambda \ll \bar{D}_{min}$	$\alpha = B_1 f + C_2 f^2 + A_0/\bar{D}$

The coefficients are labelled by subscripts indicating the power of frequency with which they are associated. The origin of the linear loss term (B_1) is a hysteresis loop in the incremental stress-strain curve for the material. It is overshadowed in the intermediate scattering range by the quadratic scattering behaviour mentioned earlier. At high frequencies the attenuation due to grain boundary scattering becomes independent of f and is inversely proportional to the grain diameter $\bar{D}$. At these higher frequencies losses due to thermoelastic damping (C_2), which were swamped at lower frequencies by scattering, begin to become important [2.2.11]. Although for polycrystalline materials the effect has long before become irrelevant with regard to applications this is not the case for a single crystal material. Accordingly the next section is devoted to discussing this effect. In passing it should be noted that the onset of the f^4 scattering dependence is controlled by the grain size and that α is particularly sensitive to the elastic wave velocities. The latter dependence causes low velocity materials to have significantly higher attenuation and causes shear waves to be attenuated more than longitudinal waves.

2.2.3.2. Thermoelastic Attenuation

Thermoelastic attenuation is one of many loss mechanisms which belongs to the general class of relaxation phenomena. Both phonon-viscosity and phonon-conduction electron attenuation are also included in this category but will be discussed later.

The attenuation for a relaxation process may be shown to have the general form [2.2.12]

$$\alpha = 8.68 \frac{\Delta M}{2vM_0} \frac{\omega^2 \tau}{1+\omega^2 \tau^2} \text{ (dB cm}^{-1}) \qquad (2.2.10)$$

where ω is the frequency, τ a characteristic relaxation time and v the phase velocity. The parameters M_0 and ΔM are best described by considering the mathematical model which leads to this equation. The appropriate equation describing a viscoelastic solid (standard linear solid) is [2.2.13]

$$\tau^{-1}\sigma + \dot{\sigma} = M_1\tau^{-1}\varepsilon + M_0\dot{\varepsilon} \qquad (2.2.11)$$

where σ is the stress, ε the strain and τ the same relaxation time as appears in eqn (2.2.10). Under the action of a stress this solid behaves as shown in Fig. 2.2.8.

The exponential changes in the strain at constant stress (elastic after-effect) occur at a rate governed by $\tau_\sigma = (M_0/M_1)\tau$. From eqn (2.2.11) it is obvious that at constant strain M_1 the stress relaxes at a rate determined by $\tau_\varepsilon = \tau$. The unrelaxed and relaxed elastic moduli M_0 and M_1 may be defined in terms of the strains ε_1 and ε_2 in which case

$$M_0 = \frac{\sigma_0}{\varepsilon_1} \quad \text{and} \quad M_1 = \frac{\sigma_0}{\varepsilon_2} = \frac{\sigma_0}{\varepsilon_1 + \Delta\varepsilon} = M_0 + \Delta M, \qquad (2.2.12)$$

ΔM is the difference between M_1 and M_0. Implicit in the derivation of eqn (2.2.12) is the condition that $\Delta M \ll M_0$ (note in this limit $\tau_\sigma \approx \tau_\varepsilon$).

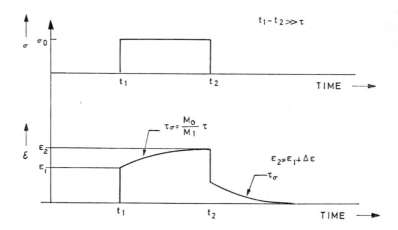

FIG. 2.2.8. Response of a standard linear solid to a stress pulse.

In terms of the unrelaxed modulus and the density ρ the phase velocity v in the attenuation formula is given by

$$v = \left(\frac{M_0}{\sigma} \right)^{\frac{1}{2}} . \tag{2.2.13}$$

For each of the different relaxation mechanisms associated with acoustic attenuation it is possible to evaluate the parameters described here and to use them to obtain estimates of the contribution of a particular process to the attenuation.

Thermoelastic attenuation is an example of a relaxation-type damping mechanism which occurs in all media that support longitudinal elastic waves. Shear waves are not attenuated by this mechanism since they produce no volume changes or heat conduction losses. It is only in the low loss region (contributions dominated by intrinsic losses) that the thermoelastic effect becomes important. The thermoelastic effect describes the heating and cooling of the compressed and rarefied regions of a longitudinal acoustic wave. The resulting heat flow between adjacent hot (compressed) and cold (rarefied) regions gives rise to an increase in entropy and a dissipation of energy, which causes the wave to be attenuated. The lifetime τ for the thermoelastic effect and the resonance frequency ω_r of the relaxation process are expressed by

$$\omega_r = \tau^{-1} = \rho C_V v_L^2 / K, \tag{2.2.14}$$

where C_V is the specific heat at constant volume, K is the thermal conductivity, v_L the longitudinal wave velocity and ρ the density. For insulators τ has the distinction of being related to the thermal phonon lifetime. This is due to the fact that in an insulator heat is conducted by the phonons and thermal resistivity is caused by phonon–phonon collisions which can be described in terms of simple kinetic theory concepts ($K = \frac{1}{3} C_V v^2 \tau_{th}$). In a metal heat is primarily conducted by the electrons while the thermal resistance is determined by electron–phonon scattering. The latter effect does not lend itself to a simple kinetic theory interpretation. An estimate of the upper limit on τ may be obtained by evaluating eqn (2.2.14) for a high conductivity material such as silver. In this case $\tau_{metal} \sim 10^{-10}$ s, which corresponds to a frequency in the gigahertz range. For insulators the relaxation time will be even shorter due to the decrease in the thermal conductivity. For the 100 KHz–1 GHz range of interest

$$\alpha_L = \frac{2\pi^2 f^2}{\rho v_L^3} \left[\frac{\gamma^2 K T}{v_L^2} \right]; \quad \gamma = \frac{3B\beta}{\rho C_V} \tag{2.2.15}$$

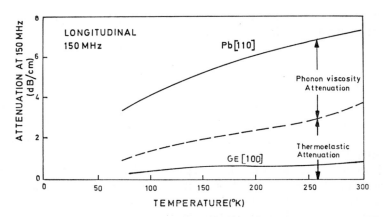

FIG. 2.2.9. Comparison of thermoelastic attenuation in lead with total losses in germanium.

where B is the bulk modulus and β the linear coefficient of expansion, and where γ is the Grüneisen constant [2.2.14] and presumably is nearly temperature independent.

When α is calculated for metals, semiconductors and insulators, it appears that the thermoelastic effect accounts only for a small fraction of the total losses (as will be discussed, the bulk of the losses at high frequencies in semiconductors and insulators can be attributed to the Akhieser effect or phonon-viscosity attenuation). For a typical metal the thermoelastic effect alone accounts for roughly $4\,\mathrm{db\,cm^{-1}}$ of attenuation which is the same order of magnitude as the total losses which occur in semiconductors and is significantly higher than the total losses which occur in insulators. This is illustrated in Fig. 2.2.9 where, albeit somewhat unfairly, the data for propagation along the [110] direction of lead [2.2.15] is compared to that for germanium along the [100] directions at 150 MHz. The data for germanium is that for $306\,\mathrm{MHz}$ corrected $(\sim f^2)$ to the frequency at which the comparison is made [2.2.16].

The slow temperature variation of thermoelastic attenuation observed in Fig. 2.2.9 is expected at high temperatures because $K \sim T^{-1}$ [2.2.15]. Because the thermal conductivity in metals is so much greater than that in semiconductors or insulators, the losses due to the thermoelastic effect in metals are significantly higher—so much so that they alone are larger than the total losses found in insulators or semiconductors. For this reason in applications involving longitudinal elastic waves at high frequencies insulator materials are favoured. The attenuation (shear and longitudinal) is determined in these materials by phonon-viscosity losses.

2.2.3.3. Akhieser or Phonon-viscosity Attenuation

For single crystal materials with few impurities Akhieser or phonon-viscosity attenuation [2.2.17] becomes an important loss mechanism at high frequencies (100 MHz–1 GHz). In the inherently low loss crystalline dielectric materials this form of relaxation attenuation dictates the total acoustic damping while in metals it is estimated to contribute about as much to damping as thermoelastic attenuation, however the thermoelastic attenuation in a metal is far greater than the total loss incurred by a semiconductor or insulator. These considerations eliminate metals as serious contenders for low loss applications.

In a crystalline solid there exist intrinsic elastic waves—thermal phonons—which are excited as the temperature, or equivalently the thermal energy, of the solid is increased. At room temperature the wavelength and the mean free path of a typical thermal phonon are, for example, a factor of 10^4 and 10^3 smaller respectively than a single wavelength of a 1 GHz ultrasonic wave. As a result an ultrasonic wave in the range of practical interest (100 KHz–1 GHz) produces what appears to be a spatially uniform strain to the thermal phonons which slowly changes with time. The effect of the uniform strain is to alter locally the dispersion relations of the thermal phonon modes. The strain ε_j due to the excited ultrasonic wave causes the energies $\hbar\omega_i$, and hence effective temperatures of various phonon modes, to become different, with the result that subsequently the non-equilibrium temperature distribution of modes relaxes back to a local equilibrium temperature. The equalization process proceeds via phonon–phonon scattering. Under the influence of a sinusoidally varying strain the attenuation is governed by the standard relaxation formula eqn (2.2.14) with (note from kinetic theory $K = Cv^2\,\tau_{th}/3$)

$$\tau_s = \tau_{th} = \frac{3K}{C_V\,\bar{v}^2} \qquad (2.2.16)$$

for shear waves and $\tau_1 = 2\tau_{th}$ for longitudinal waves where $\bar{v}$ is the average Debye velocity $\bar{v}$. The factor of two difference between relaxation of shear and longitudinal waves is not quantitatively understood. Since shear acoustic waves can interact directly with thermal phonons the thermal relaxation rate is expected in this case, but longitudinal waves couple only to thermal phonons of the same frequency which suggests that a much longer relaxation time should come into play. A factor of two, however, seems to give good agreement between experiment and theory [2.2.18]. For metals it is only the lattice thermal conductivity which comes into play in determining the relaxation time τ_{th} and since this is much less than the electronic contribution, the relaxation time is expected to be much smaller than that calculated for the thermoelastic effect based upon the total thermal conductivity. In fact since the lattice thermal conductivity in a metal is determined by electron–phonon collisions the relaxation time is expected to be the same order of magnitude as that for phonon–phonon collisions in an insulator (10^{-12} s). The attenuation for a longitudinal (shear) wave can be expressed by:

$$\alpha_{L(S)} = 8 \cdot 68 \, \frac{\bar{\gamma}_{L(S)}^2 K T \omega^2}{\rho \bar{v}^5} \, (\text{dB cm}^{-1}) \qquad (2.2.17)$$

where $\bar{\gamma}$ is a renormalized Grüneisen constant and contains the effect of mode dependence, K is the thermal conductivity. A comparison of the thermo-elastic attenuation with the Akhieser attenuation shows for semiconductors

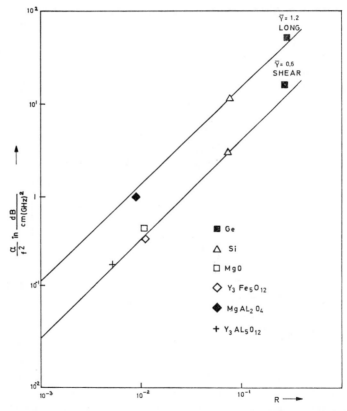

FIG. 2.2.10. Sound attenuation normalized to 1 GHz as a function of the thermal parameter R for cubic insulating materials at room temperature—propagation along the (100) directions [2.2.19].

and insulators that

$$\alpha(\text{Akhieser}) \gg \alpha \text{ (Thermoelastic)}$$

and that for metals

$$\alpha(\text{Akhieser}) \approx \alpha(\text{Thermoelastic})$$

The Akhieser attenuation at high temperatures, where $K \sim (1/T)$ for most insulators, can be described by

$$\frac{\alpha}{f^2} = 304\left(\frac{\bar{\gamma}^2}{\gamma_{th}^2}\right)R \qquad (2.2.18)$$

where γ_{th} is the average Grüneisen constant obtained from thermal conductivity, f is the frequency and R is a thermal parameter used as an acoustic figure of merit.

At high frequencies the best crystalline insulating materials with low R, will be those with (1) low thermal conductivity, (2) high Debye temperature and (3) low average volume per atom.

For $\gamma_{th} = 2$, $\bar{\gamma}_s = 0.6$ and $\bar{\gamma}_1 = 1.2$ the data for several cubic materials are plotted in Fig. 2.2.10 against the quantity R. The attenuation is normalized to 1 GHz with quadratic frequency dependence confirmed experimentally for Ge and Si down to below 100 MHz [2.2.19].

2.2.3.4. Phonon-Conduction Electron Attenuation

An ultrasonic wave propagating in a crystalline solid disturbs the periodic arrangements of atoms or ion cores thereby producing electric fields which can scatter charged carriers. In a metal it is possible for the conduction electrons to absorb energy from the ultrasonic wave via this interaction mechanism and, accordingly, produce damping much in the same way as that which occurs in a classical gas or liquid due to viscosity. As has been mentioned in connection with thermoelastic and Akhieser attenuation, damping characterized by a viscosity gives rise to an attenuation which may be regarded as arising through a relaxation process. The attenuation due to energy absorption by conduction electrons is related to the mean free path of the electrons. Therefore it is only at the very lowest temperatures ($T < 10$ K) that conduction electron attenuation makes up a significant portion of the total loss of a metal—at higher temperatures the other intrinsic mechanisms (such as arise from the thermoelastic effect or from phonon–phonon scattering) are usually dominant.

An interesting effect occurs, however, when an electric field is applied to a metal causing the electrons to drift along the direction of sound propagation (longitudinal mode assumed for discussion). Normally the electrons absorb energy from the sound wave but under the condition that the drift velocity is non-zero the reverse may occur. Theoretical predictions [2.2.20] suggest that the attenuation decreases linearly with electron drift velocity v_{drift}. Physical considerations as well as experimental results suggest that the transition from loss to gain should occur when the drift velocity just equals the longitudinal sound velocity. For a metal at low temperatures the mobility may be as high as $10^4 \text{ cm}^2 \text{ V}^{-1} \text{ s}^{-1}$ which would require a field of 10 V cm^{-1} to produce a sound velocity of 10^5 cm s^{-1}. At higher temperatures the mobility decreases rapidly due to phonon scattering requiring even larger fields to drive the carriers. In a metal it is impossible to produce such fields because of the high conductivity; however, in semiconductors fields of the required order of magnitude can be obtained. The fact that in a semiconductor the change in potential energy of an electron is directly related to strain immediately prompts comparison with piezoelectric materials for which a similar effect occurs. In a piezoelectric insulator or semiconductor an electric field is produced by a strain. This field due to an acoustic wave changes the potential energy of a conduction electron in a piezoelectric material. It can be shown that coupling between phonons and electrons will be more favourable in a piezoelectric material than in an ordinary semiconductor for all attainable frequencies.

In an insulator the number of carriers which can couple to a sound wave is small and therefore piezoelectric semiconductors might be expected to show the most promise. This is verified by experiments on CdS and other compound semiconductors which display piezoelectricity.

An acoustic plane wave produces significant electric fields which can couple to drifting electrons only when a component of piezoelectric polarization is produced along the direction of propagation. Acoustic waves satisfying this criterion by virtue of their "orientation" relative to the crystallographic axes are said to be piezoelectrically active [2.2.21] and are those which offer the best possibility for amplification. Provided the frequency of such a wave is much higher than the conductivity frequency $\omega_c = \sigma/\varepsilon$ the piezoelectric fields associated with the wave will not be cancelled since the electrons cannot respond fast enough. As a result of the additional potential energy stored in these fields, piezoelectric stiffening occurs which modifies the elastic modulus. Hence considering the interaction between phonons and electrons as a relaxation type attenuation process governed by the conductivity relaxation frequency V, which is Doppler-shifted by $\gamma = 1 - v_{\text{drift}}/v$ to account for the drift velocity of the electrons yields [2.2.22]

$$\alpha = \omega \frac{K_{\text{em}}^2}{2v} \frac{\omega_c/\gamma\omega}{1 + \omega_c/\gamma^2 \omega^2} \qquad (2.2.19)$$

where K_{em} is the electromechanical coefficient and v the wave velocity. The velocity v as well as the electromechanical coupling parameter depend upon the direction of propagation. This formula indicates that at low frequencies

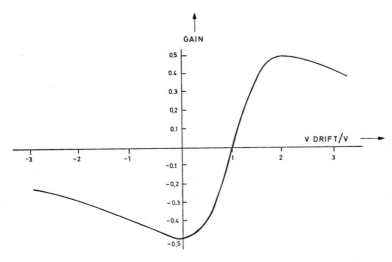

FIG. 2.2.11. Acoustic gain as a function of drift velocity when $\omega/\omega_c = 1$.

($\omega_c \gg \omega$) the effect of the piezoelectric will be small, due physically to the screening effects of the electrons. When the piezoelectric has no conductivity ($\omega_c = 0$) there are no electrons to which the acoustic wave can couple and therefore $\alpha = 0$. The most interesting situation occurs when $v < v_{\text{drift}}$ in which case $\gamma < 0$ giving rise to amplification instead of attenuation. Figure 2.2.11 shows the behaviour of α as the drift velocity is varied through positive and negative values for $\omega = \omega_c$. At the synchronous velocity $v_{\text{drift}} = v$ and there is no attenuation.

2.2.3.5. Ultrasonic Attenuation by Dislocations and Impurities

It is customary when considering crystalline solids to use as a model a highly idealized physical structure which does not include imperfections. In many cases the omission of structural defects is not important, because the physical properties of interest do not depend strongly upon them. This is fortunate since it is usually difficult to eliminate them. It so happens that, unlike most physical properties, acoustic attenuation is sensitive to these imperfections and therefore it is necessary to consider them when analysing attenuation data. Two important defects encountered in single crystal materials are dislocations and impurities both of which give rise to forms of relaxation attenuation. The relaxation time associated with dislocation damping varies slowly with temperature at low strain amplitudes while that for impurities is characterized by a strong exponential dependence. In both cases the attenuation is controlled by the concentration of defects as might be expected.

A dislocation is a linear imperfection in a crystal. It is characterized by severe distortion of a localized region of the crystal lattice. The absence of a row of atoms in the centre of the lattice produces a channel around which the deviation from regularity decreases with distance. In effect the upper two planes of lattice points have slipped past the lower ones in the region to the left of the channel causing severe distortion in the centre of the lattice and moderate distortion elsewhere. The magnitude and direction of the slip step may be characterized by a vector $\bar{b}$, the Burgers vector of the dislocation. A dislocation can move as a result of a shear strain. It can be shown that a dislocation segment of length L which has moved a distance γ produces the strain $\varepsilon_d = bL\gamma$ in a cube of unit dimensions. Hence the application of an external shear stress along the Burgers vector (in the slip plane) produces an elastic and dislocation contribution to the total strain. The elastic module which relates the stress to the strain is reduced by the presence of ε_d and the material appears more elastic than that predicted on the basis of purely elastic deformation. This fact gives a clue as to which materials are likely to have large dislocation densities and therefore large dislocation damping. Metals are important candidates since they are very ductile.

In actuality the dislocations in a solid form a network and are anchored firmly where they cross. Point defects such as impurities or vacancies pin down the dislocations at intermediate points. As a result the application of a shear stress causes a bowing of the dislocations between intermediate pinning points. So long as the stresses are not great the intermediate pinning points will not break away. In this case the dislocation behaves like a string under tension and can be described by the differential eqn [2.2.23]

$$A\frac{\partial^2 U}{\partial t^2} + B\frac{\partial U}{\partial t} - C\frac{\partial^2 U}{\partial x^2} = b\sigma \qquad (2.2.20)$$

where the displacement at intermediate points $U = U(x, y, t)$ results from the applied force per unit length $b\sigma$. The constants in the differential equation are

$$A = \pi\rho b^2 \quad \text{and} \quad C = \frac{2M_0 b^2}{\pi(1-v)} \qquad (2.2.21)$$

where ρ is the density of the crystal, M_0 is the shear modulus and v is the Poisson ratio. B is a phenomenological damping constant. In a solid with dislocations, an acoustic wave which produces an oscillatory component of shear stress σ in the slip plane drives the dislocation and loses energy through a viscous damping term. The problem is exactly analogous to a driven string vibrating in a viscous medium.

In the overdamped limit which is expected to apply to high-purity metals at room temperature a relaxation-type resonance occurs at

$$\omega_m = \tau^{-1} = \frac{\pi^2 C}{BL^2} \tag{2.2.22}$$

where L is the average distance between intermediate pinning points (loop length) and the two other parameters B and C have been defined previously. An estimate of this frequency indicates that it falls in the low megahertz range ($f_m \approx 15$ MHz for $L = 10^{-4}$ cm, $B = 5 \times 10^{-4}$ dyne-s cm^{-2} and $C = 10^{-4}$ dyne) for unworked crystals. Experimental measurements of the decrement at room temperature indicate that values of 3 MHz, 100 MHz, 70 MHz are representative of copper, NaCl, and LiF respectively. It should be noted, however, that the resonance frequency ω_m depends strongly upon the metallurgical state of the single crystal through L. This fact can be used to test the validity of eqn (2.2.22) by measuring the frequency dependence of the decrement as a function of irradiation time. The effect of high energy radiation is to produce defects such as interstitials or vacancies which further pin down the dislocations thereby reducing L and hence increasing ω_m.

The attenuation of an acoustic wave due to the presence of dislocations is given by the relaxation formula

$$\alpha = \Omega \left(\frac{4M_0 b^2}{4\pi C} \right) \Lambda L^2 \, \omega_m \, \frac{(\omega/\omega_m)^2}{1 + (\omega/\omega_m)^2} \tag{2.2.23}$$

where Λ is a measure of the dislocation density and is defined as the total length of movable dislocation line in a unit cube. The orientation factor Ω takes into account the fact that only shear stresses in the slip plane will be effective in driving dislocations. In order to determine the correct attenuation it is necessary to resolve the stresses associated with a propagating longitudinal or shear wave into shear components along the slip plane. Since there are usually many slip planes in a crystal the orientation of the propagation vector relative to each of these planes is important. The factor Ω implicitly contains all of this geometrical information. The verification of the behaviour predicted by eqns (2.2.22) and (2.2.23) is shown in Fig. 2.2.12 for copper [2.2.24]. Here the dislocation decrement ($\delta = \pi Q^{-1} = \lambda \alpha / 8.68$) has been plotted against frequency for compressional waves propagating in the [100] direction. The solid was irradiated with gamma rays which gives rise to the series of data points, each labelled with an exposure time. Under the assumption that the only parameter to change during exposure is the loop length L, theoretical curves have been computed on the basis of a linear dependence of L with time and appear in Fig. 2.2.12 as the solid curves. It is evident that the behaviour is described very well by eqns (2.2.22) and (2.2.23).

D

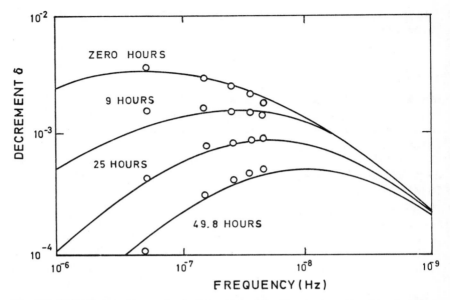

Fig. 2.2.12. Dislocation decrement δ of gamma-irradiated copper as a function of exposure time and frequency. The data appear as circles and the solid curves are the theoretical predictions [2.2.24].

As the loop length decreases with increased pinning due to point defects, the position of the frequency maximum increases inversely with L^2 while the value of the corresponding minimum decreases directly with L^2. Notice that at high frequencies the theoretical curves predict that the attenuation becomes independent of L. The decrement data shown in Fig. 2.2.12 for the unexposed specimen corresponds to an attenuation of about $4\,dB\,cm^{-1}$ at 500 MHz. These numbers are comparable to the total losses which occur in silicon or germanium and are very much larger than those that occur in low loss dielectric materials. Since other contributions to the attenuation such as discussed previously continue to rise quadratically with frequency where the dislocation contribution begins to level off (near f_m), at extremely high frequencies the relative contribution of dislocations to the attenuation will be small. The effects of dislocations are expected to be seen primarily in the vicinity of f_m. For some ionic crystals which can also have large dislocation densities this resonance frequency is observed to be fairly large. Since ω_m is controlled in part by the elastic shear modulus M_0 one might expect that high shear velocity materials such as diamond would have a high resonance frequency. While this may be the case the importance of dislocation attenuation at high frequencies in these and in fact in all materials is controlled by Λ or equivalently the dislocation density. Presumably in diamond the density is small which would imply low dislocation loss. In most materials the dislocation density depends on the metallurgical state of the specimen. A typical value for Λ in an unworked metal such as copper is 10^{-7} cm^2. While pinning of dislocations can be achieved through irradiation, additional dislocations can be produced by plastically deforming a solid. Studies of dislocation attenuation as a function of plastic deformation agree well with predictions based on eqn (2.2.23).

The simple discussion of dislocation damping presented here is valid so long as the stress associated with the acoustic wave does not cause the dislocations to break away from their intermediate pinning points. At high stress amplitudes this is not the case, and attenuation will be much larger.

2.2.3.6. Survey of Materials

The results of the previous sections can be summarized by plotting attenuation versus frequency data for a number of representative materials. This has been done in Fig. 2.2.13. Represented in this figure are polycrystalline, amorphous and single crystal materials; metals, semiconductors and insulators. As the intended use of these materials is for delay line applications, the data presented is that for room temperature or thereabouts. A cursory examination of the data reveals that the attenuation for a solid increases with frequency in the megahertz range at a rate roughly between f and f^4. The shear wave curve for fused quartz (curve 3) [2.2.25] provides a natural dividing line between low and high loss materials. Traversing the attenuation curves at a fixed frequency (≈ 100 MHz) in order of increasing loss one finds crystalline insulators such as rutile (curve 1) [2.2.26] in the low loss region followed by crystalline semiconductors such as silicon (curve 2) [2.2.16] as one approaches the intermediate loss region, which contains low loss amorphous materials such as fused quartz (curve 3) and crystalline metals, such as aluminium (curve 4) [2.2.27]. Following these materials at still greater attenuation one finds amorphous materials such as glass (curve 5) [2.2.28] and fine grained polycrystalline metals such as stainless steel (curve 6) [2.2.29].

For crystalline materials the attenuation is by and large quadratic in frequency when f is greater than 100 MHz reflecting either phonon-viscosity attenuation in dielectrics or presumably a combination of phonon-viscosity and thermoelastic attenuation in metals. Since the temperature dependence of the attenuation in crystalline materials is determined primarily by the product of the thermal conductivity K and the temperature T, the attenuation is expected to be slowly varying in the vicinity of room temperature where $K \sim 1/T$. For non-crystalline materials the temperature dependence of the acoustic loss is determined by a large number of factors and accordingly

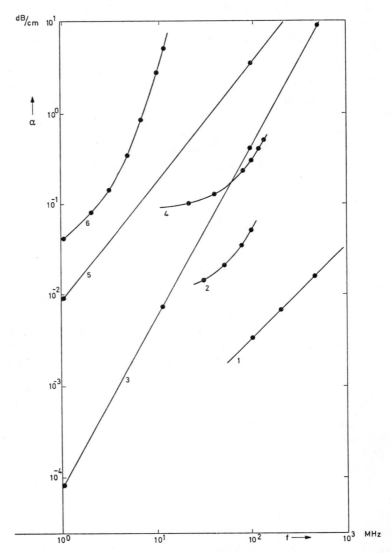

FIG. 2 2.13. Frequency dependence of attenuation for representative acoustic materials: (1) rutile c-axis shear [2.2.26], (2) silicon (111) long. [2.2.16], (3) fused quartz, shear, (4) crystal aluminium (111) long. [2.2.27], (5) T-40 glass, shear [2.2.28] and (6) stainless steel, long. [2.2.29].

experimental measurements are the most convenient way to determine the temperature dependence. In digital delay lines a low temperature coefficient of attenuation is important so that the frequency characteristic does not change during operation possibly causing a loss of information. Generally the temperature coefficient of delay which depends on the temperature dependence of the propagation velocity and the length of the delay line is more of a problem. The effects of a change in delay time due to temperature can be avoided entirely by leaving a short time gap after the pulse sequence and by using marker pulses to gate the timing and counting circuits on and off.

Returning to Fig. 2.2.13 the role of crystalline metals should be mentioned. Since the attenuation for these materials falls in the intermediate loss range, they are loss competitive with fused quartz. The fact that they correspond to a more metallurgically refined state however, makes them economically unfavourable. By far the most economically competitive materials are the polycrystalline metals.

2.3. ULTRASONIC BULK WAVE DELAY LINES

2.3.1. WAVE PROPAGATION IN UNBOUNDED MEDIA

It is important when constructing an ultrasonic delay line device to understand what type of bulk modes propagate in a solid and how these are affected by the presence of boundaries. In view of the recent trend to use anisotropic crystalline materials for high frequency device applications, bulk wave propagation in unbounded media of this type will be considered first [2.3.1]. Two types of waves exist in unbounded media: those for which the particle motion may be described as being transverse to the propagation direction and those for which it is parallel. These so-called transverse and longitudinal waves may be characterized by the elastic stiffness constants c_{ijkl} which relate stress and strain in the solid via Hooke's law (implied summations on repeated indices):

$$\sigma_{ij} = c_{ijkl}\, \varepsilon_{kl} . \qquad (2.3.1)$$

Here σ_{ij} is the stress (force per unit area) acting in the ith coordinate direction on a surface normal to the jth direction. ε_{kl} is the corresponding strain (normalized displacement). Knowledge of the elastic constants c_{ijkl} and the density ρ for a particular material allows one to determine the phase velocity v of the transverse and longitudinal waves as a function of direction. One finds three mutually orthogonal modes of propagation, two of which are transverse and the other longitudinal. The relationship between transverse and longitudinal velocity for a given direction is nearly invariant. Typically the velocity of a transverse wave v_s is of the order of $3 \times 10^3 \text{ m s}^{-1}$ and is roughly a factor of two less than v_l. This is found to be true independent of the crystal system. Expressions for the velocity of a transverse or longitudinal mode propagating in an arbitrary direction in more complicated crystal systems have been derived and can be found in literature [2.3.2]. Each mode has a distinct velocity and the polarization of the longitudinal mode need not coincide with the propagation vector as is the case for principle directions in the cubic system. The corresponding modes are neither transverse nor longitudinal in the strict sense but still are referred to as being such.

A further complication occurs when the solid is piezoelectric [2.3.3]. In this case Hooke's law must be generalized to include the effects of the piezoelectric fields. The appropriate equations become

$$\left.\begin{array}{l} \sigma_{ij} = c_{ijkl}\, \varepsilon_{kl} - e_{ijm}\, E_m \\[2mm] D_n = e_{nkl}\, \varepsilon_{kl} + \varepsilon_{nm}\, E_m \end{array}\right\} \qquad (2.3.2)$$

where the e_{ijm} are the piezoelectric constants which relate the electric field E to the stress and the ε_{nm} are the elements of the dielectric permittivity matrix which relates the electric field to the electric displacement D. As a result of the coupling between elastic and electric systems an electric wave now accompanies the elastic wave. The additional energy stored in the electric fields stiffens the solid and accordingly increases the longitudinal wave velocity. The transverse waves are unaffected since no electric fields couple to them. The effect of a finite conductivity is to introduce attenuation and dispersion (frequency-dependent phase velocity) into the system. So long as $\omega \gg \omega_c$ ($\omega_c = \sigma/\varepsilon$) the charge carriers cannot respond fast enough to screen out the piezoelectric fields and the elastic modulus remains at the stiffened value. This was mentioned previously in connection with amplification in piezoelectric materials. The qualitative aspects of this discussion are expected to extend to more complex situations where coupling between shear strains and electric fields occur. For a real solid the problem of wave propagation in a piezoelectric crystal becomes difficult to do analytically and it is necessary to resort to computer calculations to obtain the phase velocity.

Up to this point the effects of boundaries on the propagation velocity have been completely ignored. In device applications it is convenient to confine the elastic waves to a restricted region in space for economic and packaging reasons. The influence of the boundaries under such circumstances cannot be ignored. In general the phase velocity no longer remains independent of frequency with the result that an acoustic pulse (many frequency components) will spread in space (or time) as it propagates.

The presence of a boundary modifies the simple unbounded problem by imposing the condition that at a "free" surface the particle motion must be

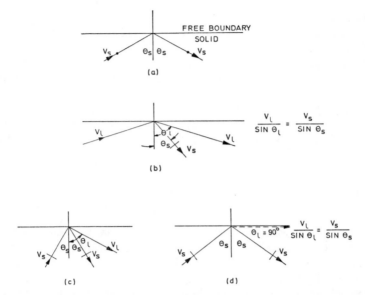

Fig. 2.3.1. Reflection of a plane wave at a free boundary: (a) horizontally polarized shear wave, (b) longitudinal wave, (c) vertically polarized shear wave $\theta_1 < 90°$ and (d) $\theta_1 = 90°$.

such that the normal and shear components of the stress vanish. This has the effect of coupling different modes of propagation together as can be seen by considering the results of various reflection processes at an interface [2.3.4]. Figure 2.3.1 summarizes the three possible situations. In case (a) a transverse wave polarized horizontally is incident upon a free surface. Here the boundary conditions dictate that the angle of incidence must equal the angle of reflection and that the polarization and amplitude remain unchanged after reflection. No mode conversion occurs. A longitudinal wave reflected under similar circumstances is partially converted to a transverse wave with polarization parallel to the page as shown in case (b). The angles θ_1 and θ_s are related by Snell's law $v_1/\sin\theta_1 = v_s/\sin\theta_s$, i.e. the components of the phase velocities along the boundary are equal. Mode conversion also occurs when a transverse wave polarized vertically strikes the free surface as in case (c) and (d). A longitudinally polarized wave is then reflected at an angle $\theta_1 = \sin^{-1}\left((v_1/v_s)\sin\theta_s\right) > \theta_s$. Since $v_1 > v_s$ it is possible for total internal reflection of the longitudinal wave to occur (see case (d)). Generally when $\theta_1 = 90°$, θ_s lies between 30° and 40° depending on Poisson's ratio $\sigma = \frac{1}{2}(v_1^2 - 2v_s^2)/(v_1^2 - v_s^2)$. Beyond this critical angle no longitudinal wave is reflected. The relative amplitudes of the incident and reflected waves in cases (b), (c) and (d) may be determined by solving the boundary value problem and in each case depend on the angle of incidence, the phase velocities, and Poisson's ratio. Reflection problems of this type can and have been solved for particular crystal classes. These simple free surface reflection considerations enable one to understand the modes which propagate in an acoustic waveguide. By thinking of a mode as one or more simple plane waves reflecting in a zigzag path between free surfaces, it is possible to present the results of solving the wave equation subject to the free surface boundary conditions without going into mathematical detail. The following discussion of guided waves applies to isotropic homogeneous solids.

2.3.2. GUIDED WAVE PROPAGATION IN SIMPLE STRUCTURES (SHEAR AND TORSIONAL MODES)

Since a transverse wave polarized parallel to a free boundary is reflected without mode conversion, interpretation of the corresponding guided wave modes is very simple. Figure 2.3.2(a) shows an infinite plate and the according particle displacements for the first three horizontally polarized shear modes which propagate in it. The boundary conditions at the plate surfaces can be satisfied without the presence of longitudinal waves and therefore these shear modes can be interpreted entirely in terms of bulk shear waves. The lowest order mode is non-dispersive and propagates straight down the

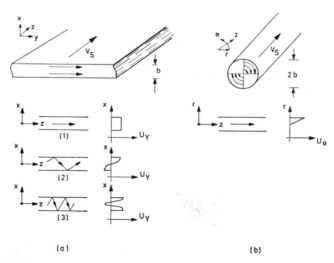

FIG. 2.3.2. Horizontal shear modes: (a) in a plate and (b) the analogous non-dispersive torsional mode in a cylinder with corresponding particle displacements.

guide with velocity v_s. Figure 2.3.2(a) (case 1) shows that the particle motion is uniform over the cross-section and, as is the case for all modes, this pattern does not change with distance along the polarization direction. Above the lowest cut-off frequency $f = v_s/2b$ (which corresponds to the condition $\lambda/2 = b$) the second order mode can propagate. It is dispersive and corresponds, as do all higher order modes, to a shear wave being reflected back and forth between the plate surfaces. The particle motion is sinusoidal over the cross-section as indicated by Fig. 2.3.2(a) (case 2). The third and higher modes are generalizations of the second with more oscillations in the displacement profiles. In terms of delay line operation the non-dispersive mode is ideally suited for digital applications. It is clear that by choosing the thickness b of the plate sufficiently small it is possible to operate in a frequency region such that all modes except the first are cutoff and therefore will not propagate. For $b = 0.1$ cm the cutoff frequency corresponds to several megahertz which suggests that the non-dispersive mode can be used for low frequency digital applications. This was recognized by Meitzler [2.3.5] who constructed an approximation to an infinite plate by using a thin metal strip to guide acoustic waves. The width was made much larger than the thickness and the minor surfaces were coated with an absorbing material to reduce reflections. This type of mechanical waveguide has been operated successfully up to about 10 MHz using piezoelectric shear transducers and polycrystalline aluminium strips and forms the basis for the strip delay line. To conserve space the strip is coiled into a helix—the operation of the device is unaffected by this modification so long as the curvature is not great. Figure 2.3.3(a) shows a strip digital delay line employing the non-dispersive mode. This type of delay line was studied extensively at Bell laboratories. There, devices with delay times spanning the millisecond range with corresponding capacities of up to 20 000 bits were constructed. A typical device with 4.2 ms delay has a 34 dB mid-band insertion loss. Since most of these devices were operated below 10 MHz the bandwidth was usually less than a few megahertz. Bit rates of 2–5 MHz were typical. A great advantage of this type of device was the relatively low cost that could be obtained by using polycrystalline aluminium strip as the delay medium. As an alternative to the aluminium strip a thick glass plate can be used to achieve higher frequency operation. The non-dispersive mode can be selectively excited by optimizing the transducer height.

A difficulty arises in the latter case when one attempts to fold the delay path by machining reflecting facets on the plate perpendicular to the flat surfaces. Since the shear mode is polarized horizontally it will undergo mode conversion upon reflection unless the angle of incidence is greater than the critical angle $\theta_c = \sin^{-1}(v_s/v_l)$. The latter effect places severe limitations on the possible configurations that can be used and has led to a special class of

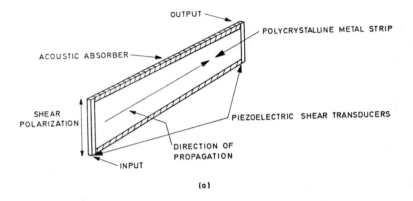

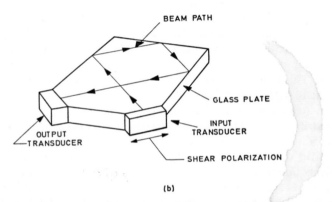

FIG. 2.3.3. Delay lines employing the non-dispersive horizontal shear mode in a chip (a) or plate (b).

devices. The fact that the critical angle in most delay media is less than 45° has inspired wave guides of rectangular symmetry [2.3.6] as shown in Fig. 2.3.3(b).

The horizontal shear modes of a plate have an analogue in the torsional modes of a cylinder. This is to be expected since the particle motion is again parallel to the boundary. The lowest order dispersive mode cut-off is at $f_c = 5.136 \, v_s/2\pi b$ where b is the radius of the cylinder. The non-dispersive mode propagates with the shear velocity v_s and the displacement profile is linear with radius as shown in Fig. 2.3.2(b). Since this mode is exactly analogous to that found in a plate it can and has been used successfully in low frequency magnetostrictive delay lines [2.3.7]. Since at 10 MHz the largest possible diameter is of the order of 0.1 cm the delay medium invariably takes the form of a piece of metal (beryllium copper) wire coiled into a helix. Memories storing 20 000 bits at 1.5 MHz have been constructed. Besides the simple shear and torsional modes in plates and cylinders, compressional and flexural modes can also exist. These modes may be interpreted in terms of a mixture of longitudinal and transverse plane waves which are produced via mode coupling at the surfaces. In some high frequency delay lines these modes are used.

2.3.3. BULK WAVE TRANSDUCERS

2.3.3.1. Piezoelectric Transducers and Transducer Materials

(i) *Phenomenological description of piezoelectricity.* As was suggested in the discussion of amplification by piezoelectric semiconductors, the phenomena of piezoelectricity is associated with the occurrence of a strain (or possibly a stress) in a material when subject to an electric field. Historically the converse effect in which charge is produced in proportion to an applied pressure was discovered first. The physical basis for the latter effect is suggested schematically in Fig. 2.3.4 by the net electric dipole moment which is produced by distortion of a structure, which has a three-fold rotation axis. The importance of atomic symmetry is accentuated by this illustration to convey the point that the occurrence of piezoelectricity and crystal symmetry are intimately related. It is convenient, for the moment, to consider only single crystal materials and in this case it is necessary for the existence of piezoelectric behaviour that the structure does not possess a centre of symmetry. The implied anisotropy which must result is a consequence of the linear relationship between electrical and mechanical parameters which cannot exist otherwise. Of the 32 crystal classes only 20 satisfy the criterion of being non-centrosymmetrical and only a handful of these are represented by materials used in actual devices. The description of these materials has been facilitated by a phenomenological approach to piezoelectricity which

FIG. 2.3.4. Strain-induced charge-polarization.

incorporates the effects of crystal symmetry into the observed linear relationships between electrical and mechanical variables. More fundamental approaches which attempt to predict the values of the interrelating parameters have received less interest due to the difficulties involved in assessing the atomic nature of bonds and due to the simplicity with which practical measurements determining these parameters can be made.

The electrical state of a dielectric is determined when the electric field (E) or the electric displacement (D) vector is specified. The elastic conditions are specified by the stress σ and the strain ε components. In a piezoelectric material any of the state variables may be related linearly to any of the remaining parameters giving rise to electro-elastic matrices describing the material.

Although single crystal materials can be used to make transducers, polycrystalline ferroelectric materials in the form of ceramics [2.3.8] offer the potential for much greater versatility. Variation of chemical composition can be used conveniently to optimize the piezoelectric properties and therefore these materials have found widespread application. In a ceramic many small crystallites are sintered together with their crystallographic axes oriented randomly. The application of a poling field aligns the spontaneous polarization of these crystallites thereby rendering the ceramic piezoelectric.

(ii) *Piezoelectric materials and crystal classes.* Of the 20 possible crystal classes in which the piezoelectric effect can actually occur, 5 form the basis for the majority of transducers used in ultrasonic applications.

Important materials belonging to each class are listed below.

Class 6 mm (hexagonal system): CdS, ZnO, ZnS, CdSe, CdTe, ZnTe, ZnSe. Ceramics: $BaTiO_3$, $PbZr_x Ti_{1-x}O_3$, $PbNb_2O_6$.

Class $\bar{4}3$ m (cubic system): GaAs, InSb, ZnS, CdS.

Class 32 (trigonal system): αSiO_2, HgS.

Class 3 m (trigonal system): $LiNbO_3$, $LiTaO_3$.

Class 2 mm (orthorhombic system); $LiGaO_2$.

As an illustration of how these materials can be used, consider the crystal class 6 mm [2.3.9]. In this case the axes x_1, x_2 and x_3 (Fig. 2.3.5) are mutually orthogonal with x_1 and x_2 lying in planes of reflection symmetry and x_3 coinciding with the 6-fold rotation axis of the hexagonal lattice. An electric field E_1 applied perpendicular to a thin plate (X-cut) of this material will cause it to shear (σ_5) along an axis perpendicular to x_1. This effect can be used to generate shear waves as illustrated in Fig. 2.3.5 by applying an oscillating electric field at a frequency such that the thickness dimension d represents one half wavelength of a shear wave in the material. When this

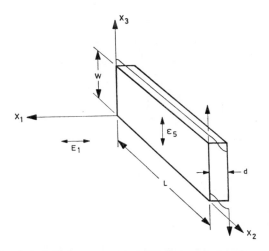

FIG. 2.3.5. Shear wave generation in crystal class 6 mm.

plate is mounted on a delay medium the motion is governed by the equation for ε_5 and both stress and strain oscillate with time. The application of an electric field E_2 perpendicular to a plate lying in the x_1, x_3 plane (Y-cut) produces a strain ε_5 which can be used to generate shear waves in a similar manner. In fact due to the symmetry of the crystal, all directions perpendicular to the x_3 axis are equivalent in so far as elastic and piezoelectric properties are concerned and therefore it is not necessary to specify the orientation of the electric field in the x_1, x_2 plane. Longitudinal waves may be produced by applying a field E_3 parallel to the 6-fold rotation axis and perpendicular to a plate lying in the x_1, x_2 plane. The effect of this field is to produce compressive or dilatational stresses along all three axes, the plate becomes shorter and narrower as it gets thicker. This effect can be used to generate longitudinal waves by mounting the plate on its flat face and applying an oscillating electric field such that the plate thickness corresponds to one half wavelength of a longitudinal wave in the material. Similar considerations for the crystal class $\bar{4}3$ m indicate that longitudinal waves can be excited by an electric field in the [111] direction oriented parallel to the thickness dimension of a plate. Shear waves polarized in the [001] direction may be excited in a plate oriented perpendicular to the [110] direction. The X-cut crystal of class 3 mm (in the form of α-quartz) may be used to generate longitudinal waves. Shear waves may be generated by Y- or rotated Y-cuts. Since PZT transducers can be used to produce both shear and longitudinal waves with less conversion loss, the role of quartz in ordinary transducer applications has become minor. The principle use for

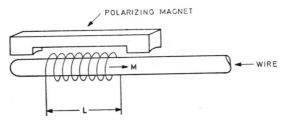

FIG. 2.3.6. Idealized magnetostrictive longitudinal mode transducer.

quartz lies in frequency control applications where extreme frequency stability is important. The temperature coefficient of frequency for a quartz oscillator can be minimized over a broad temperature range by correctly orienting the cut of a plate relative to the crystal axes.

2.3.3.2. Magnetostrictive Transducers and Materials

The application of a magnetic field to a ferromagnetic or ferrimagnetic material can, under the proper conditions, cause a strain analogous to that produced in a piezoelectric [2.3.7]. Although the microscopic origin of this effect is fundamentally different in these cases, there exists a formal parallel between the two which can be used to an advantage.

In a magnetic material the elastic relationship between stress and strain established through the elastic compliance tensor or its inverse the stiffness tensor must be supplemented by variables describing the magnetic state of the system. The magnetic field intensity H and the magnetic flux density B are the counterparts of the electric variables E and D respectively and are related by the permeability tensor μ. As in the case of piezoelectric materials the direct and converse effects can be combined into a 9×9 magnetoelastic matrix. The polycrystalline materials are of the most technological importance. Generally it is assumed that these materials are elastically isotropic and that the piezomagnetic constant matrix is equivalent to that for crystal class 6 mm. Longitudinal waves can be generated by driving a polycrystalline material parallel to the magnetization axis as shown in Fig. 2.3.6. Such transducers have been used in connection with longitudinal and torsional wire delay lines. Combining two longitudinal magnetostrictive transducers (using thin tapes instead of wires) into a push-pull arrangement, the torsional mode can also be excited. A principal drawback of this type of magnetostrictive devices lies in the fact that a bulky coil is required to produce the necessary magnetic field and optimum coupling to elastic waves occurs when $\lambda = 2L$ which restricts the maximum frequency of operation due to geometrical considerations. It is difficult to make coils small enough to generate and receive high frequency (1 MHz) elastic waves.

2.4. SURFACE WAVE DELAY LINES

2.4.1. SURFACE WAVE PROPAGATION

The propagation of bulk acoustic waves in an infinite medium was considered in connection with and as an introduction to waves in bounded media in Section 2.3.1. There is another type of elastic wave which can exist on the surface of a semi-infinite solid, the so-called surface wave [2.4.1, 2.4.2]. It has the advantage that it is easily accessible which permits the realization of a wide range of devices involving coupling between the surface wave and external electric fields. Since the generation, detection, and guidance of these waves can be performed with surface structures, planar processing techniques developed for the manufacture of integrated circuits can be used to fabricate the required components. Whereas transducer bonding is troublesome in bulk wave devices, the associated problem for surface wave devices can be avoided by depositing the transducers on a substrate using evaporation techniques. These and other advantages weigh in favour of surface as opposed to bulk waves and account in part for the current interest in this area. As for their bulk wave counterpart, surface waves can be generated and detected piezoelectrically and amplified in piezoelectric semiconductors. Since surface wave losses do not differ significantly from bulk wave losses, materials which were useful for bulk wave devices also find application in surface wave work.

In an unbounded isotropic material there exist three independent bulk waves which can propagate in any given direction. Two of these are transverse waves with their particle displacements transverse to the direction of propagation and orthogonal to each other. The third is a longitudinal wave with particle motion along the direction of propagation. These waves are non-dispersive with their phase velocity determined by the elastic stiffness constants and the density of the solid. To achieve the stress free conditions required at the boundary surface of a semi-infinite medium it is necessary that there be two components of motion associated with a surface wave; one in the direction of propagation and one normal to the free surface. In general a particle near the surface moves in an elliptical path with the amplitude of the motion decaying exponentially with depth. The latter effect can be attributed to the fact that the particles in the interior are restrained more than those at the surface. As a result the surface wave velocity is less than the bulk wave velocities in the same medium and these waves cannot exist anywhere but at the surface. As in the case of bulk waves the surface wave velocity is independent of frequency and direction for an isotropic solid. In anisotropic media the particle motions may include three orthogonal components and the velocity may be a function of direction with the complication that in some directions the surface wave velocity may be higher than that of a particularly slow bulk wave mode thereby causing a transfer of energy from the surface to the interior. The exponential decay constants which govern the dependence of the particle displacements upon distance from the surface may become complex thus causing oscillatory decay. Surface waves which exhibit this behaviour are called generalized Rayleigh waves. Finally, it should be mentioned that in anisotropic materials the phase and group velocity vectors are not always collinear. It is convenient when building devices to choose "pure mode directions" in which the two velocity vectors are parallel. So as to avoid the complications associated with anisotropy the following discussion will be based on isotropic or transversely isotropic materials. In the latter media the surface wave velocity is independent of direction in the plane of the surface. Crystals of the hexagonal class and poled ferroelectric ceramics (equivalent elastically to 6 mm) oriented with their symmetry axes normal to the free surface are transversely isotropic.

The velocity v_R of a straight-crested surface wave propagation on an isotropic semi-infinite solid is given by [2.4.3]

$$\frac{v_R}{v_s} = \frac{0.87 + 1.12\sigma}{1 + \sigma} \tag{2.4.1}$$

in which v_s is the shear wave velocity and the Poisson's ratio σ is given by

$$\sigma = \tfrac{1}{2} \frac{v_1^2 - 2v_s^2}{v_1^2 - v_s^2} \tag{2.4.2}$$

in which v_1 is the longitudinal wave velocity. From (2.4.1) it follows, that v_R lies between $0.87\,v_s$ and $0.96\,v_s$ and increases monotonically with σ. For wave propagation along the x_1 axis the displacements take the form

$$u_1 = \tilde{u}_1(x_2)\sin(kx_1 - v_R t) \quad u_2 = \tilde{u}_2(x_2)\cos(kx_1 + v_R t) \tag{2.4.3}$$

indicating that the wave has an infinite lateral extent and that the components are $\pi/2$ out of phase. Figure 2.4.1 in which the amplitudes of $\tilde{u}_1$ and $\tilde{u}_2$ are plotted as a function of depth shows that the particle motion is in general elliptical with the amplitudes decaying exponentially at large distances from the surface. The major axis of the ellipse is perpendicular to the boundary of the medium, and at about $0.18\,\lambda$ the motion is entirely along the x_2 direction. Since $\tilde{u}_1$ changes sign at $0.18\,\lambda$, the direction of particle motion reverses at this depth. The behaviour illustrated in Fig. 2.4.1 is representative of surface waves in isotropic non-piezoelectric solids.

For a piezoelectric material not only must the elastic boundary conditions be satisfied at $x_2 = 0$, but the electromagnetic boundary conditions must be met there also. The net effect is to generalize the form of the surface wave solution slightly. Practically, it appears that the addition of the piezoelectric

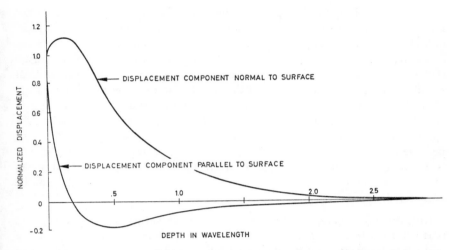

FIG. 2.4.1. Normalized particle displacements for a surface wave in an elastically isotropic medium. Poisson's ratio is 0.34 for this case.

fields has a rather minor effect on the general form of the particle displacements. Adding a thin metal film to the surface has the effect of shorting out the piezoelectric fields in the neighbourhood of the surface and is equivalent to turning off part of the electromechanical coupling. The effect on the particle displacements is found to be small. For a weaker coupling material such as CdS no significant difference in displacements occurs on addition of a metallic coating.

2.4.2. GUIDING AND FOLDING

2.4.2.1. Guiding Surface Waves

The surface waves introduced in the previous section extend an unlimited distance in the transverse (x_3) direction. In practical applications a source of finite transverse width may be used to generate these waves and presents no difficulties so long as the width is sufficiently large so that diffraction losses are negligible (see Section 2.3). The reliance on "line of sight" paths associated with unguided surface waves while feasible for some applications is unduly restrictive. It is far more convenient to be able to guide surface waves over more general prescribed paths while at the same time confining the lateral extent of the acoustic field to a few wavelengths. The surface wave guide has been introduced with this goal in mind. Thin layer guides have been studied most extensively as they show particular promise from the

E

technological viewpoint. The techniques for depositing layers of different materials on a substrate are well understood from microelectronics technology. Topographical guides have been studied to a lesser degree probably as a consequence of the mathematical difficulties associated with any realistic structure of this type. Inlayed or sandwiched structures should be capable of guiding action but have received little experimental or theoretical attention. In the following subsections each of the different types of surface wave guide is briefly discussed. The physical basis for confinement in all cases is a spatial phase velocity differential which causes the slower guided wave to become evanescent in regions of higher velocity. The principle of guidance is the same as that used to realize electromagnetic dielectric wave guides. As in the discussion of bulk wave devices, only isotropic materials will be considered.

(i) *Thin layer guides.* The thin layer guides shown in Fig. 2.4.2 are particularly attractive for guiding surface waves since the thin layers can be fabricated by using evaporation or sputtering techniques. Where low losses are required the substrates of these guides can be chosen to be a single crystal material, and the layers can be deposited epitaxially. In the case of the slot guide, epitaxial growth may not be necessary since the bulk of the surface wave resides in the substrate. The analysis of these wave guides involves solving the wave equation subject to a much more complicated set of boundary conditions than occurs for the comparatively simple case of Rayleigh waves on a plated semi-infinite solid [2.4.4]. As is to be expected the nature of the guided wave is quite different. Whereas the simple Rayleigh wave extends indefinitely in the x_3 direction the guided wave is confined to the vicinity of the strip or slot. For films thinner than a wavelength the amplitude of the crest varies trigonometrically in this region and decays exponentially outside. The criterion for confinement is that Rayleigh surface wave velocity of the film v_{Rf} be smaller than that of the substrate v_{Rs} in case (a) and the reverse must be true for case (b). Accordingly the terminology slow-on-fast and fast-on-slow has come to describe the two different types of wave guide in

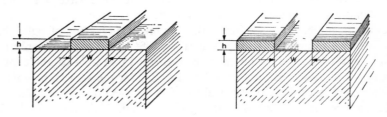

FIG. 2.4.2. Thin film guides: (a) slow-on-fast strip and (b) fast-on-slow slot guide.

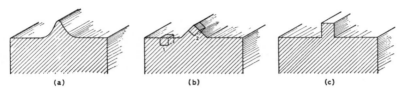

FIG. 2.4.3. Variations on topographical guides: (a) continuous ridge, (b) triangular ridge and (c) rectangular ridge.

Fig. 2.4.2. The essence of the confinement problem is to "surround" a slow velocity region by a fast velocity one.

(ii) *Topographical guides.* The elastic restoring forces which act near the surface of a solid are smaller than those in the bulk material due to the absence of stresses on the free surface. This fact accounts for the existence of straight crested surface waves which propagate with velocity slower than bulk shear waves. Using this concept it is possible, by properly contouring a surface, to produce a velocity differential which acts to confine surface waves just as in the case of a strip [2.4.5]. The advantage of the topographical guide lies in the fact that it requires only one material which can easily be chosen on the basis of loss considerations. Three examples appear in Fig. 2.4.3 to illustrate this type of wave guide. Comparison of the two volume elements in the figure for the triangular guide indicates that half as many of the surfaces are restrained for element 2 as for element 1. Hence the phase velocity of an elastic wave in the neighbourhood of the ridge will be less than that of the surroundings and the structure can be used to guide surface waves. Similar considerations apply to the other geometries. Cutting parallel slots in a material to form a channel produces a guidance system equivalent to that in Fig. 2.4.3(c).

(iii) *Inlay and sandwich guides.* Two interesting variations on the thin layer guides are the inlay and sandwich structures. The inlay guide can be thought of as a strip guide in which the slow region, instead of being evaporated on the substrate, is diffused or grown in the material. If the slow region extends to such a depth that the substrate is essentially subdivided into three regions, fast-slow-fast, one obtains the sandwich guide. The cross-sections for these guides are shown in Fig. 2.4.4. Both of these systems are expected to produce significant guiding action although there seems to be little experimental confirmation of this point. The criterion for binding, presumably, is the same as for the other cases. Recently the construction and operation of an inlay guide similar to that in Fig. 2.4.4(a) based upon a piezoelectrically stiffened substrate has been reported [2.4.6]. The structure

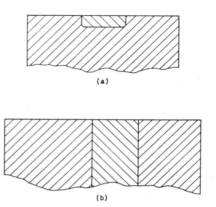

FIG. 2.4.4. Variations on thin layer guides: (a) inlay and (b) sandwich structures.

consists of an unpolarized ferroelectric channel imbedded in a polarized ferroelectric substrate and may be altered electrically.

2.4.2.2. Reflection of Surface Waves

In large capacity delay lines it is usually necessary to fold the sound path to conserve space. In a multiple reflection device a bulk wave is reflected between facets which have been machined on a blank. The comparable process in which a surface wave is reflected from an edge or a corner will be discussed here along with reflection from artificial boundaries such as strips or slots. The earliest interest in this area arose in connection with geophysical studies and there has been relatively little research done in areas related to surface wave devices. A problem is that, upon reflection, usually a part of the energy is converted into bulk waves. This form of mode conversion is characteristic of surface waves and is a consequence of the fact that in general the collection of incident, reflected, and transmitted Rayleigh waves do not satisfy the boundary conditions on the flat surfaces of the edge.

In general any discontinuity in wave velocity or surface contour will cause partial reflection of surface waves. This fact can be used to advantage in making artificial reflectors by introducing loading or stiffening strips or by cutting parallel slots in the substrate. A single strip or slot oriented at an angle θ_I relative to the incident beam will cause partial reflection at an angle θ_R such that $\theta_I = \theta_R$. If additional reflectors are added parallel to the first and spaced according to the Bragg condition $2d \sin \theta = n\lambda$, the waves reflected from each strip or slot will add in phase to produce a strong reflected signal. As was mentioned previously, conducting strips on a piezoelectric material behave similarly to a loading strip and therefore can be used conveniently in

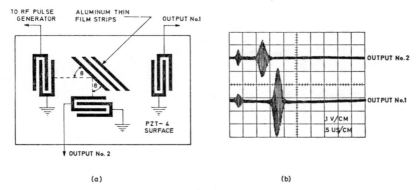

FIG. 2.4.5. Bragg reflection of surface waves by a metallic thin-film grating on a piezoelectric substrate: (a) experimental arrangement of transducers and grating and (b) output waveforms at transducers 1 and 2 [2.4.8].

such applications. The conducting strips can be isolated electrically or interconnected with reactive or active elements [2.4.7] to control the reflectivity. If desired a net gain can be produced in the latter case. Figure 2.4.5(a) shows a reflection experiment utilizing three interdigital transducers and a Bragg thin film grating evaporated on a PZT-4 substrate [2.4.8]. In order to bring more energy into the pass band of the device an RF pulse generator drives the input transducer. The output reflected and transmitted waveforms are shown in Fig. 2.4.5(b). The grating in this case operates much like a beam splitter and could, if desired, be used to tap information from a delay line.

2.4.3. SURFACE WAVE TRANSDUCERS AND AMPLIFIERS

2.4.3.1. Surface Wave Transducers

The strain in the piezoelectric material between a pair of electrodes caused by a passing surface wave generates electric fields which can be used to detect acoustic signals. The application of a voltage to a pair of electrodes produces the reverse effect and can be used to generate surface waves. When the alternating electrodes of a grating on a piezoelectric substrate are connected together to form two separate contacts, the electric fields or strains associated with a surface wave with $\lambda = 2L$ (electrode spacing) add coherently and the resulting device forms the basis of the interdigital transducer [2.4.1]. Figure 2.4.6 shows a three section interdigital transducer along with the hypothetical field configuration under the electrodes at a particular instant of time. Qualitatively the operation of this device can be understood

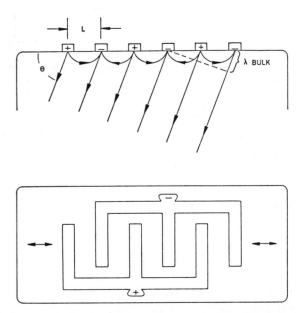

FIG. 2.4.6. Interdigital electrode array transducer and electric field configuration under the electrodes at a particular instant of time.

very simply. Each pair of electrodes sets up a strain pattern roughly consistent with a half wavelength of a surface wave. The alternation of the field components between electrodes favours the production of waves with $\lambda = 2L$. Alternatively each pair of electrodes can be regarded as an elementary source–constructive interference between the waves from all the sources occurs when the frequency is such that the wavelength equals twice the electrode spacing. The latter argument suggests that adding more electrodes will increase the conversion efficiency, and this is in fact realized in practice, but at the expense of bandwidth. When the number of electrodes is increased, more complete cancellation of waves outside of the array occurs at frequencies which deviate from the value $f = v_R/2L$. Since constructive interference occurs at harmonics of the fundamental frequency, these arrays can be operated in overtones. The electric field symmetry between electrodes is consistent with odd harmonic generation only and couples poorly to the higher frequency waves resulting in lower conversion efficiency in harmonic operation. This is somewhat unfortunate because for extremely high frequencies (small spacing) one has to push the photoprocessing and deposition techniques, which can be used to construct the electrodes, beyond their limits. The minimum electrode width which can be achieved by optical photoresist methods is on the order of 1 μm which corresponds to about 1 GHz on lithium niobate. These interdigital transducers have been operated at frequencies ranging from less than 1 MHz to 3 GHz, the upper limit corresponding to a 5th harmonic overtone on Y-cut Z-oriented LiNbO$_3$.

A surface wave alone will not in general satisfy the required boundary conditions in the vicinity of the electrode fingers of an interdigital transducer. As a result there exist bulk waves which when generated by each electrode pair will interfere constructively at certain angles relative to the surface. Examination of Fig. 2.4.6 indicates that the condition for constructive interference is met when (isotropic material assumed)

$$f = v/2L \cos \theta. \tag{2.4.4}$$

When $\theta = 0$ and v is taken to be the surface wave velocity, the frequency at which constructive interference occurs corresponds to $\lambda = 2L$. Since the bulk wave transverse and longitudinal velocities are higher than v_R, coupling to these bulk modes occurs at higher frequencies.

For most delay line applications the interdigital electrode transducer provides a simple and practical means of generating and receiving surface waves. When it is inconvenient to have a piezoelectric substrate, the electrodes can be deposited on a driving surface and a piezoelectric material in the form of a thin film or a block can be placed over the array. The basic principles of operation of such a device are the same as the interdigital transducer of Fig. 2.4.6 except that the film or block now behaves as though it were the substrate. Enhanced coupling in the latter case may be obtained by using a thin liquid film to make acoustic contact between the piezoelectric block and the substrate—this arrangement being particularly useful in exploratory work.

All the above array transducers are bidirectional. They generate and receive surface waves in both the forward and backward directions. In some circumstances it is desirable to have unidirectional transduction. This can be achieved by producing cancellation of one of the radiated waves via interference. Driving two identical constant pitch arrays separated by $(n+\frac{1}{4})\lambda$ (where n is an integer) with electrical signals 90° out of phase will generate waves travelling to the right and cause cancellation to the left. Similarly terminating one of these two arrays with an inductor such that it resonates at the operating frequency produces reflected waves which interfere constructively. In both cases conversion efficiency is improved as might be expected since waves radiate in only one direction. As an added benefit waves incident upon the unidirectional transducer are not as strongly reflected as from the bidirectional array—thus improving triple transit suppression in delay lines employing these transducers. Unfortunately these improvements are offset by a reduction in bandwidth.

2.4.3.2. Surface Wave Amplification

Because the electric fields generated by a surface wave in a piezoelectric material are easily accessible, coupling between drifting charge carriers and elastic waves is possible which like the bulk wave counterpart can produce amplification. Since fields existing both inside and outside the piezoelectric material can be utilized, this affords the construction of a variety of devices not possible for bulk wave amplifiers and allows separation of the semiconductor and acoustic materials into configurations which offer greater versatility. These surface wave amplifiers may be used in delay lines to compensate for the acoustic attenuation in the delay medium and the conversion losses incurred at the transducers. Since amplification in such a device depends on the direction of surface wave propagation relative to the charge motion, it is non-reciprocal and therefore can be used to eliminate spurious signals which result from reflections from the output transducer. Triple transit signals which are particularly troublesome in low insertion loss delay lines can be eliminated in this way. Since the added flexibility which comes with amplification is desirable, three of the more successful piezoelectric semiconductor device configurations will be discussed in this section.

The initial experiments carried out in connection with bulk wave amplification used a piezoelectric semiconductor material and an electric field was applied to this which caused the mobile carriers to drift faster than the acoustic wave velocity. The natural generalization of this effect to apply to surface wave devices has led to what is referred to as the combined medium amplifier [2.4.9]. Figure 2.4.7 shows part of a piezoelectric semiconductor substrate in which a thin sheet near the surface of the material has been

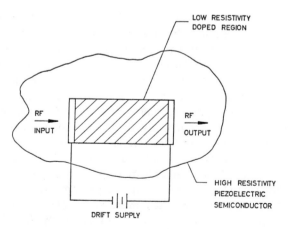

FIG. 2.4.7. Monolithic surface wave amplifier.

made highly conductive by doping. The drift electrodes cause coupling between carriers and acoustic wave to occur within one region, similar to bulk wave devices. This configuration has the advantage that the electric fields which lie below the surface extend to a greater depth than those outside and accordingly greater coupling can be achieved. A difficulty of this type of amplifier lies in the conflicting choice of a material with optimum piezoelectric (high electromechanical coupling constant K, low acoustic loss) and semiconductor (high mobility, wide conductivity range) properties. As a result the separated medium amplifier which optimizes these properties separately has become important. In this case semiconductor and piezo-electric materials are arranged spatially adjacent so that the external fields produced by the surface wave in the piezoelectric solid enter the semi-conductor and the interaction with drifting carriers can take place. Since the external fields decay within half a wavelength, the two materials must lie less than a few hundred Ångströms apart at frequencies above 100 MHz. In order for the Rayleigh wave to propagate, the elastic medium must be traction-free at its surface which means that the semiconductor and piezo-electric materials must be separated by an air gap. Figure 2.4.8(a) illustrates such a device in which dielectric spacers are used to provide this separation. The essential features of this amplifier are a piezoelectric acoustic substrate, a thin-film single-crystal semiconductor-on-insulator structure and an oxide dielectric spacer. The relatively high dc voltages required across the semi-conductor region to produce terminal gain can cause bulk power dissipation problems and for this reason the semiconductor-on-insulator thin-film structure is necessary. A particularly convenient arrangement is to grow n-silicon epitaxially on sapphire (SOS). Figure 2.4.8(b) shows a typical gain characteristic for an SOS composite amplifier operating in conjunction with a lithium niobate substrate [2.4.9]. A swing of more than 100 dB in output can be obtained.

While the separated medium amplifier provides abundant gain for device applications its fabrication puts severe demands on fabrication technology particularly at high frequencies where the spacing between acoustic substrate and semiconductor becomes very small. The desirability of placing the semi-conductor directly on the substrate so as to avoid these difficulties has prompted research on the monolithic thin-film amplifier for which net terminal gain has been reported. One of the earliest investigations in this area [2.4.10] was made on a dispersive surface-wave delay line consisting of a cadmium-selenide film on a lithium-niobate substrate.

2.4.4. DIGITAL DELAY LINE MEMORIES

The three basic surface wave components, transducer, amplifier, and wave

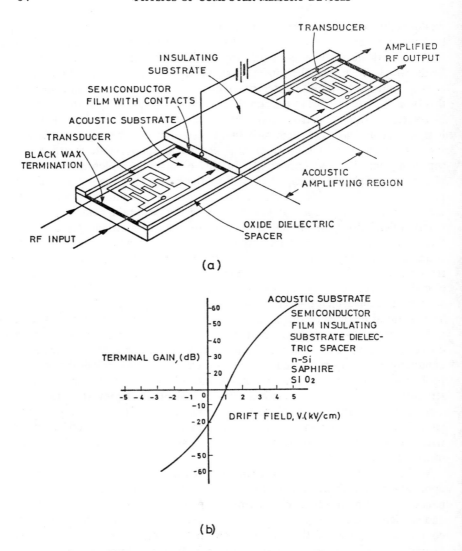

FIG. 2.4.8. Separated medium surface wave amplifier: (a) device configuration and (b) gain characteristic [2.4.9].

guide can be combined to form a variety of devices useful in storing digital information. In this section a few of these systems will be described. In an attempt to anticipate future developments the discussion will include proposed as well as already realized devices. Whether or not some of these devices

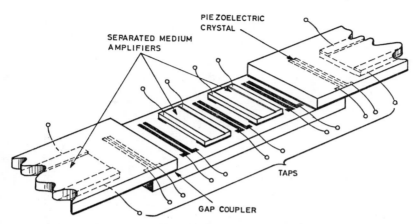

FIG. 2.4.9. Extended surface wave delay line with taps and amplifiers [2.4.11].

become a reality will depend to a large degree upon the advances made in materials technology. Operation at high frequencies requires the use of single crystal materials in devices. Heteroepitaxial growth techniques are likely to become extremely important in this respect. Silicon on sapphire, ZnO on sapphire, and GaAs on BeO are important combinations which are currently available for acoustic applications. The advances made in competing digital technologies will also determine whether surface wave storage techniques become important. If the material costs become less with improvements in technology, as is expected, then digital surface wave storage techniques will be potentially very inexpensive since comparatively little processing is required to be able to store a large amount of information on a flat surface and the techniques available for this processing have already been refined in connection with semiconductor technology. The evaporation of an interdigital transducer on a flat substrate is a much simpler process than that involved in bonding a bulk wave transducer to the end of a crystalline block. In the simplest bulk wave device it is necessary to process two surfaces as opposed to one in a surface wave device. These and other aspects favour surface wave devices over their bulk wave counterparts and suggest that in the future surface waves will play an important role in storage applications.

A section of a straight delay line memory with taps and amplifiers is shown in Fig. 2.4.9 [2.4.11]. The signal from one piezoelectric substrate is coupled via external electric fields to the adjacent crystal and the separated medium amplifiers compensate for losses and suppress reflections. Similar arrangements can be made with piezoelectric channel or strip structures, but when large quantities of data are to be stored it is much simpler to fold th

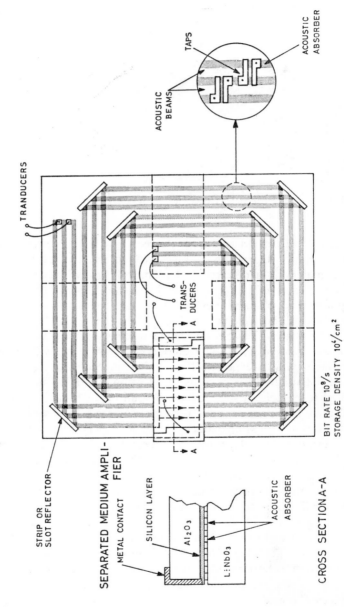

FIG. 2.4.10. Multiple reflection–multiple path surface wave delay line with amplifier and taps [2.4.12].

path. This can be accomplished by forming serpentine, spiral, or other space saving patterns. A basic limitation on these configurations is, of course, that the radius of curvature be large compared to an acoustic wavelength. Presumably less restrictive a criteri will apply to graded guides. The pattern for a channel guide can be made on a planar surface by etching grooves in a substrate. Thin-film overlay patterns can be formed using standard photolithographic techniques. Low frequency channel devices have been constructed by machining a helical slot in a cylinder.

The use of the Rayleigh wave reflectors allows the versatility of folding an unguided beam. Figure 2.4.10 shows a parallel delay line in which strip or slot reflectors are used to confine the beams to a square chip [2.4.12]. Acoustic absorbers are used to minimize cross-talk between beams and the separated medium amplifiers make up for the losses incurred due to propagation and reflection. The single amplifier spans six sound paths and produces gain in the signal level of a single channel at three different locations. The drift field in the amplifier causes electrons in the silicon layer to move parallel to the direction of sound propagation. On such a surface wave delay line at 100 MHz it should be possible to store as many as 10^4 bits cm^{-2} while at the 1 GHz photolithographic limit the storage of 10^6 bits cm^{-2} becomes feasible.

REFERENCES

[2.1.1] J. P. Eckert, A survey of digital computer memory systems, *Proc. IRE*, **41**, 1393–1406, 1953.

[2.1.2] D. L. Arenburg, Ultrasonic solid delay lines, *J. Acoust. Soc. Am.*, **20**, 1–26, 1948.

[2.1.3] J. R. Anderson, Electrical delay lines for digital computer applications, *IRE Trans. Electr. Comp.*, **EC-2**, 5–13, 1953.

[2.2.1] W. P. Mason, "Electromechanical Transducers and Wave Filters", D. van Nostrand Co., Princeton, pp. 185–224, 1948.

[2.2.2] C. F. Brockelsby, J. S. Palfreeman and R. W. Gibson, "Ultrasonic Delay Lines", Iliffe Books Ltd., London, pp. 33–56, 1963.

[2.2.3] P. S. Fuss and R. M. Lauver, Cause and correction of phase distortion in pulse excited long ultrasonic delay lines", *Wescon Conv. Record*, **6**, §5.4, 1–5, 1962.

[2.2.4] E. K. Sittig, High-speed ultrasonic digital delay line design: a restatement of some basic considerations, *Proc. IEEE*, **56**, 1194–1202, 1968.

[2.2.5] A. H. Meitzler, Ultrasonic delay lines for digital data storage, *IRE Trans. Ultrason. Eng.*, **UE-9**, 30–37, 1962.

[2.2.6] R. N. Thurston, Effect of electrical and mechanical terminating resistances on loss and bandwidth according to the conventional equivalent circuit of a piezoelectric transducer, *IRE Trans. Ultrason. Eng.*, **UE-7**, 16–25, 1960.

[2.2.7] A. Rothbart, A non-return to zero (NRZ) mode of operation for a magnetostrictive delay line, *Proc IRE (corr.)*, **48**, 1486–1487, 1960.

[2.2.8] E. P. Papadakis, Ultrasonic attenuation caused by scattering in poly-crystalline media, *in* "Physical Acoustics", Vol. 4B (ed. W. P. Mason), Academic Press Inc., New York, 269–328, 1968.

[2.2.9] A. H. Meitzler, Ultrasonic delay lines using shear modes in strips, *IRE Trans. Ultrason. Eng.*, **UE-7**, 35–43, 1960.

[2.2.10] C. Zener, Internal friction in solids II. General theory of thermoelastic internal friction, *Phys. Rev.*, **53**, 91–99, 1938.

[2.2.11] L. G. Merkulov, Absorption and diffusive scattering of ultrasonic waves in metals, *Sov. Phys.-Tech. Phys.*, **2**, 953–957, 1956.

[2.2.12] K. Lücke, Ultrasonic attenuation caused by thermoelastic heat flow, *J. Appl. Phys.*, **27** 1433–1438, 1956.

[2.2.13] C. Zener, "Elasticity and Anelasticity of Metals", University of Chicago Press, Chicago, 89–96, 1948.

[2.2.14] M. W. Zemansky, "Heat and Thermodynamics", McGraw–Hill Book Co., New York, 334, 1968.

[2.2.15] W. P. Mason and T. B. Bateman, Relation between third-order elastic moduli and the thermal attenuation of ultrasonic waves in nonconducting and metallic crystals, *J. Acoust. Soc. Am.*, **40**, 852–862, 1966.

[2.2.16] J. Lamb, M. Redwood and Z. Shteinshleifer, Absorption of compressional waves in solids from 100 to 1000 Mc/sec, *Phys. Rev. Lett.*, **3**, 28–29, 1959.

[2.2.17] A. Akhieser, On the absorption of sound in solids, *J. Phys. (U.S.S.R.)*, **1**, 277–287, 1939.

[2.2.18] W. P. Mason, Effect of impurities and phonon processes on the ultrasonic attenuation of germanium, crystal quartz, and silicon, *in* "Physical Acoustics", Vol. 3B (ed. W. P. Mason), Academic Press Inc., New York, 235–286, 1965.

[2.2.19] D. W. Oliver and G. A. Slack, Ultrasonic attenuation in insulators at room temperature, *J. Appl. Phys.*, **37**, 1542–1548, 1966.

[2.2.20] H. N. Spector, Amplification of acoustic waves through interaction with conduction electrons, *Phys. Rev.*, **127**, 1054–1090, 1963.

[2.2.21] J. H. McFee, Transmission and amplification of acoustic waves in piezo-electric semiconductors, *in* "Physical Acoustics", Vol. 4A (ed. W. P. Mason), Academic Press Inc., New York, 1–45, 1966.

[2.2.22] D. L. White, Amplification of ultrasonic waves in piezoelectric semi-conductors, *J. Appl. Phys.*, **33**, 2547–2554, 1962.

[2.2.23] A. V. Granato and K. Lücke, The vibrating string model of dislocation damping, *in* "Physical Acoustics", Vol. 4A (ed. W. P. Mason), Academic Press Inc., New York, 225–276, 1966.

[2.2.24] A. V. Granato and R. Stern, Dislocation damping in copper at kilocycle and megacycle per second frequencies, *J, Appl. Phys.*, **33**, 2880–2883, 1962.

[2.2.25] D. B. Fraser, J. T. Krause and A. H. Meitzler, Physical limitations on the performance of vitreous silica in high-frequency ultrasonic and acousto-optical devices, *Appl. Phys. Lett.* **11**, 308–309, 1967.

[2.2.26] T. A. Midford and S. Wanuga, Ultrasonic attenuation in rutile at uhf and room temperature, *J. Appl. Phys. (Comm.)*, **36**, 3362–3363, 1965.

[2.2.27] W. D. Sylwestrowicz, Mechanism of ultrasonic loss in silicon and aluminium, *J. Appl. Phys.*, **37**, 535–541, 1966.

[2.2.28] D. E. Chapin, Frequency and temperature dependence of shear wave attenuation in Bausch and Lomb T–40 glass, *IEEE Trans. Son. and Ultrason.*, **SU–15**, 178–181, 1968.

[2.2.29] C. E. Fitch, jr, New methods for measuring ultrasonic attenuation, *J. Acoust. Soc. Am.* **40**, 989–997, 1966.

[2.3.1] R. N. Thurston, Wave propagation in fluids and normal solids, *in* "Physical Acoustics" Vol. 1A (ed. W. P. Mason), Academic Press Inc., New York, 1–110, 1964.

[2.3.2] V. T. Buchwald, Elastic waves in anisotropic media, *Proc. R. Soc. Lond.*, **A253**, 563–580, 1959.

[2.3.3] A. R. Hutson and D. L. White, Elastic wave propagation in piezoelectric semiconductors, *J. Appl. Phys.*, **33**, 40–47, 1962.

[2.3.4] D. L. Arenberg, Ultrasonic delay lines, *J. Acoust. Soc. Am.*, **20**, 1–26, 1948.

[2.3.5] A. H. Meitzler, Ultrasonic delay lines using shear modes in strips, *IRE Trans. Ultrason. Eng.*, **UE–7**, 35–43, 1960.

[2.3.6] J. H. Evelth, A survey of ultrasonic delay lines operating below 100 Mc/s, *Proc. IEEE*, **53**, 1406–1428, 1965.

[2.3.7] G. G. Scarrott and R. Naylor, Wire type acoustic delay lines for digital storage, *Proc. IEEE Lond.*, **103B**, 497–508, 1956.

[2.3.8] D. A. Berlincourt, D. R. Curran and H. Jaffe, Piezoelectric and piezomagnetic materials and their function in transducers, *in* "Physical Acoustics" Vol. 1A (ed. W. P. Mason), Academic Press Inc., New York, 169–270, 1964.

[2.3.9] D. A. Berlincourt, Delay line transducer materials, *IEEE Natl. Conv. Record*, **15** (part II), 61–68, 1967.

[2.4.1] R. M. White, Surface elastic waves, *Proc. IEEE*, **58**, 1238–1276, 1970.

[2.4.2] G. W. Farnell, Properties of elastic surface waves, *in* "Physical Acoustics" vol. 6 (ed. W. P. Mason), Academic Press Inc., 109–166, 1970.

[2.4.3] I. Aviktorov, "Rayleigh and Lamb Waves", Plenum Press, New York, 1967.

[2.4.4] H. F. Tiersten, Elastic surface waves guided by thin films, *J. Appl. Phys.*, **40**, 770–789, 1969.

[2.4.5] E. A. Ash and D. Morgan, Realisation of microwave circuit functions using acoustic surface waves, *Electron. Lett.*, **3**, 462–464, 1967.

[2.4.6] M. Yamanishi and K. Yoshida, A new type of surface acoustic waveguide, *Jap. J. Appl. Phys.*, **9**, 1276, 1970.

[2.4.7] R. Y. C. Ho and A. J. Bahr, Active impedance matching for microwave acoustic delay lines, *IEEE Trans. on Microw. Theory and Techn.* (*corr.*), **MTT–17**, 1041–1042, 1969.

[2.4.8] C. C. Tseng, Elastic surface waves on free surface and metallized surface of CdS, ZNO, and PZT–4, *J. Appl. Phys.*, **38**, 4281–4284, 1967.

[2.4.9] R. M. White and F. W. Voltmer, Ultrasonic surface wave amplification in cadmium sulfide, *Appl. Phys. Lett.*, **8**, 40–42, 1966.

[2.4.10] H. Hanebrekke and K. A. Ingebrigtsen, Acoustoelectric amplification of surface waves in structure of cadmium-selenide film on lithium niobate, *Electron. Lett.*, **6**, 520–521, 1970.

[2.4.11] J. H. Collins, H. M. Gerard, and H. J. Shaw, High performance lithium niobate acoustic surface wave transducers and delay lines, *Appl. Phys. Lett.*, **13**, 312–313, 1968.

[2.4.12] E. Stern, Microsound components, circuits, and applications, *IEEE Trans. Microw. Theory and Techn.* **MTT–17**, 835–844, 1969.

Chapter 3

MATRIX MEMORIES

3.1. INTRODUCTION

Matrix memories are memories, in which the memory cells, such as cores, films, flip-flops etc., are physically arranged in rows and columns in such a way that the result looks like a mathematical matrix (Fig. 3.1.1). The separate cells are interconnected to the outside world by a complex system of wires. Depending on the wiring scheme, one speaks of 3D, $2\frac{1}{2}$D or 2D memories [3.1.1, 3.1.2]. These terms were first used when dealing with ferrite core memories, but were also used later on for other types of memory cells.

It is for this reason that in this introductory section attention is paid to the different organizational structures without at this stage defining the physical nature of the memory cell itself.

3.1.1. MEMORY ORGANIZATIONS

3.1.1.1. 1D-Memory Organization

In general the writing operation consists of two actions. First, with the help of an address, the desired memory cell is chosen and secondly the information to be stored is fed to the cell. In computers this information is a binary "one" or a "zero".

One of the least desirable and most expensive ways of doing this is sketched in Fig. 3.1.1. Each memory cell is connected by two independent wires. When the memory matrix consists of N cells, $2N$ wires are needed. The N horizontal wires are connected to a bucket full of electronics called an address decoder, which on command of a binary coded address can select and activate one of the cells. By means of the N vertical lines and another decoder the binary "zero" or "one" is supplied to the chosen cell. It is apparent from Fig. 3.1.1. that a considerable reduction of electronic circuitry can be gained when the binary information is fed not to the separate cells but to the address decoder for the horizontal drive lines (dotted line). In the case of a binary "one" the chosen cell is switched, in the case of a "zero", the cell is not activated at all.

70

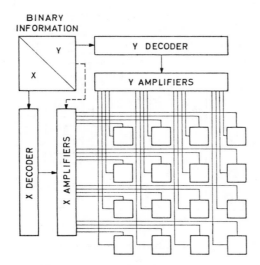

FIG. 3.1.1. 1D-memory organization.

Nevertheless, the peripheral electronic circuitry for this kind of memory organization is so excessive that it is less expensive to make the memory of electronic flip-flops and to do away with the memory cell altogether.

3.1.1.2. 2D-Memory Organization

A more economic solution can be obtained when a part of the address decoding is performed in the memory matrix itself, thereby reducing the peripheral electronics.

The simplest, though historically not the first, scheme used is referred to as the 2D, linear-select system. Figure 3.1.2 shows its block diagram. All memory cells of the rows are connected to horizontal lines and the cells of the columns to vertical lines. In the case of a square matrix ($N \times N$ cells) we will need $2\sqrt{N}$ wires to make each cell attainable. When we send a current through or place a voltage on, depending on the physical nature of the memory cell, one horizontal and one vertical drive line, only one cell experiences both X and Y signals, and $2(N-1)$ cells are selected by only one signal.

In contrast to the 1D-memory organization, now the memory cell has to fulfill the condition that its state is only altered when both signals are coincident and that it does not change noticeably when the cell is subjected to only a half select pulse.

In fast modern computers the information is handled in the form of a group of bits, which is called a word. The bits of this word are always

F

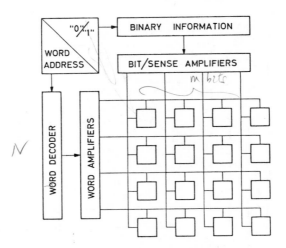

FIG. 3.1.2. 2D-memory organization.

shifted, transported and also stored simultaneously. In our 2D selection scheme such a word is written in the following way. A word address arrives at the word address decoder. A half select signal is generated by the word drivers on one of the horizontal word lines. Simultaneously, the word content arrives at the bit register and is transmitted simultaneously by the bit drivers to the vertical bit lines. The coincidence of the word and bit pulses will cause the memory cell to be set to the "one" state. If the bit signal on a bit line is absent, the memory cell will remain in the "zero" state. The elegance of the 2D system is that for the writing operation the matrix has both a storage and a selection property.

Reading the stored word in a 2D scheme is accomplished by generating a signal only on the word line. Depending on the physical nature of the cell this signal might be larger than and parallel or opposite to the write word signal. Due to this read word signal, output signals are generated on the bit lines in accordance with the information stored in the different bits which form the word. The use of the bit lines as sense lines requires some additional peripheral electronic circuitry to separate the bit drivers from the sense amplifiers at the right moment. It is also possible to add separate and isolated sense lines, as in activating the word line all sense signals appear simultaneously on the bit sense lines.

It is interesting to investigate how large the saving in peripheral circuitry is for the 2D scheme compared to the 1D scheme.

To store N words each of m bits, the 1D scheme requires two address decoders, which are each capable of selecting one out of $N \times m$ lines, moreover, $2N \times m$ drive amplifiers are required, as well as $N \times m$ sense amplifiers (not shown on Fig. 3.1.1).

In the 2D scheme N words of m bits require a decoder capable of selecting one out of N word lines whereas no decoding is required for the bit lines. In addition N word drivers, m bit drivers and m sense amplifiers are necessary.

Assuming a practical example of a memory consisting of 256,000 bits, 2000 words each 128 bits long, we find for the 1D memory not counting the decoders, $3N \times m = 768\,000$ and for the 2D memory only $N + 2m = 2256$ amplifiers. Though the memory cell in the 2D scheme is subject to some restrictions, the saving in electronics is formidable.

3.1.1.3. 2½D-Memory Organization

The savings due to performing the address decoding partly by the memory matrix in the case of the 2D scheme justifies the expectation that even more can be saved by a still more inventive memory organization. Historically, the 3D-memory organization to be treated in the next section was put into practice first. When requirements increased during the course of years, the so called 2½D scheme was proposed. It is a memory structure intermediate between the 3D and 2D organization (Fig. 3.1.3). The 2½D system consists of a large matrix subdivided into a number of m submatrices each consisting of N memory cells. N is the number of words to be stored in the whole matrix and m is the number of bits per word. To select a word, one of the horizontal drivers and one vertical driver of each plane is activated.

The physical nature of the memory cell is chosen in such a way that only a "one" is written in those cells (shaded in Fig. 3.1.3) where the horizontal and vertical drive pulses are coincident. If only the horizontal signal is

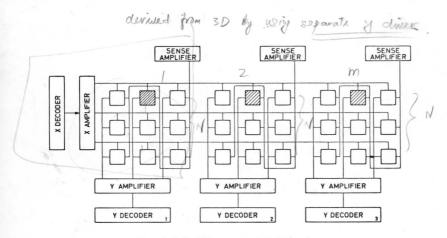

FIG. 3.1.3. 2½D-memory organization.

present, the memory cell will remain in the "zero" state. Reading is accomplished by sending half select signals through the horizontal wires and all the separate y wires. A sense signal results only from those cells where signal coincidence occurs. In each memory submatrix this is only one cell. This makes it possible to connect one sense wire to all the cells of one submatrix as is shown in Fig. 3.1.3. In order to rate the value of the $2\frac{1}{2}$D scheme, we assume again that we want to store 256 000 bits. As the word length has an important impact on the economy of a certain system, (for the 2D system long words are favourable) we do not make a choice yet and assume N words of m bits, so that $N \times m = 256\,000$. The number of words is equal to the number of cells per submatrix, which is equal to $N_x \times N_y = N$. The number of necessary x drivers is N_x, the number of y drivers is $N_y \times m$ and the number of sense amplifiers is m. The total number of amplifiers is then $N_x + m N_y + m$. It is easy to see that for a favourable $2\frac{1}{2}$D system it is necessary to increase N_x at the expense of N_y and to keep the word length m short. With $N_x = 1000$, $N_y = 8$ and $m = 32$ the total number of amplifiers is 1288, which is smaller than the 2256 amplifiers needed in the 2D scheme to store the same 256 000 bits.

3.1.1.4. 3D-Memory Organization

The use of a memory cell that changes its state only when two signals are coincident allows the use of the matrix partly as an address decoder, leading to appreciable savings. It can be expected that a cell that switches only upon the coincidence of 3 signals might lead to even more cost reduction [3.1.3]. The most obvious memory structure based on such a cell would consist of a

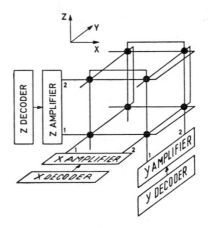

FIG. 3.1.4. True 3D-memory organization. The cube contains the first bits of eight words.

large number of matrices stacked on top of each other. The cells would be interconnected as shown for 8 cells in Fig. 3.1.4 by x, y and z drive wires, and each cell of the 3D structure would be independently accessible. Imagine that we want to store the same 256 000 bits as mentioned in the preceding sections. We divide them up into 8000 words each 32 bits long. To store these words we use 32 small 3D-memory cubes each consisting of $20 \times 20 \times 20$ cells. All the x drive lines of these 32 cubes are interconnected and so are the y and z lines. When a certain x, y and z line is activated, 32 cells, one per cube, will switch. Since we also want to write "zeros", it is necessary to add a drive line to each cube, which is interconnected to all the cells of one cube. With this line, called the inhibit line, a signal which is opposite to the x, y and z signal in that cube, can be produced in case a "zero" is desired, thereby preventing the cell from switching. This inhibit line can also be used as a sense line during reading. To store the 8000 words of 32 bits, we need 20 x-drivers, 20 y-drivers, 20 z-drivers, 32 inhibit drivers and 32 sense amplifiers, which makes a total of only 124 amplifiers. Although such a 3D memory looks very favourable to the research and development engineer, it is the manufacturing engineer who has to produce it and these people have a very negative attitude toward producing three dimensional structures. In fact they just manage to make reasonable two dimensional matrices.

A 3D-memory organization which became very popular and which eliminates the threading of wires in the z direction is shown in Fig. 3.1.5. The memory consists of a stack of, in fact, 2D matrices of which the x drive lines as well as the y drive lines of all the matrices are interconnected. All cells of one plane are connected by an inhibit line and/or sense line. The stack consists of as many matrices as the word contains bits. The words are stored vertically in the cube and the number of words N is equal to the number of cells in one matrix, which is $N_x \times N_y$. To store 8000 words of 32 bits each, the matrix may consist of 80 rows and 100 columns. As the x and y wires are interconnected we need only 80 x-drivers, 100 y-drivers, 32 inhibit drivers and 32 sense amplifiers. As a result we need only a total of 244 amplifiers which compares favourably with the 2D- and $2\frac{1}{2}$D-memory organization hardware.

3.1.1.5. Other Memory Organizations

At this moment the question is justified of whether or not it is possible to further reduce the electronic circuitry by making a more sophisticated cell organization. The answer to this question has to be yes. On paper a 4D, 5D or even a 10D organization is feasible. For instance in an 8D organization it is possible to read or write $5^8 = 390\,635$ cells by means of only $5 \times 8 = 40$ wires. In such a memory the physical nature of the cell must be something from another planet because it should change its state only on coincidence of

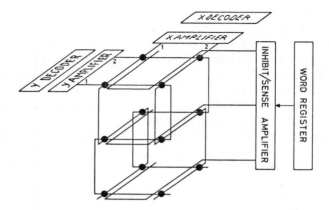

FIG. 3.1.5. Common 3D-memory organization. The memory contains four words of three bits each.

8 pulses and should not switch when only $8 - 1 = 7$ pulses or less arrive simultaneously. Moreover the wiring pattern is extremely complicated. In general one can say that when the amount of peripheral electronic circuitry is reduced by increasing the address decoding capability of the memory structure, the requirements on the memory cell and the problems of manufacturing soar. In todays computers the most complicated structure used is the 3D organization and as the requirements with respect to speed, size and cost increase, the tendency is to go to the $2\frac{1}{2}$D and 2D structures. In the following sections this will be amply illustrated.

In the preceding sections each cell of the memory system could be accessed in an identical way. With the advent of the semiconductor memory a new kind of memory organization was invented in which each cell of the matrix structure did not contain just one bit, but a large number of bits, which were read in series upon addressing that memory position. The cell consisted of a semiconductor shift register. Also a delay line as discussed in Chapter 2 of this book is possible. The characteristics of such structures will be treated in Section 3.4.

3.1.2. GENERAL MATRIX MEMORY TERMS AND DEFINITIONS

In the literature on matrix memories a number of terms and definitions are used which are not specific to a certain cell but generally apply to all matrix organizations.

(i) *Destructive read out (DRO) and non-destructive read out (NDRO)*. In order to read a memory cell, two drive amplifiers are activated and the cell where the signals coincide will change its information state causing an output signal on the sense line.

With respect to the response of the cell to the read signals one can distinguish between two types of cells. In one case called destructive read out (DRO) the information state of the cell is permanently changed by the read signals and when the information has to be re-used, rewriting is necessary. Most ferrite cores behave in that way. A cell which allows non-destructive readout (NDRO) will not change its state and makes a rewriting operation superfluous, which allows faster memory operation.

(ii) *Cycle time and access time.* A computer memory and the memory cells are often judged and compared on the basis of their cycle time and access time.

It is not easy to give a precise definition of cycle time, but in general the cycle time is defined as the time between the moment of entering a first binary address in the address decoder, after which the information in the selected address is read and the new or old information is written or rewritten, and the moment of entering the next address in the decoder. The read access time is the time between entering the address in the decoder up to the moment the sense signal has been produced. For some cells the read access time is small compared to the cycle time and it is evident that if such a cell has NDRO property, the cycle time can be noticeably reduced.

(iii) *Random access.* Most matrix memories allow random access to any stored word in the memory structure. This means that the access time does not depend on which address is selected. This makes the life of a computer programmer much more pleasant, since he can specify the word address in a completely random manner.

(iv) *Read only memory (ROM).* For certain applications as storing tables, read only memories are needed. In reality each matrix memory can be used as a ROM by just writing information in it once and never changing it again. However, an element which is capable of doing more than just store information is unnecessarily complicated and expensive and it is no wonder that engineers looked for simpler and less expensive devices which could perform as well. A large number of resistive, capacitive and inductive coupling elements were proposed in the past twenty years. The principle of most ROM organizations is that at a crosspoint of the drive wires a coupling element is mounted when a binary "one" is desired, and no coupling element is present in case of a "zero". When computer architects got accustomed to these ROM structures, they started to think that a little bit of alteration of the contents of such a memory would be pleasant. Alterable read only memories are now offered under the name read mostly memories (RMM).

(v) *Volatility*. For a number of computer applications it is very inconvenient, when information stored in a memory cell is lost during power failure. For such an application one demands non-volatility. When magnetic devices are used, this non-volatility does not pose a problem because a magnetization direction remains stable even without the supply of energy. For memory cells consisting of semiconductor flip-flops this is not the case. It appears however, that the number of applications where volatility is important is restricted and that computer architects want to spend only 5% of the total price of the main memory system to assure non-volatility [3.1.4].

(vi) *General requirements of the memory cell*. In the next sections the most important memory cells will be discussed. However, in the literature one finds many more devices, very often presented with great cogency, which never were nor will be used. The reason is that although these devices had certain definite advantages, the devices also had properties which prevented their use. Some of the most important requirements a memory cell has to satisfy are as follows:

THRESHOLD. As in a matrix the device should only change when two or more drive signals coincide. It is desirable that the memory cell switch sharply at a certain critical value of voltage or current.

TWO STATE DEVICE. Since modern computers operate on the binary system at least two different stable states should be available.

STABILITY. When in a certain memory cell a "zero" or "one" is stored, we would like to find that this memory state remains even after a very long time. The cell should only change, when its content is rewritten on command. However, the cell is subject to many perturbations like temperature variations, mechanical shocks and most annoying, also to changing electric or magnetic fields. In a matrix memory it is unavoidable that when a specific cell is interrogated, many other cells will receive a half-select signal. A few half-select signals in the "zero" direction will not change a "one" state, but when 10^6 disturb pulses pass, many cells proposed with great triumph behave in a very disappointing manner.

SEPARATION OF DRIVE AND SENSE LINES. A sense signal should only reflect the contents of the read cell in a matrix, but very often it contains many spurious signals. A two port device like a tunnel diode is very difficult to use in this respect. In a ferrite core the situation is much more favourable as the sense and drive wires make no electrical contact at all.

SPEED. The speed of a modern computer is limited by the memory cycle time of the main memory. And as fast computers can be more economically used the switching speed of a memory device is very important.

LARGE SENSE SIGNAL. In order to reduce the peripheral sense circuitry and to be able to use simple noise cancellation systems, the sense signal should be as large as possible.

ENERGY CONSUMPTION. Computer memories consist of very many cells. When each cell produces some heat, the total memory might be an efficient stove and extensive cooling is needed. One can distinguish between two types of cells, those that only consume energy when the energy state is changed, like ferrite cores, or those that have a continuous energy consumption, like flip-flops. Today great advances with respect to this problem can be expected.

VOLATILITY. The larger the memory capacity the more non-volatility is preferred.

NDRO. Because of the savings with respect to the cycle time of the memory this is always a much applauded property.

CAPACITY. In computers aside from some small special memories, the main memory should have a very large capacity. The size is usually mentioned in the computer maker's advertisements and is a selling point. Memory cells which behave well on a laboratory scale very often are not suitable for mass production. Moreover, the size of the memory cell should not be too large.

LOW COST. A requirement readily overlooked by enthusiastic scientists is the price, usually given as the cost per bit. No matter how fast, small, non-volatile, etc. a memory cell may be, when the anticipated price is not evidently lower than of already known products, the device will give a nice publication, but will never go into production.

SIMPLE TECHNOLOGY. Related to the cost is the simplicity with which the memory cell can be manufactured. It is clear that the manufacturing of a ferrite core poses less problems than that of a complicated IC memory matrix.

COMPATIBILITY OF TECHNOLOGY. The main frame of computers consists of logic building blocks and the memory. Today it is without a doubt that the logic circuits are, and also in the future will be, made of semiconductors. Therefore, a computer manufacturer will always have extensive experience with respect to semiconductor technology. When this experience can also be used for the memory cell a very desirable situation arises. Moreover, it becomes fairly easy to distribute parts of the memory when necessary, throughout the logic system. In contrast, ferrite cores, superconductive cryotrons and ferroelectric cells have the disadvantage that they require additional research and development effort, because their technology is not compatible.

TABLE 3·1·1. Comparison of matrix memory cells.

Cryotron	OVONIC cell	MOSFET cell	Bipolar cell	Tunneldiode	Ferroelectr. cell	Plated wire	Planar film	Twistor	Ferrite plane	Ferrite core	
+	+	++	++	+	−−	+	+	++	+	++	THRESHOLD
+	+	++	++	+	+	++	++	++	+	++	TWO STATE DEVICE
+	−	++	++	+	−−	−−	−−	++	+	++	STABILITY
−	−	++	++		−	++	++	++	+	++	SEPARATION OF DRIVE AND SENSE LINES
−	−	+	++	++	−	+	++	−−	+	+	SPEED
+	++	++	++	++	+	+	−	+	+	+	LARGE SENSE SIGNAL
+	−	+	−	−	+	+	+	+	+	+	ENERGY CONSUMPTION
−−	−−	−−	−−	−−	−	++	++	++	++	++	VOLATILITY
+	+	++	++	+	−	−	−	−	−	−	NDRO
+	+	++	+	+	−−	+	+	−	+	+	SIZE
−−	+	+	+	−−	−−	−	−−	+	−	++	LOW COST
−−	+	+	−	−−	−−	−	−−	+	−	++	SIMPLE TECHNOLOGY
−−	+	++	++	+	−−	−−	−−	−−	−−	−−	COMPATIBLE TECHNOLOGY

As already stated, not all kinds of memory cells are treated in the next sections. To justify our selection, in Table 3.1.1. the different proposed matrix memory cells are compared with the requirements just described. A double + + indicates very good, one + good, one − unsuitable, whereas the double − − means very unsuitable. It is evident that the treatment of memory devices in the next sections is related to the plus points in the most important columns of the survey. The physics of twistors, consisting of a strip of magnetic material around a conductor [3.1.5] or ferrite planes, consisting of a monolithic sheet of ferrite with embedded conductors [3.1.6] will not be treated in detail.

3.2. MAGNETIC MEMORIES

3.2.1. INTRODUCTION

In their search for physical effects which could be used for the storage of binary digits, it occurred quite early to the computer designers that the direction of a magnetization could be related to a memory state. As only two bits are used in computers, only two magnetization directions are required. It is evident that the energy and field necessary to switch from the "0" to the "1" state should be as low as possible. This precludes the use of hard magnetic materials. However, a disadvantage of soft magnetic materials in which small fields are sufficient to change the direction of magnetization is that demagnetization effects play a dominating role. For instance, a bar will demagnetize in such a way that the resultant magnetization component in any direction is only a fraction of the total possible saturation magnetization so that the storage state is indefinite.

In order to circumvent the demagnetization problems, one is forced to use "closed flux" devices of which the core (Section 3.2.2) is the simplest or to reduce one dimension of the device with respect to the others to obtain a small demagnetization constant perpendicular to that direction, as is applied in planar magnetic films (Section 3.2.3). As experiments have shown, even in thin magnetic films demagnetization effects have a detrimental effect on the memory operation, so that also "closed flux" thin film structures (plated wires Section 3.2.3) have definite advantages.

A region in which the magnetization direction is parallel is called a domain. In the above devices during the storage state the whole storage device consists more or less of one domain. However, it is also possible to store binary information by means of small domains in a large ferromagnetic plane. Many such proposals were made, the most important of which will be discussed in Section 3.2.3. Finally in Section 3.2.4 magnetic bubble memories will be discussed.

3.2.2. FERRITE CORE MEMORIES

Without doubt the most important and successful memory device is the ferrite core. Today about 95% of all computer main memories consist of ferrite cores and the yearly world production of these cores is estimated to be about $2-3 \times 10^{10}$ cores [3.2.1]. Roughly half of all ferrite material produced is used for these tiny cores. It is always difficult in the case of such an important invention to trace in the literature who made the first suggestions. In general the names of J. W. Forrester and W. N. Papion, both at that time at MIT in Boston [3.2.2], are connected to the first ideas, with respect to the coincident current selection method of core memories. The first cores consisted of many turns of nickel-iron tape wound on a spool and as vacuum tubes were to be used for driving, the driving windings consisted of many turns (Fig. 3.2.2.1). Forrester as well as Rajchman of RCA suggested in their early papers [3.2.2], [3.2.3] the use of non-metallic ferrite cores to increase the switching speed of the memory cells. The first experimental computer with a ferrite core memory was the Whirlwind I. It was built at the Lincoln laboratory at M.I.T. in 1953. This computer so convincingly showed the potential of ferrite core memories that at many laboratories throughout the world an intensive research and development program

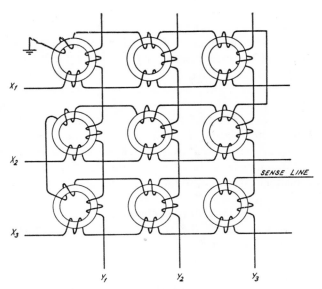

FIG. 3.2.2.1. First coincident current matrix plane showing many turns of the drive windings. (From [3.2.3].)

on ferrite cores started. The first commercial computer which contained besides a magnetic drum memory, a ferrite core memory of about 100 000 cores with a cycle time of 17 μs, was the IBM 705. It was delivered in the latter part of 1955 [3.2.4].

3.2.2.1. Principle of Coincident Current Selection

Nickel-iron and also ferrite cores can be made in such a way that their hysteresis loop looks almost rectangular (Fig. 3.2.2.2(a)). When a large current is sent along a wire through the core, the core is saturated in the direction given by the magnetic field and remains saturated even when the current is switched off. A large current in the opposite direction would set the core magnetization in the opposite direction. The two states represent the stored "1" and the stored "0". In a coincident current matrix plane the core is threaded by two drive wires (Fig. 3.2.2.2(b)). In order to store a "one", currents are passed through both wires. The polarities of both currents are chosen such that the fields due to the currents add. The magnitude of the currents is chosen so that the core will not switch when only one wire is activated, but will switch from the "0" to the "1" state when both currents coincide. For reading currents of equal magnitude but of opposite direction

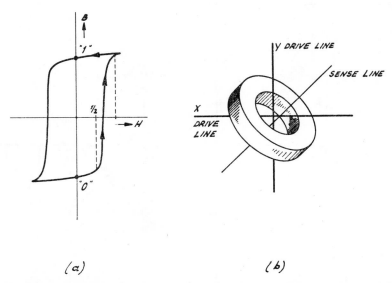

(a) *(b)*

FIG. 3.2.2.2. (a) Ferrite core hysteresis loop indicating half and full select fields and (b) core with drive and sense lines.

are sent through the windings. When the core returns to the "0" state a voltage pulse will be induced in a third wire, the so-called sense wire. In case a "0" is stored, the read currents will not produce a signal or will only produce a very small signal on the sense wire.

3.2.2.2. Ferrite Core Memory Organization

The coincident current principle can be used in many different memory systems. In the course of time bit organized 3D memories, word organized 2D memories and 2½D memories were constructed. These will be briefly reviewed [3.2.5].

(i) *3D-memory system.* This kind of memory consists of a number of core matrices stacked on top of each other. The number of cores of one matrix is equal to the number of words which have to be stored, whereas the number of matrices is equal to the number of bits in the words. A typical

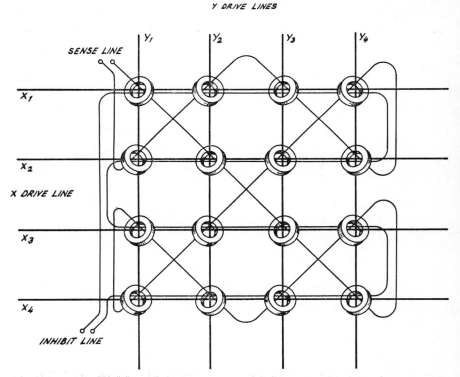

FIG. 3.2.2.3. Four-wire 3D-core-memory matrix.

design stores 4096 words of 32 bits in 32 64 × 64 matrix planes. Each core of the matrix is threaded by three or four wires as shown in Fig. 3.2.2.3 for 16 cores. Each core in the matrix plane can be uniquely selected by the coincident application of half select current pulses in one of the x and one of the y wires. When no current is passed along the third wire, called the inhibit line, which threads all cores of one plane, the half select x and y currents will set the core in the "1" state. However, if a half current pulse is passed through the inhibit line in such a way that the magnetic field it produces is anti-parallel to the x and y fields, the core remains in the "0" state. It is the inhibit line that determines what binary information is stored in a core, which is selected by the x and y wires. For reading a core, half select currents pulses are sent through one of the x and one of the y wires. The polarity of the currents is such as to bring the core into the "0" state. During reading the inhibit line is not activated. In case the core was already in the "0" state, only a very small signal is induced on a fourth line, the so-called sense line. When the core was originally in the "1" state a large sense signal is produced. The sense wire is not threaded in the same simple way as the inhibit wire. The reason is that the hysteresis loop of a ferrite core is not as rectangular as is desired. During reading all cores on the x and y lines are subjected to half select current pulses and no signal should be induced. However, in practice a small voltage is observed. If the sense wire in a 64 × 64 matrix were threaded in a straightforward manner, 126 such small voltage pulses would add up and the sense signal would become indetectable. The sense wire in a standard 3D memory is therefore threaded and the cores arranged in such a way that the small voltages oppose one another. However, the use of the very small fast cores of today forces the memory designer to reduce the number of wires. Since the inhibit wire is only used during writing and the sense wire is only used during reading and both wires thread all cores of one plane, the inhibit line and sense wires can be combined. This however imposes very stringent requirements on the peripheral electronic circuitry. The different systems are known in the literature as the four-wire and the three-wire 3D-memory system. In a 3D-memory organization matrix, planes as shown in Fig. 3.2.2.3 are stacked on top of each other. The x and y drive lines of all matrix planes are connected as shown in Fig. 3.2.2.4. The bits of one word are positioned vertically above one another and in the stack the number of words is equal to the number of cores in the matrix plane.

The main advantage of the 3D-memory organization is the small number of drivers necessary to select the cores. In the case of a square matrix of N cores, only $2\sqrt{N}$ drivers are necessary, which means only $2\sqrt{N}$ drivers per bit. Matrix planes with a large number of cores seem favourable. Due to noise, signal attenuation and delay on the sense line this number is limited

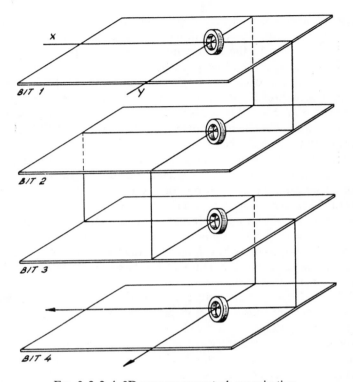

FIG. 3.2.2.4. 3D-core-memory stack organization.

and 4096 seems to be a maximum. For larger capacities the memory is divided into several segments so that the cost per bit does not decrease beyond 4096 words.

(ii) *2D-memory system.* A much more costly though faster operating memory organization is the so-called word-organized or 2D memory. As opposed to the 3D memory all the bits of one word lie in one matrix plane (Fig. 3.2.2.5). A core is switched to the "1" state by the coincidence of half-select pulses on the horizontal word lines and the vertical bit lines. If the bit current is absent, the core stays in the "0" state. The number of words is equal to the number of horizontal lines and the number of bits is equal to the number of cores per word line. An inhibit line as used in the 3D memory is not needed. During reading, one of the word lines is selected and a current opposite to the writing currents is passed. The current can be arbitrarily high because only the cores belonging to one word will be switched, all other words are unaffected. The cores will switch very rapidly, which makes a 2D

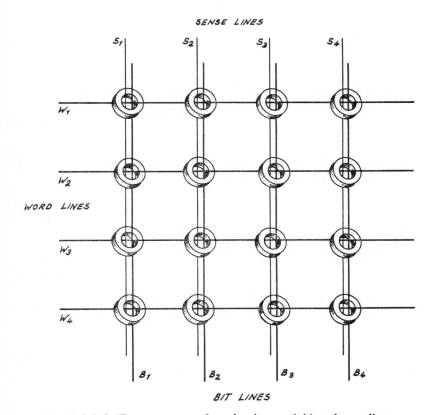

FIG. 3.2.2.5. 2D-core-memory plane showing word, bit and sense lines.

memory fast. The read signals are induced on the bit lines when a common bit-sense system is used or on separate sense lines.

Because the selection of the word lines during reading occurs in the peripheral electronic circuitry and not in the core matrix itself as in the 3D system, the costs of a 2D system are much higher. As the word decoding circuitry is more expensive than the sense-bit circuitry, long words reduce the cost per bit. A limit to the word length is given by the information-dependent back voltage on the word line when the cores switch simultaneously.

A typical 2D memory would consist of 2000 words each of 128 bits. Because of their high cost, 2D memories have only been used in applications where speed and not capacity was most important, for instance in scratch-pad memories (Chapter 1.1) as part of a memory hierarchy.

G

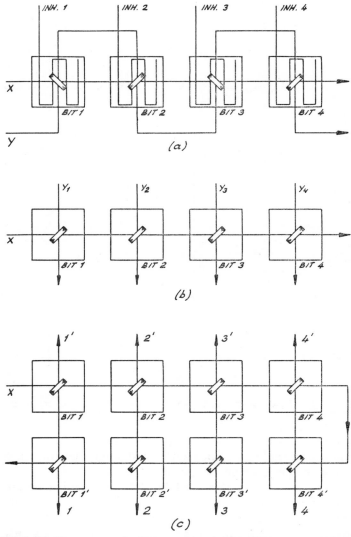

FIG. 3.2.2.6. (a) 3D memory, (b) $2\frac{1}{2}$D memory and (c) $2\frac{1}{2}$D memory with bit current phasing.

(iii) *$2\frac{1}{2}$D-memory system*. A compromise between the economy of a 3D-memory system and the speed of a 2D-memory system is a system that has come to be known as the $2\frac{1}{2}$D system [3.2.6]. It was proposed as early as 1951 but it first came into use in 1954 and today is generally used for bulk core memories. In the $2\frac{1}{2}$D system writing occurs similar to that in the 2D system, whereas reading information conforms to the 3D-memory system. In order to understand how the $2\frac{1}{2}$D system operates, it is useful to compare it with the 3D system. Figure 3.2.2.6(a) shows the previously discussed 3D system but for clarity the core matrices which in reality are on top of each other are drawn side by side. One core of each plane is threaded by a particular x and a y line. For writing, the x and y lines are energized and by means of a counteracting inhibit line the resulting core magnetization direction is set. Without one inhibit line per matrix plane, it would not be possible to store "0s" and "1s" simultaneously in different planes. In order to reduce the number of wires through each core, in the $2\frac{1}{2}$D system, the y line is no longer interconnected. Each plane has its own y selection line increasing the electronic circuits for selection. For writing a "1" in a certain plane the x line and y line are activated and the core switches due to the coincidence of the current pulses. A "0" is stored by simply not activating the relevant y line. An inhibit line is no longer required, but the number of y drivers multiplies with the number of bits per word. The number of words is equal to the number of cores per plane and as the x lines are much more economically used than the y lines since they connect the cores of all the planes, in a $2\frac{1}{2}$D memory the planes are very asymmetric. The number of cores in the x direction is much larger than the number in the y direction. As a result it is not necessary to mount the different planes on top of each other. In a $2\frac{1}{2}$D memory the rectangular bit planes are mounted side by side in a large frame. A variation of the $2\frac{1}{2}$D system is possible which results in twice as many cores being selected by about the same electronic circuitry. As is shown in Fig. 3.2.2.6(c) the total core plane is doubled and the x lines loop around in a U shape to thread twice as many cores as before.

During writing the polarity of the bit current pulse determines if a "1" will be stored in the upper or lower half of the double core plane.

With respect to the reading process, in a $2\frac{1}{2}$D-memory system one distinguishes between the two wire and the three wire $2\frac{1}{2}$D-system.

In the early days of ferrite core memories the cost of the electronic circuitry was much higher than that of the core matrix planes. In the course of time magnetics were getting more expensive because of the smaller cores used, and the cost of the electronic circuits decreased rapidly because of the advent of the integrated circuits. When new generations of computers had to be equipped with bulk core memories, the advantage of the $2\frac{1}{2}$D system in which no inhibit line is needed for selection made this system very suitable for bulk stores. Moreover, the y lines of Fig. 3.2.2.6(b) can be used as sense lines, so that only two drive lines perpendicular to each other have to pass each core. This makes the production of very inexpensive memory planes possible. Reading in a two wire $2\frac{1}{2}$D system is accomplished by sending half select currents along one x line and along one of the y lines of each core matrix. The penalty of the two wire $2\frac{1}{2}$D-memory system is a relatively large cycle time because it takes some time to separate the sense signal from the y line driving noise.

A typical two wire $2\frac{1}{2}$D-memory consists of 32 (word length) core planes each of 4096×32 cores totalling roughly 5×10^6 cores. The cycle time of such a memory is typically 2.8 μs [3.2.7].

For faster $2\frac{1}{2}$D memories a common drive sense line can no longer be used and a separate sense line has to be threaded through all the cores of one bit plane. This sense wire is generally inserted parallel to the y drive wires in order to reduce the stringing costs. A typical three wire $2\frac{1}{2}$D memory consists of 32 (word length) core planes each of 512×16 cores, totalling roughly 2.5×10^5 cores. The cycle time of this memory is shorter than that of a 3D memory of the same size and is typically about 0.35 μs.

3.2.2.3. Manufacturing Technology

The use of ferrite cores as memory cells poses formidable problems for the manufacturing engineer. First millions of very tiny brittle cores have to be fabricated with very uniform magnetic and crystallographic properties as well as dimensions and secondly, these tiny cores have to be threaded by 2, 3 or 4 tiny wires to obtain the well known matrix planes. The demand of the computer industry around 1955 for large, fast and reliable memories was so urgent that many large companies started investing huge sums of money in the development of core memories with great success. It is very probable that if the ferrite core had been invented today and not 15 years ago this investment would not have been made.

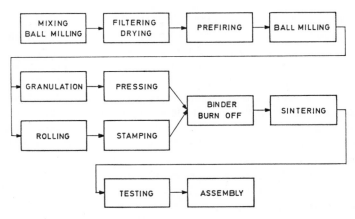

Fig. 3.2.2.7. Flow-chart of core memory production.

(i) *Preparation of bulk material.* As will be amply discussed in the next sections, the so-called ferrites consist of mixtures of iron oxide and oxides of other metals such as magnesium (Mg), manganese (Mn), copper (Cu), nickel (Ni), zinc (Zn), lithium (Li), etc. In the first step high purity raw materials for instance, fine-grained oxides are mixed in a water suspension in vibratory steel-ball mills [3.2.8] (Fig. 3.2.2.7). After milling the mixture is filtered and dried and subsequently prefired at temperatures around 600°C. During this firing cycle an incomplete reaction takes place between the ferrites. The resulting material is again broken up and milled for the second time to improve the homogeneity and to reduce the final grain size. The composition of the ferrite has to be very accurately determined; even the iron oxide content has to be adjusted for the wear of the steel balls of the mills.

The final particle size is of the order of magnitude of a few microns. In the next step the ferrite powder is mixed with an organic binder such as polyvinyl alcohol and granulated by spray drying. The resultant granules are spherical, with the smallest 10 μm (0.4 mil) in diameter. The material is then ready to be pressed. The amount of material prepared at one time is typically large enough for the production of some one million cores.

(ii) *Pressing step.* The pressing step has become a very critical part of the process since the core diameter has to be very small for fast operation. The first employed ferrite cores had outer diameters of 90 mils (2.25 mm). Today cores with a diameter of only 16 mils (0.4 mm) are produced. The pressing operation is done on rotary type presses. A cylindrical die is filled with the ferrite granules and a punch compresses the powder into the core shape. The pressure is so high that the core is very homogeneous and the granule boundaries are hardly observable. Today a multistation press is capable of shaping thousands of cores per minute. The smaller the cores the shorter the life of the pressing tool. Moreover, it is increasingly difficult to control the core dimensions and to maintain a constant density of the cores. To circumvent these problems, ferrite cores are made in an alternate way today. The prefired ferrite is mixed with a relatively large amount of organic binder and rolled out into large sheets [3.2.9]. The density and thickness of this sheet can be easily controlled. The cores are then stamped out of the sheet like cookies. The process is suitable for producing the cores for the two wire 2½D mass memories.

(iii) *The sintering process.* The pressed cores are loaded onto boats which automatically move through tunnel kilns in which zones exist with different, very accurately controlled temperatures. The temperatures used are between 1050°C and 1350°C. During the sintering process the organic binder is burned out and in the case where the new stamping process is used which employs a high content of binder this burn off has to be very well controlled.

Further the ferrite grains grow in size and coalesce so that a very dense material results without pores. The sintering process occurs in a neutral, slightly reducing or in an air atmosphere depending on the kind of ferrite and on the temperature. The most appropriate sintering process giving the desired magnetic properties is found empirically and varies from manufacturer to manufacturer.

(iv) *Core testing.* The next phase of the fabrication process is the testing of the individual cores. Since it is very difficult and costly to replace a core, after a memory plane is completed it is justifiable to test all the cores before they are assembled. Due to the huge number of cores which have to be tested, this operation is automated. In a standard machine the cores are moved and oriented by a vibratory feeder to the test station where two sets of pressure contacts make the drive and sense circuit connections. The magnetic and switching parameters are determined and the cores are either dropped in an "accept" or "reject" collector. Because the whole operation is mechanical it is very slow; a typical machine tests only sixteen cores per second.

(v) *Core plane assembly.* After the cores are tested they are assembled into memory planes. In the beginning this was done manually and it took days, today the operation is partly mechanized and takes only hours [3.2.5]. A sheet of plastic is used which contains small rectangular holes into which the cores are sucked in such a way that the core holes are above the surface. In the next step a number of hollow needles are driven through the cores of a row or a column of the matrix and wires are fed through the needles. The wires are clamped and the hollow needles withdrawn. Since the inhibit line in the 3D memory and the sense line in 3D and $2\frac{1}{2}$D memories take less straightforward paths these wires are still predominantly done by hand. It is rather improbable that assembly of core matrices can be completely automatized in the future. It is for this reason that some industries have their core planes assembled in low wage areas such as Hong Kong and Taiwan.

3.2.2.4. Single Core Testing for Memory Application

In this section we will discuss the method by which ferrite cores are tested and we will indicate the relationships between the resulting switching parameters and the hysteretic properties of the core material. One distinguishes between three different kinds of core test procedures.

Uniformity testing. In the final phase of the ferrite core production process each core is tested and compared with the specifications to ensure production uniformity and to enable immediate intervention in the fabrication process when switching parameters change.

Single core testing. Ferrite cores might also be subjected to extensive test programs in order to find the optimum operating conditions and to investigate the sensitivity of the devices to large numbers of half select drive currents. This test will be applied especially when new core dimensions or materials are introduced.

Array testing. Cores are used in large matrices and are connected by a complex wiring pattern. This causes all kinds of coupling and transmission line effects. Moreover, the spurious signals occurring on the sense lines, generally called delta noise, are memory content dependent and it is not always easy to imagine the worst case pattern. It is no wonder that computer methods have to be used to solve these memory array test programs [3.2.10]. As we are mainly interested in the physical parameters which determine core behaviour, we will focus on the second test procedure.

In Section 3.2.2.2 the different core memory organizations have been discussed. Because of the different write and read cycles of these organizations the requirements the cores have to satisfy also differ. It appears that the 3D-memory organization is the most demanding since in it the participation of the matrix in the selection function is the largest. In a 3D memory the coincidence of two half select currents causes the complete switching of a core, whereas one half select pulse should preferably cause no change at all and no output signal on the sense line. A core test pulse train should contain pulses with amplitudes equal to the half select current pulses and equal to twice this current. When a specific core in a 3D matrix is addressed, other cores in the matrix experience half select drive currents. During writing of a "one", all the cores on the X and Y lines which intersect at the location of the selected core are subjected to half select "one" currents. It is conceivable that these cores are all in the "zero" state. When the hysteresis loop of the ferrite core is perfectly square, these half select pulses will cause no change. In practice the loops are rounded off and half select pulses cause many problems.

When a "zero" is written in a core the inhibit line of a matrix is activated and all cores of that plane experience a half select current pulse in the "0" direction. Cores which are in the "one" direction will change their magnetization state slightly and cause small sense signals also.

To test the sensitivity of a ferrite core with respect to these different disturb situations a core is subjected to a standard, generally accepted, pulse program, which is shown in Fig. 3.2.2.8.

The pulse sequence starts with a large write pulse I_w, with which the core is set into the "1" direction. The next pulse I_r has the same magnitude but opposite polarity and the core is reset to the "0" state. The corresponding magnetization changes are indicated in Fig. 3.2.2.9(a). Resetting to the "0" state induces a signal uV_1 on the sense line through the core as is shown

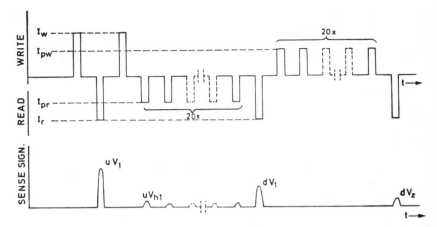

FIG. 3.2.2.8. Generally accepted pulse sequence for testing memory cores.

in Fig. 3.2.2.10. In order to improve the surveyability of figures like Fig. 3.2.2.10., a system of symbols to designate the various sense signals was agreed upon [3.1.1]. Only sense signals caused by the leading edges of the drive pulses are considered. A sense signal is indicated by three characters. The prescript describes the prior magnetic history. The character u means undisturbed since last full current. The second character V indicates a response voltage and the post-subscript 1 describes the information state the core had just before reversal started, in this case the "one" state.

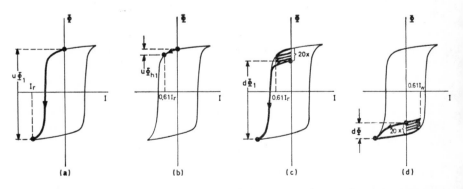

FIG. 3.2.2.9. (a) Flux change during reading of the undisturbed "one" state, (b) flux change caused by half select read current pulse, (c) flux change during reading of a disturbed "one" state and (d) flux change during reading of a disturbed "zero" state.

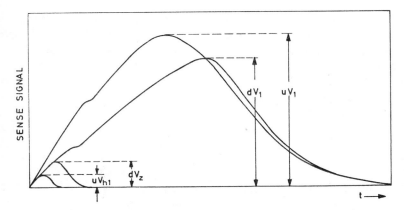

FIG. 3.2.2.10. Characteristic sense signals of a core that is subjected to the test program of Fig. 3.2.2.8.

Following the full read current the core is again switched to the "one" state by a second current pulse I_w. In order to learn how a core responds to a half select pulse such a pulse I_{pr} is applied to the "0" or read direction. The subscript pr means partial read current. In the case of an ideal rectangular hysteresis loop no signal would be induced on the sense line. For a real core a small signal appears designated with uV_{h1}, in which the h stands for half select. In a 3D memory a core might be subjected to many half select currents so that the I_{pr} pulse is followed by a large train of pulses of the same magnitude. These pulses in the "0" direction tend to destroy the "1" state. Since the significant magnetization changes occur only during the first tens of pulses, in most test programs a pulse train of about 20 pulses is used (Fig. 3.2.2.9(c)). Following the train of disturb pulses the core is again interrogated by a read current pulse I_r. For a good core, the resulting sense signal dV_1 (the prescript d means 20 disturbs of a polarity, which tends to drive the core toward the opposite state) should be equal to the undisturbed signal uV_1. For bad cores or at improper operation conditions the disturbed signal is smaller and might even be equal to uV_{h1}, so that the signal due to an interrogated core cannot be distinguished from a signal due to one of the other non-addressed cores on the x or y lines.

The first part of the pulse sequence serves to test the reaction of an undisturbed and a disturbed "one" state to a full select and a half select read current, in the second part the "zero" state is tested. For this purpose a half select current pulse train with amplitude I_{pw} in the "1" or write direction and subsequently a full read current I_r are applied. A read signal dV_z (z indicates that the "zero" state is interrogated) appears on the sense line and it is evident that this signal has to be small in a good memory. In a coincident current memory the full select pulses are twice as large as the half select pulses. However, in the worst case condition it is possible for the full select pulse to be smaller than, and the half select pulse to be larger than, the nominal values. A 10% margin is usually accepted. The ratio between I_{pr} and I_r or between I_{pw} and I_w, the so-called selection ratio R_s, is then in a standard test program:

$$R_s = \frac{I_{pr}}{I_r} = \frac{I_{pw}}{I_w} = \frac{0.5 + 10\%}{1.0 - 10\%} = \frac{0.55}{0.9} = 0.61 \qquad (3.2.2.1)$$

It is usual to plot the magnitude of the above described sense signals uV_1, dV_1 and dV_z as a function of the magnitude of the full select drive current in order to find the optimal operation conditions (Fig. 3.2.2.11). The dependence of the uV_1 signal on the driving current amplitude is a straight line. Since the sense signal amplitude is proportional to the rate of change of magnetization, a ferrite composition with high saturation magnetization gives rise to a large output.

When the uV_1 line is extrapolated to the current axis, one finds a current below which no significant magnetization changes occur. This current is related to the coercive force of the ferrite core hysteresis loop. The dV_1 signal plot is very close to the uV_1 line until at a certain current, the signal starts to decrease. This decrease is due to the series of disturb pulses in the "zero" direction. When the amplitude of these disturb current pulses

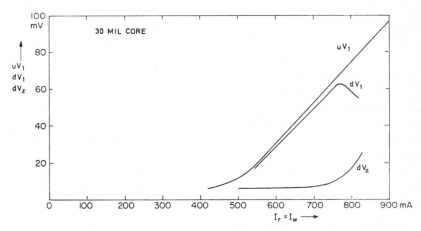

FIG. 3.2.2.11. The most important sense signal amplitudes as a function of the magnitude of the full select pulse $I_r = I_w$.

$(0.61 \times I_r)$ is close to the current, which causes magnetization reversal, the core is partially switched to the "0" state after the application of the full I_{write} (Fig. 3.2.2.8). The current I_w at which dV_1 starts to decrease should be about 1.64 (10 : 6.1) times the current amplitude at which the uV_1 line intersects with the current axis and is again related to the coercive force. The dV_z dependence on I_r is a line parallel to the current axis for small currents until at a certain I_r, dV_2 starts to increase. The current pulse amplitude at which this increase sets in is equal to the current at which dV_1 starts to decrease. This is to be expected for symmetry reasons, because the magnitude of the disturb field in the "0" direction to disturb the "1" state should be equal to the magnitude of the disturb field in the "1" direction to disturb the "0" state.

Cores with ideal rectangular hysteresis loops should, for small current pulses, show no dV_z signal at all, as the "zero" state should not change. In less ideal cores as is shown in Fig. 3.2.2.9(d) the disturb pulses cause the traversing of minor loops, which lead to a small dV_z. The dV_z signal as such is an indication of the quality of the core and, in physical terms, of the loop rectangularity of the ferrite core material. So far the time in which the core switches has not been discussed but of course it plays a very important role. All the signals discussed so far are observed at the leading edge of the switching current pulse and the pulse length has to be long enough so that the trailing edge appears after the switching process takes place. It is the switching time of the core which determines the access and cycle times of the core memory.

From the above discussion the following physical parameters evolve which determine the switching parameters of the core:

Saturation magnetization

Coercive force

Loop rectangularity

Switching time

During operation of the memory the temperature of the core may increase due to the hysteresis energy dissipation in the core and resistance heating of the drive lines. A temperature increase might be deleterious to the core characteristics, so we have to study as a fifth significant physical parameter:

Temperature dependence

The last parameter to be investigated is

Stress sensitivity.

Due to the wiring of the memory matrix the cores might be under stress. When the core material shows magnetostriction the switching parameters will be affected.

In the next section the physical parameters as just enumerated will be amply treated.

3.2.2.5. Relation Between Physical and Device Parameters

(i) *Introduction.* The first cores tested in a memory matrix consisted of many turns of high permeability nickel-iron tape wound on a spool. Apart from the high costs of such a device the switching speed of metal cores is relatively low. Consequently from the beginning interest was concentrated on cores made of ferrites.

Ferrites are complex refractory compounds containing in each case oxides of iron and also oxides of other metals such as magnesium, manganese, cobalt, nickel, lithium, barium, yttrium, etc.

Crystallographically, four structures are distinguishable:

the ferrites with hexagonal symmetry, like barium ferrite, which are used for permanent magnets

the orthoferrites with orthorhombic symmetry

the garnets containing rare earth oxides showing cubic symmetry and

the spinels which also show cubic symmetry and which in this context are the only structures of interest as all memory core materials have this structure.

The mineral spinel ($MgAl_2O_4$) consists of oxygen ions which are packed into a face-centred cubic lattice with magnesium and aluminium ions occupying the interstices between the relatively large oxygen ions. In spinel ferrites the Al ions are substituted by trivalent Fe^{3+} ions. The Mg ion can be replaced by a divalent metal ion such as Mn, Ni, Co, Fe etc., so that the general formula of a spinel ferrite has the form $Me^{2+}Fe_2^{3+}O_4$.

In a spinel lattice two kinds of interstices exist:

A-sites, which are surrounded by four oxygen ions that lie on the corners of a tetrahedron (Fig. 3.2.2.12(a)) and

B-sites, which are surrounded by six oxygen ions that lie on the corners of an octahedron (Fig. 3.2.2.12(b)).

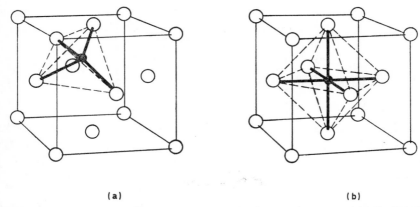

(a)   (b)

FIG. 3.2.2.12. Interstices between oxygen ions in the spinel structure: (a) A-site with tetrahedral symmetry and (b) B-site with octrahedral symmetry.

The magnetic properties of the different ferrites depend mainly on the distribution of the divalent metal and trivalent Fe^{3+} ions among the two types of interstices. The general formula for a spinel ferrite is then:

$$Me_x^{2+} Fe_{1-x}^{3+}(Me_{1-x}^{2+} Fe_{1+x}^{3+})O_4$$

in which the B-sites are indicated by the parentheses [3.2.8]. When $x = 1$ all the divalent Me^{2+} ions are on the A-sites and all the trivalent Fe^{3+} ions are on the B-sites, such a structure is called a normal spinel:

$$Me^{2+}(Fe_2^{3+})O_4$$

These ferrites are nonmagnetic. In the other limiting case, when $x = 0$, half of the trivalent Fe^{3+} ions are on A-sites and half are on B-sites, further all the divalent Me^{2+} ions are on the B-sites. In this case the ferrite structure is designated an inverse spinel $Fe^{3+}(Me^{2+} Fe^{3+})O_4$ and is ferrimagnetic. When $1 > x > 0$ the structure is called partially inverse. For memory purposes many compounds were investigated; single ferrite spinels containing only one divalent Me^{2+} are seldom used. In the next sections the different physical parameters of ferrites will be reviewed.

(ii) *Saturation magnetization.* In order to sense the information stored in a ferrite core, a magnetic field is produced by the x and y wire so that the magnetization in the core is reversed to the "0" direction. The signal amplitude induced on the sense line is given by the induction law:

$$uV_1 = -\frac{d\phi}{dt} = -\alpha\frac{M_s O}{\tau} \qquad (3.2.2.2)$$

where

M_s = saturation magnetization of the core material

O = cross-section of the core

τ = switching time

α = a constant dependent on the sense signal pulse shape.

In this section we will discuss the origin of M_s and its dependence on the composition. The theory of ferrimagnetism is mainly due to the French scientist L. Néel, for which he earned the Nobel prize in 1970. Néel showed that in ferrites the interactions between the ions in the A- and B-sites are antiferromagnetic, which means that the spins of the A- and B-ions are antiparallel. The net saturation magnetization is due to an incomplete cancellation of the moments of the A- and B-ions. It is for this reason that the saturation magnetization of ferrites is much lower than that of single metals. It is also possible to change the saturation magnetization by replacing the metal ions on the A- or B-sites.

To understand Néel's theory it is more convenient to work with the magnetic moment per ion expressed in Bohr magnetons, rather than using the bulk property of the material called saturation magnetization.

In Table 3.2.2.1 the spin structure and magnetic moments of some ions used in spinel ferrites are shown. Because of electrostatic Coulomb interactions between the electrons in the 3d shell, the spins fill the shell parallel according to Hund's rule until the maximum of five places is occupied, (Fe^{3+}, Mn^{2+}). The next electron will have its spin antiparallel to the first five spins, as is the case in the divalent Fe^{2+}. The net magnetic moment of

TABLE 3.2.2.1. Atomic structure and magnetic moments of ions used in ferrites.

ion	atomic number	number electrons	electron configuration 3d	4s	net moment in Bohr magnetons	site preference
Fe	26	26	↑↓ ↑ ↑ ↑ ↑	↑↓	4	—
Fe^{3+}	26	23	↑ ↑ ↑ ↑ ↑	—	5	A, B
Mn^{2+}	25	23	↑ ↑ ↑ ↑ ↑	—	5	A, B
Fe^{2+}	26	24	↑↓ ↑ ↑ ↑ ↑	—	4	B
Co^{2+}	27	25	↑↓ ↑↓ ↑ ↑ ↑	—	3	B
Ni^{2+}	28	26	↑↓ ↑↓ ↑↓ ↑ ↑	—	2	B
Cu^{2+}	29	27	↑↓ ↑↓ ↑↓ ↑↓ ↑	—	1	A, B
Zn^{2+}	30	28	↑↓ ↑↓ ↑↓ ↑↓ ↑↓	—	0	A

an ion is equal to the number of unpaired spins in Bohr magnetons. The result for the different ions is shown in Table 3.2.2.1. The next moment is only due to 3d spins, whereas the moment due to the orbital motion of the electrons is negligible. As a consequence the net magnetic moment of the Zn^{2+} ion with 10 electrons in the 3d shell is zero. In a spinel ferrite the different ions occupy A- or B-sites in an oxygen lattice. Therefore the distance between the metal ions is quite large and the direct exchange interaction, which is responsible for ferromagnetism in metals, is very weak. Still, a large indirect exchange coupling is observed, which is called superexchange [3.2.11]. The interaction between the metal ions on opposite sides of the oxygen ion takes place by means of an interaction with the electrons of the oxygen ion. When the orbits of the 3d electrons of the metal ion and the 2p electrons of the oxygen ion overlap, which is the case for instance, when the Fe^{3+} ion on an A-site, the oxygen ion and the Fe^{3+} ion on a B-site are in a straight line, the superexchange is a maximum. The 5 spins of the Fe^{3+} ion on the A-site are antiparallel to the one 2p electron of the oxygen ion and the 5 spins of the Fe^{3+} ion on the B-site are antiparallel to the other 2p electron of the oxygen ion. As the 2p spins of the oxygen ion are antiparallel according to the Pauli principle, the moments of the A- and B-site Fe^{3+} ions are also antiparallel and cancel each other as is shown in Fig. 3.2.2.13. However, in a spinel ferrite the Fe^{3+} and O^{2-} ions do not lie on straight lines. Actually one finds an angle of 125° for the A–O–B combination, 80° for the A–O–A combination and 90° for the B–O–B combination. As the overlap and thus the superexchange decreases for decreasing angles, only the superexchange between the A- and B-sites counts.

It is now possible, knowing the net moments of the different metal ions and the occupancy of the A- and B-sites, to calculate the net moment in Bohr magnetons of the ferrite molecule. In Table 3.2.2.2 this is demonstrated for some simple single ferrites [3.2.12, 3.2.13].

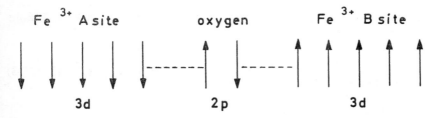

FIG. 3.2.2.13. Superexchange interaction between Fe^{3+} ions on opposite sides of an oxygen ion.

TABLE 3.2.2.2. Net magnetic moment of ferrite molecules.

Ferrite	A-site	B-site	magnetic moment			
			A-site	B-site	net	measured
$MnFe_2O_4$	$Mn^{2+} Fe^{3+}$	Fe^{3+}	5	5+5	5	4·6
$FeFe_2O_4$	Fe^{3+}	Fe^{2+}, Fe^{3+}	5	4+5	4	4·1
$CoFe_2O_4$	Fe^{3+}	Co^{2+}, Fe^{3+}	5	3+5	3	3·7
$NiFe_2O_4$	Fe^{3+}	Ni^{2+}, Fe^{3+}	5	2+5	2	2·3
$CuFe_2O_4$	Fe^{3+}	Cu^{2+}, Fe^{3+}	5	1+5	1	1·2
$ZnFe_2O_4$	Zn^{2+}	Fe^{3+}, Fe^{3+}	0	5+5	10	0

The deviation between the calculated and measured values of the net magnetic moment is relatively small and is due to a small contribution of orbital moments and a deviation from the ideal inverse spinel structure (In $MnFe_2O_4$ 80% of the Mn^{2+} ions are on A-sites and the rest are on B-sites). The Zn ferrite is a special case. Because Zn has a zero net magnetic moment, there is no exchange between the A- and B-sites. For the resulting moment the small superexchange between the B-sites is important, this interaction is also negative with the result that the moments of the Fe^{3+} ions are antiparallel and cancel each other. The Zn ferrite is nonmagnetic. The relative ease with which the net moments of ferrites can be predicted shows that Néel's theory is a good description of the interatomic interactions in simple ferrites. This is not the case in ferromagnetic metals. From Table 3.2.2.1 we expect 4 Bohr magnetons for the net magnetic moment of iron, whereas we find only 2.2 by experiment.

This is due to the close proximity of the interaction atoms, which causes a deformation of the electron configurations, which is theoretically much more difficult to understand.

It is not difficult to calculate the saturation magnetization of a ferrite. In the simple Fe^{3+} $(Fe^{2+}Fe^{3+})$ O_4 the edge of the unit cube is 8.39 Å as determined by X-ray analysis and the unit cube contains 8 molecules each contributing 4 Bohr magnetons. The saturation magnetization is (1 Bohr magneton $= 1.165 \times 10^{-29}$ Wb m)

$$I_s = \frac{8 \times 4}{(8.39 \times 10^{-10})^3} \frac{\text{Bohr magnetons}}{m^3} = 0.6 \text{ Wb m}^{-2} \quad (3.2.2.3)$$

which is close to the measured value. (4π $M_s = 6000$ Gauss)

In actual cores a mixture of ferrites is used to obtain an optimization of device parameters. The systems used for memory cores are the magnesium-manganese-zinc ferrites, the copper-manganese ferrites and the lithium-manganese ferrites, [3.2.14, 3.2.15]. The saturation magnetization is sufficiently high to ensure a large sense signal. (A 30 mil core e.g. produces a signal of the order of 50 mV at a cycle time of $1.5\,\mu$s.). Because of the problems of core heating and transmission line loading even in the case of smaller cores, the interest in searching for high saturation magnetization materials is not large. Parameters treated in the next sections are more important in determining the composition.

(iii) *Coercive force.* In a ferrite core memory a core is supposed to switch from the "0" to the "1" state when two half select current pulses are coincident. The amplitudes of these pulses are, as expected, related to the magnetic field at which magnetization reversal occurs in the core. The field at which 50% of the core volume is reversed is called the coercive force H_c. In order to be able to optimize the core memory, it is important to understand what parameters have an influence on H_c. One has to know how the magnetization reversal processes occur in the ferrite core. The study of reversal processes in magnetic materials is often facilitated by techniques which enable the direct observation of domains and wall motion. As cores consist of very small grains and have rough surfaces, these techniques do not work and nearly all information about the reversal processes has been obtained indirectly from electrical measurements and it is no wonder that contradicting theories exist. As we have seen in Section 3.2.2.3 cores are pressed from granules and subsequently sintered. During the sintering process the material recrystallizes; the resulting grain size depends on the sinter temperature and the sinter duration. On one side the overall magnetic behaviour of a ferrite core is determined by the magnetic properties of the single grains and, on the other hand, by macroscopic considerations such as the shape of the core and the magnetostatic coupling between the grains. As the grains are monocrystalline there exist preferred directions for the magnetization in the grains which will be isotropically distributed in space. However, due to the magnetostatic coupling between grains, the magnetization directions in adjacent grains must be parallel to prevent the forming of free magnetic poles on the grain boundaries. For the same reason the magnetization will be parallel to the surface of the core and thus circular. The behaviour of the core will depend mainly on the relative strengths of the crystalline and macroscopic properties.

When we assume that the preference of the magnetization for certain directions in the grain is very weak, which in physical terms means that the crystal anisotropy energy and the stress anisotropy energy are very small, the magnetization will be circular throughout the core. The dispersion of the magnetization directions will be a minimum. When a circular magnetic

H

field is applied antiparallel to the magnetization by means of a wire through the core, this field will be largest at the inner diameter of the core. When the surface of the core is very smooth, it will take a relatively large field to nucleate a wall at the inner diameter.

This wall is parallel to the inner diameter (Fig. 3.2.2.14(a)) and as the wall nucleation field H_n is larger than the wall motion field H_w, the wall will move rapidly to the outer diameter thereby reversing the total core magnetization. The core will have an ideal rectangular hysteresis loop with $H_c = H_n$ (Fig. 3.2.2.14(b)).

In normal, less ideal cores, the core surface is quite rough and it can be expected that even in the absence of an external field tiny domains in which the magnetization is antiparallel to the magnetization in the rest of the core will exist at the inner diameter of the core.

When a field is applied these small domains will start to grow as soon as the field H_{id} at the inner diameter reaches the wall motion field H_w. When the current is increased the circular wall will move to the outer diameter. When the wall is half way and when the inner and the outer diameter radii are not too different, roughly 50% of the core is reversed. In displaying the hysteresis loop of a core on the horizontal scale, the field acting in the centre of the core is normally plotted. In the case where 50% of the core is

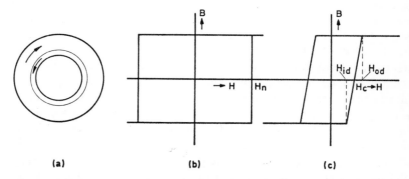

(a)   (b)   (c)

FIG. 3.2.2.14. (a) Circular wall in a ferrite core, (b) hysteresis loop of a very homogeneous core in which magnetization reversal starts by the nucleation of a wall at the inner diameter and (c) shearing of the hysteresis loop of a core with finite thickness. Wall motion at the inner diameter starts at

$$H_1 = \frac{2r_{id}}{r_{id} + r_{od}} H_c$$

and ends at the outer diameter at

$$H_2 = \frac{2r_{od}}{r_{id} + r_{od}} H_c.$$

switched, this field is equal to H_w and is called H_c (Fig. 2.3.2.14(c)) . When the current is further increased, the circular wall reaches the outer diameter. The field in the centre of the core, which is plotted on the horizontal axis is then

$$H_{\text{centre}} = \frac{r_{\text{od}}}{r_{\text{centre}}} H_{\text{od}} = \frac{2r_{\text{od}}}{r_{\text{id}} + r_{\text{od}}} H_c \qquad (3.2.2.4)$$

Due to the finite thickness of the core the hysteresis loop is sheared as is shown in Fig. 3.2.2.14(c). As we assumed the core was very homogeneous, it must be expected that the wall motion field is very low.

In practical cores, as the reader might expect, the situation is quite different. In the first place the compositions used are such that in the tiny crystallites which compose the core, preferred directions of magnetization occur. This causes some dispersion of the magnetization directions. To reduce the free poles due to this dispersion at the grain boundaries, small domains will occur here of which the magnetization is always antiparallel to the main magnetization direction in the grain. These domains will also be formed to reduce the free poles and associated energy of small pores in the material. When such a non-ideal core is subjected to a magnetic field, the small domains at the inner diameter will again be the first to grow. Again a circular wall will be formed which will move to the outer diameter when the field is increased. However, due to the dispersion of the magnetization and the small domains at the grain boundaries and pores, the wall will show small kinks bypassing grain boundaries. The wall motion field will be definitely higher than in the ideal core, as some friction occurs due to the magneto-static irregularities. The wall motion field, as one might expect, will be higher for smaller grains and for higher crystal anisotropy energy. This is indeed experimentally found; the grain size dependence of H_c is shown in Fig. 3.2.2.15 for a MnMgZn ferrite [3.2.16].

(iv) *Loop squareness.* Any magnetic material shows magnetic hysteresis and the remanent points of the hysteresis loop can be used as the "0" and "1" storage states. However, such a material is not necessarily suitable for a memory based on the coincident current principle. For this principle requires that the magnetization state of the material be unaffected by half-select drive currents. This is reached only when the hysteresis loop is nearly square. No wonder physicists and chemists tried very hard to understand and reproduce the parameters influencing the loops squareness. The first ferrites with reasonably square loops were discovered by Albers–Schoenberg [3.2.17] in 1951, just in time to be used by the coincident current memory people. In this section, we will discuss the different definitions of the square-ness ratio R, the physical parameters determining R and some materials most suitable for coincident current memories.

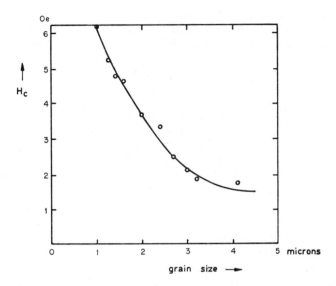

FIG. 3.2.2.15. Coercive force H_c as a function of grain size for a MnMgZn ferrite (adapted from [3.2.16]).

(a) *Squareness ratio.* The definition of this important parameter is not the same for all people and some care is necessary in comparing the results of different publications. The engineer will use a definition of the squareness ratio which gives a direct indication about the usability of the ferrite core or the core material in a memory. As has been discussed in Section 3.2.2.4 in an actual memory a ferrite core is subjected to a large number of positive and negative pulses (Fig. 3.2.2.8), which lead to different magnetization states of the cores (Fig. 3.2.2.9). The disturbed "1" state signal dV_1 should be as large as possible, the disturbed "0" state signal dV_z should be as small as possible. Therefore the ratio dV_1/dV_z is a measure for the quality of the core and, as can be seen in Fig. 3.2.2.11, it depends on the drive current amplitude. To relate this ratio to actual magnetization changes the output signals must be integrated and one obtains the ratio

$$\frac{\int_0^\infty dV_1 \, dt}{\int_0^\infty dV_z \, dt} = \frac{d\phi_1}{d\phi_z} \qquad (3.2.2.5)$$

which for good cores will lie in the range between 10 and 50. This ratio is low when the hysteresis loop is rounded off. This leads to another definition of the squareness ratio, which is more often used:

$$R_m = \frac{B(-\alpha H_m)}{B_m} \qquad (3.2.2.6)$$

As demonstrated in Fig. 3.2.2.16 B_m is the flux density at the maximum applied field H_m and $B(-\alpha H_m)$ is the flux density at $-\alpha H_m$, where $\alpha = 0.61$ and is equal to the selection ratio (see Section 3.2.2.4). R_m depends on the maximum field H_m and the cited ratios in the literature are the maximum squareness ratios obtained for the material. The squareness ratio, more often used by physicists, is the ratio $R_0 = B_r/B_s$, which is easier to relate to the physical parameters of the material. B_s is the saturation flux density at large field and B_r the remanent flux density of the hysteresis loop. Materials with large R_0 also have a large R_m.

(b) *Physical conditions for square hysteresis loops.* Different physical models have been proposed in the course of the years of which the so-called Wijn-model is the most generally accepted. In an ideal ferrite core the magnetization direction in the grains is not dictated by the crystal or stress anisotropies, but by the shape of the core. The magnetization follows a circular path and

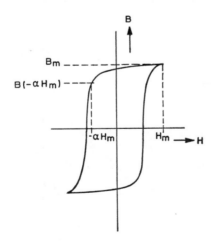

FIG. 3.2.2.16. Definition of squareness ratio

$$R_m = \frac{B(-\alpha H_m)}{B_m}.$$

the hysteresis loop is very square, with a squareness ratio R_0 of unity. Such ideal cores have been approached by using ferrite materials showing negative magnetostriction. The cores were subjected to a radial compression which was achieved by surrounding the core by a glass or a resin [3.2.18]. Though the squareness ratio of these cores improved significantly, the resulting H_c and switching speed prevented their use. The loop squareness of even ideal cores might be detrimentally influenced when the outer and the inner diameters of the core are very different (Fig. 3.2.2.14), when the grain size and therefore H_c vary throughout the core or when small pores or even cracks occur. Due to these structural defects, free magnetic poles occur inside the material leading to a demagnetizing field equal to

$$H_n = -NM_s \qquad (3.2.2.7)$$

For a core with an outer diameter $\phi_{od} \approx 0.3\,\text{mm}$ and a crack of only $1\,\mu\text{m}$ and with $4\pi M_s = 5000$ Gauss the demagnetization field H_N is equal to $5\,\text{Oe}$, which is about equal to the coercive force of the ferrite core. The shearing of the hysteresis loop due to the crack is shown in Fig. 3.2.2.17. Such a core can not be used in a coincident current scheme because the magnetization change due to the half select current pulse will be very large.

When the crystal and stress anisotropies in the grains are not neglected, the hysteresis loop assumes a much less square appearance. This is due to the fact that in each grain the magnetization tends to align to resulting easy directions in the grain. The inverse spinel ferrites used for memory cores

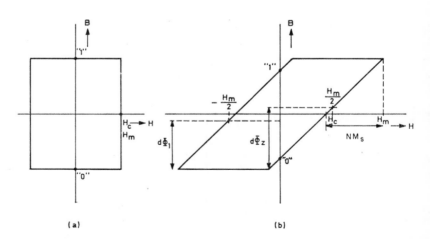

FIG. 3.2.2.17. (a) Hysteresis loop of an ideal core and (b) hysteresis loop of an ideal core with a crack. Because of shearing the disturbed "zero" flux $d\Phi_z$ is larger than the disturbed "one" flux $d\Phi_1$. (See also Fig. 3.2.2.9.)

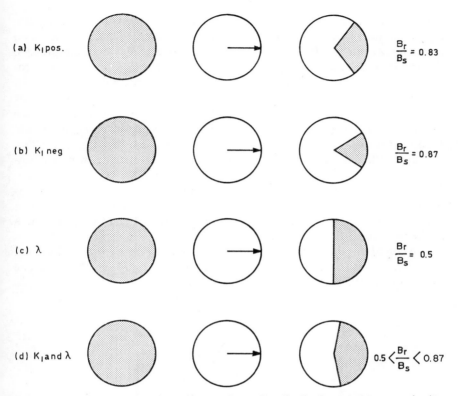

(a) K_1 pos.

(b) K_1 neg

(c) λ

(d) K_1 and λ

$\dfrac{B_r}{B_s} = 0.83$

$\dfrac{B_r}{B_s} = 0.87$

$\dfrac{B_r}{B_s} = 0.5$

$0.5 < \dfrac{B_r}{B_s} < 0.87$

FIG. 3.2.2.18. Schematic representation of angular distribution of the magnetization directions in the grains: (a) positive crystal anisotropy constant, (b) negative crystal anisotropy constant, (c) random oriented strain and finite magnetostriction coefficient and (d) both crystal and stress anisotropy present. From left to right: field zero and no hysteresis, large saturating field and field again zero.

show cubic crystal symmetry. In such crystals easy axes of magnetization are the cube axes when the magneto-crystalline anisotropy constant K_1 is positive. Such crystals show 6 preferred directions of magnetization. When the crystal orientation of the grains is at random and when we subject the core to a large field, which is subsequently reduced, the magnetization in the grains will rotate to the nearest easy direction in the grains (Fig. 3.2.2.18(a)). For this situation a squareness ratio of $R_0 = 0.83$ has been calculated. However, in most ferrite compositions the magneto-crystalline anisotropy constant is negative and in such crystals the easy directions for the magnetization are parallel to the cube diagonals. The calculated square-ness ratio appears to be $R_0 = 0.87$, which is larger than in the other case (Fig. 3.2.2.18(b)). Thus for square loop ferrites it is advantageous to use material with a negative K_1. When we assume that stress and not magneto-crystalline anisotropy dictates the final magnetization direction in a grain, a squareness ratio of $R_0 = 0.5$ is calculated. Due to the sintering process, the grains in the core are subjected to compressive strain; when the magneto-striction coefficient is negative in the grain, two easy directions exist parallel to the strain. When the strains are randomly oriented in the core the low squareness ratio of 0.5 is the result (Fig. 3.2.2.18(c)). When both crystalline anisotropy and stress anisotropy are determining the remanent magnetization state, squareness ratios between 0.5 and 0.87 can be expected (Fig. 3.2.2.18(d)). Therefore it is desirable to use material with a low magnetization coefficient. This constant is a function of the direction in the crystal. In the most favourable material (K_1 negative) the remanent state is distinguished by the fact that in each grain the magnetization is parallel to a [111] direction. This state should not be disturbed by stresses, so that a $\lambda_{111} = 0$ is most favourable.

The conditions of K_1 negative and not too small and $\lambda_{111} = 0$ as discussed above were first stated by Wijn and co-workers [3.2.19] and therefore one speaks of the Wijn-model.

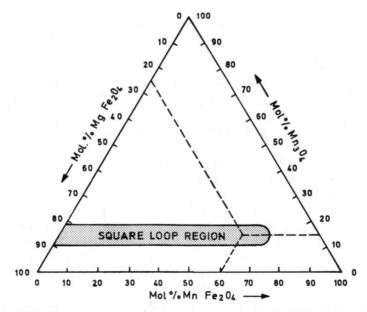

FIG. 3.2.2.19. Diagram showing square loop region in the MgMnFe system [3.2.15]. Interpretation of the diagram is shown for a $25\,MgFe_2O_4$–$60\,Fe_2O_4$–$15\,Mn_3O_4$ compound (broken lines).

(c) *Square loop materials*. In order to test the Wijn-model, it is necessary to measure the squareness ratio of polycrystalline samples and the constants K_1 and λ_{111} of monocrystalline samples for many compositions. Because of the large amount of work connected with such a programme, this is never performed and proof of the Wijn-model depends on a number of direct or indirect experiments. Wijn and co-workers showed that in an

$$x\text{NiFe}_2\text{O}_4(1-x)\,\text{Fe}_3\text{O}_4$$

system a maximum squareness ratio occurred for $x = 0.7$, where $\lambda_{111} \to 0$ and K_1 is negative.

The Japanese scientists Ohta and Kobayashi [3.2.20] showed that MnZnFe ferrites with 10% ZnO and 40% Fe_2O_3 had a very low λ_{111} constant, a negative K_1 and showed good square loops. Many other square loop ferrites were found by changing the composition and empirically determining the squareness ratio. The results are often plotted in diagrams such as is shown in Fig. 3.2.2.19 for the MgMnFe system [3.2.15].

Many other square loop ferrites are found containing Li, Cu and Zn ions. The theoretical squareness ratio of 0.87 is not reached in the usual poly-crystalline ferrites. This is not surprising as the model leading to the factor 0.87 is too simple. In actual ferrite materials small reverse domains will occur at grain boundaries and pores, thereby reducing B_r. On the other hand magnetostatic coupling between the grains will tend to align the magnetiza-tion in the grains, thereby increasing B_r. In order to obtain the proper H_c values for memory cores, the anisotropy constant K_1 must be negative and not too small and the grain size must also be small (Fig. 3.2.2.15). It seems that under these circumstances the favourable effect of the magneto-static coupling between the grains on the squareness ratio is very weak.

(v) *Switching time*. Besides capacity and cost, the speed or cycle time of a ferrite core memory is of great interest to the computer system designer. Great advances have been made with respect to the processor-electronics, which caused a continuous pressure on the core people to improve the switching speed of the ferrite core. In the usual DRO core memory a reading operation is always followed by a writing operation in order to rewrite the information. Therefore the cycle time of a memory will always be at least a factor of two larger than the switching time of the core. In practice in a 3D-organized core memory of moderate size (some 100 000 bits) the cycle time is about four times the switching time, whereas for the $2\frac{1}{2}$D organization a factor of 3 is observed [3.2.21].

In this section we will discuss the definition of the switching time, the physical processes determining the switching speed and the maximum switch-ing time that can be obtained with ferrite cores.

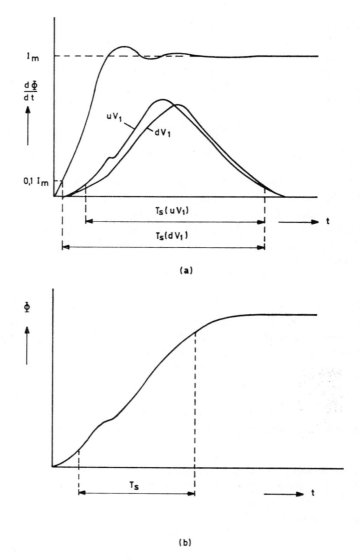

FIG. 3.2.2.20. Definitions of switching time (see text).

(a) *Switching-time definition and switching curve.* Different definitions of the switching time T_s are used by different authors. Some are more related to physical descriptions of the reversal process and others give a value directly usable for memory applications.

A typical output signal of a core is shown in Fig. 3.2.2.20. The double maximum in the output voltage is seen when the rise time of the current pulse is not too long and later on we will discuss the physics leading to this behaviour.

One definition of the switching time is based on the uV_1 signal which is observed when an undisturbed "1" state is reversed to the "0" direction. The switching time is defined as the time between the moment the output voltage has risen to 10% of its second maximum and the moment the signal decays again to 10% (Fig. 3.2.2.20(a)). Another, more memory oriented, definition is based on the dV_1 signal which occurs when a "1" state which is disturbed by half select read current pulses is reversed to the "0" state. The time between the moment the read current pulse reaches 10% of its maximum and the moment the dV_1 signal decays to 10% of its maximum amplitude is defined as the switching time (Fig. 3.2.2.20(a)).

Still others consider the total flux switched and define the switching time to be between the moments 10 and 90% of the flux has been reversed. (Fig. 3.2.2.20(b)). Great care must be taken in comparing switching time given by different authors.

Very often the inverse of the switching time $1/T_s$ is plotted, for reasons which will be explained later, as a function of the driving current or field.

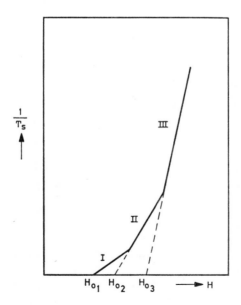

FIG. 3.2.2.21. Schematic drawing showing the three different reversal regions.

When very large drive currents are applied, the switching curve of Fig. 3.2.2.21 is obtained. The switching curve consists of three, linear regions, which makes one suspect that three, different reversal mechanisms occur in a ferrite core. Quite a bit of disagreement between different authors about the exact nature of these processes exists in the literature. The linear regions can be presented by the following relations:

$$\frac{1}{T_s} = \frac{1}{S_{wi}} (H - H_{oi}) \quad i = 1, 2, 3 \tag{3.2.2.8}$$

S_w is called the switching coefficient and depends on the field region and on the definition of T_s. A core material switches fast when S_w is a small number. H_{oi} is called the threshold field and is the intersection of the region of the switching curve in question with the field axes. In the next section we will discuss the switching phenomena in more detail.

(b) *Elastic flux switching.* As already discussed ferrite cores always show hysteresis loops which are rounded off (Fig. 3.2.2.9). This means already that at fields much smaller than H_c and even at negative fields, some magneti-

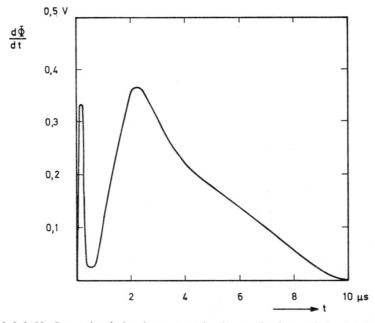

FIG. 3.2.2.22. Sense signal showing two peaks due to the fast and the slow reversal process in a Co ferrite core [3.2.22].

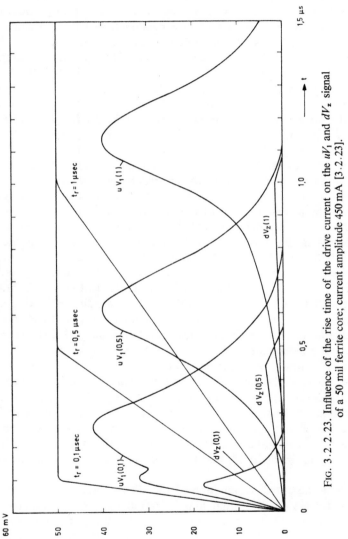

FIG. 3.2.2.23. Influence of the rise time of the drive current on the uV_1 and dV_z signal of a 50 mil ferrite core; current amplitude 450 mA [3.2.23].

zation change always takes place at slowly changing fields. When pulse fields with an amplitude below H_c are applied to a core, a small output voltage is observed. The switching time is equal to that of the first peak voltage which is observed, when the pulse amplitude is larger than H_c. This justifies the assumption that we are dealing here with the same kind of reversal process. The switching time of the initial reversal process also seems to be much smaller than the switching time of the second switching process as can be seen in Fig. 3.2.2.20 or even better in Fig. 3.2.2.22, which is taken from an early paper of Van der Heide *et al.* [3.2.22] showing the sense voltage for a rather slow Co ferrite. Reversal here occurs very clearly by a fast and a slow process. At the trailing edge of the driving pulse a sense signal is observed again. This signal is similar to the signal due to the fast process at the leading edge of the pulse. The similarity indicates that we are dealing partly with a reversible or an elastic switching process, whereas the second sense signal maximum is due to an irreversible switching process. The difference in switching speed of both processes is also very convincingly illustrated by a measurement of the output voltage maximum as a function of the rise time of the drive current. Instead of measuring the peak due to the fast process in the output signal it is more convenient to examine the dV_z signal amplitude. This signal represents the flux changed by a number of half select write field pulses, which are each smaller than H_c and should cause the fast reversal process (see Fig. 3.2.2.9). In Fig. 3.2.2.23 the drive current pulse the uV_1 and the dV_z output signals are shown for three different rise times. In Fig. 3.2.2.24 the maximum of uV_1 and dV_z are plotted as a function of the rise time as measured by Olson [3.2.23]. Whereas uV_1 is practically independent of the rise time of the drive pulse, which means that the switching time of the second and main reversal process at this pulse amplitude is much larger than the rise time. This does not apply for the fast reversal process represented by dV_z; here the signal amplitude is inversely proportional to the rise time, as follows from Fig. 3.2.2.24. This indicates that the flux change $d\phi/dt$ is solely determined by the pulse rise time, and the reversal process must be an extremely fast one. From the work of Stegmeier [3.2.24] it can be deduced, that these fast processes can even occur within $0.01 \ \mu s$.

The most accepted explanation of the above observations relates the fast reversal process to the initial magnetization state at the remanent point. As we have seen in the preceding section, the magnetization directions in the core show some dispersion due to the magneto-crystalline anisotropies in the grains. When K_1 is negative the squareness ratio is $R_0 = B_r/B_s = 0.87$. When a magnetic field is applied antiparallel to the main magnetization direction, the dispersion of the magnetization will increase causing a sense signal. As the increase of the dispersion is reached by small rotations of the

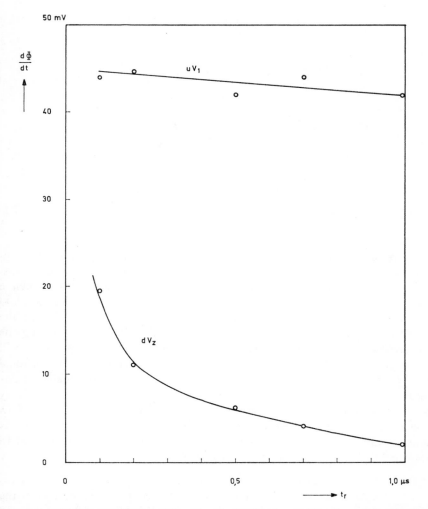

FIG. 3.2.2.24. The amplitude of the uV_1 and dV_z signals as a function of the rise time of the drive current.

magnetizations in the grains, the flux change is reversible and fast and will follow the rise time of the drive pulse. However, the total flux change caused by this process is too small to explain the whole first peak in the sense signal. As shown beautifully by Knowles [3.2.25], by means of the Bitter technique, the grain boundaries and pores are decorated with so-called Néel spikes, in the remanent state (Fig. 3.2.2.25). In these Néel spikes the magnetization

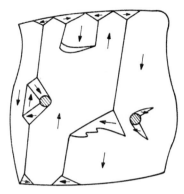

FIG. 3.2.2.25. Schematic drawing of domain structures in a ferrite grain. (After [3.2.25].)

is perpendicular to the main magnetization in the grain. The Néel spikes are necessary to reduce the magneto-static energy associated with the discontinuities in the magnetization at the pores and boundaries. When a pulse field is applied, these Néel spikes can easily and quickly increase and decrease, causing a reversible and an irreversible flux change. When the pulse amplitude is further increased, 180° Bloch walls occur reversing the magnetization in the grains. This process is comparatively slow as we will see in the next section. As the dV_z signal amplitude is inversely proportional to the rise time of the drive current pulse and increases for smaller grains and thus increasing magnetization discontinuities, it becomes increasingly more difficult to discriminate between disturb and read signals in the modern fast core memories. However, because the maximum in the dV_z signal is reached much earlier than in the dV_1 signal, pulse strobing can be used to improve the discrimination.

(c) *Irreversible switching processes.* As the first elastic switching process occurs very rapidly, the measured switching times are representative of the second irreversible process. The switching curve shows three different regions, with three different switching constants. In order to explain three regions, Gyorgy [3.2.26] assumed that in region I reversal occurred by domain wall motion, in region II by a non-uniform rotation process in which the magnetization rotates in a spiral mode to reduce magneto-static energy and in region III by a uniform rotation process. Many experiments have been performed to test these assumptions of which those by Tancrell and McMahon [3.2.27] are most revealing. They started their experiment by saturating the core with a very high write current before the application of each read current pulse. The amplitude of the read current pulse was varied. In Fig. 3.2.2.26 the

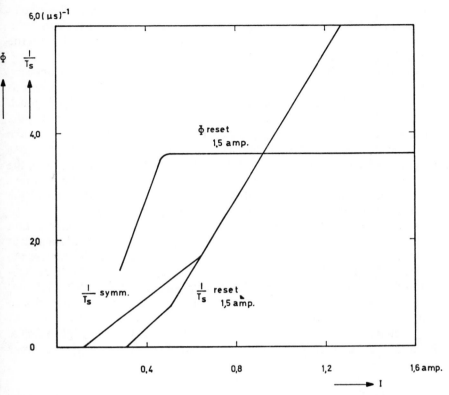

FIG. 3.2.2.26. Switching curve for large reset and symmetrical reset compared with curve relating total switched flux with current amplitude [3.2.27].

resulting switching curve, leaving out the measurement points, is shown. At the same time they integrated the sense signal in order to determine the total flux switched by the drive pulse. This flux is plotted in the same figure. Comparison of the two curves showed that the core is not fully reversed unless the read current is larger than the current at the break in the switching curve. From this they concluded that the reversal processes in region I and region II are the same, but that in region I the reversal only occurs in a part of the core. The field in the core is due to a current passing through a wire in the centre hole and it is evident that the field at the inside diameter is smaller than the one at the outside. The first sense signal will occur when the field at the inside diameter first reaches the coercive force. The break in the switching curve will occur when the field at the outside diameter reaches H_c. By drilling holes at different distances from the centre in a large core and

I

measuring the sense signals occurring on the sense wire through these holes Tancrell and McMahon were able to prove the correctness of their assumptions. In an actual memory cores are not completely saturated by a write current, but the read and write amplitudes are always equal.

When the switching curve is measured under this condition, it appears, that the break between region I and II occurs at about the same current as can be seen in Fig. 3.2.2.26, but that the threshold current H_{01} is much lower. This suggests that the coercive force depends on the reset amplitude. This is indeed observed, as is shown by Fig. 3.2.2.27. The coercive force of the hysteresis loop depends on the amplitude of the driving current. As in a computer memory, the cores are always operated on a minor loop, the second switching curve of Fig. 3.2.2.26 must be used. The threshold current of the second curve is then equal to the current for which the field at the inside diameter reaches the coercive force of the minor loop.

In general an extended region I is disadvantageous for the construction of fast core memories, as is illustrated in Fig. 3.2.2.28. In a coincident current memory it is required that the half select pulse does not reverse the core and therefore this pulse field must be smaller than H_{01}. The T_s belonging to $2H_{01}$ gives the shortest switching time possible. As Fig. 3.2.2.28 shows, an extended region I leads to low switching speeds. Therefore one tries to suppress region I by reducing the od:id ratio and by using materials without low coercive force minor loops. By adding Pb or ThO_2 to a MgMn ferrite Baba [3.2.28] succeeded in improving the switching time at $2H_{01}$ by a factor of 4.

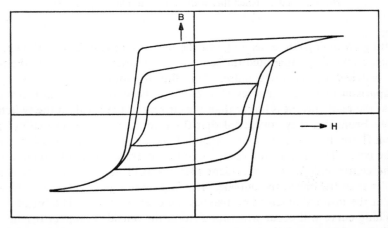

FIG. 3.2.2.27. Hysteresis loop of a ferrite core as a function of the drive field amplitude.

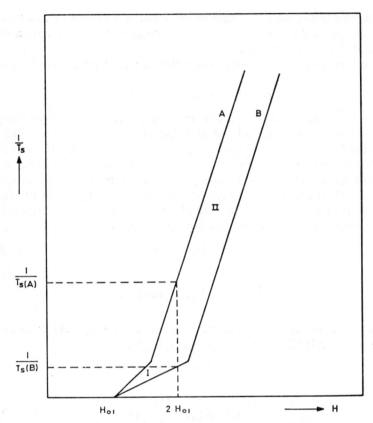

FIG. 3.2.2.28. Schematic drawing of two switching curves, showing that a short field region I leads to small switching times.

The relation between T_s and the magnetic field is a straight line which is worth investigating to see if it is possible to explain this straight line relationship with a simple model and to predict values for S_w. Qualitatively, one assumes that in region II the following reversal process occurs. Nucleation centres, the so-called Néel spikes, are present in the remanent state in each grain. When a field roughly equal to H_c is applied the Néel spikes grow and form one or more 180° walls which move through the grain. As two grains with opposite magnetization directions give a large magnetostatic energy, when these grains lie in the magnetization direction it can be expected that the wall reversal process will occur simultaneously in chains of grains parallel to the main magnetization direction. When we want to calculate the switching speed, we must examine the speed of wall motion as a function of the applied field and we must know the number of walls in a grain or the average distance one wall traverses in a grain.

The general equation of motion for a 180° domain wall is given by Döring [3.2.29] as

$$m_w(dv/dt) + \beta v + c_1 = 2M_s H \qquad (3.2.2.9)$$

in which m_w is the wall mass per unit area, v the wall velocity, β the damping coefficient, c_1 a constant and $2M_s H$ is the pressure on the wall. The first term is the force necessary to accelerate the wall and is negligible for the wall velocities occurring in ferrites at the fields considered here. The second term represents the friction the moving wall is subjected to. When an applied field is equal to the threshold field of the first region H_{01} the wall velocity is zero, so it follows that c_1 is equal to $2M_s H_{01}$. The above equation reduces then to what is called "the viscous flow approximation".

$$\beta v = 2M_s(H - H_{01}) \qquad (3.2.2.10)$$

or

$$v = \frac{2M_s}{\beta}(H - H_{01}) = m(H - H_{01})$$

in which m is the so-called wall mobility. When the average distance one wall moves is called d, the switching time T_s is given by

$$T_s = d/v$$

and

$$\frac{1}{T_s} = \frac{M}{d}(H - H_{01}) = \frac{1}{S_{w1}}(H - H_{01}). \qquad (3.2.2.11)$$

From these relations we find, that

$$S_w = d/m. \qquad (3.2.2.12)$$

The switching speed of a ferrite core in a memory matrix increases when the average distance each wall has to move is short and the friction of the wall with its surroundings is large.

Because it is quite complex to relate m to the material parameters, we will follow here a more qualitative approach. As shown in Fig. 3.2.2.29 in a domain wall the magnetization rotates from one magnetization direction in one domain to the magnetization direction in the neighbouring domain. When the total angle is 180° we speak of a 180° domain wall. Also 90° domain walls exist, for instance surrounding the Néel spikes of Fig. 3.2.2.25. When a wall is displaced in a direction perpendicular to the magnetization direction all spins in the wall rotate across a small angle. If

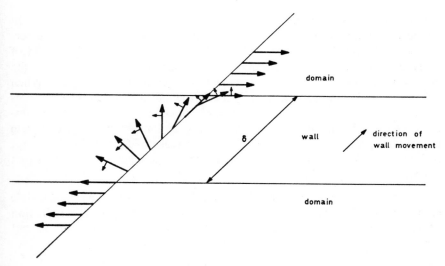

FIG. 3.2.2.29. Magnetization distribution in a Bloch wall. During wall movement the magnetization rotates about an axis perpendicular to the wall surface as indicated by the small arrows.

the wall width is δ and the displacement of the wall is Δ, then all spins will rotate across Δ/δ 180°. The damping the wall experiences is in fact a damping of the spin rotations in the wall. The same damping is observed in spin resonance experiments and is today not very well understood. Eddy-current damping, as is observed in metallic magnetic materials, is not observed because ferrites are insulators. The smaller the wall width, δ, the faster the spins have to rotate to realize the same wall displacement, Δ. From this it follows that wide walls are fast moving walls. Using early calculations by Kittel [3.2.30] one can derive the following relation for the switching coefficient.

$$S_w = k \frac{d\alpha}{\delta\gamma} \qquad (3.2.2.13)$$

in which k is a constant depending on the kind of wall, d is the average distance each wall moves during the reversal process, α is the phenomenological damping constant and γ is the gyromagnetic ratio which is constant and relates the magnetic and angular momentum of a spin. Because α, δ and γ are constants and when we assume that d is field independent, then it follows that S_w is a constant. We can expect a linear relationship between $1/T_s$ and H. This relationship is indeed found (Fig. 3.2.2.21). However, besides region I, two regions are found with different S_w. To explain this behaviour one assumes that the average distance d is not equal for both regions. In region II the number of walls involved in the reversal of one grain is determined by the number of Néel spikes, which can enlarge on application of a moderate field. One suspects that these are the spikes which decorate the grain boundaries, as there the magnetization discontinuity is largest. When larger field pulses are applied, (region III) the spikes decorating the pores in the grain can grow also and create additional 180° walls. When the number of walls is larger, the average distances they have to move to complete the reversal process are smaller, causing a decrease of S_w. Region III is not of interest to the memory designer, as at these large fields coincident current operation is not possible.

(d) *Minimization of the switching speed.* Having obtained a plausible expression for S_w, it is of interest to investigate by what means a reduction of S_w can be obtained. In fact we are more interested in T_s than in S_w and for the switching time T_s we can write:

$$T_s = S_w \frac{1}{(H - H_o)} \ .$$

In a coincident current memory it is necessary for the half select field to be smaller than H_o, the maximum writing field is then a little bit smaller than $2H_o$. Combining the expression for S_w with the above relation we obtain:

$$T_s = k \frac{d\alpha}{\delta \gamma H_o} \ .$$

In order to minimize T_s we have to study the different parameters in detail.

γ Is the gyromagnetic ratio and a fundamental constant which cannot be changed.

α Is the phenomenological damping constant. This constant is known from resonance experiments and does not depend very much on the composition. One can expect that parameters which increase the density of discontinuities will also cause a slight increase in α.

H_o From the relation for T_s it follows that a large threshold field is advantageous. However, H_o is limited by the possible drive currents and the electronic circuitry. When the core diameter is reduced, the same threshold field can be obtained with smaller currents. For the same drive current a smaller switching time is measured [3.2.31] for smaller cores, as is shown in Fig. 3.2.2.30. Smaller cores allow the use of higher threshold fields. The threshold field is strongly related to the coercive force and, as is shown in Fig. 3.2.2.15, H_c can be increased by decreasing the grain size.

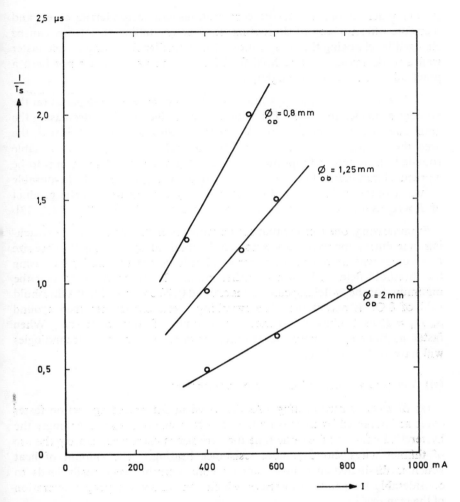

FIG. 3.2.2.30. Switching curves for ferrite cores of identical material but different diameters.

δ The wall width is in the denominator, which means that wide walls give fast cores. The wall width is proportional to $(A/K_1)^{\frac{1}{2}}$ where A is the exchange constant and K_1 is the magneto-crystalline anisotropy constant. The constant A is a measure of the molecular field, which forces the spins to be parallel. A large Curie temperature T_c, which stands also for a strong molecular field, implies a large A.   However, neither T_c nor

A vary much among the ferrite compositions usable for ferrite cores, and therefore offer no way of decreasing T_s. The crystalline anisotropy can be changed by changing the composition. But a smaller K_1 giving a wide faster wall also decreases the threshold field H_o. Up to now K_1 has not been a practical parameter for changing T_s.

d The average distance a wall moves during core reversal depends on the number of nucleation sites. This number can be increased by decreasing the grain size and the pore density. When too small grains are fabricated, the area the nucleation spikes occupy becomes relatively large and unusable rounded off hysteresis loops are observed. A grain size of 2 μm seems to be a practical minimum. Because H_o also changes with grain size, the favourable influence of the grain size on d is only observable when we plot the product of $T_s \times H_o$ as a function of the grain size as is done in Fig. 3.2.2.31 [3.2.32].

Summarizing, one can say that the advances in the reduction of the switching time during the past years were mainly obtained by reducing the core size (even cores with an outside diameter of 12 mils were tried) and by increasing the threshold field H_o by using smaller grains. It can be expected that the minimum for the switching constant is around 0.20 μs Oe and that a threshold field of 8 Oe is acceptable. The switching speed barrier lies then around $S_w/H_o \approx 25$ ns leading to memory cycle times of around 100 ns. When faster memory cycle times are required, it is clear that other technologies will have to be employed.

(vi) *Temperature dependence of core parameters*

(a) *Sources of core heating.* As discussed in the preceding section faster cores are obtained by increasing the coercive force and also unwillingly the hysteresis losses. At the same time the core size is decreased, causing the use of thinner wires showing more resistance heating. The amount of heat which is dissipated in a fast compact core assembly very easily leads to considerable temperature increases which can hinder the proper operation of the memory.

Hysteresis heating occurs locally in a core which is repeatedly addressed, whereas resistive heating occurs along the whole drive line. Temperature increases of 50°C are easily possible and even higher temperatures can be expected for cycle times on the order of 500 ns. Due to the inhibit currents resistive heating is more important in the 3D memories than in $2\frac{1}{2}$D memories.

(b) *Temperature dependence of the physical parameters.* Although the damping constant α and the exchange constant A in the interesting range do not change very much as a function of the temperature, such parameters as coercive force H_c, anisotropy constant K_1 and the saturation magnetization

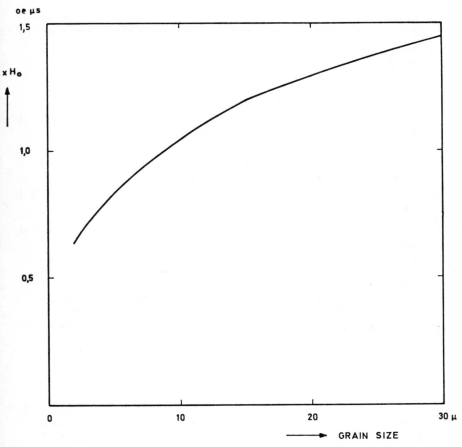

oe µs

x H_o

FIG. 3.2.2.31. The product $T_s \times H_o$, which is proportional to the switching coefficient S_w as a function of the grain size for a Li-ferrite.

M_s show a large temperature dependence. At the Curie temperature T_c (Fig. 3.2.2.32) the magnetization is zero and it appears that dH_c/dT, dK_1/dT, dM_s/dT are large for materials with low Curie temperatures. As discussed in a previous section the coercive force of a material depends on the crystal anisotropy constant and the grain size. The dependence of K_1 on temperature often shows positive as well as negative regions for dK_1/dT. As $K_1 = 0$ at the Curie temperature, dK_1/dT is usually negative for low T_c materials at room temperatures. This results in a decrease of the H_c for increasing temperatures. Fig. 3.2.2.33 shows the T dependence for a low and a high T_c ferrite material. Also the saturation magnetization

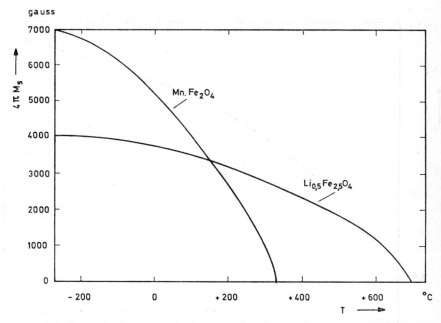

FIG. 3.2.2.32. Saturation magnetization as a function of the temperature for low T_c (Mn ferrite) and a high T_c (Li ferrite) material [3.2.33].

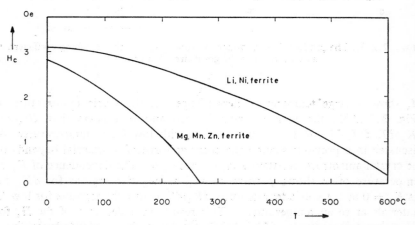

FIG. 3.2.2.33. Coercive force as a function of temperature for a MgMnZn ferrite and a LiNi ferrite [3.2.21].

decreases for increasing temperature. Then one would also expect the output signals to decrease for increasing temperatures. In practice this does not happen. The fields used in memory operation are such that the core operates on a minor loop. When H_c decreases, another minor loop with larger B_r is traversed giving a larger output signal. Moreover, the switching time decreases for decreasing H_c and constant drive current amplitude, so that the total output signal increases for increasing temperature.

(c) *Temperature dependence of core parameters.* As is discussed in Section 3.2.2.4 on single core testing, the uV_1, dV_1 and dV_z signal amplitudes are usually plotted as a function of the drive current amplitude (Fig. 3.2.2.11). The optimal drive current is obtained when dV_1/dV_z is a maximum. When the temperature increases causing a decrease in H_c, the dV_1 signal will decrease and the dV_z signal will increase, with the result that the core cannot be used for the originally chosen drive current amplitudes. Temperature sensitive cores, therefore require a very precise temperature control. In Fig. 3.2.2.34 the dependence of uV_1, dV_1 and dV_z as a function of temperature the sensitive MgMn ferrite and for a temperature insensitive Li ferrite memory core are shown. The MgMn ferrite core cannot be operated above 50°C. In order

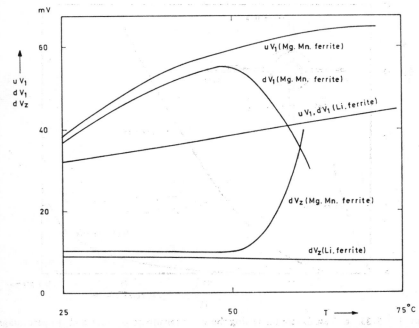

FIG. 3.2.2.34. Signal amplitudes uV_1, dV_1 and dV_z as a function of the temperature for a MgMn ferrite and a Li ferrite [3.2.34].

to compare different materials some various temperature coefficients are defined. The coefficient generally used is C_f which indicates how much the drive current must be changed to maintain a constant uV_1

$$C_f = \left(\frac{dI}{d\theta}\right)_{uV_1} = \text{constant.}$$

If the temperature of the whole core matrix would increase uniformly, the temperature range of operation could be slightly increased by the application of some kind of current compensation. As C_f is negative the compensation should reduce the drive amplitude for higher temperatures. However, hysteresis heating is rather local, so that current compensation is ineffective and other temperature insensitive core materials have to be used. As illustrated by the figures, only Li-containing ferrites have higher Curie temperatures and consequently show less temperature sensitivity [3.2.33, 3.2.34]. Cores made of some Li ferrites are called WT (wide temperature range) cores, they are operable from $-50°$ to $+150°C$. A disadvantage is

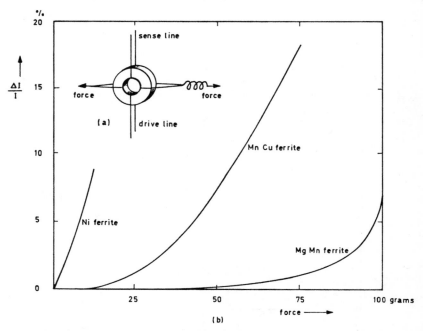

Fig. 3.2.2.35. (a) Test fixture for testing the stress sensitivity of cores and (b) percentage change of the full select current to maintain a constant uV_1 amplitude as a function of the applied force [3.1.1].

that the switching coefficient S_w is usually somewhat larger than for the more temperature sensitive ferrite compositions.

(vii) *Stress sensitivity of ferrite cores.* Ferrite cores in memory matrices are subjected to mechanical stresses which can have undesirable influences on the core parameters. Moreover, it is possible for stress sensitive cores which are cycled by read-write pulses, to start vibrating mechanically, thus producing spurious signals on the sense line.

(a) *Stress sensitivity of core parameters.* Faster memories require smaller cores and it becomes increasingly difficult to weave the wires through the core holes. The stresses due to these wires will be quite inhomogeneous and not very reproducible from core to core. In order to fix the position of the cores with respect to the wires, the matrices are often coated with a lacquer. This material may cause a compressive strain and when the magnetostriction coefficient is negative the strain will induce a uniaxial anisotropy of which the easy axis will be circular.

In general the addition of a uniaxial anisotropy caused by the compressive strain with the easy axis parallel to the magnetization will reduce the dispersion of the directions of magnetizations at the remanence point. The result is a better loop rectangularity. The decrease in dispersion will decrease

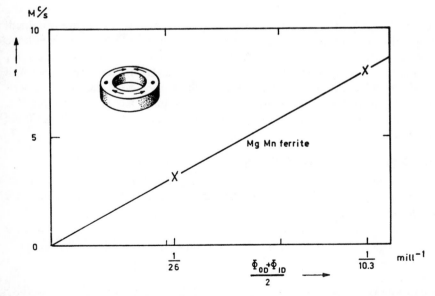

FIG. 3.2 2.36. Magnetostrictive oscillation frequency as a function of the inverse of the mean core diameter for the longitudinal mode [3.2.36].

the coercive force. Moreover, it can be expected that the average distance one wall moves during the switching process becomes larger, which leads to a larger switching coefficient S_w as shown by Steinbeiss [3.2.35].

It is much more difficult to analyse the influence of inhomogeneous stresses on the core behaviour. The best approach is the experimental one as performed by Reese Brown [3.1.1]. As shown in Fig. 3.2.2.35(a), he subjected the cores to stresses in a special test fixture. The parameter measured was the percent change $\Delta I/I$ in the full select current necessary to maintain a constant uV_1 amplitude as a function of the applied tensile force. The measurements were done on 30 mil cores of different ferrite compositions. The change appears to be always positive (Fig. 3.2.2.35(b)) and small for MgMn or Li ferrites, medium for MnCu or MgMnZn ferrites and large for Ni ferrites. The magnetostriction coefficient increases in the same order.

(b) *Magnetostrictive ringing.* Stress sensitive cores which are subjected to repetitive current pulse signals can start to vibrate at a magneto-acoustic resonant frequency. This frequency is of the order of a few MHz and depends on the vibration mode, the core size and the mechanical properties of the ferrite material. Boyd [3.2.36] measured the resonance frequency as a function of core diameter for different modes. His results are shown for the longitudinal mode, as indicated in the inset in Fig. 3.2.2.36 for two MgMn ferrite cores with a mean diameter of 26 and 10.3 mils. We find that the magnetostrictive oscillation frequency is proportional to the inverse of the mean diameter. For the other vibration modes similar results are obtained. Boyd also found that the amplitude of the vibration and the ringing voltage are proportional to $M_s \lambda_s/K_1$. A large crystalline anisotropy constant K_1 means that the magnetization directions in the crystallites are rather well fixed; consequently a stress has no large effect on these directions. Experimentally, it was indeed found that large K_1 materials show less ringing. Magnetostrictive ringing can be suppressed by coating the cores with suitable materials.

3.2.2.6. Are Faster and Less Expensive Core Memories Possible?

Today's knowledge of the physics governing the core parameters and the ability to suppress noise signals in the various memory organization schemes made it possible to construct the following memories:

use	scheme	cycle time	capacity	price/bit
main memory	3D	$1.0\ \mu s$	10^6	6 cents/bit
bulk memory	$2\frac{1}{2}$D	$4.0\ \mu s$	10^7	3 cents/bit
scratch pad memory	2D	$0.2\ \mu s$	2×10^5	10 cents/bit

Under the pressure of the demands of the computer architects and the presence of the other new technologies, the engineers and scientists involved in the development of ferrite core memories tried to come up with new techniques promising still faster and less expensive memories. In this last section on ferrite cores, we will discuss some of the more interesting approaches to realizing these goals.

(i) *Faster memories.* In the course of years much progress has been made with respect to the speed of the electronic logic circuitry of the processor unit of a computer. This made it compulsory either to also speed up memory or, at least, to invent some kind of sophisticated memory hierarchy in which a part of the memory system has a very small cycle time. Different possibilities of reducing the cycle time were investigated.

(a) *Grain size.* As we have discussed in a preceding section, the switching time of a core is small when the average distance a wall has to move during the switching process is also very small. The smaller the grains, the more walls will participate in the switching process leading to a smaller switching coefficient S_w. Figure 3.2.2.31 shows the favourable effect of the grain size on the switching speed. It is possible with todays technology to make usable cores with grain sizes of the order of 2 μm. When the grain size is further decreased, the volume of the nuclei with a magnetization direction different from the main magnetization direction in the core becomes too large. The squareness ratio rapidly decreases below a grain size of 1–2 μm, so that satisfactory coincident current operation is no longer guaranteed. It seems that a smaller switching coefficient S_w cannot be obtained by decreasing grain size further.

(b) *Core size.* Smaller cores allow larger switching thresholds H_0 to be used for equal drive current amplitudes. As the switching time is inversely proportional to H_0, it is advantageous to reduce the size of the cores. In the last twenty years the core size came down from 90 mils to 12 mils, while the switching time decreased from 1.5 μs to 0.1 μs (Fig. 3.2.2.37). With respect to the difficulties in pressing such tiny cores and in fitting two or three wires through the tiny hole, it seems very unlikely that faster memories can be made by a further reduction in core size.

(c) *Partial switching of ferrite cores.* When a core is switched from the "0" to the "1" direction by a dc current the amount of flux switched depends only on the magnitude of the current as indicated by the hysteresis loop of Fig. 3.3.2.38. However, when a current pulse is used, the final state also depends on the pulse width, when this width is of the order of the switching time of the core, as is shown for a pulse duration of respectively 25, 30 and 35 ns (also in Fig. 3.2.2.38) [3.2.37]. It is now possible to use one remanent state to

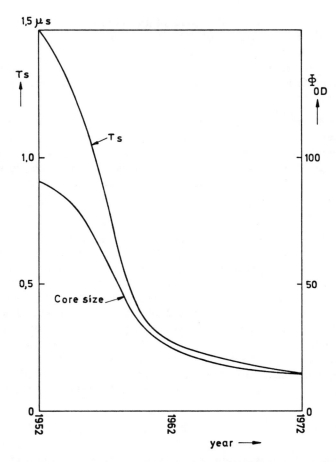

Fig. 3.2.2.37. Decrease of switching time and core size during the last 20 years. (After [3.2.15].)

indicate the "0" and to use a partially switched state as the "1". Since the sense signal depends strongly on the current amplitude and the pulse width, as can be seen from Fig. 3.2.2.38, partial switching can be employed much more favourably in a 2D two core per bit scheme, (Fig. 3.2.2.39). The word and the bit lines are so oriented that in one core the bit current aids and in the other core opposes the write current. When writing, the direction of the bit current determines the information stored.   When the current pulse amplitude and width are chosen properly, the magnetization states indicating a "0" and a "1" are those shown in Fig. 3.2.2.39(b).

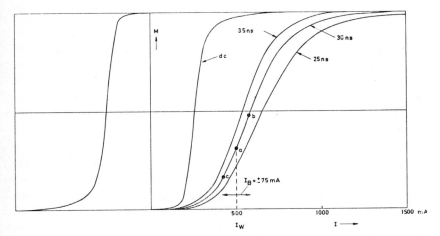

FIG. 3.2.2.38. Magnetization as a function of the drive current amplitude. Pulse duration resp. ∞, 35, 30 and 25 ns [3.2.37].

During the reading process a large current pulse is sent along the word line in a direction opposite to the write pulse, thereby resetting both cores to the "0" state. The sense signals on the common bit sense line due to both cores are opposite but unequal. The polarity of the resulting signal will depend on the information stored. Based on this principle Werner and Whalen [3.2.37] were able to design a memory consisting of 8192 words of

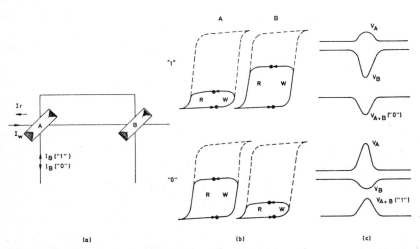

FIG. 3.2.2.39. (a) 2D two core/bit scheme, (b) magnetization state of core A and B for a "0" and a "1" and (c) sense signals.

J

72 bits with a cycle time of 110 ns. They used a word write pulse of 500 mA and a duration of 30 ns. The bit write current was 75 mA, so that the points b and c in Fig. 3.2.2.38 represent the partially switched states of both cores representing the binary information. As a 2D selection scheme requires extensive peripheral electronic circuitry and because of the two cores per bit scheme the bit density is not large, it is evident that in this capacity and cycle time range the monolithic semiconductor memory is much more attractive.

(d) *Nondestructive read out*. During reading, the information stored in a ferrite core memory is destroyed, so that a subsequent write operation is required to store again the original information. The cycle time of a memory could be reduced roughly by a factor of two if the cores could be interrogated nondestructively. When a core is subjected to small, narrow pulses the magnetization changes can be reversible. A small sense signal is obtained, but the information state is not changed. As expected, the permeability of a core depends on its magnetization state. The permeability is low for the remanent state and large for a partially switched state. Feasibility of NDRO has been shown [3.2.38, 3.2.39] on ferrite core memories which where organized in a 2D one or two cores per bit scheme. The restrictions with respect to core and driving parameters do not make it plausible that faster memories will be realized using this permeability sensing method.

(ii) *Less expensive memories*. Ferrite core memories are still rather expensive boxes full of wires and ferrite rings, even though a single core is very inexpensive. Therefore, it is evident that the possibility of decreasing the production costs (tooling and labour) has been extensively investigated. Two approaches have been discussed in literature. In one approach the production of single cores was improved, whereas the other approach tried to batch fabricate whole matrices.

(a) *Stamping instead of pressing cores*. As already discussed in Section 3.2.2.3 Wiechec [3.2.9] developed a technique in which the cores are stamped out of large sheets of ferrite material mixed with a binder, whereas the standard techniques are based on pressing the single cores one by one. The stamping process seems to be especially suitable for production of inexpensive cores for application in $2\frac{1}{2}$D bulk memories.

(b) *Batch fabrication of ferrite planes*. One of the cost increasing operations during memory production is certainly the assembly of the cores into matrices. The 3D scheme with four wires per bit requires much manual labour especially. Therefore batch fabrication of the entire wiring scheme and the ferrite looks very attractive. One approach [3.1.6] starts with spreading a ferrite slurry by means of a blade into sheets. In these sheets a set of parallel

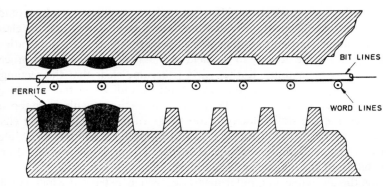

FIG. 3.2.2.40. Cross sectional view of a Flute memory plane showing grid of drive lines between grooved dies filled with ferrite material.

drive lines is embedded. Two sheets with their drive lines perpendicular to each other and a sheet without drive lines are pressed together and sintered. The storage positions in this laminated structure are the crossovers of the perpendicular lines. As the amount of flux which switches is not as defined in the usual ferrite cores, a two intersection per bit 2D selection has to be used. Though the feasibility of small matrices operating with rather small cycle times and small drive currents has been shown, the future of laminated ferrite memories looks dim.

The other element considered is called Flute [3.2.40] and consists of a bar of ferrite surrounding a axial word line. The bit lines are perpendicular to the word line. The entire memory consists of a large number of parallel bars. The memory is fabricated by sandwiching a grid of wires between a mixture of a ferrite and a binder which fill the grooves of two dies as is shown in Fig. 3.2.2.40. In the next heating cycle the binder is removed and the ferrite sintered. This memory is also operated in a 2D scheme. The material requirements are still severe and it is very difficult to obtain matrices with 100 % usable bit positions.

3.2.3. THIN MAGNETIC FILM MEMORIES

3.2.3.1. Introduction

In the year that commercial computers with ferrite core memories started to find wide acceptance, a publication on magnetic films by Blois [3.2.41] drew much attention. He found that when a planar magnetic film of a Ni-Fe alloy was deposited by evaporation in vacuum on glass in the presence of a magnetic field, such a film exhibited a square hysteresis loop parallel to the field direction during evaporation. This meant that a magnetic film could be used as a bistable element, provided the time necessary to switch the element from one stable state to the other was sufficiently short. The publication by Blois started a large activity in the field of magnetic films, reversal processes and switching behaviour. Rather early it became clear that the rectangular hysteresis loop of magnetic films could not be utilized in the same way as those of ferrite cores had been. Domain walls in magnetic films are too small in number and the wall velocity is too slow. In order to utilize the characteristic properties, in 1959 Raffel [3.2.42] proposed a different principle for the use of magnetic films as storage elements. His principle was based on the fast rotation of the magnetization in films.

Using this principle, computer memories were constructed which consisted of a number of planes each containing a large number of small film dots. In order to write or read the information, sheets of mylar with conductors were mounted on top of the planes. Memories constructed in this way produced a rather small signal and worse yet had a large disturb sensitivity. When a certain element was activated many times, neighbouring elements also changed their information state.

Using the principle of Raffel, it also became possible to make memories which consisted of wires electrochemically plated with Ni-Fe. These memories produced large signals, were less disturb sensitive and were less expensive to produce. Only one computer manufacturer, namely the Sperry Rand Corporation, started volume production of these so called "plated wire memories" for their UNIVAC system and used them to replace ferrite core memories [3.2.43].

Today the same company is replacing the plated wire memories with semiconductor memories. Only in special, generally military applications, are the thin magnetic films still used or anticipated, but it is quite certain that the magnetic film never will replace the ferrite core in the manner originally expected by almost everyone in the memory field. It is for this reason that the treatment of magnetic films will not be too detailed in this chapter. For more information refer to recent review articles [3.2.44–47]. In the next section we will describe the Raffel memory principle and compare it with other principles. A short section follows with a presentation of the most important steps of the manufacturing technology of planar and wire memories. In the final section the relations between the parameters characterizing a memory element and the physical parameters of the material will be discussed.

3.2.3.2. Thin Magnetic Film Memory Principle

(i) *Selection scheme based on parallel fields in the easy direction.* As already mentioned, magnetic Ni-Fe films evaporated in the presence of a magnetic

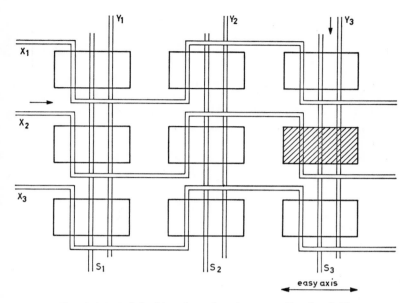

FIG. 3.2.3.1. Selection scheme based on easy direction fields.

field show in one direction, the so-called easy direction, square hysteresis loops. Bitter or magneto-optic Kerr observations show that the edges of a rectangular film are decorated with tiny triangular domains which start to grow when a field equal to the coercive force is applied. This situation is not very different from the reversal mechanism in ferrite cores and the first film memory selection scheme therefore was derived from that of the core memory and is shown in Fig. 3.2.3.1. Two drive conductors on mylar sheets are mounted perpendicularly to the easy axis. Each produces a field in the easy direction slightly smaller than the wall motion coercive force of the film material. When both lines are activated at a film spot, the magnetization will be reversed and a sense signal induced in the sense line which is also perpendicular to the easy axis.

Aside from the large inductive coupling between the sense and drive lines, this memory system is not very attractive because wall motion is a too slow process.

By means of the magneto-optic Kerr effect it is possible to measure the velocity of a domain wall in a magnetic film as a function of the applied field [3.2.48]. Figure 3.2.3.2 shows such a curve for a 600 Å Ni-Fe film. The threshold field is equal to the coercive force H_c. The curve shows two slopes for which up to now no satisfactory explanation exists. During bit

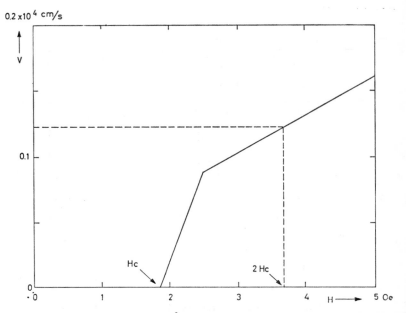

FIG. 3.2.3.2. Wall velocity in a 600 Å film as a function of the field pulse amplitude.

reversal the total applied field will be roughly equal to $2H_c$ and at this field the wall velocity is about 10^3 cm s^{-1}. When we assume that during reversal the number of moving walls is such that each wall has to traverse a distance of 10^{-2} cm, the switching time is 10 μs. This is much too long and the signal induced in the sense line will be too small to be detected reliably.

(ii) *Selection schemes based on perpendicular fields.* A better selection scheme was presented by Raffel [3.2.42], which employed perpendicular drive lines (Fig. 3.2.3.3).

When the hysteresis loop of a magnetic film is measured with the applied field normal to the easy axis, a straight line is observed which saturates at a field H_k. As different methods show, in the hard direction reversal takes place by magnetization rotation instead of by wall motion. The selection scheme of Raffel takes advantage of the rotation process in the following way.

When no external field is applied the magnetization in the elements can point in one of the easy directions or the element can be in an intermediate state with a large number of domains.

When a pulse field is applied by means of one of the horizontal word lines ($W_1 - W_3$), the magnetization rotates toward the hard direction and a positive or negative pulse signal is induced in the sense lines ($S_1 - S_3$). When

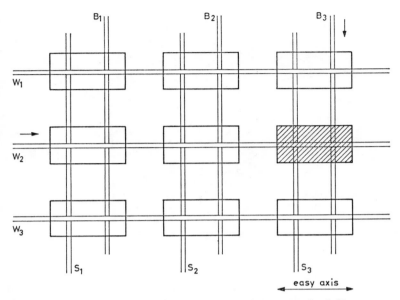

FIG. 3.2.3.3. Selection scheme based on perpendicular fields.

the pulse field is small, the magnetization turns through a very small angle only and returns to the initial state after the field has been switched off. Non-destructive readout (NDRO) can be realized in this way, however, the signal is very small. When a word field is applied which is larger than the saturation field H_k, the magnetization rotates fully to the hard direction. When subsequently the word field is reduced, the magnetization vector becomes unstable, and it is uncertain as to which of the two easy directions the magnetization will return. Usually an element splits up into domains and does not represent either a "0" or a "1". To avoid the occurrence of this indefinite state, a small bit field is applied parallel to one of the easy directions by means of the bit drive lines $(B_1 - B_3)$ at the moment when the word field decreases below H_k. The information state depends on the direction of the bit field.

The storage of information requires word fields which are larger than H_k. These fields are applied to all elements of one horizontal word, which means that the information in all elements belonging to one word is erased. All bit drive lines must carry a signal; otherwise the information state of the elements becomes indefinite. All elements of a word are always simultaneously interrogated. A memory operated with this selection scheme is word organized and requires expensive electronic circuitry.

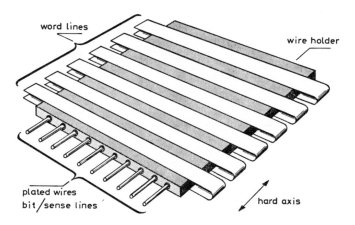

FIG. 3.2.3.4. Plated wire memory plane.

Most of the thin film application work was focused on the realization of planar film arrays with high bit densities and moderate drive requirements. Although actual operating systems could be built, the advantages with respect to the already very well established core technology never were very convincing. The processing costs were high and the yield very low, because in contrast to cores, one bad element on a memory plane made the whole plane useless. This disadvantage does not apply so much to a different memory construction; the so-called "plated" wire memory, first suggested by Long [3.2.49] in 1960. The operation is also based on the Raffel scheme, but the shapes of the films and drive lines are completely different. As Fig. 3.2.3.4 shows, the memory consists of a number of wires which are covered with Ni-Fe by means of electro-deposition. The easy axis of the material is circumferential and the bit current passes through the wires. Conductors through which the word currents flow are arranged perpendicularly to the plated wires. The word fields are parallel to the plated wires and also to the hard direction, as is required for the Raffel selection scheme. The plated wire memory has the important advantage that each wire can be separately tested, which improves the yield considerably. The plated wire also shows a larger output signal and a smaller disturb sensitivity. It was these advantages which made possible the thin film memories which were finally used on a small scale in actual computers.

(iii) *Memory test program.* In order to test whether planar film or plated wire arrays satisfy the device requirements, many different test programs have been considered. A simple program which allows a quick evaluation

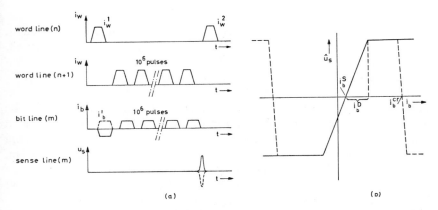

FIG. 3.2.3.5. Test program for evaluation of skew, angular dispersion and disturb sensitivity: (a) used pulse sequence and (b) sense signal amplitude as a function of the bit pulse.

and also allows one to relate the physical and device parameters will be briefly described.

As shown in Fig. 3.2.3.5(a) a first element on word line 1 is subjected to a word pulse of a given fixed amplitude i_w^1. At the trailing edge of this pulse a bit-pulse i_b^1 of variable amplitude positive or negative, is applied. The first write word pulse is followed by a second read word pulse i_w^2, and the sense signal amplitude is measured at the leading edge of this second word pulse. Figure 3.2.3.5(b) shows this amplitude (solid line).

When the magnetic field due to the write word pulse is exactly parallel to the hard axis of the bit element and this field is decreased in the absence of a bit field, the element will split up into equal domains with antiparallel magnetization. The read word pulse will not produce a signal on the sense line. Very often, however, it was observed that the field and hard direction in certain elements are not parallel and domain splitting only occurs when a small bit field i_b^s is applied. The angle between the hard axis and the word field direction is known as skew and it gave memory designers a lot of problems.

Furthermore, it was found that even when no skew is present a certain minimum bit field i_b^d is necessary to ensure that the full sense signal is obtained. This means that a symmetric domain splitting also occurs when the bit field is too small. When an element shows skew, the total minimum bit fields for the "0" and "1" directions are different, which is disagreeable from a tolerance point of view. The existence of a minimum bit field is due to the existence of a so-called "dispersion" of the microscopic hard directions inside a film element (skew is due to a macroscopic deviation of the hard axis). The minimum bit field is necessary to ensure that the whole element, including the locations where the deviation of the hard direction is largest, rotates in the proper information direction. The skew and the dispersion depend very sensitively on the preparation conditions.

When the test program is extended it is also possible to obtain an impression about the disturb sensitivity of the elements. In an actual memory the situation can arise where the element (w $= n+1$, b $= m$) is interrogated many times; this should not affect the information state of surrounding elements such as (w $= n$, b $= m$). In order to test this in a worst case program, element $(n+1, m)$ is written many times (10^6) with the opposite information of that stored in the test bit (n, m). These write pulses on line $n+1$ and bit line m fit in between the write and read pulses for element (n, m).

With this program it is possible to subject the test bit to the full opposite bit field and to the reduced stray word field due to the neighbouring word line. The observed reduction of the sense signal (dashed line in Fig. 3.2.3.5(b) occurred at bit fields i_b^{cr} which were much smaller than originally anticipated and are due to a physical process called wall creeping. The goal of the memory designers is to construct a memory with the largest possible distance between $(i_b^s + i_b^d)$ and i_b^{cr}, yet with an acceptable sense signal and bit density. They only succeeded in marginally reaching this goal for plated wire memories. In the last section of this chapter the physical parameters which determine the device operation will be discussed in more detail.

3.2.3.3. Manufacturing Technology of Planar and Plated Wire Memories

For both plated and planar film memories a composition of roughly 80% Ni and 20% Fe has been found to be most advantageous. This alloy is characterized by the fact that the magnetocrystalline anisotropy constant as well as the magnetostriction coefficient are both relatively small. When the films are properly prepared, they show rather small coercive forces, (1–5 Oe). The method by which 80/20 films are deposited is very different for planar and plated films and, therefore, will be described separately.

Two techniques have been successfully employed to make planar films i.e. vacuum evaporation from an alumina crucible and sputtering from a Ni-Fe cathode.

(i) *Vacuum evaporation.* In a bell jar (Fig. 3.2.3.6) with a vacuum of 10^{-5} Torr or better an alumina crucible with the material to be evaporated is placed in an RF induction coil. Since the metals Fe and Ni do not have the same vapour pressures, the charge in the crucible should be a little bit different from the desired composition in the final planar film. In thin film memories it is important that the magnetostriction coefficient λ_s be zero;

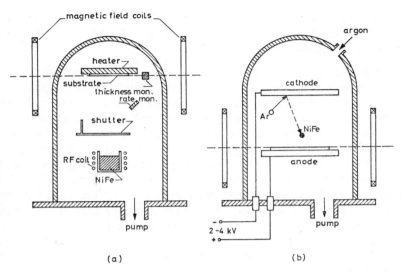

FIG. 3.2.3.6. Schematic diagram of thin film: (a) evaporation and (b) sputtering system.

this is obtained when the charge consists of 82.7% Ni and 17.3% Fe. This can easily be achieved by using two types of Ni-Fe wires with 80/20 and 85/15 Ni-Fe compositions and by weighing and mixing appropriate amounts of each wire [3.2.50].

The crucible is heated to a temperature of approximately 1600°C. The crucible can also be heated by means of electron bombardment. In one case the alumina crucible is placed in a molybdenum crucible which is on a high voltage and which is surrounded by a heated tungsten cathode wire. In the other case the electrons are focused electrostatically or with magnetic fields directly onto the evaporant. The substrate is mounted above the evaporation source and is usually heated by an electrically heated substrate holder. For Ni-Fe films, 250°C is common.

During deposition and subsequent cooling a magnetic field of about 50 Oe is applied, preferably by Helmholtz coils outside the bell jar. The films obtain an easy axis parallel to the applied field. Before mounting, the substrates must be carefully cleaned. Many cleaning procedures have been suggested and because this is a bit of alchemy, each laboratory has its own "best" method. The thickness of the film is accurately monitored during deposition by measuring the resonance frequency of a quartz-crystal oscillator which is mounted close to the substrate holder. Since the physical parameters of the films also depend on the evaporation rate, this parameter is monitored by an ionization-rate monitor.

After many years of experimenting, most laboratories finally succeeded in making 5 cm by 5 cm planar films with reproducible properties by the evaporation technique.

(ii) *Cathode sputtering.* This process is based on an electrical discharge in argon at a pressure between 10^{-4} and 10^{-1} Torr. Positive argon ions in the glow discharge are accelerated by a voltage of between 2000 and 4000 V toward a cathode (Fig. 3.2.3.6(b)) which is made of the same composition as the alloy to be sputtered. The argon ions transfer energies to the cathode atoms thus causing them to be emitted and deposited on the substrate mounted on the anode. The main advantage of the sputtering process is that due to the nature of the process, the composition of the deposited film is the same as that of the starting cathode material even when rather complex compounds have to be deposited. A disadvantage is the difficulty of substrate temperature control. During sputtering the cathode and anode have to be water cooled. Moreover, the rather low deposition rate causes a large sensitivity of the magnetic properties to impurities, in particular to water vapour and oxygen.

Despite these disadvantages, the sputtering process is capable of producing 5 cm by 5 cm planar films with the desired properties.

(iii) *Preparation of plated wire.* While research on magnetic films has concentrated on planar layers because these films can be investigated much easier, practical memories have been realized with plated wires. The preference for plated wires is due to two important facts. First the yield of plated wire memory elements can be high, since the preparation process easily allows the selection of parts of the wires which satisfy the element specifications. Secondly, the film can be thicker than in the case of the planar films, which gives larger sense signals.

The plated wire fabrication process starts with a beryllium-copper wire that is 125 μm in diameter [3.2.51, 3.2.52]. The wire is first prepared by

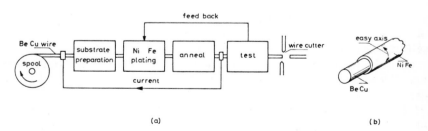

(a)   (b)

FIG. 3.2.3.7. (a) Plated wire fabrication line and (b) easy axis in plated wire.

electrocleaning, electropolishing and copper-plating to adjust the smoothness of the wire substrate (Fig. 3.2.3.7(a)). Secondly, the Ni-Fe film is electroplated onto the substrate. The nickel to iron ratio in the bath is adjusted to give films with a zero magnetostriction coefficient, which are not strain sensitive. During the plating process, a current flows through the wire producing a circumferential easy axis (Fig. 3.2.3.7(b)).

In the third step the temperature of the wire is increased to 300 °C for one minute which results in a stabilization of the physical parameters of the film. Films which are not subjected to an annealing step show aging effects, which easily lead to a malfunction of the device. The preceding sequence is usually performed in a continuous processing line at the end of which a device test stage directly controls the device parameters. In case the measurement results do not satisfy the requirements, the plating bath can be adjusted immediately. It is also possible to cut the defect areas out of the completed wire which gives a significant yield advantage compared to planar films [3.2.43]. Compared to vacuum evaporation, electrodeposition is a rather complicated process and requires a great deal of experience in the field. The electroplating bath must contain: (1) cations of the required metals, like Ni and Fe and sometimes Co, (2) anions like sulphates, chlorides, etc. to obtain advantageous deposition conditions, and (3) additives to influence stresses, composition gradients, etc. in the bath and the film. Because of the many parameters it is difficult to relate the process and device parameters to each other.

3.2.3.4. Relation Between Physical and Device Parameters

(i) *Signal amplitude.* In order to read the information stored in a film element in the Raffel selection scheme, a large word field pulse is applied normally to the easy axis. This forces the magnetization to rotate toward the hard axis and a positive or negative signal is induced in the sense line parallel to the hard axis. In the plated wire memory, the wire is the sense line. According to the induction law the signal is given by:

$$e = -\frac{d\phi}{dt} = -\frac{M_s D a}{\tau} \qquad (3.2.3.1)$$

in which M_s is the saturation magnetization for Ni-Fe, $M_s = 10\ 000$ Gauss, D is the film thickness, a is the dimension of the film along the hard axis and τ is the switching time.

From the above relation, it seems, that a large signal-to-noise ratio can be obtained for thick films. Unfortunately this is not true for planar films, since they, in contrast to ferrite cores, do not provide a closed flux path. When the coercive force is low, demagnetizing fields caused by the magnetic poles at the edges of the film partly reverse the film in the opposite direction. When the hard axis field is applied, the signal due to such a partly demagnetized film is not larger than that of a non-demagnetized thin film. In experimental thin film memories the thickness usually was less than 1000 Å. Attempts have been made to fabricate closed flux planar structures [3.2.53]. These so-called coupled film elements were obtained by a sequence of plating or evaporating steps resulting in a device consisting of two magnetic layers, which enclosed, with proper film isolation, the bit line. Such films indeed allowed the use of thicker films and the generation of larger signals, but the increased complexity of this device handicapped its chances of success. Plated wires are by their very nature closed flux devices like cores. The thickness of such films can be made much thicker without causing easy axis demagnetization effects. Plated wires often employ a film thickness between 5000 Å and 10 000 Å. The other parameter which is important for the sense signal is the switching time τ. This is the time necessary to rotate the magnetization from the easy direction toward the hard direction. Switching times are usually calculated with the Gilbert equation:

$$\dot{\mathbf{M}} = \gamma(\mathbf{M} \times \mathbf{H}) + \frac{\alpha}{M}(\mathbf{M} \times \dot{\mathbf{M}}) \qquad (3.2.3.2)$$

in which γ is the gyromagnetic ratio and α is the damping-constant. In a thin film as a result of the first term the magnetization $\mathbf{M}$ starts to precess around $\mathbf{H}$. However, as soon as $\mathbf{M}$ turns out of the film plane a large demagnetizing field occurs normal to the film plane. This demagnetizing field is much larger than the applied field, so that the magnetization now starts to rotate quickly around this demagnetizing field toward the hard direction parallel to the applied field.

Because of the second damping term, the hard direction switching process is very fast and can occur within 1 ns depending on the field amplitude. It was this fast switching process that really triggered the huge research effort on thin films in the last decade.

In practical memories the reversal time τ is not limited by the film switching time, but by the rise times of the used drive pulses. These rise times are often of the order of 20 ns. The third parameter is the width of the element in the hard direction, which is practically equal to the width of the word line. Because of demagnetization effects this width cannot be increased without limit. In Fig. 3.2.3.8 the results of a careful analysis by Stein [3.2.54] are summarized. The signal switching time product is shown as a function of the width of the word strip line a and the film thickness D. The heavy lines indicate feasible memory elements for planar "open flux" and planar "closed flux" structures. At the top of the figure, the relating bit densities are

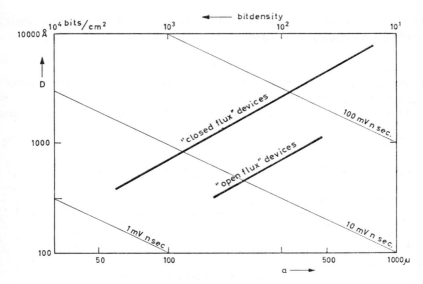

FIG. 3.2.3.8. Diagram indicating the signal switching time product as a function of the width a of the word line and the film thickness D for "closed flux" and "open flux" memory devices. (After [3.2.54].)

indicated. It appears that the output signals are rather small for those bit densities, which are of interest from the application point of view.

(ii) *Word field amplitude.* To store or read information in a film element it is necessary to apply a word field pulse first in the hard direction. This field must be large enough to completely rotate the magnetization toward the hard axis. The amplitude of the word field is determined by the magnitude of the uniaxial anisotropy and by the shape of the memory element.

When the film is deposited in the presence of a magnetic field, a uniaxial anisotropy results with the easy axis parallel to the field. The origin of this anisotropy has been the subject of many investigations. Today it is assumed that the anisotropy is caused by a number of physical effects. Directional ordering of the Fe atom pairs in the Ni lattice due to the magnetic field has been experimentally verified. The experimentally determined dependence on the composition agrees with theory.

Since pure Fe films can also display uniaxial anisotropy, other physical effects must be active. The present belief is that besides the orientation of Fe-atom pairs, the orientation of vacancies, dislocations and impurity atoms can also contribute to the anisotropy. The anisotropy constant can be changed by annealing in a magnetic field. If the field is in the hard direction, then the anisotropy constant will decrease. The anisotropy energy E per unit volume can be expressed by:

$$E = K \sin^2 \theta \qquad (3.2.3.3)$$

in which K is the anisotropy constant and θ the angle between the magnetization and the easy axis.

When a field H_y is applied in the hard direction, the total energy per unit volume is

$$E = -M_s H_y \sin \theta + K \sin^2 \theta. \qquad (3.2.3.4)$$

For a given H_y that angle θ is stable for which $\partial E/\partial \theta = 0$ and $\partial^2 E/\partial \theta^2 > 0$, that is

$$\frac{\partial E}{\partial \theta} = -M_s H_y \cos \theta + 2K \sin \theta \cos \theta = 0 \qquad (3.2.3.5)$$

and

$$\frac{\partial^2 E}{\partial \theta^2} = M_s H_y \sin \theta + 2K(\cos^2 \theta - \sin^2 \theta). \qquad (3.2.3.6)$$

The solutions are $M_s H_y = 2K \sin \theta$ and $\cos \theta = 0$. The field H_y necessary to saturate in the hard direction is

$$H_y = \frac{2K}{M_s}.$$

Depending on the deposition parameters, we find that H_y can have almost any value. Typical values are around 5 Oe. Also the minimum word field usually depends on the length to width ratio of the film element. When the magnetization is in the hard direction, the magnetic poles at the edges parallel to the easy axis will cause a demagnetizing field antiparallel to the magnetization and the applied field must be corrected for this field.

The total demagnetizing energy is

$$E = \tfrac{1}{2} N_x M_s^2 \cos^2 \theta + \tfrac{1}{2} N_y M_s^2 \sin^2 \theta \qquad (3.2.3.7)$$

in which N_x and N_y are the demagnetizing factors in the easy and hard directions respectively. The energy can also be written as

$$E = \tfrac{1}{2}(N_y - N_x) M_s^2 \sin^2 \theta + \tfrac{1}{2} N_x M_s^2. \qquad (3.2.3.8)$$

The first term leads to a shape anisotropy field

$$H_{\text{shape}} = (N_y - N_x) M_s. \qquad (3.2.3.9)$$

The field is non-existent when circular or square elements are used, since $N_y = N_x$. In elongated elements and more so in coupled films and plated wire elements, H_{shape} can have a large value since N_x is small. To reduce the word drive current, keepers have been used in actual memory designs. These keepers consisted of magnetic rubber or flat ferrite plates and provided some closure of the hard direction flux thereby decreasing N_y and H_{shape}.

(iii) *Skew and dispersion.* When a large word field is decreased and no bit field is applied, it can be expected that the film splits up into domains such that the resulting magnetization in the easy direction is zero. When a word field is applied during reread no sense signal is observed. In a planar thin film memory this will be the case for many elements, but for some elements positioned near the edges of the plane a small positive or negative signal will be obtained. These unwanted signals are created because the word field and the hard axis are not parallel in the elements. The angle between them is called skew. When a word field is decreased, the magnetization rotates back preferentially to that easy direction which makes the smallest angle with the word field. In the test program described in Section 3.2.3.2, a bit current $i_b{}^s$ must be applied to compensate for the skew.

Skew is caused by a number of effects. When the magnetostriction coefficient λ is not very small, skew may arise from stresses due to the mounting of the memory plane and from the temperature gradients in the substrate. Also, inhomogeneous magnetic fields during evaporation and the angle of incidence effect may result in skew.

The effect is more severe in planar memory structures than in plated wire stores due to their different preparation techniques. In memories skew must be kept as small as possible. The disturb curve (dashed in Fig. 3.2.3.5(b)) as will be discussed in the next section is independent of skew. Therefore, in memories with large skew the operating margin for the bit field amplitude becomes very small. Even when skew is absent, a certain positive or negative bit current $i_b{}^d$ is necessary to obtain the maximum sense signal amplitude as shown in Fig. 3.2.3.5(b). This bit current is a result of the existence of a certain angular dispersion of the hard axis, which is symmetrically distributed around the field direction during deposition. In plated films this dispersion is usually larger than the dispersion in evaporated films [3.2.55]. Many physical effects for the dispersion can be indicated. Thin magnetic films are polycrystalline. The crystallite size is of the order of the film thickness. In Ni-Fe films these crystallites are face-centred cubic. Since the non-magnetostrictive composition 81.4% Ni−18.6% Fe is preferred for memory applications, the easy axes of the small crystallites are parallel to the body diagonals [111]. The crystal axes are randomly distributed, and since the resulting anisotropy in a crystallite is the sum of the small magnetocrystalline anisotropy and the induced anisotropy, the occurrence of an angular dispersion of the easy axis appears plausible.

K

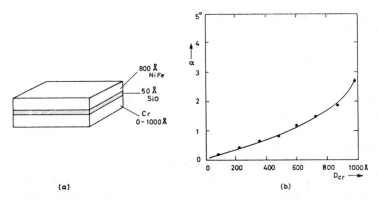

(a)　　　　　　　　　　　　　　　　　　　(b)

Fig. 3.2.3.9. Angular dispersion in NiFe/SiO/Cr sandwich films: (a) structure and (b) dependence of angular dispersion on Cr film thickness.

When the magnetostriction coefficient is not zero, randomly distributed uniaxial stresses which arise during cooling after deposition will lead to randomly distributed easy axes. Theoretically, one can expect Ni-Fe compositions around 80/20, which have small magneto-crystalline anisotropies and small magnetostriction coefficients, to show a minimum in angular dispersion, this indeed is observed.

Structural imperfections such as holes, film thickness variations and scratches can also cause anisotropy dispersion. This influence is demonstrated in Fig. 3.2.3.9, where the angular dispersion α of a non-magnetostrictive 800 Å film is given as a function of the thickness of a Cr substrate layer between glass and film [3.2.44]. As indicated in Fig. 3.2.3.9(a), a very thin SiO layer is used between the Ni-Fe and Cr layer. The experiment shows that if the substrate is made rough artificially, dispersion increases rapidly. The roughness of the Be-Cu wires in plated wires also contributes to dispersion.

In theoretically determining the anisotropy dispersion, early workers assumed that a film consisted of a large number of non-interacting crystallites. Today it is known that this assumption is not correct [3.2.56]. In fact the crystallites are very tightly coupled as a result of both exchange coupling and magnetostatic coupling. The exchange coupling causes the magnetization of neighbouring crystallites to be as parallel as possible thereby reducing the effective angular dispersion of the magnetization. The magnetostatic coupling is caused by the occurrence of the poles when the magnetizations in two neighbouring crystallites are not parallel. Whereas the exchange coupling is isotropic, the magnetostatic coupling is large in a direction normal to the average magnetization direction and small parallel to the

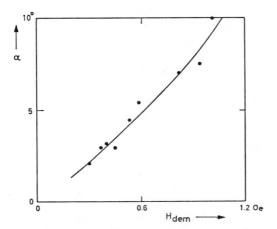

FIG. 3 2 3.10. Angular dispersion α in a 890 Å NiFe film as a function of the demagnetizing field in the easy direction. (After [3.2.44].)

magnetization. The anisotropy of the magnetostatic coupling causes the occurrence of elongated areas perpendicular to the magnetization direction in which the magnetization has the same deviation from the easy axis. Experimentally, these domains have been made visible by electron micro- scopy. As a result of the magnetostatic and exchange coupling, the effective angular dispersion is much smaller than the originally expected one, which is fortunate from a device point of view. The measured angular dispersion is a quantity which is significant for the application of the film, but does not give the true physical dispersion. In planar film memories another source of dispersion is related to demagnetizing effects. When the hard direction field is reduced the magnetization starts to rotate toward the easy axis. Due to the occurring poles at the edges of the element, a demagnetizing field antiparallel to the magnetization appears and reverses a part of the element. To overcome this effect a minimum bit field must be measured as a function of the calculated demagnetizing field in the easy direction [3.2.44], as is shown in Fig. 3.2.3.10. For closed flux plated wire elements this effect is much less. In a practical situation a memory designer must choose the element size and the physical parameters of the deposition step in such a way that the bit field margin in Fig. 3.2.3.5(b) is large enough to assure that each bit can be properly interrogated. It proved to be much more difficult to satisfy this requirement for evaporated planar films than it was for plated wires.

(iv) *Disturb sensitivity.* During the write cycle in a thin film memory, the selected film element is subjected to a word field and a bit field of the proper directions. When the film elements are situated at short distances from each other, film elements along the bit line will be subjected to the full bit field and also to a stray word field due to the neighbouring word line. In a satisfactorily operating memory these latter fields should not cause any change in the magnetization. When work began on film memories, people were rather confident with respect to this problem, because it was assumed, that in the easy direction a magnetic film could only switch by a uniform rotation of the magnetization in the film. The field at which this should occur can easily be calculated from energy considerations.

When H_x is a field in the easy direction, the total energy is given by:

$$E = -M_s H_x \cos \theta + K \sin^2 \theta \tag{3.2.3.10}$$

and

$$\frac{\partial E}{\partial \theta} = +M_s H_x \sin \theta + 2K \sin \theta \cos \theta = 0 \tag{3.2.3.11}$$

with the solutions $M_s H_x = -2K \cos \theta$ and $\sin \theta = 0$. The first solution is never stable, whereas the second solution gives $\theta = 0$ and $\theta = \pi$. Transition between these directions occurs for

$$\frac{\partial^2 E}{\partial \theta^2} = M_s H_x \cos \theta + 2K = 0 \tag{3.2.3.12}$$

when $\theta = \pi, H_x = 2K/M_s$ This is the same field for which saturation in the hard direction is achieved. Since the bit field has only to overcome the angular dispersion and skew, it can be much smaller than H_k and the disturb sensitivity of the film elements should not pose a problem. However, very soon it appeared that magnetization reversal in the easy direction of magnetic films did not occur by uniform rotation but by wall motion. This wall motion occurred at fields which were usually much smaller than H_k. At the edges of planar film elements, small triangular domains exist which start to grow at the wall motion coercive force of the film H_w (Fig. 3.2.3.11).

In order to increase the operating margins of a memory element, the wall motion coercive force was the subject of many theoretical and experimental studies. Though no conclusive theory exists, one can say that the coercive force is due to the angular dispersion found in all films. The dispersion in turn can be caused by magneto-crystalline and magneto-strictive anisotropies and also by surface roughness. By changing the evaporation or plating conditions it is always possible to obtain suitable coercive forces. Because the stray word field is also active on a neighbouring bit, one measures the wall motion coercive force in the easy direction as a function of the hard axis. Such a so-called critical curve for wall motion is displayed in Fig.

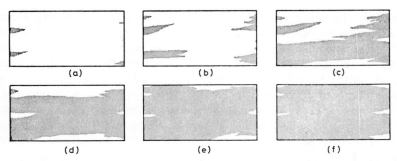

FIG. 3.2.3.11. Magnetization reversal by wall motion caused by a magnetic field H_w in the easy direction.

3.2.3.12. In most films the dependence of H_w on a hard direction field is not very strong for small fields. Around 1960 it was generally believed that the bit current i_b^{cr} at which information disturbance occurred was directly related to H_w^1 in Fig. 3.2.3.12. Therefore one assumed that though coherent magnetization reversal in the easy direction did not occur, H_c could be made large enough to warrant disturb free operation in films.

The shock came, when it appeared that after a neighbouring bit was disturbed many times, 10^6 as in the test programme of Fig. 3.2.3.5(a) the disturb bit field H_b^{cr} was much smaller than H_w and the bit field. As a consequence the operating margins were very much smaller than had been

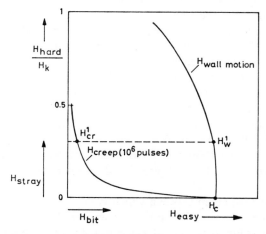

FIG. 3.2.3.12. Critical curves for wall motion H_w and wall creep H_{cr}. At a stray field H_{stray} in the hard direction, the maximum H_{bit} reduces from H_w' to H_{cr}' which is smaller than the necessary minimum H_{bit} to overcome skew and angular dispersion.

expected. The disappointing disturb sensitivity is due to a magnetization reversal process called wall creeping, which hitherto was not observed in other magnetic materials [3.2.57, 3.2.58]. It has been shown that when dc fields are applied in the easy and hard direction and the resulting field vector lies within the H_w critical curve, wall motion will not take place. If the dc field in the hard direction is replaced by a pulse or an ac field then the H_{cr} critical curve applies. The speed of the creep reversal process depends on the amplitude of the pulse field in the hard direction, the magnitude of the dc field in the easy direction and the pulse repetition frequency. Wall creep consists of two small wall jumps during the rise and fall of the hard direction pulse field. The resulting wall velocity is proportional to the pulse frequency as has been experimentally verified.

Although no full agreement between the different authors exists with respect to the exact wall creep mechanism, a reasonable understanding is now available. Let us consider a straight wall with a length l parallel to the easy axis which is shifted across a small distance dy by a field H_x in a film of thickness D. The increase of the free energy of the wall must be equal to the work performed on it, thus:

$$d(\gamma Dl) = 2H_x M_s lD \, dy \qquad (3.2.1.13)$$

or

$$H_x = \frac{1}{2M_s lD} \frac{d(\gamma Dl)}{dy} \, . \qquad (3.2.3.14)$$

In a film $d(\gamma Dl)/dy$ varies from place to place (Fig. 3.2.3.13) and so does the field necessary to move the wall.

The maximum value will correspond to H_c. When a field H_1 smaller than H_c is applied, the wall will move to some place y_1. As long as the applied field does not exceed H_2 an irreversible wall motion cannot occur. When a hard direction field is now applied of proper amplitude, the domain wall undergoes a structural change as is well known from many experiments [3.2.59]. The new wall configuration leads to a different, for instance reversed, dependence of H_x on y as is sketched in Fig. 3.2.3.13 (dashed line). The wall will jump now to position y_2. When the hard direction field is switched off the wall obtains its original configuration although some transition hysteresis has been observed and another jump to y_3 occurs, and so on.

Although this wall creep process, which is only observed in thin magnetic layers, is scientifically very interesting, it was at the same time the death-blow to the planar film memory. Because of the wall creep process operating margins of a thin film memory became very tight. The requirements with respect to element size, distance, skew, etc. were so strict that planar film

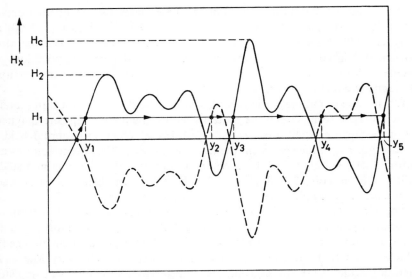

FIG. 3.2.3.13. Explanation of hard direction field induced wall creeping. The critical field for wall motion varies in the y-direction in two ways: with hard direction field switched on (solid line) and off (dashed line).

memories were economically not attractive compared to other technologies such as semiconductor memories. Since plated wires are closed flux devices, wall creep was less serious, but also present [3.2.55]. Therefore it is no surprise, today that, except for special purposes, the plated wire memory lost ground in favour of the semiconductor memory.

3.2.4. MAGNETIC BUBBLE MEMORIES

3.2.4.1. Introduction

Magnetic-disk memory systems are widely used as external high capacity storage and at present are the best solution for inexpensive data storage with acceptable access times. As the systems are mechanical, they are not as reliable as internal ferrite core or semiconductor memories and therefore the search for non-mechanical external memories, which offer low cost data storage, is still going on.

Magnetic bubble memories might be the answer, if a number of technical problems can be solved. In most magnetic materials easy directions for the magnetization can be observed. In a number of materials such as hexagonal ferrites, orthoferrites, garnets and MnBi these easy directions can be normal to the surface of thin platelets of films of these materials. Magnetic domain structures in such platelets were described by Kooy and Enz [3.2.60] as early as 1960. A renewed interest in these domain structures occurred after Bobeck published his paper on the properties and device applications of magnetic domains in orthoferrites in 1967 [3.2.61]. Today many sessions at magnetic conferences are devoted to this subject.

When no external magnetic field is applied, the domains in a thin platelet of orthoferrite form serpentine patterns with domains of opposite magnetization occupying equal areas (Fig. 3.2.4.1(a)). When an external field is applied normal to the specimen, the domains in which the magnetizations are antiparallel to the applied field contract into cylindrical domains usually called bubbles (Fig. 3.2.4.1(b)). The size of the bubbles ranges between 1 μm and 100 μm and depends on the material properties.

The idea occurred to Bobeck and his colleagues at the Bell Telephone laboratory to use these bubbles for storing data. It appeared that the bubbles could be moved through the platelet easily by means of a magnetic needle, which meant that the coercive force of the materials was very low. The methods, which were subsequently developed to make bubble shift registers can be divided into two groups. In the first group, called conductor access methods, conductor loops are laid down on the platelet by photolithographic techniques (Fig. 3.2.4.2(a)). A "1" is represented by a bubble and this bubble can be moved by properly energizing the conductor loops. The second group includes all the so-called field access methods. Soft magnetic structures

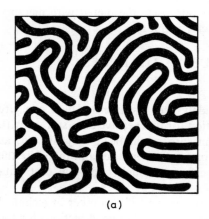
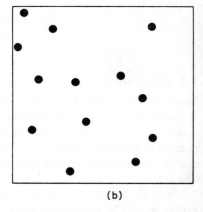

(a)   (b)

FIG. 3.2.4.1. (a) Strip domains in a platelet of orthoferrite viewed by the Faraday effect, (b) when a bias field is applied antiparallel to the magnetization in the dark domains, bubbles appear.

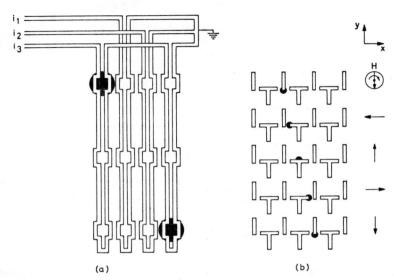

FIG. 3.2.4.2. Magnetic bubble shift register based on: (a) conductor access method and (b) field access method.

are laid down on the platelets; these structures are magnetized by an external rotating magnetic field, in such a way that the bubble is attracted by the patterns in the proper sequence (Fig. 3.2.4.2(b)). For a memory system, besides propagation, other functions such as bubble generation, annihilation, replication and detection are also necessary. It proved possible to realize these functions in the conductor access method as well as in the field access method which will be discussed in the next sections.

In the first years of bubble memory research, most work was done on orthoferrites; more recently the different garnet materials have proved to have better combinations of physical properties. Today most bubble work is performed on epitaxial garnet films, which are grown either by the liquid phase epitaxy technique (LPE) or by chemical vapour deposition (CVD) on non-magnetic garnet substrates. In Sections 3.2.4.3 and 3.2.4.4 the different preparation methods and the relation between physical and device parameters will be described.

As a prototype for a bubble mass-memory the Bell people built a "telephone repertory dialer", a device which can contain for instance 100 frequently called telephone numbers [3.2.62].

Such a repertory dialer consists mainly of a large number of minor bubble shift registers which can be coupled to a major shift register on command (Fig. 3.2.4.3). Using the same principle, magnetic bubble mass memories

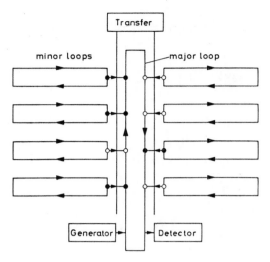

FIG. 3.2.4.3. Organization of bubble mass memory with one major loop and a multitude of minor loops.

have been designed which contain up to 56 garnet chips. Each chip has 70 minor loops, each with 293 bit positions giving a total storage capacity of more than one million bits [3.2.63, 3.2.64].

3.2.4.2. Generation, Propagation and Detection of Cylindrical Domains

In this section the different logic functions which are necessary to build a memory system will be discussed. Of the different devices, the current access variant will always be discussed first; some devices have both current and field access features.

(i) *Bubble generator*. Any logic system using bubbles requires a method for generating bubbles on demand. In the first proposals by Bobeck *et al.* [3.2.65] bubble generation in platelets of orthoferrite was effected by a hairpin conductor circuit (Fig. 3.2.4.4). This was possible because the bubbles in the used orthoferrites were rather large, about 100 μm in diameter. In the first step a bubble is moved from the left to a place beneath the hairpin by sending a current through the outer conductor. In the second step a large current (about 1A) is sent through the inner conductor which produces a field (about 100 Oe) that is now anti-parallel to the bubble magnetization. This field splits the bubble into two bubbles which are moved to the surrounding conductor loops by providing currents of proper sign through these loops. The left bubble can be used to generate new bubbles, whereas the

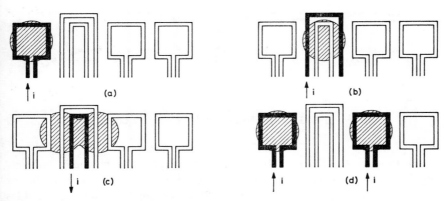

FIG. 3.2.4.4. Conductor access bubble generator: (a) start position of seed domain, (b) bubble under hairpin, (c) bubble splitting and (d) resultant two bubbles.

second bubble is propagated to the right by a sequence of currents in the adjacent loops.

A field access bubble generator [3.2.66] consists of a square permalloy disk (Fig. 3.2.4.5), about 9000 Å thick. The disk maintains a domain which stays in contact with, for instance, the positive poles on the disk which are generated by the rotating horizontal field. When the field is rotated counter-clockwise, the domain is forced to the positive pole on the horizontal bar. When the field is rotated further, the domain is stretched because the domain stays attached to the vertical bar. At a certain moment the domain becomes unstable and suddenly ruptures into two portions, one remaining on the disk and the other in the shift register. In general the minimum rotating field amplitude for domain generation is larger than the minimum rotating field for propagation; therefore, the generation of bubbles can be controlled by adjusting this amplitude.

A disadvantage of both bubble generators is that in the beginning bubbles must already be present beneath the current loop or permalloy disk. To remove this uncertainty, bubble generators have been proposed [3.2.67] which consist of a permalloy disk and a current loop. The current loop can be used: (1) to divide an already existing bubble maintained by the disk or (2) to inhibit the propagation of a bubble generated by a disk generator, which is normally on or (3) to nucleate a bubble beneath a permalloy disk. In Fig. 3.2.4.6 such a device is shown, it consists of a permalloy disk and a hairpin shaped conductor etched from a 4000 Å gold conductor. The conductor field is antiparallel to the bias field. Rather large currents are required, but this poses no serious problem because the nucleation function is very rarely required.

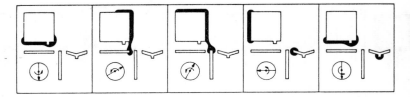

FIG. 3.2.4.5. Field access bubble generator.

(ii) *Propagation circuits*. In order to propagate the magnetic bubbles, highly localized magnetic fields are required at specific points. The conductor circuits used first by Bobeck *et al*. [3.2.65] on orthoferrites with large bubbles are shown in Fig. 3.2.4.2(a). The sizes of the bubble and the conductors are chosen in such a way that the bubble is in contact with the field gradient of the next loop. To prevent reverse motion of bubbles, a three phase system is needed. The bubble is shifted by the sequential application of currents through the loops. A three phase system requires electrical insulation between the connections of the conductor loops. This is a disadvantage from the technological point of view. This problem is overcome with the two phase system as shown in Fig. 3.2.4.7. Directionality is achieved with the help of permalloy dots. Because of flux closure the bubble domain prefers a location which is symmetric with respect to the dots. When the next current loop is activated, the bubble is closest to one loop so that the propagation direction is defined. By connecting the current loops at both sides of the register electrical insulation is superfluous as no conductor crossovers occur.

A disadvantage of current access is that one flaw in a conductor of a complicated memory circuit makes the whole device worthless. This problem is much less severe in field access propagation circuits and therefore today bubble propagation circuits are all based on the field access method. The first field access propagation device proposed, was the so-called "angel fish"

FIG. 3.2.4.6. Bubble generator based on nucleation by a current through a hairpin conductor.

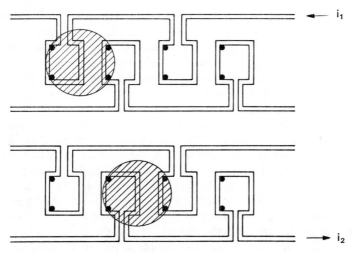

FIG. 3.2.4.7. Two-phase current access propagation circuit.

bubble mover (Fig. 3.2.4.8). This device is based on the fact that the bubble diameter is a function of the bias field. The device consists of permalloy wedges between two permalloy rails. The interaction between bubbles and wedges is such that a bubble is more easily moved off the point rather than off the blunt end of the permalloy wedge. When the bias field is decreased, the bubble increases and the leading domain wall reaches out to latch onto the blunt edge of the next wedge. When the bias field is decreased, the trailing domain wall slides off the point of the wedge. By periodically modulating

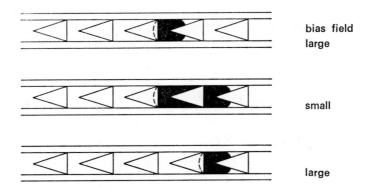

FIG. 3.2.4.8. Expansion and contraction of a bubble in an "angel fish" propagation circuit.

the bias field, a unidirectional motion of bubbles can be ensured. The permalloy rails are necessary to cause the bubbles to expand along the direction of motion. "Angel fish shift registers" have been built on ortho-ferrite platelets [3.2.65]. In the second field access method, a combination of permalloy patterns and an in-plane rotating field is used [3.2.66]. A variety of permalloy patterns can be used such as T-BARs, Y-BARs and CHEVRONS. The operation of the T-BAR is pictured in Fig. 3.2.4.2(b). The bias field normal to the platelet is chosen to maintain bubble domains with negative magnetic charge at the pattern side of the platelet. When the in-plane field is in the negative y-direction, the bubble moves to the positive pole end of the permalloy bar. When the in-plane field is rotated clockwise to the negative x-direction, the bubble moves to the left tip of the T-BAR. The field gradient between the permalloy structures forces the bubble to the right. This sequence repeats itself as the field is further rotated resulting in a continuous propagation of the bubble to the right. When the in-plane field is rotated counter-clockwise, the bubble moves to the left. In the first experiments on orthoferrites the T-BAR structures were very large (about 100 μm), because the bubbles in these materials had large dimensions also. However, it has proven possible to reduce the size of the T-BARs for the new garnet materials which work with much smaller (6 μm) bubble domains.

Another structure, which is often used, is the so-called Y-BAR [3.2.68]. Such a register consists of vertical bars with Y-BARs between, as shown in Fig. 3.2.4.9. As in the case of the T-BAR, a bubble is propagated along this structure by rotating an in-plane magnetic field as shown in Fig. 3.2.4.9. In more recent bubble memory designs a structure is used which is called a chevron. This structure was first proposed by Bobeck et al. [3.2.69]; it also allows simple logic operations.

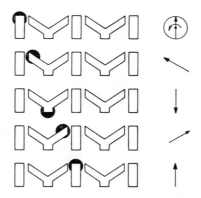

FIG. 3.2.4.9. Propagation of a bubble domain along a Y-BAR circuit.

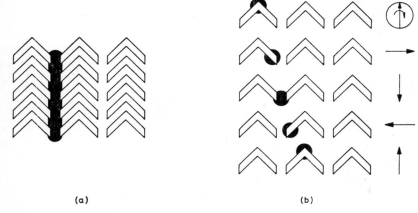

(a)   (b)

FIG. 3.2.4.10. (a) Strip domain in a multi chevron propagation circuit, and (b) bubble propagation along a single chevron circuit.

As is shown in Fig. 3.2.4.10(a), the circuit consists of an array of closely spaced chevrons. Many registers have been built with one to five chevrons per position. The propagation of a bubble along a single chevron structure is indicated in Fig. 3.2.4.10(b).

When many chevrons are used per position, the effective bias field can be decreased and vertical strip domains can also be propagated under control of the in-plane field. Because of a redundancy of drive elements, defects in the permalloy structure or in the bubble material can be more readily tolerated. A disadvantage is the larger area needed for the single positions.

In order to compare different materials and structures operating margins are determined. In Fig. 3.2.4.11 this is illustrated for a 2-Bar chevron circuit. Vertically the bias field H_z and horizontally the amplitude H_x of the in-plane horizontal field are plotted. When the bias field is too large, the bubbles are no longer stable and collapse, whereas, when the bias field is too small, the bubbles strip out beyond the propagation structure. When the horizontal field is too small, the permalloy structures are not properly switched, and the bubble cannot propagate. The data of Fig. 3.2.4.11 are obtained by very slowly rotating the in-plane field; when higher frequencies are used the operating margins reduce.

(iii) *Transfer circuits.* Bubble memory designs are based mainly on the cooperation of many minor bubble shift registers with one major shift register. During reading or writing the bubbles must be transferred between the minor and major loops. A large number of devices for the transfer of bubbles have been invented. Two examples will be discussed, one is based on

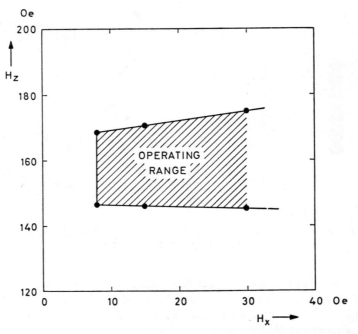

FIG. 3.2.4.11. Low frequency operating range of a two-bar chevron propagation circuit on a garnet film [3.2.69].

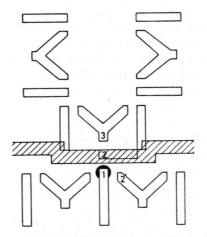

FIG. 3.2.4.12. Major loop–minor loop transfer device. A current through the conductor (dashed) determines whether the bubble goes from 1 to 2 or to 2′ [3.2.70].

a local magnetic field generated by a conductor loop [3.2.70] and the other is a true field access device without conductor loops [3.2.71].

The current access transfer device is shown in Fig. 3.2.4.12. The major loop is vertical and consists of Y-BAR propagation circuits. A bubble at position 1 can propagate from position 1 to position 2 or 2' when the rotating field is going counter-clockwise. When a current is sent through the conductor, the polarity of the current and accompanying magnetic field determine whether the bubble is going to 2 and further to 3 or to 2'. In the first case transfer from the major loop to the minor loop takes place. By reversing the sense of the rotating field and by properly timing the current through the conductor a bubble transfer from the minor loop to the major loop is also possible as can be easily seen. The other transfer device is shown in Fig. 3.2.4.13 and is called a bias modulation switch [3.2.71]. A single bar is positioned between a minor and major loop. When the external field is rotated clockwise, a bubble originally at position 1 will be attracted by the magnetic pole at position 2. When the magnetic field is further rotated, the bubble can go to position 3 and 4 successively or to position 5. The propagation direction depends on the size of the bubble. A small bubble will not leave the Y-BAR and propagates to 5, whereas a large bubble sufficiently interacts with the magnetic pole at 2 and will be transferred to the other loop. Because the bubble diameter is a function of the bias field normal to the film, modulation of the bias field affects the bubble size and also the transfer of bubbles between minor and major loops.

(iv) *Bubble detection devices.* A memory consisting of major and minor loops as indicated in Fig. 3.2.4.3 requires a method for detecting the presence or absence of bubbles at the output. Several principles have been investigated. Detection can be performed by electromagnetic induction, by the magneto-resistance effect, by the Hall effect and by direct optical sensing.

In the electromagnetic induction method, the detector consists of a pickup loop on which a weak electric voltage is induced when a bubble passes the loop. Because of the weak signal this method is not generally used. The most

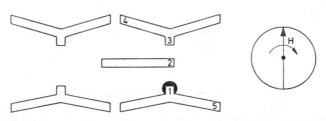

FIG. 3.2.4.13. Bias modulation major loop–minor loop transfer device [3.2.71].

L

popular magneto-resistance method is based on the change of the resistance of a thin permalloy strip when this strip is subjected to the stray field of a bubble. Less popular though usable is the Hall effect, where a voltage appears across a semiconducting film carrying a current when the bubble and its field come near the semiconductor film. Because the Faraday effect in the usual bubble materials is rather low, the fourth method of optical sensing is also not used unless high powered gas lasers are available.

Since the magneto-resistance detection technique seems to be the most generally accepted one, the effect will be further illuminated here. The change of resistance of a conducting material in a magnetic field is called the magneto-resistance effect. This effect is due to the fact that when a magnetic field is applied the electron paths become curved. This reduces the component of motion in the direction of the applied electric field and therefore the resistance of the conductor will be higher. In ordinary conductors this effect is very small and cannot be used for bubble detectors. In ferromagnetic conductors the magneto-resistance effect is much larger (about 4% is possible) due to high internal magnetic fields. The direction of these fields, which are coupled to the magnetization, can easily be changed in soft permalloy films by applying rather small external magnetic fields. Almasi *et al.* [3.2.72] were among the first to use the magneto-resistance effect in thin permalloy films for the detection of bubbles. As shown in Fig. 3.2.4.14(a) a thin permalloy strip is placed close to the bubble propagation path with the easy axis vertical. The stray field of the bubble rotates the magnetization toward the hard direction and changes the resistance. Very thin permalloy is used to ensure that the detector does not interfere with the bubble motion. The sense signal is proportional to $j\Delta\rho l$ where j is the current density, $\Delta\rho$ is the change in the resistivity and l is the detector length. As long as large bubbles are used the sense signal is more than sufficient. In order to increase the bit density in

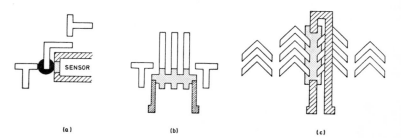

(a)   (b)   (c)

FIG. 3.2.4.14. Magnetoresistive sensing of bubbles domains: (a) The stray field of the bubble rotates the magnetization of the sensor from the easy to the hard direction [3.2.72], (b) thin permalloy "Chinese letter" bubble stretcher [3.2.69] and (c) thin permalloy chevron bubble stretcher.

present memory chips the bubble size has been reduced toward about 5 μm and this has caused the signal-to-noise ratio to become problematic. A method to increase the signal is called bubble stretching. The propagation structure in the neighbourhood of the detector is changed in such a way that the bubble is stretched. Bobeck *et al.* [3.2.69] introduced the "Chinese letter" detector as shown in Fig. 3.2.4.14(b). The additional three bars stretch the bubble along the permalloy film thereby increasing the flux available for detection. The output signal is about 2.5 times larger than it would be if a single detector element were used. A disadvantage of the above domain stretcher is that the bubble is elongated in the propagation direction. This requires a velocity increase at the detector. As the bubble velocity cannot be increased indefinitely, this detector will have a detrimental effect on the data rate of the bubble registers.

This effect can be overcome by stretching the bubble domain normal to the propagation direction. Such a detector, which is due to Archer *et al.* [3.2.73] is sketched in Fig. 3.2.4.14(c). The propagation is caused by chevrons and the number of chevrons is increased at the detector location. The permalloy strip is positioned between the chevrons and normal to the bubble propagation path. The advantage of the stretcher is that its output can be increased by increasing the number of chevrons to much more than three in a column without affecting the maximum obtainable data rate too much.

After detection the bubble will generally be returned to the proper minor loops. However; sometimes new data is used to replace the old ones. In that case the bubbles will be propagated to a so-called bubble annihilator. Such a device consists of a conductor loop which produces a field that is added to the bias field and reduces the bubbles to less than their minimum stable diameter.

(v) *Bubble logic devices.* When new physical phenomena appear which can be used for data storage, usually their utility for logic is also investigated. It is even possible that the inclusion of some logic operations on a memory chip will improve its versatility.

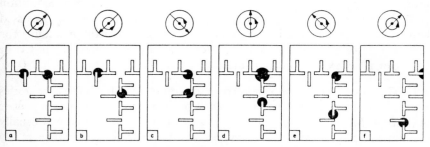

FIG. 3.2.4.15. Divide-by-two circuit with bubbles.

The physical effect, which can be used for bubble logic, is the bubble-bubble magnetostatic interaction. A divide-by-two circuit based on this effect is illustrated in Fig. 3.2.4.15 [3.2.74].

In a simple T-BAR propagation circuit a second vertical circuit is placed normal to the first one in such a way that single bubbles tend to go to the second circuit (Fig. 3.2.4.15(a, b)). The bubble is then captured by the idler consisting of two opposite bars (Fig. 3.2.4.15(c)). The presence of this bubble in the idler forces a second bubble to stay in the horizontal propagation circuit, due to magnetostatic repulsion (Fig. 3.2.4.15(d)), whereas, at the same time the first bubble is pushed out of the idler and continues to propagate along the vertical circuit (Fig. 3.2.4.15(e, f)).

It is clear that the dimensions of the T-BAR circuit elements and their intermediate distances must be very well tuned to the bubble diameter and magnetization. Also AND and OR operations can be realized in a similar way, however this area of activity has not attracted much research effort thus far.

3.2.4.3. Preparation of Bubble Memory Materials

Application of bubble domains to computer storage was first investigated with the help of a group of materials commonly known as orthoferrites [3.2.61]. The general formula of these materials is $MFeO_3$ where M is a rare earth ion. Platelets with the proper crystallographic orientation can support bubble domains, which move easily through the platelet on applying proper magnetic fields. Because the bubbles were rather large ($\approx 100 \, \mu m$) in orthoferrites, a search began for materials which support much smaller bubbles ($\approx 6 \, \mu m$) and enable the construction of memories with a large packing density.

The materials having small bubbles and also a relatively large mobility are known as garnets. The general formula of the simple garnets is $M_3Fe_5O_{12}$ in which M is a rare earth ion.

Instead of using platelets, thin magnetic garnet layers are epitaxially grown on non-magnetic garnet substrates by chemical vapour deposition (CVD) or liquid phase epitaxy (LPE) processes which will be discussed hereafter. Another material which more recently proved to be suitable for bubble memories is obtained by sputtering amorphous films of Gd-Co or Gd-Fe on a large variety of substrates.

(i) *Chemical vapour deposition.* The garnet films used for bubble memories generally must have a rather complex composition in order to obtain proper anisotropy constants and saturation magnetizations. The garnet will usually contain more than one rare earth ion and the iron ions might be partly substituted by gallium ions. Such a gallium substituted garnet with M, N

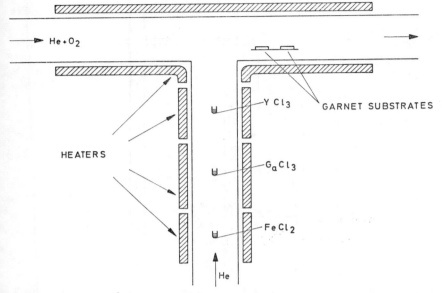

FIG. 3.2.4.16. "T"-shaped reactor for epitaxial garnet deposition of gallium substituted yttrium iron garnet layers by chemical vapour deposition (CVD).

and P rare earth ions is represented by the general formula

$$M_{3-y-z} N_y P_z Ga_x Fe_{5-x} O_{12}.$$

As the physical and device parameters depend strongly on the ratio of the different ions, the preparation method must allow an accurate control of these ratios. One of the methods giving reasonably reproducible layers is the so-called chemical vapour deposition method, introduced by J. E. Mee [3.2.75] and others.

Chemical vapour deposition is performed in a T-shaped reactor (Fig. 3.2.4.16). In the reactor metal halide vapours are oxidized according to

$$MX_n + (n/4)O_2 \rightarrow MO_{n/2} + (n/2) X_2$$

in which M is the metal and X represents F, Cl, Br or I. The oxide $MO_{n/2}$ is deposited on a single crystal substrate. In the case of a complex garnet, oxidation of more than one metal halide occurs simultaneously.

The metal halides are maintained in separate temperature zones in the vertical chamber of the reactor. Helium is used to transport the halide vapours into the reaction zone, which is in the right part of the horizontal chamber. Helium and oxygen are injected into the horizontal chamber.

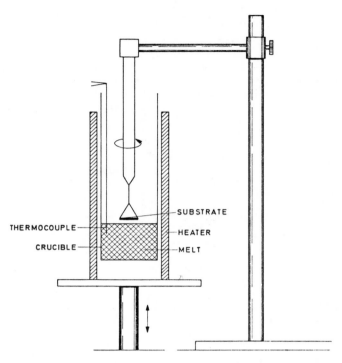

FIG. 3.2.4.17. Apparatus for the growth of epitaxial garnet films by liquid phase epitaxy (LPE).

The exact garnet composition is obtained by choosing the proper metal halides and by adjusting the temperatures at the different places in the reactor and the different flow rates. Since a large lattice constant mismatch between film and substrate will not allow proper epitaxial growth, garnet films are grown on nonmagnetic single crystal garnet substrates. Although a huge number of different garnet compositions have been prepared and the reproducibility was promising with the CVD technique, more recently another technique called liquid phase epitaxy (LPE) has superseded CVD.

(ii) *Liquid phase epitaxy.* This technique is based on the well known fact, that melts containing different components can be supercooled. This effect is observed when one of the components does not start to freeze out at a temperature at which it is expected to according to the phase diagram.

The simple apparatus used for the growth of epitaxial garnet films is shown in Fig. 3.2.4.17 [3.2.76]. It consists of a furnace with a platinum crucible which can be moved vertically. The crucible contains the melt, which consists of a rare earth oxide like Sm_2O_3, Y_2O_3, Eu_2O_3 etc. and the oxides Ga_2O_3 and Fe_2O_3 dissolved in a mixture of PbO and B_2O_5. The temperature of the melt is just below its freeze out temperature ($10°$–$30°C$ supercooling).

The furnace with melt is moved up in such a way that a nonmagnetic garnet substrate is just above the melt, so that the substrate attains the melt temperature. By raising the melt, the substrate is inserted. When the melt is supercooled, the substrate, which is rotated for reasons of homogeneity, is covered by a single crystal garnet layer of the desired composition. By lowering the furnace, the film growth is again terminated. Since many parameters like temperature, melt composition, rotating speed, substrate treatment, etc. have a strong influence on the final epitaxial film, the process variables must be adjusted very carefully. Moreover, during the subsequent fabrication of many films the film composition will change due to the change of the melt composition. Nevertheless it has been proven that with liquid phase epitaxy large reproducible garnet films for bubble memories can be fabricated with very few defects.

(iii) *Substrates.* Though many substrate compositions can be used for CVD as well as for LPE, gallium substituted gadolinium garnet substrates with the composition $Gd_3Ga_5O_{12}$(GGG) are dominant in the bubble field. This is because GGG is non-magnetic, provides good lattice match to the epitaxial garnet films and can be grown with high quality [3.2.77].

Garnets are very complex materials, they crystallize in the cubic system and have a body-centred cubic lattice. In non-substituted garnets the interstitial sites between the oxygen ions are occupied in such a way that Fe ions occupy tetrahedral sites (d-sites) and octahedral sites (a-sites), whereas the rare earth ions are on dodecahedral sites (c-sites) with 12 fold symmetry. The iron ions are antiferromagnetically coupled and the resultant magnetic moment is parallel to that of the d-site Fe ions. The rare earth ions in turn are antiferromagnetically coupled to this resultant iron moment. In gallium substituted garnets all the Fe ions are replaced by trivalent Ga ions, which do not have a resultant magnetic moment. Since exchange coupling between the rare earth ions and the Ga ions cannot take place, GGG is non-magnetic and therefore suitable as a substrate material. Single crystal boules are grown using the standard Czochralski pulling technique. These boules usually have a diameter of one inch, although larger diameters are feasible.

From the boules, wafers are cut which are polished mechanically and chemically so that smooth, defect-and strain-free surfaces are obtained. The preparation of GGG wafers appears to be quite similar to that known from the semiconductor industry.

(iv) *Amorphous metallic films.* Though the preparation of suitable layers for bubble applications has been mastered as just described, the methods are still rather expensive and it is no wonder that alternative materials and preparation methods receive continued attention.

A very promising material was presented by Chaudhari *et al.* [3.2.78]. It consists of metallic $Gd_{1-x}Co_x$ or $Gd_{1-x}Fe_x$ of which amorphous layers are deposited on a wide variety of substrates by the sputtering technique. The resulting magnetization arises from the antiferromagnetic coupling between the spins of the Gd and Co atoms in the amorphous alloy. At one composition exact compensation occurs. The net magnetization M is given by

$$M = (1-x)M_{Gd} - xM_{Co}$$

When we use $M_{Gd} = 7.1\ \mu_B$ and $M_{Co} = 1.72\ \mu_B$, for the compensation composition we find $Gd_{0.195}Co_{0.805}$, which is very close to the experimentally found one as shown in Fig. 3.2.4.18 [3.2.79].

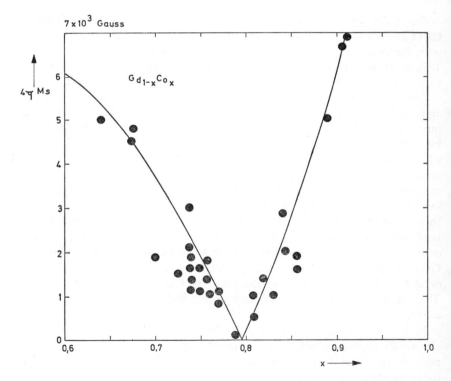

FIG. 3.2.4.18. Room temperature saturation magnetization as a function of film composition in amorphous Gd–Co alloys [3.2.79].

The advantage of the material is that it can be deposited on a wide variety of substrates, even on flexible plastic substrates, and that the composition and so the magnetization can easily be chosen.

(v) *Fabrication of permalloy propagation and detector structures.* In a bubble memory permalloy structures are used for propagation and for magneto-resistive sensing.

For propagation the permalloy should have a low coercive force and no magnetically preferential directions. Moreover it should be thick enough for satisfactory magnetostatic interaction with the bubbles. Many possibilities exist for the preparation of permalloy films as there are evaporation, sputtering or electroplating and each laboratory has its own preference.

In one process [3.2.80] a non-magnetic separating layer of vacuum deposited Al_2O_3 or chemical vapour deposited phosphorous doped SiO_2, having a thickness between 0.5 and 1 μm, is first applied to the garnet layer. Then a 3500 Å permalloy film is vacuum evaporated on top of the oxide. By using standard photoresist techniques the propagation structures are delineated by etching with ferric chloride.

For the detector a much thinner permalloy film is required, as otherwise unwanted interference with bubble domain propagation would occur. Moreover, a thin detector has a larger resistance, which leads to a larger output signal. The difference in thickness of the propagation and detector structures makes a separate permalloy deposition, photoresist step and etching necessary. For the detector a thickness of 300 Å is often used. Finally, current carrying conductors are applied, typically 8000 Å thick and consisting of a 400 Å thin layer of titanium and the rest of gold. The layers are deposited by vacuum evaporation and are delineated by applying photoresist and etching.

By using the above processing steps, it has proven feasible to produce 10^4 bits per chip samples with good reproducibility and yield.

3.2.4.4. Relation between Device Parameters and Physical Properties

(i) *Introduction.* Thin plates or layers of materials like orthoferrites, hexagonal ferrites, manganese bismuth and garnets display cylindrical or bubble domains when they are subjected to a proper bias field normal to the layer. In the bubble domain the magnetization is normal to the layer, leading to large demagnetizing fields, which tend to rotate the magnetization to a direction in the plane of the layer. All the above materials have in common the display of a uniaxial anisotropy with an easy axis normal to the layer. When this anisotropy is sufficiently large, it can overcome the demagnetizing field so that the magnetization direction normal to the layer is a stable one.

The stability and size of bubble domains have been considered in detail by Bobeck [3.2.61, 3.2.65] and Thiele [3.2.81] and will be presented in this chapter. In a memory the velocity with which the stable bubble domains can be propagated determines the serial data processing rate. Theoretically it appears to be possible to calculate the dependence of the bubble mobility on the physical parameters and the wall structure, which will also be discussed here. The chapter concludes with a description of how the required physical parameters like anisotropy constant, saturation magnetization and their respective temperature dependences can be obtained by adjusting the material parameters, like rare earth and gallium content, growth temperature etc.

(ii) *Theory of stability of bubble domains.* First we will consider the condition under which the direction normal to a thin layer is a stable magnetization direction. When the easy axis is parallel to the normal and the angle between magnetization and normal is ψ, the anisotropy energy can be expressed by the relation

$$E_k = K_u \sin^2 \psi \qquad (3.2.4.1)$$

in which K_u is the anisotropy constant.

The magnetostatic energy can be expressed by

$$E_s = \tfrac{1}{2} N M_s^2 \cos^2 \psi \qquad (3.2.4.2)$$

in which N is the demagnetizing factor and $M_s \cos \psi$ is the normal component of the saturation magnetization. For a direction normal to an infinite layer $N = 4\pi$, therefore the total energy is

$$E_{tot} = K_u \sin^2 \psi + \tfrac{1}{2} N M_s^2 \cos^2 \psi = K_u \sin^2 \psi + 2\pi M_s^2 \cos^2 \psi \qquad (3.2.4.3)$$

Stable solutions for $\psi = 0$ or π only occur when $K_u > 2\pi M_s^2$.

As already indicated in an earlier chapter, in general a layer will not be uniformly magnetized normal to the layer, but will display stripe domains (Fig. 3.2.4.1(a)). These domains are separated by domain walls, which also have an energy. When this wall energy is taken into account, it is not difficult to calculate the equilibrium domain width as a function of the anisotropy constant, magnetization and layer thickness [3.2.61].

When a bias field is applied normally to the film, the stripe domains antiparallel to the field shrink, until cylindrical domains remain. Two bias fields are of interest to the application, the decreasing field at which the cylindrical bubble will transfer to an elliptical one, the so-called elliptical instability field, and the (increasing) field beyond which the cylindrical domain collapses, the so-called radial instability field. Besides these bias fields, which indicate the field region in which stable cylindrical domains can be obtained, the dependence of the size of the bubble on the physical parameters must also be known. Since the bit density must be as large as possible for economic and data rate reasons, one is interested in working with the smallest bubbles possible. A lower limit is given by the accuracy with which

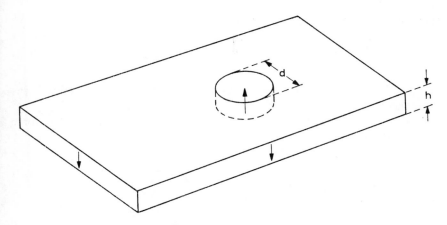

FIG. 3.2.4.19. A bubble domain with diameter d in a layer of thickness h.

the propagation structures can be fabricated by the standard photolithography. Today bubbles with a diameter of 6 μm leading to propagation circuits with a periodicity of 25 μm seem feasible. The instability fields and bubble size can be calculated in the following way as shown by Bobeck and Thiele. Consider a cylindrical bubble domain as shown in Fig. 3.2.4.19. We assume the wall width to be negligible and bubble diameter d not to be a function of the z co-ordinate. The total energy E_T can be written as

$$E_T = E_W + E_H + E_D \qquad (3.2.4.4)$$

in which E_w is the energy due to the circular wall, E_H is the energy due to the interaction of the magnetization of the bubble with the externally applied bias field and E_D is the internal magnetostatic energy due to the magnetic poles on the surface of the layer. Relation (3.2.4.4.) can be written as

$$E_T = \pi d h \sigma_w + \tfrac{1}{2} M_s H \, \pi d^2 h + E_D \qquad (3.2.4.5)$$

in which σ_w is the wall energy density and h the thickness of the layer. It has proved to be helpful in comparison of materials to use a characteristic materials parameter

$$l = \frac{\sigma_w}{4\pi M_s^2} \qquad (3.2.4.6)$$

so that (3.2.4.5) becomes

$$E_T = 4\pi^2 M_s^2 \, dhl + \tfrac{1}{2} M_s H \pi d^2 \, h + E_D \qquad (3.2.4.7)$$

In equilibrium the partial derivative of the total energy with respect to the diameter d of the bubble must be zero

$$\frac{\partial E_T}{\partial d} = 4\pi^2 M_s^2 hl + \pi M_s Hdh + \frac{\partial E_D}{\partial d} = 0 \qquad (3.2.4.8)$$

The wall energy and the field energy reduce for decreasing diameter, whereas the magnetostatic energy increases.

When we divide (3.2.4.8) by $4\pi^2 M_s^2 h^2$ we obtain the normalized force equation of Thiele [3.2.81].

$$\frac{l}{h} + \frac{d}{h} \frac{H}{4\pi M_s} - F\left(\frac{d}{h}\right) = 0 \qquad (3.2.4.9)$$

in which

$$F\left(\frac{d}{h}\right) = -\frac{1}{4\pi^2 M_s^2 h^2} \frac{\partial E_d}{\partial d}. \qquad (3.2.4.10)$$

and represents a rather lengthy and complex function of (d/h). A determination of the bubble diameter as a function of l, M_s, H and h can be

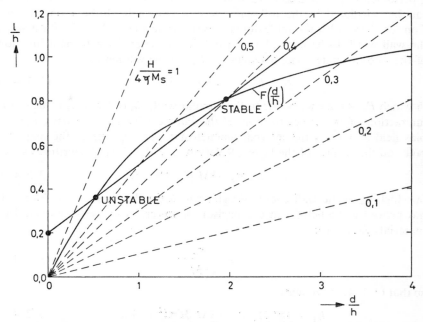

FIG. 3.2.4.20. Graphical determination of the bubble diameter [3.2.81]. Solid line indicates solution for $l = 0.2h$ and a bias field $H = 1.2\,\pi M_s$.

obtained with Fig. 3.2.4.20, in which the different derivatives are plotted. The construction starts with drawing a straight line through the point l/h on the vertical axis. The slope of the line is $H/(4\pi M_s)$ and is proportional to the applied field. When the field is zero, the line is horizontal (the dashed lines have numerical slopes between 0.1 and 1.0). As the $F(d/h)$ curve is plotted also, the intersections of the straight line with the $F(d/h)$ curve are solutions to (3.2.4.9). When a small field is applied, two solutions occur of which, by considering the second derivative, the small diameter appears to be the unstable and the large diameter to be the stable solution. When the field is zero or negative there is no stable solution and this is also true for fields which are larger than the field for which the straight line is tangential to the $F(d/h)$ curve, and the bubble collapses. It is also possible as Thiele [3.2.81] has shown to calculate the largest bubble diameter at which a bubble will transfer to an elliptical bubble.

The results of these calculations are summarized in Fig. 3.2.4.21. The upper curve shows the bubble diameter in units of l at which a circular bubble transfers to an elliptical one as a function of the film thickness in units of l. At the lower curve the bubble collapses. From the curves some interesting conclusions can be drawn.

(a) The minimum bubble diameter for a given material is $3.9l$ and occurs at a thickness of $3.3l$.

(b) Thin layers show large bubbles.

(c) The width of the stable region is not very thickness dependent.

(d) The diameter of a bubble just before becoming elliptic is about three times the diameter at collapse.

With this information, for a particular application it is possible to choose the material and the film thickness. In a later section we will discuss the physical parameters of a number of bubble materials.

(iii) *Wall mobility*. Another important parameter, worth analysing, is the wall velocity. The data processing rate depends on the time which is necessary to propagate the bubbles between the separate elements of the propagation structures. As experimentally shown the bubble velocity depends strongly on the physical parameter of the epitaxial layers used. Because of the rotating field the bubbles are subjected to field gradients between the propagation elements. When a bubble is in a field gradient as shown in Fig. 3.2.4.22, the small field H_2 causes a pressure P_2 on the bubble to the left whereas the large field H_1 causes a pressure P_1 to the right. Since $P_2 > P_1$ the bubbles move to the right. In the wall of the bubble the magnetization

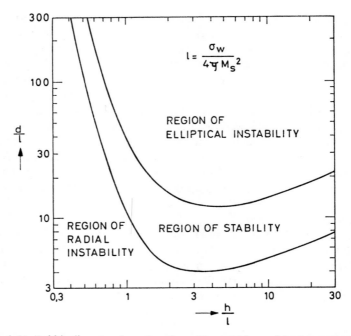

FIG. 3.2.4.21. Bubble diameter d as a function of layer thickness h both expressed in units of the characteristic length l for the three regions of stability as calculated by Thiele [3.2.81].

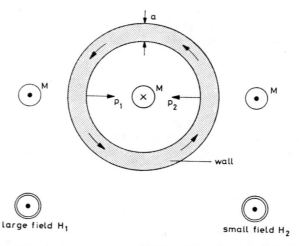

FIG. 3.2.4.22. Bubble propagation due to a field gradient. The bubble moves to the right when $H_1 > H_2$ and thus $P_1 > P_2$.

rotates from one normal to the other. In the middle of the wall the magnetization lies in the plane of the layer. When the bubble moves, the spins in the wall will rotate very fast over an angle of 180°. The bubble velocity depends of course on the applied field gradient and on the rotating speed of the spins in the wall. For two bubbles with the same diameter and propagation velocity, the bubble with the smallest wall width will show the largest spin rotation speed and damping. For fast bubble velocity wide walls are thus advantageous. However, it is clear that the wall width cannot be larger than the bubble diameter.

In general spin rotation is described by the well-known Gilbert equation of motion [3.2.82]:

$$\frac{d\mathbf{M}}{dt} = \gamma \mathbf{M} \times \mathbf{H} - \frac{\gamma \alpha}{M} \frac{d\mathbf{M}}{dt} \qquad (3.2.4.11)$$

where $\mathbf{M}$ is the magnetization vector, $\mathbf{H}$ the effective field, γ is the gyro magnetic constant and α is a damping constant which depends on material parameters.

The first term represents the precession of the magnetization around the field vector $\mathbf{H}$. This precession would continue forever if the second term representing damping effects did not exist. As a result of this term the magnetization becomes parallel to $\mathbf{H}$.

When the bias field is increased the magnetization in the wall starts to precess around this field so that a magnetization component normal to the wall occurs. Due to the surface poles which appear because of this normal component, a large demagnetizing field originates normal to the wall, which is much larger than the applied field. The magnetization starts to precess quickly around this demagnetizing field, which leads to a fast motion of the wall in the desired direction.

From the Gilbert equation of motion the following expression for the wall velocity can be deduced:

$$v = \frac{\gamma}{\alpha} \frac{a}{\pi} H. \qquad (3.2.4.12)$$

The wall width a can be expressed in terms of the uniaxial anisotropy constant K_u and the exchange constant A by

$$a = \pi \left(\frac{A}{K_u}\right)^{\frac{1}{2}}. \qquad (3.2.4.13)$$

Combining (3.2.4.12) and (3.2.4.13) leads to

$$v = \frac{\gamma}{\alpha} \left(\frac{A}{K_u}\right)^{\frac{1}{2}} H. \qquad (3.2.4.14)$$

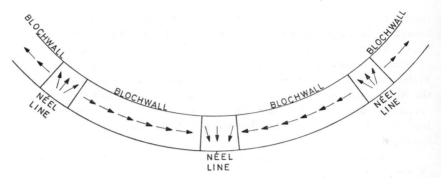

FIG. 3.2.4.23. Schematic representation of a bubble wall consisting of Bloch walls with different polarities separated by Néel lines.

Materials with a small uniaxial anisotropy constant will display a large wall velocity. However, this requirement is in contradiction with the requirement for bubble stability, which is that K_u must be large. In practice one chooses the anisotropy constant as small as possible, but large enough to warrant bubble stability.

Expression (3.2.4.12) gives a linear relationship for the wall velocity. In many experiments this is indeed observed. However, many materials have also been found which display nonlinearities and even velocity saturation for larger fields has been observed.

One of the reasons for the nonlinearity and the much too low wall mobilities, with respect to theory, is that the simple wall structure as indicated in Fig. 3.2.4.22 only occurs under very special conditions. Usually the domain walls will have structures as indicated in Fig. 3.2.4.23. Bloch wall sections with clockwise and counter-clockwise rotation of the spins are separated by Néel segments in which the magnetization is normal to the wall [3.2.83]. The rotation of the spins is such that the Bloch wall sections cannot be removed by simply shifting the Néel lines together. When a bubble is shifted by a field gradient all the Néel lines are also moved. These Néel lines have two effects. In the first place the bubble velocity in the direction of the field gradient decreases very much depending on the number of Néel lines and secondly the Néel lines cause the bubble to move sideways i.e. the bubble has a velocity component normal to the field gradient. Occasionally in a fast shift register the bubble even leaves the propagation line. Bubbles with Néel lines are called hard bubbles for apparent reasons.

The occurrence of hard bubbles can be detected by several experiments. One easy means of detection is the measurement of the field dependence on the bubble diameter. Because the Néel lines contribute some extra energy, the

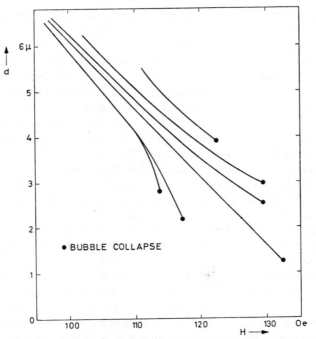

FIG. 3.2.4.24. Bubble diameters d as a function of bias field H in a (Eu$_{0.65}$, Yb$_{0.15}$Y$_{2.2}$) (Ga$_{1.1}$Fe$_{3.9}$)O$_{12}$ film (thickness = 7 μm). (After [3.2.84].)

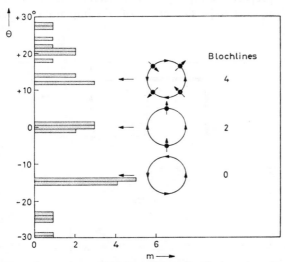

FIG. 3.2.4.25. Histogram of hard bubble deflection angles θ and the relationship between bubble structures and the peaks at $\theta = +13° \pm 1°$, $0°$, $-14° \pm 1°$ [3.2.85].

M

field region in which bubbles are stable is much larger and also the field at which the bubble collapses is much larger. In Fig. 3.2.4.24 this is illustrated by measurements of Malozemoff [3.2.84]. Another very elegant way of investigating hard bubbles and the influence of a small number of Néel lines on bubble motion is by measurement of the deflection angle in a field gradient [3.2.85]. When a histogram of the different deflection angles is made as shown in Fig. 3.2.4.25 it appears that quantization of the deflection angle occurs. Since deflection is due to Néel lines and these lines can only occur in pairs, the above experiment is a very convincing proof of the influence of Néel lines on the wall mobility. A more precise consideration of this effect shows that the normal bubble, that is the bubble which moves parallel to the field gradient contains two Néel lines such that the magnetizations in the left and right Bloch wall segments are parallel. The discovery of Néel lines and hard bubbles with their low mobility led to some pessimism with respect to the application of bubbles to computer memories. However, recently methods were found with which the occurrence of hard bubbles can be prevented or at least their influence reduced.

These methods are based on the preparation of a second layer on top of the first main layer. The physical parameters of the second layer are chosen in such a way that at the bias field used the second layer is completely saturated and the first layer contains bubbles. The second layer can be deposited with the LPE technique; the melt composition will be changed in such a way that a film with a much lower saturation magnetization occurs [3.2.86]. It is also possible to prepare the top layer by subjecting the garnet film to proton ion implantation [3.2.87]. The effect of ion implantation seems to be a

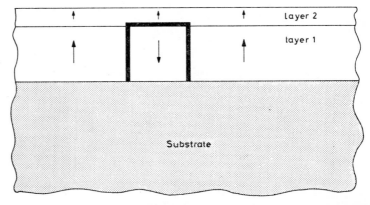

Fig. 3.2.4.26. Magnetization distribution in a double garnet layer showing hard bubble suppression [3.2.88].

change of the garnet lattice such that an easy axis occurs in the plane of the film.

Though the exact mechanism by which the hard bubbles are suppressed by the second layer is not clear, it seems that the wall between the bubble in the first layer and the totally saturated top layer (Fig. 3.2.4.26) makes the unwinding of the Bloch-Néel transitions possible [3.2.88]. The extra processing step connected with the top layer will have a negative influence on the cost and yield of memory chips.

3.2.4.5. Materials for Bubble Domain Applications

In the preceding sections the different physical parameters which govern bubble size, stability and mobility have been discussed. In this section the materials will be presented which most properly satisfy the device requirements.

For bubbles to exist a uniaxial anisotropy is required with an easy axis normal to the layer. Therefore materials displaying a natural uniaxial anisotropy were first examined for bubble applications. These materials are the orthoferrites, the hexagonal ferrites, hexagonal manganese bismuth and hexagonal cobalt. The orthoferrites, especially, were very much studied in the early years of bubble research.

Orthoferrites have the general formula $MFeO_3$, where M is any rare earth ion. They have an orthorhombic structure with the c side about twice as large as the a or b side. The easy axis of orthoferrites is parallel to the c-axis. The saturation magnetization is rather low: $4\pi M_s \approx 100\,\mathrm{G}$, whereas the anisotropy constant is on the order of $K_u \approx 10^5\,\mathrm{erg\,cm^{-3}}$. As shown by Thiele the minimum bubble diameter obtainable by choosing the proper layer thickness is $3.9\,l$ in which l is the characteristic length. For orthoferrites this minimum diameter is around 50 μm. In order to compare different materials, Bobeck and Scovil [3.2.74] and Gianola et al. [3.2.89] constructed charts from which this minimum diameter can be taken for different groups of materials distinguished by their respective uniaxial anisotropy constants and saturation magnetizations.

In Fig. 3.2.4.27 their results are collected in a slightly altered form. The minimum bubble diameter for orthoferrites like $GdFeO_3$, $TbFeO_3$, $HoFeO_3$, $ErFeO_3$ etc. is much too large for the pursued bit densities and means were sought to decrease the anisotropy constant of orthoferrites. This decrease was made possible by partly replacing rare earth ions with Sm ions. Mixed Sm orthoferrites like $Sm_{0.5}Gd_{0.5}FeO_3$, $Sm_{0.5}Y_{0.5}FeO_3$ etc. indeed show much smaller bubble diameters. However, the large temperature dependence of the physical parameters of these materials makes them impractical.

Another group of materials being considered is the group of hexagonal ferrites. These materials have a large uniaxial anisotropy with the easy axis

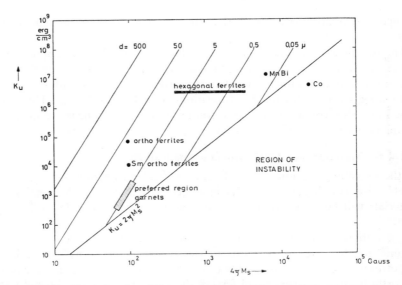

FIG. 3.2.4.27.   Chart showing different bubble materials with their anisotropy constant and saturation magnetization.   Using an exchange constant $A = 0.4 \times 10^{-6}\,\mathrm{erg\,cm^{-1}}$ the minimum bubble diameter is calculated for each K_u and M_s and plotted as lines.

parallel to the c-axis.   Depending on the saturation magnetization bubble sizes of about 5 μm, as required for application, can be obtained in certain $PbAl_xFe_{12-x}O_{19}$ compositions.

As shown in the section on wall mobility, the wall velocity can be expressed by

$$v = \frac{\gamma}{\alpha} \left(\frac{A}{K_u} \right)^{\frac{1}{2}} H. \qquad (3.2.4.14)$$

This means that a small K_u leads to a large wall mobility.   Though the hexagonal ferrites can be made in such a way that the bubble diameter is around 5 μm, the uniaxial anisotropy constant is of the order of $10^6\,\mathrm{erg\,cm^{-3}}$ which leads to domain walls and bubble velocities that are too narrow and too low, respectively.   The same applies to MnBi layers.   The bubble size, as is shown in Fig. 3.2.4.27, is very small, too small with respect to today's photolithographic capabilities.   Moreover, the large anisotropy constant leads to slow wall motion.   Adding a third component to MnBi eventually might result in films with much lower anistropy constants and saturation magnetizations.

When it became clear that materials with a natural uniaxial anisotropy could not be used for bubble applications, because bubble mobility and size did not satisfy the requirements, interest started to concentrate on cubic materials which have no uniaxial anisotropy for symmetry reasons. However, it was expected that by proper preparation techniques or appropriate substitutions in the lattice these materials could be made uniaxial.

Rare earth garnet materials were selected, since previous experiments showed that the physical parameters of these materials could be easily modified. The resulting parameters were in the preferred region of 5 μm bubble size and had large mobility. Garnets have the general formula

$$M_{3-y-z}N_yP_zGa_xFe_{5-x}O_{12}$$

in which M, N and P are rare earth ions, Ga can also be replaced by Al. By properly choosing the constituents of the garnet compound, it is possible to tailor the important physical parameters: the saturation magnetization M_s and its temperature dependence, the uniaxial anisotropy constant K_u and its temperature dependence and the damping constant α. Up to now a vast amount of literature describing a wealth of different garnet compositions exists. The essential results will be summarized in the following subsections.

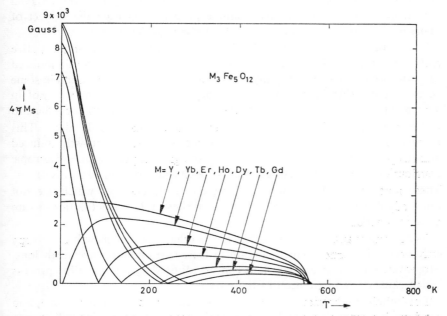

FIG. 3.2.4.28. Temperature dependence of the saturation magnetization $4\pi M_s$ of different garnet materials.

(i) *Saturation magnetization* M_s *of garnets.* In garnets the net magnetizations of the iron sublattice and the rare earth sublattice are opposite to each other due to the antiferromagnetic coupling. At a certain temperature the sublattice magnetizations exactly balance each other and the net magnetization becomes zero. This temperature is called the compensation point (T_{cp}) and depends upon the rare earth ions present (Fig. 3.2.4.28).

Below the compensation point the magnetization is mainly due to the rare earth ions, whereas above this point the Fe ions are the determining factor [3.2.90]. By choosing the proper rare earth ions, the magnetization can be adjusted. Though more important is the fact that the temperature dependence of the magnetization can be made very small by means of the rare earth content. Beyond T_{cp} the magnetization curves are rather flat and it is wise to choose a composition with a T_{cp} below room temperature. In order to obtain this, solutions of two or three rare earth ions have to be used. When the proper T_{cp} is chosen, the magnetization might still be too large. A reduction of $4\pi M_s$ can be obtained by replacing the Fe ions by non-magnetic Ga or Al ions and this will have no large influence on the position of T_{cp}.

(ii) *Uniaxial anisotropy constant* K_u *of garnets.* Garnets are cubic and have four equivalent easy [111] axes and, under normal circumstances, no uniaxial anisotropy. Yet many garnet platelets and epitaxial layers show uniaxial anisotropy. The cause for this desirable property has been the subject of many investigations, and many possible mechanisms have been found.

The lattice constant of an epitaxial layer usually will not fit the lattice constant of the GGG substrate. Due to this lattice mismatch a strain induced anisotropy can occur in the epilayer. This anisotropy has been found in some cases, but in other layers the sign of the anisotropy constant was not in agreement with the strain in the epilayer and the magnetostriction coefficient. It became evident that another mechanism must play a role also. This mechanism is generally indicated with the expression "growth induced anisotropy". One believes that simply by the growth process an anisotropic distribution of ions in the garnets occurs which leads to a uniaxial anisotropy. These ions can be Pb impurities from the melt, Ga ions which are not randomly distributed over the dodecahedral sites in the garnet lattice or rare earth ions which form pairs preferentially.

The last mechanism is supported by the fact that a certain growth anisotropy only occurs in garnets which contain at least two or more rare earth ions. Moreover, the anisotropy constant can be adjusted by an annealing process which causes a redistribution of the ions.

For bubble applications garnet compositions with a zero magnetostriction are desirable, since then the danger is small that wafer processing will change the anisotropy constant. However, for ion implantation processing a negative magnetostriction is required. All garnet compositions have negative magneto-striction constants except for those with Eu and Tb ions. A zero λ composition therefore must contain some of these ions [3.2.91].

(iii) *Damping constant.* By able material engineering it is possible to adjust M_s and K_u in such a way that the bubble size is around 5 μm and that the bubble walls are as wide as possible to warrant a large wall mobility. Yet different materials satisfying the above requirements will often show different wall mobilities, because the damping constant α is different. As shown by experiments [3.2.92], the damping constant is a function of the kind of rare earth ions and the Ga or Al content. In the following sequence, α increases from left to right—Eu, Tm, Yb, Er, Nd, Pr, Sm, Dy, Ho, Tb. Large mobility materials cannot contain many elements from Nd to Tb according to this list. The effect of Ga on the mobility is favourable, though the underlying mechanism is not quite clear [3.2.93].

(iv) *Outlook.* It has been proven that garnet epitaxial layers can be fabricated which can be tailored to device requirements with great precision. Also, the growth method LPE is so well developed that reproducibility is no longer a severe problem. This leads to the expectation that small serial memories can be fabricated today at reasonable cost. The main advantage of bubble memories over semiconductor memories is their non-volatility of information. Not clear at the time of writing (1975) is whether or not large bubble memories as replacements of disks can be made in the future. The lack of reproducibility and homogeneity and the crystal defect density of large garnet wafers might prevent large scale application of bubble memories in the future. It does not seem that the newly introduced amorphous layer will change this situation very much.

3.3. FERROELECTRIC MATRIX MEMORIES

3.3.1. INTRODUCTION

When a dielectric material is placed in an electric field the electrostatic dipoles, when present, will try to align parallel to the electric field. Alignment is opposed by the thermal motion of the atoms. Analogous to the magnetization of a magnetic material we can define a dielectric polarization P. The electric flux density D is related to P by

$$D = \varepsilon_0 E + P \qquad (3.3.1)$$

in which ε_0 is the dielectric constant of vacuum and E is the electric field. When the temperature is not too low and the electric field is not too high, the polarization is proportional to the electric field for most materials.

When the electric field is switched off the thermal activation restores the random orientation of the electric dipoles, so that the resultant polarization becomes zero. The electric flux density D can be expressed by

$$D = \varepsilon_0\,\varepsilon_r\,E \qquad (3.3.2)$$

in which the ε_r is the relative dielectric constant. When the electric flux density D is plotted as a function of the electric field with the help of an oscilloscope, a straight line is observed for most materials.

However, some materials show a different behaviour. When such materials are subjected to an electric field by sandwiching them between two electrodes the P–E loop shows hysteresis as shown in Fig. 3.3.1 [3.3.1]. At zero field two polarization states are possible, and that the possibility of using ferroelectric materials for computer stores is self evident. However, the advantages of magnetic materials in comparison to ferroelectric materials were so convincing that not much applied research has been done on ferroelectric stores and they are not used in any computer application presently.

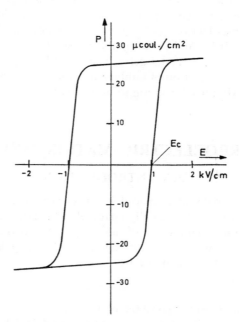

FIG. 3.3.1. Relation between the polarization P and the electric field E of a ferroelectric BaTiO$_3$ single crystal platelet (50 c/s) [3.3.1].

3.3.2 FERROELECTRICITY

The most well-known and thoroughly studied ferroelectric material is barium titanate ($BaTiO_3$) but some one hundred other compounds are also known to show hysteresis [3.3.2]. Figure 3.3.2 shows the cubic unit cell of barium titanate. The barium ions are on the corners of the cubic lattice and the oxygen ions are in the centres of the planes. Above the so-called Curie-point, which for $BaTiO_3$ is 120°C the titanium ion is in the centre of the unit cell.

Below the Curie point the titanium ion is displaced from the centre toward one of the six face centres. The centre of gravity of the negative charges no longer coincides with that of the positive charges and a net dipole moment occurs. Above the Curie point the net moment is zero. The reason for the Ti displacement is as follows. When at a certain temperature the Ti ion is displaced by thermal agitation, a dipole moment occurs causing a small internal field at the location of the Ti-ion. If the temperature is below the Curie point, then this internal field is large enough to overcome the thermal agitation, and a permanent displacement of the Ti-ion results. As the internal field also acts on neighbouring Ti-ions, domains occur in which all the electric dipole moments are parallel in one of the six possible directions in $BaTiO_3$. The domains are separated by domain walls and depending on the polarization on opposite sides of the wall, 90° or 180° walls will occur. When an electric field is applied, the domains in which the direction of the electric polarization is closest to the field direction will enlarge at the expense of the other domains until the whole crystal is saturated. Since the polarization remains in the easy direction closest to the field direction, hysteresis occurs. The polarization can be changed by an electric field opposite to the polarization and this occurs at the coercive force of the ferroelectric material.

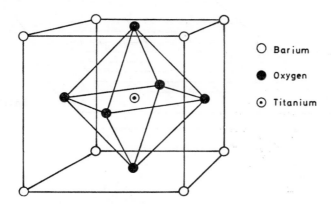

○ Barium

● Oxygen

◉ Titanium

FIG. 3.3.2. Cubic unit cell of $BaTiO_3$ above the Curie point (120°C). The titanium ion is in the centre of the oxygen octahedron.

3.3.3. FERROELECTRIC MEMORY SYSTEM

When the two remanent polarization states are used to present the digit "0" and "1", a word-organized random access memory can be constructed as shown in Fig. 3.3.3. A thin sheet of ferroelectric material which has a square hysteresis loop perpendicular to its plane, is covered on one side with bit electrodes normal to the word conductors. The information is stored in an element by coincidence of two voltage pulses, neither of which is sufficient to change the polarization state because of the rectangularity of the hysteresis loop. At each bit location the information can be stored by choosing the appropriate word and bit lines. Reading is not done by the coincidence of voltage pulses, but by applying one large voltage pulse to one word line thereby reversing all bits on the word line back to the "0" state. When the element is in the "0" state initially, the polarization change is small and so is the current through the load resistor. However, if the element is initially in the "1" state, the current will be large.

The main advantage of a ferroelectric store is its simple structure. The essential part consists only of a thin ferroelectric slab with electrodes at both sides. With the help of modern photolithography the electrodes can be as narrow as 5 μm. When the distance between the electrodes is chosen to be 5 μm, also a bit density of 10^4 mm^{-2} seems attainable.

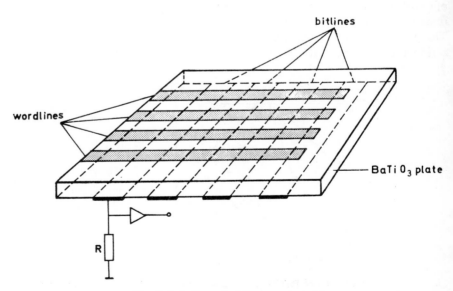

FIG. 3.3.3. Ferroelectric memory matrix.

Notwithstanding the "on first sight" appealing features of such a ferro-electric memory such memories are not incorporated in any computer system as of now. Some of the main reasons for this situation will be discussed in the next section.

3.3.4. UNDESIRABLE FERROELECTRIC PROPERTIES

In a ferrite core information is stored by the coincidence of two half select currents. In a ferroelectric cell writing would be performed by the coincidence of two voltage pulses. The sum of the voltage pulses must lead to a field that is larger than the critical electric field E_c, (Fig. 3.3.1), whereas one field pulse must be smaller. For proper memory operation one desires, that at electric fields below E_c, no polarization changes occur even when a large number of such pulses are applied. The E_c field should be a true threshold field. As discussed in Section 3.2.2. the coercive force in ferri-magnetic materials appears to be such a true threshold.

In order to be able to use ferroelectric materials for coincidence voltage memories, it was necessary to investigate the nature of the critical electric field. For this reason Merz [3.3.2] measured the switching time for a "0"

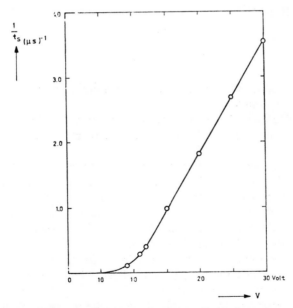

FIG. 3.3.4. Reciprocal switching time $1/t_s$ versus applied voltage for a 75 μm BaTiO$_3$ platelet [3.3.2].

to "1" reversal as a function of the electric field for $BaTiO_3$ and found the curve shown in Fig. 3.3.4. At first sight the relation between the inverse switching time and the applied voltage seems to be a straight line intersecting with the voltage axis at a certain threshold voltage similar to the situation with ferrite cores. However, when the low voltage part of the curve is more accurately examined, it appears that the curve bends toward the origin. This means that when a very small voltage is applied for a sufficiently long time, the ferroelectric cell will change its information. In a ferroelectric memory very long pulses will not occur, but because writing is performed by voltage coincidence, a neighbouring cell might be subjected to a large number of half select voltage pulses and these pulses will change the polarization state. Because of the absence of a real threshold, the disturb sensitivity of the ferroelectric memory cell is very large. The hysteresis loop of Fig. 3.3.1 is obtained with a 50 Hz alternating field. When the frequency is decreased, E_c would also decrease.

When the inverse of the switching time t_s is plotted as a function of the inverse of the electric field, a straight line is obtained. This indicates, that the relation between t_s and E has the following form

$$t_s = t_0 \exp(\alpha/E) \tag{3.3.3}$$

in which α and t_0 are constants. The relation does not contain a threshold voltage in contrast to the relation for the switching time of ferrite cores:

$$t_s = S_w \frac{1}{(H - H_c)} . \tag{3.3.4}$$

The absence of a threshold is the most serious limitation to the construction of ferroelectric memory cells.

Other disadvantages have to do with the magnitude of the voltage pulse, the switching time, the high losses and the temperature and pressure sensitivity.

The electric field necessary to reverse a cell is of the order of $1–10\,kV\,cm^{-1}$. The ferroelectric layer must be made very thin ($\approx 10\,\mu m$) to allow voltages compatible with modern electronic circuitry. The preparation of sufficiently thin platelets large enough to contain enough memory cells, is a very difficult technological problem. Perhaps in the future thin layers can be made by the sputter process or by epitaxial growth.

Ferroelectric materials are usually employed for piezoelectric transducers, because they show a large piezoelectric effect. Therefore, the mounting of ferroelectric memory matrices has to be done with great care otherwise the physical properties would be changed. Also the temperature must be controlled, first because the Curie point is rather low (120°C) which leads to a large temperature sensitivity of the saturation polarization and the critical field, secondly because the memory is heated by the switching of the cells and the losses are quite high (10^{-9} Joule/cycle).

Also from an electrical point of view the ferroelectric memory does not appear very attractive. The impedance of a cell is large; in fact it is a small capacitor with a high ε_r (≈ 1000) dielectric medium. The cell is a two terminal device which requires diode or transistor isolation to decouple the cells from one another [3.3.3]. Moreover, because the ferroelectric cells are capacitive, unwanted signals are easily picked up at the output.

Summarizing, it does not appear probable that, except for a few special applications, the ferroelectric memory can seriously compete with the present ferrite core and semiconductor matrix memories. Even the discovery of new ferroelectric materials or new processes for making thin layers probably will not change this situation.

3.4. SEMICONDUCTOR MEMORIES

3.4.1. INTRODUCTION

Magnetic matrix memories, although very useful in computer systems, suffer from a number of disadvantages. A major difficulty arises when attempts are made to integrate magnetic structures. When the volume of magnetic material used to store information is reduced, the associated output signals become very small and, due to coupling between bits, the memory is prone to spurious signals. For packaging and speed it is desirable to have the memory as small as possible which, in view of the former effect, creates a conflict. A compromise has been reached in which rather expensive addressing and sensing transistor circuits are employed. These circuits become economically justifiable only when the capacity of the memory is very large. Until recently such magnetic memories—particularly cores—dominated the memory market. Advances in the area of integrated circuits and semiconductor technology, however, have made it possible to produce monolithic semiconductor memories which are now economically competitive with cores in most computer systems. Since the storage elements can be made electrically and physically compatible with the peripheral circuits, in a semiconductor memory the need for interfacing circuitry—a major cost factor in magnetic systems—is eliminated. This compatibility represents a prime motivation for interest in semiconductor devices. Furthermore, since a semiconductor storage cell consists of a few microelectronic transistors, its construction can be smaller than a core element. This has the result that it is possible to integrate a large number of these cells on a single semiconductor chip; in some cases even with peripheral circuits. This allows the construction of small versatile memory building blocks which can be combined to form a variety of more complicated systems. The organization of representative semiconductor memories will be discussed in Section 3.4.2.

The nature of the storage elements and circuit layouts allows devices to be constructed which have cycle times much smaller than cores and which have higher readout signal levels (and consequently are less prone to noise). Unfortunately, unlike a magnetic core, the semiconductor memory cell usually requires standby power to maintain its stored information. This can cause heat dissipation difficulties when the density of bits is extremely high and means that when power is lost the stored data goes with it. The volatility of a semiconductor memory is a problem and so far has been a factor in limiting the size and the use of semiconductor systems. Experimental non-volatile semiconductor devices which are currently under development are unlikely to resolve this problem in the near future since they switch very slowly and, therefore, are only suited for special purpose applications.

While it is still too early to predict where integrated circuits and the associated technologies will make the most impact in computers, it is clear that semiconductor memories offer an irresistible alternative to magnetic matrix systems particularly in view of the past research investment which has been made in the area of micro-electronics. Integrated circuits have a strong foundation in solid state physics, are amenable to batch or simultaneous processing, and can be used to perform almost any function required in electronics. As an added benefit the production of the associated geometrical patterns by photolithographic means can be automated and the pattern itself can be designed with the aid of a computer. These features supply further incentive to the development of monolithic semiconductor memories.

At the present time major interest in planar integrated circuits for memory applications is centred around two different transistor types. They are the bipolar and p-channel MOS structures both of which, along with the less popular complementary MOS structure, will be discussed in more detail in Sections 3.4.4 and 3.4.6. While the principles of operation of these devices are entirely different, their fabrication requires the same basic technological processes—epitaxial growth, diffusion, oxidation, and metallization. In both cases the memories consist of repetitive arrays of dense cells.

In general, the bipolar ICs require more process steps than the p-MOS circuits but due to their higher switching speed and current driving capabilities they are faster. This assures them a niche in the memory market. Whereas the components in a bipolar IC require an isolation diffusion, the MOS structure is inherently self-isolating which means that MOS ICs can be made with higher circuit densities. In terms of semiconductor memories this in conjunction with the fewer processing steps means low cost per bit. Hence MOS memories look like they will make their impact in the low cost and slow speed segment of the memory market. Complementary MOS ICs (hybrid *p*-channel and *n*-channel devices) cannot compete with the low cost of *p*-MOS circuits or the speed of bipolar circuits. C-MOS cell density is roughly that of a bipolar device and its speed is between bipolar and *p*-MOS devices. C-MOS memory cells, however, have the virtue that they dissipate microwatts as opposed to milliwatts for bipolar cells and hundreds of microwatts for *p*-MOS cells. This property of C-MOS insures its use in low standby power applications. A method to decrease the standby power of either bipolar or MOS memories is to interrupt the power supply. Out of this technique has evolved the dynamic memory which, in contrast to the static memory, is based upon refreshing stored information between read and write cycles. In Section 3.4.3 both bipolar and MOS memory cells will be discussed as well as dynamic and static operation.

The two main bipolar and *p*-MOS transistor structures and the special purpose C-MOS structure have been used in a number of memory organizations. Any one of many semiconductor technologies in conjunction with the basic transistor types can be used to construct these memories. The choice depends upon the application and to a large degree upon cost.

In Section 3.4.5 serial memories called charge coupled devices (CCD) are discussed, which physically consist of serially inter-connected storage cells. The operation of these devices is based on the storage and controlled transport of charge clouds along the surface in MOS type structures.

3.4.2. SEMICONDUCTOR MEMORY ORGANIZATION

3.4.2.1. Random Access Read-write Matrix Memory

Semiconductor random access read-write memories (RAM) can be constructed in direct analogy with magnetic matrix memories [3.4.1]. The magnetic storage cell is replaced by the semiconductor equivalent which is either a transistor flip-flop in the case of a static cell or a capacitor-transistor combination when a dynamic mode of storage is used (see Section 3.4.3.).

The same functional elements—decoder, word driver, bit driver and read amplifier—as used in magnetic systems are required in connection with these storage cells. The 3D and 2D organizations found in magnetic memories can also be applied to semiconductor systems. The trend seems to be to use the 2D-organization at the chip level and to use these basic building blocks in a kind of 3D-organization to construct memory systems of different sizes. Figure 3.4.2.1 shows a block diagram of a semiconductor RAM array organized as N words by M-bits or $P = N \times M$ words by 1 bit.

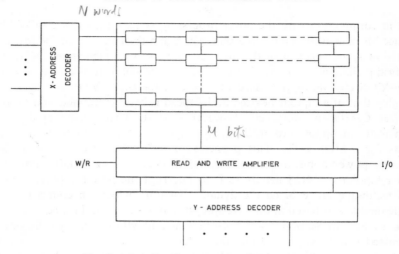

FIG. 3.4.2.1. Random access read-write memory.

Each memory cell in the two dimensional array may be accessed through the corresponding X and Y select lines. The selection of these lines is determined by a binary coded address. The selection of a particular bit allows information to be read in and out of it via the write and sense amplifier shown associated with the Y select lines in Fig. 3.4.2.1. In general the readout is designed to be non-destructive but this mode of operation is not required.

Most memory cells are capable of both non-destructive (NDRO) and destructive readout (DRO). As was mentioned previously, the basic cell can be a transistor flip-flop or a capacitor-transistor combination. In the latter case the state of the cell is determined by the charge on the capacitor. Since the charge decays with time, it becomes necessary to refresh it at periodic intervals. This requires additional circuitry which is not shown in Fig. 3.4.2.1. Memory devices which operate in this way are referred to as being dynamic (as opposed to static, see Section 3.4.3.). The block diagram of Fig. 3.4.2.1. remains essentially unchanged for these memories because the refresh operation can be combined with the read and write functions. On the whole between refresh operations the dynamic memory works just like a static one. The great advantage of the dynamic memory is, however, that the storage cell can be made very small. As many as 1024 fully decoded bits have been put on a single chip using p-channel MOS devices. This is to be compared with 512 decoded bits for the corresponding static memory.

The basic building block in Fig. 3.4.2.1. can be expanded to a P word Q bit memory by connecting the address lines and read/write controls for Q blocks in parallel. The addition of a chip select control in conjunction with a decoder allows simple expansion of the word size. When high speed not-too-large memories are required, bipolar transistor memory cells are used. The slower and less expensive dynamic MOS RAMs are ideally suited for main internal memory application [3.4.2].

3.4.2.2. The Random Access Matrix Memory with Serial Cell Store and the Serial Associative Memory

The matrix memory cells discussed in combination with the RAM and to be discussed in future sections each store one bit whether it be in a transistor flip-flop or in a capacitor in a dynamic cell. In this section a slightly different viewpoint is taken by allowing each matrix cell to contain a large number of serially organized subcells [3.4.3]. The basis of the discussion is the semiconductor shift register which will be described first.

A semiconductor shift register consists of a series of adjacent memory cells interconnected so that information may be transferred from one cell to another [3.4.4]. Fig. 3.4.2.2 shows a block diagram of a two phase shift register. The basic cells are similar to those used in static or dynamic RAMs (i.e. are flip-flops or capacitors) and are all identical. Information stored in cell 1 is transferred via an inverter or an equivalent circuit arrangement to cell 2 when a phase 1 clock pulse is applied. This bit may be shifted to cell 3 by a phase 2 pulse and so forth. A continuous sequence of pulses causes data to move from one end of the device to the other as in an acoustic delay line. If the memory cells are of the static type, the transfer may be stopped at any time without a loss of data. If the data is recirculated it can be stored indefinitely in a dynamic mode. In the latter case the block diagram for the memory is identical to that given in Fig. 2.1.1 (p. 17) but with the driver-delay-line amplifier combination replaced by a recirculating shift register. This type of system is ideally suited for integration since the geometry of the shift register is simple and repetitive and since the number of input-output contacts is small due to the form of organization.

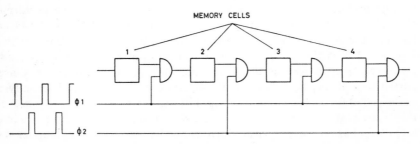

FIG. 3.4.2.2. Block diagram of a two-phase shift register.

N

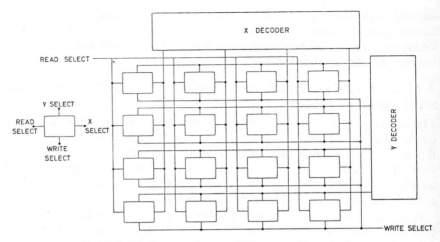

FIG. 3.4.2.3. Large scale sequential memory organization.

Depending on the technology involved, the capacity of an integrated circuit shift register can range from 4 bits per chip for a bipolar device to 1024 for a dynamic MOS register. Including the peripheral circuitry decreases the latter figure by roughly a factor of 2 which still allows low cost memory production. While the current price of a few cents per bit for MOS devices is high compared to that for drum and disk memories (0.01 cent per bit) it is expected to decrease in the future, allowing large capacity systems of this type to become competitive in the millisecond to microsecond range applications. Figure 3.4.2.3 shows a convenient form of organization for a large capacity shift register memory [3.4.5]. This arrangement allows expansion in multiples of the basic chip capacity with no increase in access time. The structure is essentially that of a random access matrix memory with the basic cell replaced by a sequential memory. For this matrix organization it is necessary for each cell to have X and Y selects which, when simultaneously chosen, enable the read and write operations to be performed. This chip select function can be introduced by connecting an AND gate between the X and Y lines and feeding the output into the R/W enable in Fig. 3.4.2.3. Although not shown, all the chip inputs and outputs for the memory plane, as well as the phase lines, are connected together. Once a particular cell has been located, the operation of the device is exactly the same as that for a simple recirculating shift register memory. An advantage of this type of large scale memory over a disk or drum magnetic store lies in the fact that it has no moving parts which eliminates the problem of maintenance. Unfortunately, however, the information stored is volatile which represents a handicap in large systems. Reducing the cost per bit of such a large scale serial semiconductor memory to that comparable to the cost per bit of magnetic surface storage will require dramatic developments in MOS technology; more than likely the choice between the two forms of storage will be based upon alternative factors. There is a need in information handling systems to be able to retrieve stored data on the basis of content rather than location. This is particularly true in data processing systems in applications such as sorting, merging and pattern recognition.

As was mentioned previously in connection with acoustic delay lines (Chapter 2), the serial mode of operation can be used to construct associative or content addressable memories. Since the shift register performs like a delay line and has the further advantage that the bit rate can be varied (when static cells are employed the data transfer may even be stopped) it would appear well-suited for this application. Figure 3.4.2.4 shows a block diagram for a serial associative memory. The operation of this device is extremely simple. As stored data becomes available at the output of the shift registers it is compared with the input information and when a match occurs the address is read out. If the input information contains only a part of a word and a match occurs the circulation may be stopped and the balance of the stored information may be read out. The disadvantage of this form of organization is that a complete search takes N/f_B seconds where N is the number of words in the registers and f_B is the bit rate (bits/sec). When N is large corresponding to optimum conditions for integration, the search time

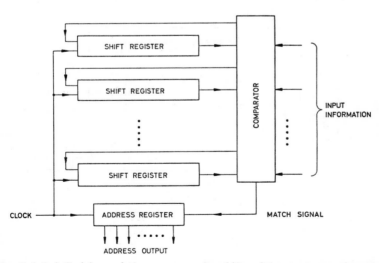

FIG. 3.4.2.4. Serial associative memory using shift registers as storage elements.

becomes rather long. For a MOS register ($f_B = 1$ MHz) with 256 bits the average access time is roughly 10^{-4} s, which is long by most memory standards. For this reason the more favourable matrix (random access) form of organization is used where high speed is desired. Since most associative memories are currently used in applications connected with the central processor, bipolar transistors are found exclusively in these arrays.

3.4.2.3. The Associative or Content-addressable Matrix Memory

The usual way of retrieving stored data on the basis of content involves taking information out of storage, looking at it quickly and returning it to storage—all of which takes time. Serial devices offer a convenient method of implementing this search but, by virtue of device physics and the serial configuration, are limited in speed. With parallel access to the memory cells allowed by the matrix form of organization, the delay time associated with serial operation can be eliminated.

Incorporating the comparison circuitry at the cell level further reduces the search time. Figure 3.4.2.5 shows a block diagram for an associative memory or associative processor [3.4.6]. Parallel access allows interrogation of all bits simultaneously, clearly an advantage over the one-by-one word search used in sequential processing. The operation of the memory depends on the state of the basic associative cells each of which are the same and which, invariably, are a modification of a transistor flip-flop circuit. Infor-

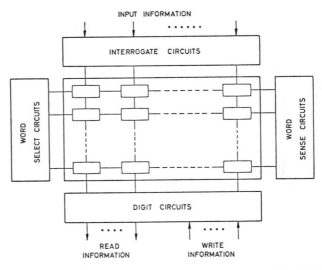

FIG. 3.4.2.5. Block diagram of associative memory or associative processor.

mation to be located in the associative memory may consist of any number of bits up to that contained in a word and enters the array through the interrogate circuits. Comparison logic at the cell level produces an output or a number of outputs at the word level indicating where matches have been obtained. These signals are sensed by the word circuits and this information is used in subsequent control operations. When the input information contains only a small portion of a word, a large number of outputs may occur. Since the corresponding group of words have in common a particular characteristic, the memory in this case may be regarded as an associative processor. New data may be read in and out of the array via the word and digit circuits just as in a random access matrix memory. Structurally, the associative matrix memory may be regarded as a RAM with additional interrogate, logic and sense circuits. The necessary control and decoding circuits have not been shown in Fig. 3.4.2.5 because they generally are not included with the array on a single chip. A major obstacle in the development of these memories has been cell size. As was mentioned previously, for high speed it is desirable to integrate the logic for detecting the mismatch between stored data and input information with the memory array. As a result even a chip with no peripheral circuitry can accommodate only a few cells which accounts in part for the high cost per bit of associative memories found today. Low cost MOS arrays which offer the highest bit densities are slow compared to their bipolar counterparts and for this reason are generally considered inferior. Efforts to develop a fast associative memory have yielded practical bipolar devices with typically 16–64 bits per chip. When a number of these devices are connected to expand the capacity, it is possible to construct very useful systems.

One of the most attractive applications of the associative memory lies in the area of memory interfacing. Many large commercial computers use a bipolar associative memory to establish liaison between a semiconductor scratch-pad memory and a slower large capacity semiconductor or core backup memory [3.4.7]. The principle of operation stems from the realization that if by arrangement desired information is always or nearly always found in the scratch-pad memory, the effective access time will be that of the faster device. By continually shifting blocks of information from the backup memory to the scratch-pad memory it is possible to arrange such a situation. It is necessary to know which blocks are currently held in the semiconductor memory. This information is stored in a coded form in an associative memory which is always consulted before going to the back-up memory. If a sought address produces a match in the associative memory, which is what generally happens, the machine goes directly to the scratch-pad memory to retrieve information thereby avoiding the backup memory entirely. The basis of this type of operation depends on the fact that the most recently used blocks are likely to contain any requested data and that these blocks are always stored in the scratch-pad memory. Similar techniques can be used to keep recently used words quickly available.

3.4.2.4. The Read only Matrix Memory

In the content-addressable or associative matrix memory a portion of each word is interrogated and on the basis of the resulting output signals the location of the desired word or words is found. The stored bits in each word are used to convert the interrogate signals to an output pulse pattern which indicates where coincidence occurs. "Ones" appear at the addresses of words which match the input information and "zeros" elsewhere. The presence of the stored information establishes a fixed relationship between the input and output signals. In an associative memory this relationship changes when new data is written into the memory array. In contrast, in the read only memory (ROM) the relationship is maintained permanently by fixing the state of each cell. As a consequence only a very simple storage element such as a diode or transistor is required. The information is built into the array by connecting or not connecting these elements to the select lines. The small size of the memory cell makes the ROM ideally suited for large scale integration. Figure 3.4.2.6 shows a block diagram of a ROM matrix at the chip level. The peripheral input–output circuits shown may conveniently be integrated with the array. For each combination of input signals the decoder establishes an address and the information stored at that address is relayed to the output buffer. An obvious application for this type of memory is as a function generator. The value of a function can be stored at the address corresponding to the binary equivalent of the independent variable or variables. Read only memories employing this one-to-one

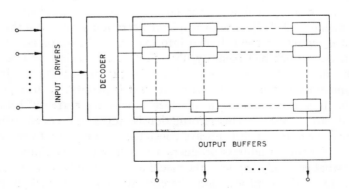

FIG. 3.4.2.6. Block diagram for read only memory.

functional concept currently perform as code converters, as logarithmic and trigonometric function generators, as character generators, and as storage for computer microprograms. From essentially the same viewpoint an output bit in a particular word position may be identified as a Boolean function of the inputs. In this sense the ROM may be regarded as an implementation of a truth table. Each of the bits in the output word can represent independent Boolean functions of the address variables. This immediately suggests that ROMs can be used for arithmetic and control logic functions. The fact that a 2048 bit read only memory is functionally equivalent to 100–200 logic gates and on a per bit basis is one of the least expensive forms of monolithic memory provides economic incentive to reorganize logic systems so that ROMs instead of arrays or assemblies of gates can be used. The compatibility of fully decoded ROMs with logic ICs further encourages the construction of such hybrid systems.

The information stored in a ROM is non-volatile in the sense that the memory array is permanently encoded—when power is supplied it will function properly. Unfortunately, in certain applications this inflexibility is not an advantage and as a result a variation of the ROM—the read mostly memory (RMM) also called reprogrammable read only memory (RePROM)—has become important [3.4.8]. The special feature of this type of memory is that the permanently stored data can be altered electrically. The distinction between an RMM and an ordinary read-write memory lies in the relative amount of time spent in the write cycle. The stored data in an RMM may be read frequently but cannot be altered at nearly the same rate. As a result the duty cycle of an RMM consists of a large number of read operations followed by infrequent data changes. The relative time spent between the read and write modes is dictated by the time constant of the write operation which in turn depends on the physical storage mechanism. One technique for constructing an RMM cell uses the charge stored in deep traps near the gate of a MOSFET to control the transistor threshold voltage. The charge can be preset by applying a gate voltage for a given duration and is retained when the voltage is removed. Charge traps are also thought to be responsible for the large conductivity changes with applied voltage observed in amorphous semiconductors which are now being used in conjunction with diodes in experimental RMM arrays.

By applying a preset voltage across the terminals of an amorphous semiconductor the material can be put into a high or low conductivity state analogous to the off or on state of a transistor. The ability to control electrically the RMM is particularly useful in microprogramming which will probably become the most important application for these devices. Data stored in a RMM can be programmed, read and reprogrammed rapidly with the advantage that it is non-volatile. Another very interesting application is in the area of computer design. Instead of using an ROM in preliminary design stages where fixed data is required it may be convenient to substitute an alterable equivalent.

Another version of an ROM is the programmable read only memory or PROM. This device is used when only small quantities of ROMs are required and the cost of generating special masks for the manufacturing of the devices is prohibitive. The PROMs are programmed by selectively and irreversibly changing connections or diodes in the matrix and this can be performed by the customer himself. Once the PROM is programmed it behaves exactly as an ROM.

3.4.3. MEMORY CELLS AND THEIR OPERATION

3.4.3.1. Introduction

The great asset of an all semiconductor memory is that the memory cell can be made compatible with the drivers and sense amplifiers which in turn can be made compatible with the system logic. There are a number of other considerations related to the cell and the system which determine whether or not a particular cell design is suited for large-scale integration. Foremost is the cell size (area) because it determines the cost per bit which determines whether or not the memory will be competitive. It is desirable to have the cell small so that the same process steps (and materials) are spread over a larger number of bits. Furthermore when the cell is small, the peripheral circuits can be included on the same chip as the array which is advantageous from a speed standpoint. Since integration of the memory cell introduces variations in the circuit parameters for large chip yields, it is important to design the cell to be insensitive to these fluctuations. Cell simplicity is a virtue both from the design and size viewpoints. At the high bit densities made possible by LSI, power dissipation becomes another important factor. A promising cell dissipates very little power thereby eliminating the need for special cooling. A somewhat contradictory requirement is that the cell output signal be large enough to drive the sensing circuits quickly—the capacitive loading of the array lines should not limit the performance. Finally in the same vein, the switching time of the cell should be fast so that it does not become a limiting factor. All of the cells to be described in this chapter have these important features. They can be subdivided into two classes on the basis of their mode of operation. In a static cell the stored information is represented by a discrete variable such as the voltage on the node of a flip-flop. So long as the power to the cell is maintained this parameter does not change and the information is retained indefinitely. In a dynamic cell the discrete variable is replaced by a continuous one such as the voltage on a slowly discharging capacitor. The voltages corresponding to the

"0" and "1" states are chosen with sufficient margin to allow partial decay of the capacitor before the state must be re-established. In contrast to the static cell, isolating a dynamic cell for an extended period of time causes a loss of information. Such dynamic cells are closely related to dynamic shift registers and are the subject of Section 3.4.3.3. A permanently encoded memory cell can be regarded as a special case of the static cell because information is stored in discrete states and may be retrieved indefinitely so long as power is maintained. Since such cells have by far the simplest configuration, we begin by considering them.

3.4.3.2. Static Memory Cells

(i) *ROM diode cell.* Monolithic semiconductor read only memories are commonly constructed using diodes and transistors as circuit elements. The presence or absence of an element between two lines establishes the stored information. Figure 3.4.3.1 shows a two dimensional diode array. One can distinguish between two types of cells in this array. The "1" and "0" cells are outlined by dashed perimeters. The formation of one or another of these cells at a particular location usually starts with the construction of a fully populated array. Either at a masking stage or after production the diodes to become "0's" are opened. The high initial cost of making custom masks favours the latter approach. Techniques for opening the metal lines include chemical etching, scratching and vaporizing. Burning out the metal lines may be done electrically as in a fusible ROM or by high intensity light

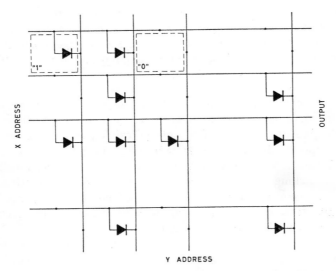

FIG. 3.4.3.1. Read only memory array with diode storage elements.

as in a laser produced ROM. Both of these approaches lend themselves to automated production [3.4.9].

The operation of the array shown in Fig. 3.4.3.1 is very simple. If a fixed current is applied to a particular cell the voltage drop across its terminals indicates whether the circuit is continuous or not. An individual cell may be singled out by driving an x line with a constant current source and holding a y line at a low voltage so that it acts like a current sink. Since the system is arranged so that the cells only conduct when accessed, no standby power is required, which is a favourable situation. The interest in large capacity diodes as well as other semiconductor ROM arrays has been limited by the fabrication techniques. The cost per bit of programmed arrays rises sharply with size. A recently reported silicon on sapphire SOS diode array has been built with a conservative 1024 bits on a 220 mil square chip. The cell size was 4.5×4.5 mils which could probably be reduced by a factor of two or four. This would make it possible to place 4096 bits on a chip of approximately the same size. The power dissipated by a selected diode is on the order of 0.28 mW. Since a good portion of the array involves "0's" this figure places an upper limit on the cell dissipation. The access time of the array alone is on the order of 50 ns with a 100 ns cycle time. A 1024 word 32 bit module using these SOS arrays with bipolar peripheral circuits has an access time of 300 ns and a cycle time of 500 ns. The unit occupies 20 cubic inches and dissipates three watts of power. The low capacitance of an SOS diode in conjunction with bipolar driving and sensing circuits makes this memory potentially faster than an all bipolar system. Whereas isolation is a problem with bipolar memory cells due to parasitic capacitances this is not the case for SOS devices. A further advantage of an SOS ROM array is that it is highly radiation resistant. Unfortunately, these advantages come at a rather high price due to the complexity of SOS technology and due to the difficulties of encoding.

(ii) *ROM ovonic cell.* The methods described previously for programming the array produce irreversible changes in the interconnection pattern. These permanent changes make the ROM both inflexible and inconvenient from a device standpoint. It would be far more convenient if the array could be reprogrammed at will, particularly if this could be done electrically. The reversible switching characteristics of amorphous semiconductor materials promise this type of operation [3.4.10]. So far only an experimental 256 bit (16×16) integrated hybrid array of amorphous and crystalline devices on a 131×122 mil^2 chip has been constructed.

Each memory cell consists of a series combination of an $p–n$ junction diode and an ovonic switch and all cells are the same. Each ovonic device consists of a film of amorphous semiconductor material between two molybdenum electrodes and has stable high and low resistance states which can be electrically activated. The purpose of the series diodes in this case is to provide cell isolation. When some ovonic devices are on (low resistance) and the others are off (high resistance) the circuit arrangement is equivalent to that shown in Fig. 3.4.3.1 and the operation is similar to a conventional monolithic diode array. The array access time is found to be about 65 ns. Programming the array can be done by external equipment or by the drive circuitry of the system itself. A low resistance state may be obtained in a particular cell by delivering about 10^{-4} J to the ovonic device in a few milliseconds. This can be done by driving an x-select line by a 5 mA current source at 25 V for a few milliseconds while holding the corresponding y-select line at ground and all other unselected y-lines at 25 V so as to reverse bias the remaining cells. To obtain a high resistance state the procedure is exactly the same except that a 200 mA current is required to deliver 10^{-6} J in 5 μs at 25 V. The slow switching times restrict the array to applications in which the information is frequently read but seldom altered (RMM). Tests indicate that the amorphous material in each cell can be repeatedly switched between the high and low resistance states without adverse effects, provided the composition is chosen correctly. The physics of the reversible phase transition is currently the subject of intensive research.

(iii) *ROM bipolar transistor cell.* Bipolar and MOS transistors can be used in read only memories in very nearly the same way as diodes [3.4.11]. Because the transistor is a three terminal device the diode configuration

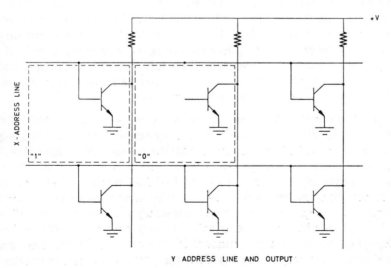

FIG. 3.4.3.2. Transistor read only memory organization.

cannot be used. Figure 3.4.3.2 shows how a bipolar transistor ROM can be organized.

Two types of cell can be distinguished just as for diode arrays. In the "0" cell the base of the transistor is disconnected from the x-address line. This may be accomplished by using any of the techniques discussed in connection with the diode array. Since in a "1" cell the transistor base is connected to an x-address line, accessing the cell by raising the line potential causes an increase in the current flowing through the series load resistor which can be detected by the change in its voltage drop. When no base connection exists, the impedance of the cell remains high and no voltage drop across the resistor occurs. If instead of encoding at the base it is done at the emitter or collector the circuit will operate under the same principles. The peripheral decoding circuits select one x-address line to drive and one y-address line to sense. The state of the cell at the coincidence of these lines determines the output. All bipolar circuitry provides extremely fast access to the stored information and due to the simplicity of the memory cell can be produced with very high bit densities. A large bipolar ROM places 4096 bits with decoding on a single chip and has a 60 ns access time.

Schottky clamping of the base collector junction helps produce this high speed (see Section 3.4.6.). The power dissipation is 0.125 mW per bit which means that the chip dissipates about 0.5 W. After packaging in a 16 pin package, probably no more than six of these devices would occupy 4 in^2; the 3 W of dissipated power does not in this case present a difficulty.

(iv) *ROM MOSFET cell.* MOS transistors can be substituted for the bipolar transistors in the array of Fig. 3.4.3.2 and it will operate under the same principles as before [3.4.12]. When MOS peripheral circuitry is employed, however, the access time rises to nearly one microsecond. Since the cell size (a fraction of a square mil) is less than that obtainable with a bipolar device and since fewer technological steps are involved in producing MOS ROMs, they are generally more economical.

(v) *FAMOS cell.* A recent development in the area of MOS-ROM technology is an electrically programmable device which uses a floating-gate avalanche injection MOS transistor (FAMOS) as a storage element [3.4.13]. A circuit schematic of a single cell is shown in Fig. 3.4.3.3. All cells in an array are physically similar. Since the FAMOS transistor behaves like a switch, the diagram has been drawn in such a way as to emphasize the similarity to an *npn* emitter (or *pnp* collector) encoded bipolar cell (see Fig. 3.4.3.2. for base encoded array). Memory operation in the read-only mode is the same as for a conventional bipolar or MOS ROM. The unique feature of this memory is the FAMOS transistor which is a normally off p-channel field effect device.

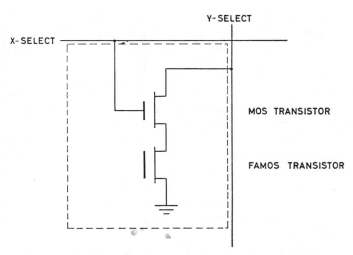

FIG. 3.4.3.3. Circuit diagram of electrically programmable memory cell.

It is constructed like a normal field effect transistor except that no electrical contact is made to the gate. The gate is formed by the deposition of poly-crystalline silicon on top of about 1000 Å of thermal oxide and is then covered by a one micron layer of vapour deposited oxide; it is therefore, completely isolated by oxide. When a large negative voltage (< -30 V) is applied to the drain of the device with the source at ground, the proximity of the floating gate to the drain causes avalanche injection of electrons through the oxide and results in the accumulation of negative charge on the gate. When this charge is sufficiently negative, it induces a p-channel inversion layer between the source and drain causing the device to have a high conductance. A -50 V, 1ms pulse on the drain causes the gate to be charged to the equivalent of -10 V on a conventional MOS transistor. After the applied voltage has been removed, the electrons on the gate are trapped by the surrounding SiO_2. The one electron volt activation energy associated with the potential well guarantees life expectancies based on 70% of the initial stored charge on the order of 10 years at 125°C and considerably longer at lower temperatures. The stored charge cannot be removed electrically but can be removed by illuminating the gate with ultraviolet or X-ray radiation either of which cause a photocurrent to flow from gate to substrate, thus restoring the initial uncharged state.

Initially a memory array consists entirely of low conductivity FAMOS transistors in series with the MOS transistors. The former devices are pro-grammed by the repeated coincident selection of x and y lines. The voltage applied to a y-line appears across the FAMOS transistor corresponding to the selected x-line and causes avalanche injection. All other memory elements are unaffected since either no pulse is applied to the y-line or the applied pulse is not transferred to the FAMOS transistor due to an open series MOS transistor on an unselected x line. In the read mode, selection of a bit is accomplished in the same way. The applied voltages are chosen smaller in magnitude so they do not inadvertently disturb the stored information. Sensing relies on the same principles employed for the bipolar array except that in this case the voltage of the y lines is multivalued to allow programming. Since examination of Fig. 3.4.3.3 reveals that it is not necessary to have the voltage source simultaneously connected to all of the y address lines for the array to operate correctly, it is common to drive only one y line at a time. Under these conditions the decoding circuitry applies either the normal read voltage or an externally generated write voltage to this line, depending on the desired mode.

An electrically programmable MOS–ROM which uses the FAMOS storage element is now commercially available. It is a fully decoded 4096 bit memory on a chip which can be operated in either the static or dynamic decoding and sensing mode. The device is fabricated using silicon gate technology (Section 3.4.4.2) which is inherently compatible with the FAMOS transistor construction as it includes formation of the polysilicon gate as a natural step in the process sequence. The memory can be read in less than 800 ns when operated in the static mode which is representative of an all MOS static system (1 μs) and can be read slightly faster (0.5 μs) in the dynamic mode. The unique features of the FAMOS storage element allow complete testing after packaging; the memory can be erased by X-radiation before shipment. Particularly important is the versatility the electrically programmable ROM offers. This type of device makes it economically feasible to produce relatively small quantities of many different patterns and therefore opens the field to applications which were once limited by the high initial costs of encoding such as associated with mask changes.

(vi) *MNOS and MAS cells.* The FAMOS storage element still suffers from the inconvenience that the high conductivity state (negative charge on the isolated gate) cannot be altered electrically. The ideal storage element should allow reversible conductivity changes to be brought about solely by electrical means as in amorphous semiconductor switching. A number of experimental devices closely related conceptually to the FAMOS element are now being studied which offer the possibility of this type of operation. Instead of using an isolated gate to store charge, these devices rely on a layer of traps in the insulating layer between the metal gate and the channel of a MOSFET. The traps can be charged or discharged by applying the appropriate potential to the gate. When the traps are occupied (by electrons) the conductivity of the channel (*p*) is high and when they are empty it is low. The parallel between the FAMOS transistor and such devices is obvious. The feasibility of this form of operation has been established by the construction of undecoded arrays of 256 bits per chip for MNOS (metal–nitride oxide–silicon) and MAS (metal–alumina–silicon) structures [3.4.14, 3.4.15]. Unfortunately, difficulties in controlling the storage dielectrics has hampered their development. The rate of charge decay from the traps is also about a thousand times faster than that from an isolated silicon gate and this causes difficulties. Once these problems are overcome, however, it is likely that this form of non-volatile semiconductor storage will become important in ROMs and possibly even in main frame and other slower, large capacity memories.

(vii) *Read-write bipolar cell.* In read-write memories it is necessary to have a storage element which can be switched rapidly from one digital state to another. The static cells used in read only memories either cannot be altered at all or can only be altered very slowly and for this reason they are not of use in such applications. From an electronics standpoint a natural choice for a two state storage element is the transistor flip-flop. Cells of this type form the basis for static read-write and associative memories and have been used in shift registers in applications where data must be retained for long periods of time without being transferred. Two basic cells are currently being used in connection with read-write memories. One configuration is optimal for bipolar transistors and the other for MOSFETs. The operational characteristics of these cells will be considered in the following paragraphs. Associative memory cells and shift register cells which rely either on slightly different sensing techniques or different cell interconnections will be discussed later.

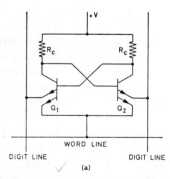 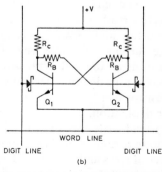

FIG. 3.4.3.4. Bipolar flip-flop memory cells: (a) emitter coupled cell and (b) Schottky diode coupled cell.

Figure 3.4.3.4(a) shows the most commonly used bipolar memory cell, the so-called emitter-coupled cell, which is nothing but a flip-flop with multiple emitter transistors arranged to allow reading and writing [3.4.1, 3.4.16]. Typically, two volts are supplied between the $+V$ terminal and the select line in the unaccessed state. The load resistors are generally made of the order of several kilohms to reduce power consumption ($\sim V^2/R_{series}$) although smaller values are used in connection with a pulsed supply technique. In standby both digit lines are held about one volt above the word select line and draw little or no current. A steady current, however, flows through one leg of the flip-flop and out the select line under these conditions. Non-destructive readout from this cell is accomplished by driving the word line positive by a few volts in which case current flow is switched from the word line to one of the digit lines depending on which transistor is conducting. The presence or absence of a signal on the digit line indicates the state of the cell. To write information into the cell, the word line is driven positive, just as for readout, but the right digit line is either held near ground to turn transistor Q_2 on or it is driven one volt or so above its standby state to turn it off. The current which flows during standby can generate several milliwatts of power loss in the cell which causes heat dissipation problems at high bit densities. Since the cell occupies about 30 mils^2 of chip area it is possible to package 1000 bits on a 150×150 mil^2 chip. The dissipation of the associated power is a consideration, therefore, for high density systems.

Array driver circuits can be constructed, however, which raise the supply voltage V from a low holding value to the normal standby level whenever a particular bit is accessed. With this technique a factor of ten in standby power can be gained. For comparison, when this type of system is used less than 100 μW per bit are required.

Another memory cell the so-called diode coupled memory cell is shown in Fig. 3.4.3.4(b). The cell is coupled to the digit lines by Schottky barrier diodes. The emitters are connected to the word selection line. Non-destructive readout from this cell is accomplished by lowering the voltage of its word line and forward biasing one of the Schottky diodes. For writing, a large current is fed into one of the bit lines through the Schottky diode which turns on the "off" transistor and turns off the "on" transistor quickly. The access time does not depend very much on the load resistor, and therefore this resistor can be larger than in the emitter coupled cell thereby reducing power dissipation.

In a read-write memory array cells of the type shown in Fig. 3.4.3.4(a) or (b) are arranged in a two dimensional matrix which may consist of any number of rows and columns. The select line and $+V$ supply input are made common to all the elements in a row, while the sense and digit lines are shared by the elements of a column. The activation of a particular select line for reading or writing causes all the cells in the corresponding row to be accessed. For reading it is necessary only to sense the output on the column sense line corresponding to the desired bit position. For writing the digit line is driven positive or negative relative to its standby value. The cells in the column which have not been selected are unaffected by these digit line pulses. The access and cycle times for a read-write memory depend on two sources of time delay. First, that which is associated with the capacitive charging and discharging of the row and column lines and with any switching delays of the cell which are referred to as array delays. This factor is strongly dependent on the size of the array through the line input capacitances. The second source of time delay is circuit delay which depends on the propagation delays of the signals through the input–output circuitry. Estimates of delays in the address decoder, word drivers and digit circuits can be made by allotting 5 ns for each logic or gain stage. For a fully decoded 1024 bit array (single chip), access times of 50 to 100 ns are typical. As a rough measure of the influence of capacity, if this chip is used as the basic building block for a larger system, these figures double for every factor of 100 in capacity. The cost per bit of this type of system is independent of size up to 100 K.

(viii) *Read-write MOSFET cell.* Static MOSFET flip-flops are also used in read-write memory arrays. They have the advantages of small cell size and of lower power dissipation over similar bipolar devices. The only circuit element required is a field effect transistor which is also used as a load. Because the multiple emitter access technique cannot be used for MOS

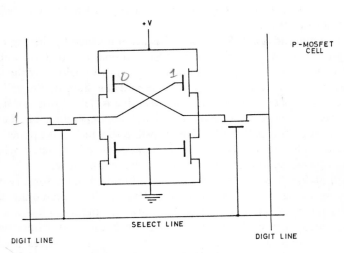

FIG. 3.4.3.5. *p*-Channel MOSFET memory cell.

o

devices, it is necessary to employ two additional transistors to connect the flip-flop to the bit lines. These transistors are used as bidirectional gates performing an AND function between the cell select line and, depending on the operation, either the digit line (write) or the flip-flop (read). A p-channel MOSFET cell is shown in Fig. 3.4.3.5. Generally V is held at about ten volts above ground as is the select line in the standby mode. The digit lines are held at ground potential and, due to the biasing, both access transistors are turned off and no current flows in the digit lines. For power dissipation reasons it is desirable to choose the series resistance of the flip-flop elements rather high. By connecting the gate of a MOS transistor to its drain a very low conductance device can be obtained. Where loads of only several kilohms are conveniently realizable with bipolar technology, "on" impedances of hundreds of kilohms are attainable with MOS technology. Typically the "on" load impedance is 40 times greater than that of the transistors with the result that the power loss in the cell is dictated by the characteristics of the load. Since the effective resistance of a MOS load can be shown to vary inversely with voltage, the power dissipated by it varies with the cube of voltage. Even with the high voltages employed with MOS circuits the low conductance of the load yields standby power losses at 10 V of typically 100 μW per cell, which is considerably smaller than that found for bipolar circuits. Reducing the supply voltage several volts reduces this figure to 50 μW. The practical operating limit for p-channel MOSFET circuits is set by the threshold voltage as will be discussed in Section 3.4.4.2. Further reduction of the power can be obtained by operating the cell in a dynamic mode. By asynchronously pulsing the supply voltage at a rate fast enough to keep the gate of the "on" transistor charged, the standby cell power can be reduced to a few microwatts per bit.

Reading from the cell in Fig. 3.4.3.5 is accomplished by driving the select line to ground in which case the accessing transistors turn on and one of the digit lines originally at ground potential is pulled positive by the flip-flop. As a result current flows in this digit line and the state of the cell may be monitored. To write into the cell, the select line is held down and a positive 10 V pulse, is applied to one of the digit lines depending on the desired state. This pulse forces the side of the flip-flop to which it is applied into the "on" state. The unique feature of bidirectionality associated with MOS transistors allows reading and writing through the same gate.

The cell of Fig. 3.4.3.5 may be used as a building block for a two dimensional array just as is done with bipolar devices. The interconnections are essentially the same. If high speed (bipolar) peripheral circuits are used to drive this array the cycle times are not much different from that for a completely bipolar device. The fact that the hybrid devices are slightly slower arises from the relatively large voltage swings required with an

MOS array. While the capacitances of the select and digit lines are slightly less than those for a bipolar array, charging to the high MOS voltages requires a relatively long time. Where the cycle time for a small bipolar memory might be 75 ns the array delays associated with a hybrid memory increase this figure to about 100 ns. The relatively high speed is due to the current driving capabilities of bipolar transistors. If MOS peripheral circuits are used instead, the cycle time rises to 1–2 μs. Commercially manufactured all-MOS static memories are now available. Fully decoded chips hold as many as 4096 bits (1024 for p-channel and 4096 for n-channel) and may be combined to form larger capacity systems. Hybrid MOS-bipolar devices have not been developed to the point of a commercial product but may prove to be more important in the future.

Along the same lines is an experimental Schottky barrier FET memory cell which as yet has not operated in an array, but promises extremely high bit densities and high speed [3.4.17]. The memory cell is essentially the same as that in Fig. 3.4.3.5 except that ordinary resistors instead of MOS loads are used and metal semiconductor field effect transistors (MESFET) are used as switches in the flip-flop. The cell requires less than 2.5 mils^2 of chip area and, due to the low threshold voltage possible with normally-off MESFETS ($V_T = 0.1$ V), the cell can be operated conveniently from a 0.9V supply. Fairly high load and channel impedances ($\sim 10^4\ \Omega$) can easily be formed in the epitaxially grown conducting layer (~ 800 Å) on which the cell is constructed giving standby power losses of 10 μW. The operation of the cell is essentially similar to that in Fig. 3.4.3.5 except that the MESFETs turn on at positive voltages. Therefore the select line is held at ground in standby and raised to a positive voltage to gain access. The digit lines are held at 0.45V relative to ground in standby and one or the other is driven negative during the write cycle. The small size and low power dissipation of this cell make it a potential candidate for digital memory applications. Estimates indicate that by using Si-MESFET technology, 4096 bits with decoding and sense circuitry could be put on a 140×140 mil^2 chip. Readout to the sense amplifier is expected to take less than 30 ns. Writing into the cell alone can be done in about 3 ns.

(ix) *Read-write C-MOS cell.* The existence of both p and n-channel MOSFETs allows the construction of complementary symmetry circuits (C-MOS) [3.4.18]. When this circuit approach is applied to memories it yields static cells which require extremely little standby power due to the fact that one FET in each of the flip-flop branches is always off. Figure 3.4.3.6 shows how the latter situation can be achieved in a memory cell with p- and n-channel MOS devices. With threshold voltages of $+1$V for the n-channel device and -1V for the p-channel device the supply voltage is

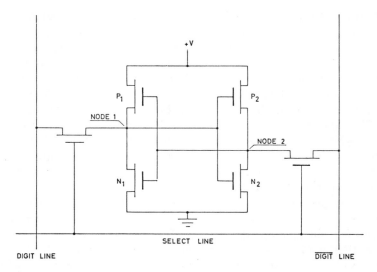

FIG. 3.4.3.6. C-MOS memory cell.

typically 10 V just as for p-MOS circuits. The access transistors can be either p-channel, in which case the select line is held at 10V in standby, or n-channel, in which case it is held at ground. Both digit lines are disconnected from the flip-flop under these circumstances. Examination of the flip-flop indicates that stable states exist with node (1) at ground and node (2) at 10V or vice versa. When node (1) is at ground, P_2 will be turned on but N_2 will be off with 10V across it, under the same circumstances P_1 will be off with 10V across it and N_1 will be on. A similar situation occurs for the other state. Hence the standby power is determined by the leakage current of the two MOSFETs with 10V across them.

An experimental complementary cell with essentially the same standby configuration has been constructed using silicon on sapphire technology and it was found to draw a leakage current on the order of 1 μA ($V_{SD} = 10V$, $V_{SG} = 0$) giving rise to a standby power of 10 μW.

In reality these figures represent an upper limit, since using improved techniques p- and n-channel transistors have been fabricated using conventional and MOS technology with leakage currents between 10^{-2} and 10^{-3} μA. The potential for extremely low power operation, therefore, lies in the complementary approach.

The read/write operation of the cell shown in Fig. 3.4.3.6 is identical to that for an ordinary p-MOS cell. A slightly more complex complementary SOS cell has been constructed and tested and appears to operate as fast as, or faster than, a bipolar cell. The write time was about 5 ns and the read time in the neighbourhood of 1 ns. Since these figures represent a small fraction of the read and write times for an array and are the consequences of a rather expensive technology, they should not be over-emphasized. By and large at the same technological level, the speed of complementary MOS arrays (with C-MOS peripheral circuits) will be the same as p-channel MOS circuits since essentially the same voltages, capacitances, and transconductances are involved. Using silicon on sapphire technology reduces the capacitances for C-MOS arrays to the point where even the poor FET drivers can cause fast voltage transitions. It will do the same for p-MOS circuits and at less cost since the C-MOS cell is comparable in size (5×5 mils^2) but requires more processing. In terms of speed, indications are that C-MOS SOS is slightly slower than bipolar circuitry. In view of its high cost, however, it is unlikely that speed will really be considered a virtue. At the conventional level, complementary MOSFETs should be compared with ordinary p-MOS circuits which are notoriously slow. Hence, at present it would appear that C-MOS memories are attractive only in special purpose applications which require extremely low standby power.

(x) *Associative bipolar cell.* With little or no modification the bipolar or MOS flip-flop cells discussed in connection with the read-write random access memory may be operated as associative cells. Referring to the bipolar cell of Fig. 3.4.3.4 one notes that in standby no current flows in the digit or sense lines because they are held at a higher potential than the word line. Readout is accomplished by driving the word line positive which causes the standby current to be diverted to either the digit or sense line. For this discussion these lines will be referred to as the digit "1" and digit "0" lines respectively. When transistor Q_1 in Fig. 3.4.3.4 conducts, it will be assumed that a "1" is stored and when Q_2 conducts, a "0" is stored. For associative operation it is convenient to interchange the standby role of the digit and word lines. This can be done by holding the word line at the potential of the digit lines and vice versa. The standby current then flows out of one of the digit lines instead of the word line. Interrogation of the cell may be accomplished by raising one of the digit lines to a potential higher than the word line. If current is flowing in the selected digit line it will be diverted to the word line and can be detected there. When no current flows in the digit line no current appears in the word line.

Normally the interrogate signal is inverted and the digit line corresponding to the resulting binary value is driven. In this case no output on the word line indicates a match. When a number of cells are connected in an array as was described for the random access memory, the absence of an output signal on a particular word line indicates that the information stored in the row of cells connected to that line matches the interrogate pattern bit by bit. The comparison is non-destructive because returning the selected digit lines to their original potential, restores each cell to its initial state. If current happens to be flowing in a transistor and the potential of the corresponding digit line is lowered, the current will continue to flow in the same transistor but in the digit instead of the word line. A non-conducting transistor is unaffected by the change in potential of the digit line. To write into a cell the potential of the word line is raised and one digit line is held at a high potential and the other at a low potential. The transistor corresponding to the low potential digit line is forced into saturation in this way and remains in this state when the word line potential is subsequently lowered. A cell may be read by driving the corresponding word line negative and sensing the change in current on one of the digit lines. Thus the basic cell of Fig. 3.4.3.4 can perform non-destructive comparison along with conventional read and write operations. If desired the cell can be operated with current flowing continuously in the word line instead of a digit line. The read and write operations are then the same as described in connection with the RAM but for associative interrogation, invariance of the word line current then indicates a match. From a practical standpoint it is more convenient to detect the presence of a current rather than a change in current and so the former mode of operation is favoured. Unfortunately, the simple cell of Fig. 3.4.3.4 is difficult to control over the temperature range ($-55\,°$C to $+125\,°$C) normally specified for memory and logic circuitry. Therefore modifications to the cell circuitry have been suggested. One of the simpler solutions to this problem is shown in Fig. 3.4.3.7 [3.4.19]. The operation of this cell

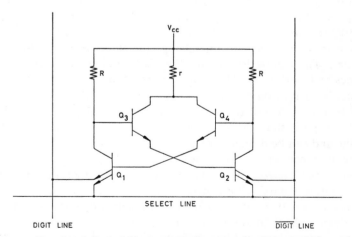

FIG. 3.4.3.7. Stabilized associative memory cell [3.4.19].

is the same as that described previously except that the stability of the cell
under associative interrogation is improved. The two additional transistors
reduce the noise sensitivity of the cell to the mismatch interrogate condition.
Since the base current of an "on" transistor is very much smaller than the
corresponding collector current, the cell dissipation will not differ much
from that for the unstabilized cell. When all resistance values are the same
order of magnitude, the single emitter transistors each form an inverter stage
between one branch of the flip-flop and the base of the opposing double
emitter transistor. An eight bit integrated circuit using the cell shown in
Fig. 3.4.3.7 has been constructed recently but no data on its operation has
been reported [3.4.19]. Presumably the speed should be nearly the same as
that for the closely related bipolar read-write RAM. The cell size of course will
be considerably larger due to the extra elements and this accounts in part for
the relatively high cost per bit of associative memories. More complicated
solutions to the bipolar associative cell problem exist than that shown in
Fig. 3.4.3.7. The basis for construction of all of these cells, however, is the
conventional transistor flip-flop.

(xi) *Associative MOSFET cell*. Just as an associative cell can be derived
from a bipolar flip-flop it can also be patterned after the MOS cell shown in
Fig. 3.4.3.5. Interest in MOS associative memory systems is now beginning
to increase. Formerly these devices were eclipsed by the much faster bipolar
systems, but as applications have diversified and a need appears to be develop-
ing for systems which operate in the 300–500 ns range. Presumably this
need will be filled by an all MOS system in the near future.

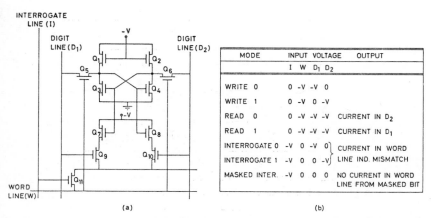

FIG. 3.4.3.8. *p*-Channel MOS content addressable memory cell: (a) cell configuration
and (b) voltage conditions required for the interrogate operations.

Figure 3.4.3.8(a) shows what appears to be the most practical cell configuration for a MOS associative memory [3.4.20]. Transistors Q_1 to Q_6 form the standard flip-flop memory element and transistors Q_7 to Q_{10} the logic circuitry required in connection with the interrogate mode of operation. Both the digit and word lines function as input and output lines which eliminate the necessity of additional interrogate and word sense lines found in associative cells with fewer transistors. Holding the interrogate line of the cell in Fig. 3.4.3.8 at ground potential (under normal operating conditions the word line voltage is 0 or $-V$) causes transistor Q_{11} to be off thus isolating the comparison circuitry (Q_7 to Q_{10}) from the flip-flop and allowing conventional read-write operation (see Table in Fig. 3.4.3.8(b)). Interrogation of the cell may be accomplished by driving the interrogate line negative ($-V$) causing the output of the comparison circuitry to be connected to the word line ($0V$) which under these conditions serves as the (word level) interrogate-sense line. The series combination of transistors Q_7–Q_9 and Q_8–Q_{10} each serve as AND gates with the flip-flop node voltages and digit-line voltages as inputs and the word line current as the output. The voltage conditions required for the interrogate operations are given in Fig. 3.4.3.8(b). Masked interrogation (i.e. no interrogation of a particular digit column) which is extremely useful in associative data processing may be accomplished by driving both digit lines to ground thereby turning transistors Q_9 and Q_{10} off and eliminating the current path through the word line to ground for that particular bit.

Very little information is currently available about arrays which have been fabricated using as their basis the cell of Fig. 3.4.3.8(a). This probably

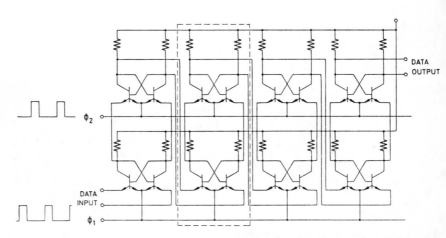

FIG. 3.4.3.9. Two-phase bipolar shift register.

can be attributed to the 400 ns cycle time which is characteristic of such arrays and which is about an order of magnitude slower than their bipolar counterparts thus making them, at present, less attractive commercially.

(xii) *Shift register cell.* Finally, one last application of static memory cells should be mentioned and that is in connection with shift registers. Figure 3.4.3.9 shows how a static two-phase shift register can be constructed by interconnecting a series of bipolar flip-flops [3.4.21]. The figure shows a four bit stage in which the basic unit is a master-slave flip-flop (see dashed line). Each cell is driven by two clock input signals which, during normal operation, alternate between a high and low voltage value but are never high simultaneously. When clock 1 is high, a differential signal on the input of the shift register sets the master flip-flop. This input information may be transferred to the slave flip-flop by reversing the role of clock 1 and clock 2. With clock 1 low the master data is stored and when clock 2 goes high this information is transferred to the slave flip-flop by the differential output signal of the first flip-flop. Continuing this process by reversing the role of clock 1 and clock 2 shifts the data to the next bit and so forth. The great advantage of this type of device is that the information flow can be stopped at any time without incurring a loss. Static MOS shift registers have also been constructed but are considerably slower than their bipolar counterparts. Dynamic MOS shift-registers which will be discussed in the next section offer an attractive alternative in so far as speed goes.

3.4.3.3. Dynamic Memory Cells

The dynamic mode of information storage is not a particularly new concept but is just now becoming extremely popular in connection with integrated circuits and semiconductor memories. Dynamic memory cells are currently being used in both serial and random access applications and in general are considerably simpler, from the standpoint of the number of elements, than their static counterparts. This means that the associated memories can be constructed with higher chip capacities and consequently lower cost per bit. The basic memory element in a dynamic cell is nothing but a capacitor which may be formed in a variety of convenient ways. For example, in a bucket brigade delay line (or shift register) it is common to enlarge the parasitic Miller capacitance between the base and collector (source and drain for a MOSFET) of a bipolar transistor and to use this as the storage element. Conventional dynamic MOS circuitry employs the parasitic gate capacitance of a MOS transistor. Due to the high input impedance of the transistor, charge can temporarily be stored on this capacitor and can be used to conditionally control the charging and discharging of other capacitors in the circuit. Since the state of the cell is dictated by the amount of charge on the storage capacitor and since this charge is depleted by leakage currents, it is necessary either to use the stored information quickly or restore it periodically. Both of these techniques are used—the former in connection with serial operation and the latter in connection with random-access type operation. This factor places a lower limit on the frequency at which a dynamic shift register can be operated and means that additional peripheral circuitry is required for read-write type memories. Since this "refresh" circuitry may be time-shared by a large number of memory cells each of which is considerably less complex than its static counterpart, the result is a system with higher capacity. Furthermore, dynamic memories have the advantage that they can be designed so that power dissipation occurs only during transient periods. In this case very little standby power is required which is an asset in large scale systems from the supply and dissipation standpoints. In terms of speed, dynamic operation is generally faster than static (same technological level) with dynamic MOS speed lying somewhere between what can be achieved by static bipolar and static MOS circuits. In view of the cell size considerations these factors make dynamic memories prime candidates for intermediate size systems. In the following a few of the more interesting semiconductor charge storage cells will be described including those employing the recently invented surface charge transistor. The simplest cells based on a single bipolar or MOS transistor will be examined first.

(i) *Bucket-brigade delay line.* As was mentioned in connection with serial memory organizations, the shift register may be used in much the same way for digital information storage as an acoustic delay line. The bucket-brigade delay line is an outgrowth of work to develop an analogue shift register as a substitute for the acoustic delay line which, not surprisingly is commonly used for analogue as well as for digital information storage [3.4.22, 3.4.23]. Since analogue wave shapes encompass digital signals, the bucket-brigade delay line is useful in digital applications as well as analogue in essentially the same way as a shift register. Figure 3.4.3.10(a) shows four stages of a bipolar bucket-brigade shift register and a blow-up of the integrated circuit realization of one stage. The storage capacitor C_{cb} is formed by enlarging the collector-base junction capacitance (Miller capacitance) by increasing the junction area. Typical capacitance values range from 5–25 pF. Only one transistor is associated with each capacitor, however, two stages are associated with the storage of one bit of information since only every alternating capacitor can be used at any one time. The clock signal amplitudes are typically 2 V and the input signal levels (required to be less than clock levels for proper operation) about 1 V. The operation of the delay line is based upon charge deficit transfer which will now be explained in connection with Fig. 3.4.3.10(a). For simplicity all the capacitors associated with the

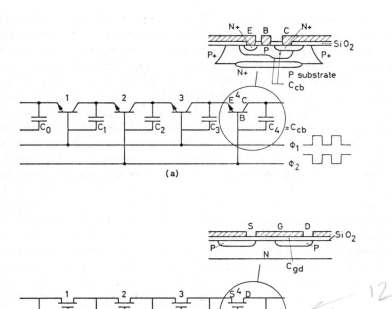

FIG. 3.4.3.10. Bucket-brigade delay lines [3.4.23]: (a) with bipolar transistors and (b) with MOSFET's.

transistors 1–4 will be assumed to be charged to the clock level of 2 V and the input capacitor to 1 V initially. Under these conditions when the phase 1 and 2 clock levels are both zero volts, all emitter-base junctions are reverse biased with the result that no current flows in the transistor collectors and the charge pattern is temporarily fixed. Raising ϕ_1 to the 2 V clock level (with $\phi_1 = 0$) forward biases the emitter-base junction of transistor 1 with the result that current flows until C_0 is charged to 2 V ($Q = C_0 \times 1$). This charge comes principally ($i_b \approx 0$) from C_1 which means its voltage is reduced to $2 - Q/C_1 = 2 - C_0/C_1$ which is 1 V if $C_0 = C_1$. Hence the voltage which was stored on C_0 is transferred to C_1 by a charge flow from C_1 to C_0 i.e. charge deficit transfer. In a similar way the voltage on C_1 may be transferred to C_2 by driving the phase 2 line positive to two volts ($\phi_1 = 0$) and so forth. Note that after each transfer the capacitor to the left of a conducting transistor becomes charged to 2 V which allows it to receive the deficit from the preceding capacitor during the next phase. Since a capacitor which is receiving charge cannot simultaneously store information (because it always recharges to 2 V), only every alternative capacitor may hold information with the result that the capacity of the delay line is half the number of transistors in it. Bipolar devices of the type shown in Fig. 3.4.3.10(a) have been constructed with typically 70 stages on an $80 \times 80 \, mil^2$ chip (includes peripheral circuitry). The rate of transfer depends on the clock rate and ranges from a minimum of 2 kHz up to a maximum of about 30 MHz. A difficulty with the bipolar transistor occurs for a large number of stages. This is the deterioration of signal due to base current. Since at each transfer the signal level is attenuated by the factor $1 - 1/\beta$ due to base current, after n stages the signal level is reduced by $(1 - 1/\beta)^n$ which can be appreciable if β is not large. Under ordinary circumstances it is necessary to include an amplification stage (or stages) on the chip to compensate for such losses. The insertion of a simple transistor-capacitor-diode amplifier circuit every n stages can be used to overcome this problem. As for many charge transfer devices a trade off exists between speed and length n for fixed attenuation. If minimum area requirements are used to determine the optimum length n, the maximum operating frequency is fixed. The use of MOSFETs instead of bipolar transistors as shown in Fig. 3.4.3.10(b) eliminates the base current problem. However, the long transients associated with the MOSFET produce essentially the same circumstances. At high frequencies voltage attenuation occurs due to incomplete transfer with the result that gain is required. Devices of this type with 16 stages have been operated at bit rates of up to 10 MHz. The cell is particularly simple to implement—allowing the gate of the MOSFET to extend out over the drain region enhances the Miller capacitances thus producing the desired cell.

(ii) *Charge-coupled shift register.* In the bucket-brigade delay line of Fig. 3.4.3.10(b) deficit charge is transferred along the semiconductor surface between metal electrodes which simultaneously perform the functions of gate electrode and storage capacitor. The direction of charge flow in this case is opposite to the direction of propagation of the signal (charge deficit transfer). If one thinks in terms of transferring charge along a semiconductor surface in the same direction as the signal, it is not a great step from the bucket-brigade configuration to imagine that this might be accomplished by constructing an array of closely spaced MOS capacitors on a uniformly doped semiconductor (i.e. eliminate the p-diffusions in a bucket-brigade delay line). Charge can then be stored in locally induced surface potential wells created by the electrodes and can be transferred from electrode to electrode by means of surface field gradients. Devices employing this form of charge storage and transfer are referred to as charge-coupled devices and represent an interesting addition to the area of semiconductor technology [3.4.24]. They show particular promise in connection with memory applications for a number of reasons. Foremost (aside from input and output connections to be discussed later) the devices are junctionless which makes processing extremely simple (no windows implies fewer masks, no diffusions, fewer etchings). Furthermore, because no connections are required to the semiconductor surface, the devices can be fabricated at higher packing densities than can be obtained with conventional MOS. Together these features suggest that in the future CCDs could show improvements in yield over conventional MOS devices. All of these advantages imply a decrease in cost per bit in terms of memory applications. The fact that no diffusions are required may have another important ramification and that is in terms of material considerations. Semiconductor materials which in the past have been ignored largely because of diffusion difficulties and which are compatible with useful insulating layers can now be used in CCDs giving an added degree of flexibility in connection with device applications.

The earliest reported charge-coupled shift registers employed rather large (by existing standards) rectangular electrodes arranged in a linear array with the width dimension perpendicular to the array length [3.4.24]. It was found quite early that the operating characteristics of such devices depended on the separation between electrodes. In an effort to eliminate the arbitrariness in surface potential between electrodes caused by the etching process an alternative two level metallization scheme has been proposed which appears to have some advantages over the single layer structure [3.4.25]. The purpose of the second level of metallization is to control the surface potential between storage wells—as an added benefit it allows the spacing between electrodes to be chosen as desired. Figure 3.4.3.11(a) shows a chip cross-section of a charge coupled shift register employing the two level metallization scheme. Oxide thicknesses are similar to those for conventional MOS being 1000 Å and 2000 Å respectively for the two sets of electrodes. The upper level of metallization overlaps the lower level to insure the correct control of inter-electrode potentials. Because the upper level electrodes act like transfer gates, the device can be operated as follows: minority charge can be inserted into the potential well of the first storage electrode (S) which will be assumed to be held at −20 V as are all other storage electrodes. With the transfer gate (G) held at 0 V a potential barrier separates the first (S) and second (D) storage electrodes and no charge transfer can take place. If the potential of the first electrode (S) is raised (10 V) relative to the second (D), transfer is energetically favourable but will not occur until the potential of the transfer gate (G) is such that the potential barrier between storage wells is eliminated (occurs at about −12.5 V). Once transfer has occurred the first electrode (S) may be returned to −20 V and the transfer gate (G) to 0 V and the process

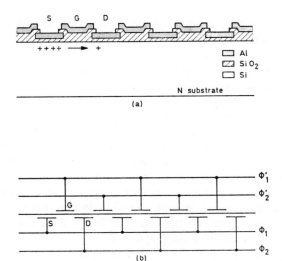

FIG. 3.4.3.11. Charge coupled delay line: (a) chip cross-section and (b) interconnection diagram.

may be repeated to transfer charge from the second storage electrode (D) to the third, etc. Proper control of the transfer gates allows charge motion from left to right or from right to left. Figure 3.4.3.11 shows a circuit diagram for the shift register, indicating the necessary interconnections required for continuous operation. As is suggested by our previous discussion, the data flow may be stopped for time intervals up to milliseconds without detrimental effect. Depending on the degree of attenuation one is willing to accept, bit rates from 1 to 100 MHz appear to be possible. On the basis of a 1–2 mil^2 cell size, chip area considerations indicate that arrays of about 30 bits between refresh operations provide optimum use of chip real estate assuming the refresh circuitry occupies 4 mil^2. For this array length the attenuation does not become severe unless frequencies exceed 10 MHz. This bit rate represents a factor of 5 increase over what can be achieved by conventional dynamic MOS. For the above cell size at 10 MHz the power dissipation should be in the neighbourhood of 10–30 μW/bit.

Although we have not mentioned it up to this point, the compatibility of MOSFETs with CCDs is extremely important for the success of charge-coupled devices in connection with memory applications. This is because MOSFETs are useful for input-output interfacing with CCDs and because they may be used to regenerate signals, which, as we have implied, is necessary at high bit rates due to incomplete charge transfer. A simple minority carrier source can be obtained by forward biasing a $p-n$ junction in the neighbourhood of the first electrode while a detector can be formed by reverse biasing a $p-n$ junction at the output of the CCD and monitoring the output current. These two examples emphasize the need for compatibility between conventional MOS technology and charge-coupled devices. Other techniques for charge generation and detection such as avalanche injection and capacitance modulation appear to be receiving less attention.

(iii) *MOSFET shift register.* Unlike charge-coupled devices, dynamic MOS shift registers rely on conventional integrated circuit logic to shift information from one storage cell to the next [3.4.26]. When reduced to its most primitive form, a dynamic MOS shift register cell consists of two inverter stages interconnecting two storage elements which in this case are parasitic gate to substrate capacitors. Figure 3.4.3.12 shows a two-phase MOS shift register circuit. Each cell has six transistors Q_1–Q_6 which are used to form two inverters and two transmission gates which serve to couple the storage capacitors shown in dashed lines. Charge deposited on the capacitors C_1 and C_2 controls the gate voltage and consequently the impedance of transistors Q_1 and Q_4. The on impedance of these transistors is

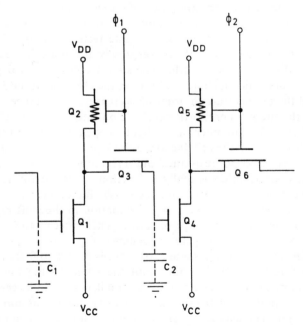

FIG. 3.4.3.12. Dynamic MOSFET shift register cell.

usually made a factor 10 smaller than that for transistors Q_2 and Q_5 in order to obtain proper inverter performance. This is suggested by the resistance symbols associated with the source to drain paths in Fig. 3.4.3.12. The impedance of the transmission gate (Q_3) is intermediate between that of Q_1 and Q_2. When the charge on C_1 is sufficiently negative (p-channel devices) to turn Q_1 on, driving ϕ_1 negative with a clock pulse causes the node formed by the three transistors Q_1 to Q_3 to approach V_{CC} (a positive voltage). Since C_2 is tied to this node through Q_3 its voltage approaches V_{CC} also. On the other hand, if the charge on C_1 is not sufficiently negative to turn Q_1 on then no current flows through it during the clock pulse and C_2 charges to V_{DD} (a negative voltage). At the end of the ϕ_1 pulse, transistor Q_3 turns off and the capacitor C_2 is isolated with either V_{CC} or V_{DD} volts across it, depending on the initial charge stored on C_1. Since V_{DD} is a negative level the voltage on C_1 is inverted as it passes from the input to the output of the first stage. Pulsing ϕ_2 negative reinverts the data and deposits it at the input to the next storage cell. Because the charge on the capacitors decay due to leakage currents, if the data is to be retained, it must be transferred from one stage to another in less than typically one millisecond. This requires a 1 kHz minimum bit rate. At higher bit rates the data flow can be stopped so long as the one millisecond holding time is not exceeded. The gain associated with the inverter stage provides the necessary regeneration of the signal at each transfer (refresh operation). A storage cell of the type shown in Fig. 3.4.3.12 requires about 10 mil^2 of chip area using silicon gate technology and 25 mil^2 with conventional technology. Both the power supply and clock drivers contribute to the power dissipated by the cell. The supply contribution depends on a number of factors which include the bit rate, the clock amplitude, the supply voltages and the temperature in order of decreasing importance. The power drawn from the supply is proportional to the bit rate and is typically 0.2 mW per bit at 1 MHz. This number varies slightly depending on the other factors. The power dissipated in the cell due to the clock pulses depends on the relative values of the driver output resistance and series input resistance to the gates. Therefore this contribution is really a function of the peripheral circuitry, and must be considered separately for each case. Increasing the driver output resistance, however, reduces the power dissipation in the shift register cells. The maximum bit rate of this type of shift register is set by the charging and discharging of the parasitic gate capacitance C_2 through the transistors Q_1 and Q_2 in series with Q_3. Gate capacitances of 0.1 to 0.2 pF and series resistances of 1000 to 10 000 ohms limit the speed to the low megahertz range. Attempts to make these resistances smaller result in larger transistors which are disadvantageous from a circuit density standpoint and which also have higher gate capacitances. Hence there is no real advantage in this approach.

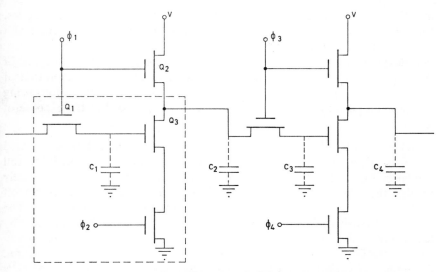

FIG. 3.4.3.13. Dynamic shift register cells (four phase).

The voltage divider logic employed in the inverters shown in Fig. 3.4.3.12 requires two different MOS impedances. These impedances are obtained by varying the layout of the individual transistors. The low impedance transistor occupies a relatively large chip area relative to the high impedance one. It is advantageous from an area standpoint to be able to use relatively high impedance transistors throughout the circuit. If the transistors are to be nearly identical it is necessary to find a form of inverter circuit other than that employed in connection with ratio logic. Four-phase techniques make it possible to use high impedance transistors in shift registers with an improvement in performance over two-phase devices [3.4.27]. Figure 3.4.3.13 shows a four-phase shift register cell which consists of two interconnected inverter stages. During operation node 2 is precharged through transistor Q_2 to the supply voltage by phase 1 independent of the input (ϕ_2 is off during ϕ_1). ϕ_2 then conditionally discharges this node depending on the state of Q_3 which forms an AND gate in conjunction with Q_2. Hence at the end of ϕ_2 the input information appears at node 2 in inverted form. The following inverter stage operates in the same way and reinverts the information before it appears at the output of the cell. An obvious advantage of this form of operation is that only dynamic power is dissipated. The use of relatively high impedance transistors allows particularly efficient cell layouts requiring typically 10 mil^2 for conventional technology making them smaller than that for two-phase devices. The smaller transistor size has a further advantage

P

and that is in connection with charging and discharging rates of the nodes. Since the associated parasitic load capacitances are smaller the overall result is an increase in speed.

Four-phase shift registers operate at approximately 10 times the speed of two-phase devices. An ultimate limit on speed is set by the generation of four non-overlapping clock pulses. Alternative inverter configurations using overlapping pulses can bring some improvement in speed at the expense of chip area.

(iv) *RAM MOSFET cell.* Random access memory cells can be operated in a dynamic mode as well as can shift registers. In fact the MOS RAM cell shown in Fig. 3.4.3.5 can be operated dynamically by simply periodically pulsing the supply voltage. Between pulses the charge stored on the off node of the flip-flop is sufficient to maintain the state of the device. The occasional pulsing of the supply restores any charge which has been lost by leakage from this node, thus re-establishing the correct cell state. Read and write operations may be performed in the same manner as for static operation. A number of variations on the simple static bipolar and MOS RAM cells exist which can be used to store information dynamically. The principal objection to many of these cells is size; they require too many transistors. For dynamic operation the flip-flop is unnecessarily redundant and it is possible to derive much simpler cells by using what amounts to half of the flip-flop. Figure 3.4.3.14(a) shows a three-transistor MOS cell [3.4.28] which, upon rearranging elements, may be recognized as part of a static flip-flop cell in which the load gate has been disconnected from the supply to form a read select line. Only three transistors are required and the storage element consists of the parasitic gate to substrate capacitance formed by the metal lead connecting transistors Q_1 and Q_2. Since cross-coupling is no

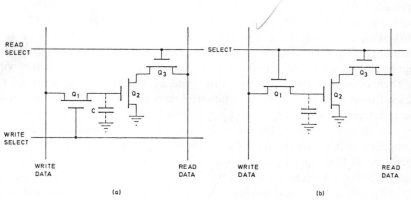

FIG. 3.4.3.14. Three transistor dynamic MOSFET cell with (a) two and (b) one select line.

longer important in the operation of this cell, the impedance ratio requirements for the flip-flop may be relaxed and the transistors may be laid out for minimum cell area. An alternative three transistor cell of the type shown in Fig. 3.4.3.14(b) exists in which a single select line is used to perform both read and write select functions. Because the operation of both cells is similar it is necessary to consider only the former one. In both cases the state of each cell is determined by the charge stored on the parasitic capacitor C. When Q_2 conducts, the cell stores a logic "1" and when it does not the cell stores a logic "0".

Writing into the cell involves driving the write select line sufficiently negative (p-channel MOS) so that transistor Q_1 conducts and the capacitor C charges to the write data line voltage. A logic "1" on the data line corresponds to a negative level and a logic "0" to ground. After C is charged the write select line is returned to ground thus turning Q_1 off and isolating the storage element. Since Q_2 is on or off depending on the stored charge, the state of the cell may be sensed by making the read data line voltage negative and turning on Q_3 with the read select line. When charge flows in the read data line, a logic "1" is stored, otherwise, a logic "0" is stored. The readout is non-destructive since the charge on the capacitor is used only to control the impedance of transistor Q_2. An important advantage of this type of cell is that it requires only three transistors which means that it can be made very small. The cell can be constructed on a chip area of 9 mil² using conventional technology. The power requirements are particularly low due to the dynamic mode of operation. The cell in Fig. 3.4.3.14(a) dissipates about 0.006 mW of standby power and 0.3 mW of operating power. These figures are well below those found for static non-complementary cells. When these cells are connected in an array a pair of read and write select lines address all the cells in a row and a pair of data lines select the cells in a column just as in static memory circuits. For a 1024 bit fully decoded p-channel chip, access and cycle times as low as 300 and 600 ns respectively have been obtained using silicon gate technology. As for dynamic shift register cells, the memory cell shown in Fig. 3.4.3.14(a) suffers from charge leakage which means that the information must be restored frequently. This is done by reading out each cell and feeding the output signal into an inverter. The output of the inverter is then returned to the cell. The original information is restored because the cell readout yields the logical complement of the stored information. The operation is similar to a one bit two-phase dynamic shift register in which the output is fed back to the input. Each cell is refreshed every 100 or so microseconds between external read and write cycles.

Examination of Fig. 3.4.3.14(a) indicates that an even simpler dynamic RAM memory cell may be constructed by omitting transistors Q_2 and Q_3. The result is shown in Fig. 3.4.3.15 where one transistor and one capacitor

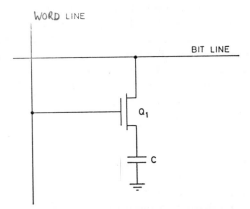

FIG. 3.4.3.15. One transistor dynamic MOSFET cell.

are required [3.4.29]. Due to the sensing requirements placed on the peripheral output circuits, the capacitor C must be chosen relatively large, which makes it impossible to use the capacitance resulting from a drain diffusion. As a consequence the capacitor C in Fig. 3.4.3.15 must be formed separately using standard thin-oxide processing. The operation of the cell is particularly simple, information may be written into the capacitor by placing a voltage on the data line and turning transistor Q_1 on; the cell may be read by turning Q_1 on thereby dumping the stored charge onto the output data line. This mode of operation is subject to two difficulties (1) the readout is destructive and (2) the output signals require special low-level sensing amplifiers. Neither of these factors should really be considered as drawbacks, particularly when it is possible to incorporate the rewrite operation with the refresh operation. As for the three-transistor cell, each cell is refreshed by reading out the stored information, amplifying it and subsequently rewriting it. Using silicon gate technology (in order to reduce the output capacitance) the cell of Fig. 3.4.3.15 requires about $3.6 \, \text{mil}^2$ per bit which puts it ahead of any of the existing RAM cells in terms of density, as many as 2048 of these decoded bits have been placed on a $138 \times 143 \, \text{mil}^2$ chip. The corresponding read access time is less than 250 ns and the cycle time is less than 400 ns. The power dissipation at the highest frequency of operation is only 150 μW per bit.

3.4.4. PHYSICS AND TECHNOLOGY OF MOS MEMORY CELLS

3.4.4.1. Introduction

Many of the MOS memory cells introduced in Section 3.4.3 employ the inverter in one form or another as a basic building block. With the exception of the MOS ROMs the static devices are all based on the transistor flip-flop which consists of two cross-coupled inverters. Each inverter in this case consists of a driver transistor connected in series with either an active (MOS) or passive load. In complementary circuits the arrangement is slightly different, with the two series interconnected transistors which make up the inverter stage functioning as active devices. The inverter also plays an important role in dynamic memory devices. As was mentioned in Section 3.4.3.3, two and four phase shift registers employ inverters to transfer information from one temporary storage cell to the next. Since the inverter forms the basis for many MOS memory cells and since it occupies a fundamental position in MOS logic which is employed in the associated peripheral circuitry it serves as an ideal basis by which to compare IC semiconductor technologies and to explore various circuit configurations [3.4.30]. It is convenient initially to consider the integrated load inverter most commonly associated with MOS LSI memories based upon the p-channel enhancement MOS device. n-Channel enhancement devices, depletion loads and complementary inverters will be discussed later in connection with the switching speed of the p-channel inverter (Section 3.4.4.3). Figure 3.4.4.1 shows a p-channel enhancement-mode inverter along with the electrical characteristics of the driver and load. A schematic integrated circuit cross-section of the MOS inverter is shown in Fig. 3.4.4.2. The steps required to fabricate the device are as follows. Initially the n-type silicon substrate is cleaned and an oxide layer (7500 Å) is formed on its surface. Where p-type diffused regions

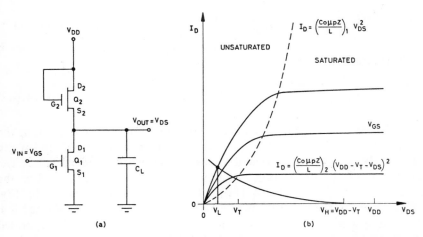

FIG. 3.4.4.1. p-Channel enhancement MOSFET inverter: (a) circuit and (b) electrical characteristics.

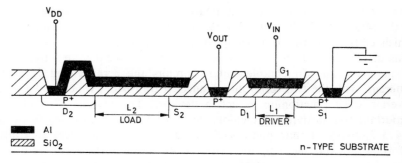

CONVENTIONAL p-CHANNEL

FIG. 3.4.4.2. Schematic integrated circuit cross-section of the MOS inverter of Fig. 3.4.4.1(a).

are later to be formed (source and drain of the MOS transistors) the oxide is removed by etching through a photomask. Boron is then deposited in these regions and an oxide layer is formed over them before or during the drive-in diffusion. A subsequent field oxidation in steam brings the oxide to its final thickness (15000 Å) and a second oxide removal defines the gate and contact regions. The gate oxide layers (1000 Å) are then formed by a dry O_2 oxidation which also covers the contact regions again. A third oxide removal opens the contact areas before an aluminium deposition followed by another photo-masking operation defines the interconnection pattern.

For p-channel MOS transistors, the electrical characteristics are given by

$$I_D = \frac{C_0 \mu_p Z}{L} \left| (V_{GS} - V_T) V_{DS} - \frac{V_{DS}^2}{2} \right| \quad |V_{DS}| \leqslant |V_{GS} - V_T| \qquad (3.4.4.1)$$

below saturation and by

$$I_D = \frac{C_0 \mu_p Z}{L} (V_{GS} - V_T)^2 \quad |V_{DS}| \geqslant |V_{GS} - V_T| \qquad (3.4.4.2)$$

when the device is saturated. C_0 is the gate capacitance per unit area, μ_p the effective surface mobility of holes, L and W the channel length and width respectively, and V_T the threshold voltage which will be defined later. The gate to source (V_{GS}) and drain to source (V_{DS}) voltages are indicated on the inverter diagram (Fig. 3.4.4.1(a)). The characteristics appear in Fig. 3.4.4.1(b) with the gate to source voltage as a parameter. The dashed line obtained by setting $V_{DS} = V_{GS} - V_T$ in eqn (3.4.4.2) separates the saturated from the unsaturated region in Fig. 3.4.4.1(b). With the gate of transistor Q_2 tied to its drain, $V_{DS} = V_{GS}$ and therefore the load Q_2 is always saturated.

The corresponding load line appears in Fig. 3.4.4.1(b) as a parabola starting at $V_{DS} = V_{DD} - V_T$. The capacitor C_L at the output of the inverter represents the load presented by other gates together with the output capacitance of the driver.

When an input voltage is applied to the inverter, the output depends on the relationship of that voltage to V_T, the voltage at which the driver transistor begins to conduct. For p-channel enhancement devices V_T is a few volts negative which means that when 0V is applied to the input gate of the inverter the driver does not turn on and the output voltage is $V_H = V_{DD} - V_T$. On the other hand when V_{in} is more negative than V_T the driver turns on and for very large input voltages the output approaches zero. The static transfer characteristics illustrating the relationship between input and output for the inverter are shown schematically in Fig. 3.4.4.3. For negative logic V_H is chosen as "1" and V_L as "0". If this inverter is used to drive another inverter stage, the "0" output voltage V_L must not accidentally become more negative than V_T or else it will produce a false output in the following stage. To insure that this is the case and to allow a wide noise margin it is desirable to choose $|V_L| \ll |V_T|$. Examination of Fig. 3.4.4.3 indicates that the relative aspect ratio of driver to load

$$K_r = \frac{(Z/L)_1}{(Z/L)_2} \quad \frac{Z}{L} = \frac{\text{channel width}}{\text{channel length}} = \text{aspect ratio} \qquad (3.4.4.3)$$

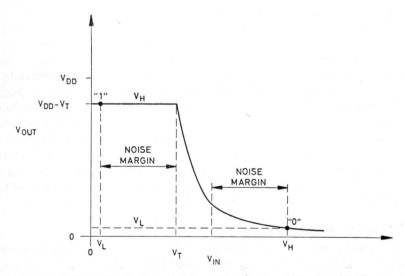

FIG. 3.4.4.3. Static characteristics of the inverter of Fig. 3.4.4.1(a)

should be high so that V_L falls near zero. If the series combination of load and saturated driver is thought of as a voltage divider this is equivalent to making the ratio of load to driver "resistance" large. Typically this ratio is on the order of 10. As the choice of the load "resistance" profoundly affects the switching speed of the inverter, the following considerations relate only to ratio logic devices unless specified otherwise. For equivalent noise immunity when the output is "1" the voltage V_H (negative) should be separated from V_T by about the same voltage as is V_L. This leads to the requirement that

$$V_H = V_{DD} - V_T \gtrsim 2V_T \qquad (3.4.4.4)$$

or

$$V_{DD} \gtrsim 3V_T \qquad (3.4.4.5)$$

which establishes the fundamental role played by the threshold voltage in determining the output voltage swing ($\sim 2V_T$), the minimum supply voltage ($\sim 3V_T$) and the noise margin ($\sim V_T$).

For conventional (111) semiconductor technology the threshold voltage V_T is in the neighbourhood of 4V and therefore the inverter requires roughly a 12–15V supply. As might be expected the power dissipated by the inverter is strongly dependent on the supply voltage. By operating at low voltages a large reduction in power may be obtained. This fact is particularly important in connection with high density MOS circuits where the high voltages associated with conventional threshold devices can cause the chips to become dissipation limited. Although reducing the supply voltage improves the power dissipation, as will be discussed later, it also degrades the speed of the inverter. However, the more relevant parameter in terms of memory applications, the speed-power product, is improved. Since the large noise margin for high threshold devices is normally not needed it becomes worthwhile to attempt to reduce the threshold voltage and consequently the supply voltage and output swing of the inverter. As an added benefit low threshold voltages simplify the task of interfacing MOS with bipolar circuits and allow lower clock levels to be used in connection with dynamic operation (in dynamic operation the gate of the load transistor is disconnected from the drain and is driven by a clock as in Fig. 3.4.3.14). A number of different techniques can be used to control the threshold voltage and these will be discussed in connection with the fundamental equation for V_T.

3.4.4.2. Threshold Voltage

As was mentioned previously, the threshold voltage V_T determines at what point the channel conductivity of a MOSFET becomes high. In terms of basic material parameters this transition occurs when the gate to source voltage becomes [3.4.31]

$$V_T = 2\phi_F + \Delta W_F - \frac{t_{ox}}{\varepsilon_{ox}} Q_{eff} \mp \frac{t_{ox}}{\varepsilon_{ox}} \{2\varepsilon_{si}qN_{a,d}(|V_s - V_{substr.}| + 2\phi_F)\}^{\frac{1}{2}} \quad (3.4.4.6)$$

where ϕ_F is the Fermi level of the silicon substrate (measured from the intrinsic level), ΔW_F is the difference in work function between the gate electrode and silicon substrate, t_{ox} is the thickness of the gate oxide which is assumed to have dielectric constant ε_{ox} and Q_{eff} is the effective surface charge at the silicon-oxide interface (includes bulk charges in the oxide) ε_{si}, is the dielectric constant of the silicon substrate and q is the basic unit of electronic charge. For this discussion the source is assumed to be held at a potential $V_s - V_{substr}$ relative to the substrate such that no current flows between the two (i.e. the source junction is reverse biased). The equation applies to both p- and n-channel devices and accordingly the doping level $N_{a,d}$ appropriate to the substrate type must be used. The plus sign applies to p-type substrates (n-channel FETs) and the minus sign to n-type substrates (p-channel FETs). A p-channel device with a negative threshold voltage such as that which was used to introduce the inverter is referred to as an enhancement transistor while the same device with a positive V_T is called a depletion transistor. For an n-channel transistor the labelling is reversed. Normally for silicon MOS transistors with low substrate doping the surface charge term dominates and is negative making n-channel devices of the depletion type and p-channel devices of the enhancement type when no substrate bias is applied. Increasing the substrate doping or equivalently the substrate bias to the point where the depletion layer charge term (square root) dominates converts an n-channel depletion transistor to an enhancement device. Since the surface charge associated with a thermally grown oxide-silicon interface is positive, depletion mode p-channel devices must be constructed using special techniques. A thin p-channel can be diffused or epitaxially grown on the n-type silicon thus producing a depletion transistor. In this case the transistor turns off when the associated space charge region extends all the way across the channel. The analysis of this type of device is complicated by the channel to substrate voltage which produces a second space charge region that reduces the effective channel depth. Hence in this discussion only those devices for which the equation holds will be considered. Examination of this equation indicates that really only six different parameters are accessible for changes and they are the following: ΔW_F, t_{ox}, ε_{ox}, Q_{eff}, $N_{a,d}$, $|V_s - V_{substr.}|$ Each of these parameters will be considered in the following subsections in relation to a particular form of semiconductor technology.

   (i) *Work function of the gate electrode.* One of the most successful techniques for reducing the threshold voltage of a MOS transistor involves controlling the work function of the gate. Referring to eqn (3.4.4.6) it is clear that for a p-channel device increasing ΔW_F which is the work function of the gate electrode with respect to the silicon substrate will produce a desirable result. Since the substrate material is fixed to a large extent by technological requirements only the gate electrode material is free to be varied. The work function of aluminium, the gate material normally used, is 4.3 eV, which yields $\Delta W_F \approx -0.3$ eV for an n-type silicon substrate with a work function of 4.0 eV (4–7 ohm cm). If a p-type silicon gate is used instead, ΔW_F would be increased to $+0.8$ eV. Thus reducing the threshold voltage by 1.1 V. Therefore using a p-type silicon gate electrode would be expected to reduce the threshold voltage of a (111) oriented transistor from about 4 to 2.9 V. This technique forms the basis for silicon gate technology [3.4.32] which will be described in more detail. In practice it is convenient to sandwich a layer of silicon nitride between the gate oxide and the p-silicon gate and as will be discussed in a later subsection this has the effect of further reducing the threshold voltage to about 2 V.

Figure 3.4.4.4 shows a series of integrated circuit cross-sections for a p-channel transistor illustrating the sequence of process steps involved in constructing a silicon gate device [3.4.33]. The sequence of steps is similar to that used in conventional technology with the important exception that the gate region is formed before the source and drain regions are diffused.

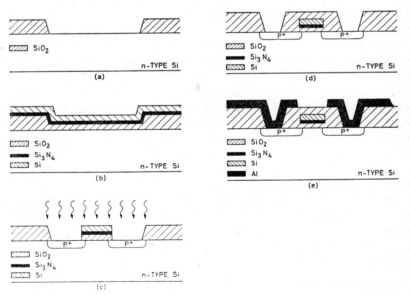

FIG. 3.4.4.4. Processing steps sequence for the production of Si-gate transistors.

As in conventional technology a relatively thick 10 000 Å silicon dioxide layer is first formed on the surface of the *n*-type silicon substrate. The regions to be occupied by the source, channel and drain are then etched away after masking the other areas so that the result appears as in Fig. 3.4.4.4(a). The thin gate oxide (1000 Å) is now formed in the window and a thin layer of silicon nitride (Si_3N_4) is deposited on top of the entire structure for reliability and to further decrease the threshold voltage. A thin layer of amorphous silicon which eventually forms the gate electrode is deposited on top of the silicon nitride and the wafer then resembles the sketch in Fig. 3.4.4.4(b). Another mask is used to define the source and drain regions and any silicon circuit interconnections which are desired. The extra silicon and silicon nitride is removed from all but the gate area and a subsequent oxide etch opens the source and drain regions in preparation for the boron diffusion (Fig. 3.4.4.4(c)). The gate region in this case serves as a self-aligning mask for the *p*-diffusion and thus reduces the gate source and gate drain overlap. Although undercutting does occur, the overlap is considerably smaller than that obtained by conventional techniques which require the gate electrode to be formed after the channel has been defined by the *p*-diffusion. As will be discussed, the reduced overlap and reduced channel length possible with these devices considerably improve the switching speed of the inverter. Following the *p*-diffusion, which also dopes the silicon gate electrode the process steps are essentially the same as for conventional technology. A thick silicon dioxide layer which serves as the support for the subsequent aluminium metallization is deposited over the entire surface. The thickness (10 000 Å) is such that the threshold voltage of parasitic transistors falls in the neighbourhood of 26 V. The corresponding parasitic threshold for silicon interconnections is about 25 V which means that for silicon gate technology the ratio of parasitic threshold to device threshold is much larger than for conventional technology (8.6 compared to 6.5), thus providing more comfortable operating margins. After oxidation, openings are etching to the diffused *p*-regions and underlying silicon gates (Fig. 3.4.4.4(d)) and an aluminium layer is evaporated which makes contact to these areas. The aluminium layer is then masked to provide the desired interconnection pattern and the remaining material is removed. Finally one last oxidation to give the interconnection pattern mechanical strength and to prevent contamination, followed by an etch which opens the contact pads, prepares the device for bonding.

Comparison of silicon gate and conventional technology indicates that the same number of masking steps (four) are required in both cases, however, more thin film depositions are required for silicon gate technology. The extra silicon deposition (the silicon nitride deposition is optional), however, provides an extra level of interconnection which in the end reduces the area of the circuits. Thus the few extra steps are well worth the effort. One of the major advantages of silicon gate technology is the protection afforded the delicate gate oxide by the silicon and thick oxide layer. The gate oxide can be subjected to high temperatures after it has been formed, which allows subsequent bipolar processing to be performed on the same substrate. This is a tremendous advantage when thinking in terms of hybrid MOS bipolar circuits.

The motivation for examining silicon-gate technology was the decrease in threshold voltage that is obtained by employing a gate electrode with a higher work function than aluminium (conventional technology). Also other conducting elements satisfy this criterion and are compatible with silicon device fabrication technology. Both molybdenum and tungsten have been used in self-aligned structures but do not give as great a threshold reduction as p-silicon nor are they as convenient to work with [3.4.34].

(ii) *Crystal orientation and surface charges.* The most poorly defined parameter in the threshold equation both in terms of technological processes and actual physical origin is the effective surface charge Q_{eff}. As used here this charge is made up of two contributions: Q_{ss} which arises from charges at the semiconductor-oxide interface and $Q_{b,o}$ a contribution which arises from space charge in the insulator. The relationship between these parameters is given by

$$Q_{eff} = Q_{ss} + Q_{b,o} = Q_{ss} + \frac{1}{t_{ox}} \int_0^{t_{ox}} x\rho(x)\,dx \qquad (3.4.4.7)$$

where $\rho(x)$ is a one-dimensional distribution, characterizing the charge density in the oxide. The variable x is measured from the gate electrode and normal to the oxide thickness. The contribution $-Q_{eff}\,t_{ox}/\varepsilon_{ox}$ as it appears in eqn (3.4.4.6) for a p-channel device is a statement of the fact that the electric field at the gate electrode arises from charges in the oxide (including Q_{ss}) and from charges in the semiconductor and that when Q_{eff} is positive (as it is normally) more negative charge is required on the gate electrode to produce the electric field necessary to cause inversion. The source of bulk charges in the oxide has been traced to alkali ionic contaminants, particularly sodium ions [3.4.35]. The motion of these ions may be indirectly observed by applying a drift field to the gate oxide of a MOS transistor and subsequently measuring the channel conductance as a function of gate voltage (transfer characteristic).

Since this characteristic depends on $V - V_T$, a systematic redistribution of charge will appear as a uniform translation of the characteristic along the voltage axis. A similar effect occurs in MOS capacitors. In this case the capacitance voltage characteristic depends on $V - V_{FB}$ where

$$V_{FB} = \Delta W_F - Q_{eff} \left(\frac{t_{ox}}{\varepsilon_{ox}} \right) \qquad (3.4.4.8)$$

and therefore, a measurement of this characteristic yields essentially the same information. Drift experiments of this type and radioactive tracer measurements suggest that the redistribution of sodium ions is responsible for shifts in the characteristics. Since the high temperature stability of MOS devices under bias is related to the motion of such ions, precautions must be taken during device fabrication to keep the gate oxide from becoming contaminated. Aside from simply keeping the fabrication process clean, the oxide can be treated with a P_2O_5 diffusion which further reduces the drift instability. By acting as a sodium getter, the P_2O_5 converts the upper portion of the oxide into phosphosilicate glass which has a much higher sodium solubility than silicon dioxide and, therefore, collects the contaminant from the underlying oxide making it unavailable for drift [3.4.36]. Elimination of the bulk charges from the oxide still leaves the surface charge Q_{ss} to effect the threshold voltage.

Even when great care is taken to prevent contaminants from entering the gate oxide, an unexpected shift in the characteristics of MOS devices occurs. The shift is attributed to a permanent surface charge, which resides in a few hundred angstroms of the oxide-silicon interface. Unlike bulk oxide charges arising from alkali ions the surface state charge exhibits no motion when subject to a drift field at high temperatures. Furthermore it cannot be charged or discharged by the application of an electric field to the oxide and appears to be relatively unaffected by changes in the oxide thickness. While impurities in the semiconductor do not significantly influence the surface charge, conditions related to the formation of the oxide do, which suggests that this charge arises from excess ionic silicon that has failed to react with oxygen atoms diffusing toward the semiconductor. For a given direction Q_{ss} depends on the type of oxidation (wet and dry) and temperature at which the process takes place. When a final anneal is used, the surface charge density is determined by this latter process so long as sufficient time is allowed for equilibrium to be reached. Since the rate of oxidation of a surface is proportional to the number of bonds per cm^2 available to react with the oxygen or water molecules it is also possible to correlate Q_{ss} with crystal orientation. Assuming that excess silicon is responsible for the surface charge and assuming that the higher the oxidation rate of a surface the greater the number of excess silicon ions, the surfaces with the most available bonds per area will have the largest Q_{ss} after oxidation. For silicon a (111) surface exposes about 12×10^{14} bonds cm^{-2} and a (100) surface

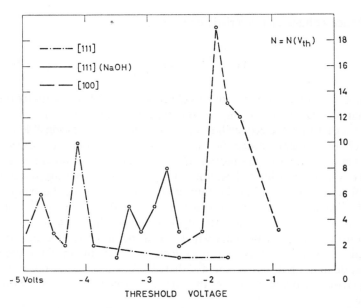

FIG. 3.4.4.5. Number of MOS devices N as a function of threshold voltage with crystal orientation as a parameter [3.4.37].

roughly half that number. Since the surface charge density for the [111] direction is of the order of 10^{12} cm^{-2} after oxidation, it should be possible to observe a change in the threshold voltage of a MOSFET with crystal orientation. Figure 3.4.4.5 shows the experimental verification of this effect for a number of p-channel devices fabricated on [111] and [100] oriented n-type silicon substrates (10 ohm cm) [3.4.37]. The oxides were grown in dry oxygen at 1200°C and the devices were subsequently annealed in N$_2$ for 30 minutes at 1100°C before metallization. No special precautions were taken to prevent alkali-ion contamination, nor was the oxide stabilized by a phosphosilicate glass layer. The distribution of device thresholds for the [111] and [100] directions reflects the difference in surface charge at the interfaces. The large surface charge associated with the [111] direction produces a more negative threshold voltage (-4V). For comparison the distribution for [111] devices etched with 10% NaOH prior to oxidation so as to favour development of the (100) faces is shown in Fig. 3.4.4.5 as in the [111] (NaOH) curve. As is expected, the peak of this distribution falls between the two other peaks at -2 and -4 V. Contamination of the oxide by the NaOH etch would shift the [111] distribution to more negative voltages. Similar curves for devices with molybdenum instead of aluminium gates annealed at 380°C for 62 hours after metallization show a reduction in the threshold voltage for all directions indicating a decrease in the corresponding surface charge.

The experimental data in Fig. 3.4.4.5 indicates that for conventional technology about a two volt reduction in the threshold voltage should be expected for typical oxide thicknesses in going from a [111] to a [100] oriented device. Unfortunately this reduction in device threshold is also reflected in the parasitic threshold which in the case of (100) transistors is about 10–17 V. For about the same threshold voltage, silicon gate technology produces devices with significantly higher parasitic thresholds. Combining silicon gate technology with the [100] orientation, however, can be used to produce extremely low threshold devices (0.4 V) with rather high parasitic margins (factor of 20–40).

(iii) *Dielectric constant of the oxide.* For p-channel enhancement devices (Si–SiO$_2$) a large portion of the threshold voltage is determined by the sum of the last two terms in eqn (3.4.4.6). For typical impurity concentrations (10^{15} cm^{-3}) the effective surface charge term is 3 to 5 times larger than the depletion region term depending on conditions at the oxide–silicon interface. Since both are divided by the gate capacitance per unit area $C_0 = \varepsilon_{ox}/t_{ox}$ it is convenient to lump them together when considering the effect of the dielectric constant on the threshold voltage. Hence for the following discussion it is not necessary to understand the physical origin of the depletion region term. This term will be considered in more detail in a later section in connection with its dependence on impurity concentration and substrate voltage.

Since the gate capacitance C_0 depends on two parameters, the dielectric constant of the oxide ε_{ox} and the oxide thickness t_{ox}, either of these can be used to reduce the threshold voltage. The difficulty with reducing the threshold voltage by decreasing the oxide thickness lies in the process yields which drop off rapidly below 1000 Å. The other alternative is to select an insulating material with a higher dielectric constant than SiO$_2$. In view of the care required when using the SiO$_2$-Si system this approach is not entirely unreasonable. SiO$_2$ also has the disadvantage that it is rather sensitive to ionizing radiation. Induced space charge in the oxide can produce a shift in the threshold voltage just as do ionic contaminants and surface charges. The ultraclean fabrication procedures normally required to control ionic contamination (and consequently the ionic drift instability) could possibly be eliminated if a dielectric material could be found which avoids the problem of impurity redistribution. The low diffusivity of impurities in silicon nitride (Si$_3$N$_4$) suggests that it might be a good alternative to SiO$_2$ [3.4.14]. Of particular importance is the fact that the drift of sodium ions under temperature-bias conditions is considerably lower in silicon nitride than in silicon dioxide. Other purported advantages of silicon nitride based on its highly inert chemical nature include improved stability and control of the surface charge at the silicon nitride-silicon interface. Since the relative dielectric constant of silicon nitride is about 6.5 (roughly 1.5 times larger than that for silicon dioxide) for the same insulator thickness and the same surface charge, a reduction in the threshold voltage can be obtained over an oxide device. For $V_{sx} = Q_{ss}/C_0$ between 1.5 and 3.75 (typical range for [111] direction) a 0.5–1.0 V improvement is possible (ignoring the effect of the smaller depletion term). A still larger reduction may be obtained by using aluminium oxide (Al_2O_3) which has a higher relative dielectric constant (7.6) than Si_3N_4 and which also has the advantage that it is comparatively immune to ionizing radiation [3.4.15]. When silicon nitride is used directly on silicon, charge instabilities at the interface result in a hysteresis behaviour of the threshold voltage as a function of applied gate voltage. This behaviour persists even when a thin oxide layer (< 500 Å) is inserted between the silicon nitride and the silicon substrate and is believed to be due in this case to the charging and discharging of traps at the Si_3N_4–SiO_2 interface. By increasing the thickness of the oxide layer and decreasing the conductivity of the silicon nitride, the charge transport mechanisms in the insulators may be suppressed and in this way the threshold voltage may be stabilized. When no charge accumulation occurs at the interface the device behaves like a conventional MOS field effect transistor and the threshold voltage is given by eqn (3.4.4.6) with the effective oxide thickness determined by

$$t_{ox}^{eff} = t_{ox} + \frac{\varepsilon_{ox}}{\varepsilon_n} t_n \qquad (3.4.4.9)$$

where ε_n is the dielectric constant of the silicon nitride and t_n is the thickness of the Si_3N_4 layer. Obviously, the importance of the dielectric constant ε_n with respect to the threshold voltage diminishes as t_{ox} increases relative to t_n. Since stability requires that the oxide be relatively thick ($t_{ox} \approx 500$ Å compared to $t_n \approx 500$ Å) the role played by the dielectric constant in this case is minor. Whether or not the extra process steps required are worthwhile is questionable even in view of the excellent passivation properties of the silicon nitride layer. If the oxide layer could be completely eliminated with either no change or a decrease in the surface charge density the threshold voltage should be substantially reduced.

The charge instability of the Si_3N_4–SiO_2 interface is rather more interesting from another standpoint and that is in connection with non-volatile semiconductor memories. This effect may be employed in the construction of non-volatile MNOS transistors by reducing the thickness of the oxide so that direct electron tunnelling into the interface traps is possible [3.4.38].

In this case the properties of the device are quite different from a conventional MOSFET. Accumulated charge Q at the interface modifies the threshold voltage by the factor

$$\Delta V_{\mathrm{T}} = -\frac{Q - Q(0)}{C_{\mathrm{n}}} \qquad (3.4.4.10)$$

where $Q(0)$ is the initial charge per unit area at the Si_3N_4–SiO_2 interface and $C_{\mathrm{n}} = \varepsilon_{\mathrm{n}}/t_{\mathrm{n}}$ is the capacitance per unit area of the nitride layer. The effective insulator thickness to be used in connection with the surface charge (and depletion layer) term is given as before by eqn (3.4.4.9). The application of a large positive voltage to the gate of a MNOSFET causes a negative charge to build up on the Si_3N_4–SiO_2 interface and thus shifts the threshold voltage to more positive values. Since the oxide tunnelling current shows a sharp rise with field, a critical gate voltage V_{CT} is required before significant charging will occur. A gate voltage below this value will not cause changes in the threshold voltage. A similar situation occurs for a negative bias in which case electrons must tunnel from the traps into the semiconductor. Figure 3.4.4.6 shows the threshold hysteresis characteristic for a p-channel MNOSFET along with the device cross-section. This computed characteristic is for a device with $t_{\mathrm{ox}} = 15$ Å and $t_{\mathrm{n}} = 600$ Å that is designed to switch in 100 μs, when ± 25 V is applied to the gate. An attempt to realize this device has been moderately successful yielding a positive threshold (transistor normally on) for the "0" state instead of the computed -1 V threshold, and yielding an improved switching speed of 1 μs. Since the conductivity of the nitride layer determines the long term discharge rate of the traps it must be made very low to produce reliable devices. For the device reported the

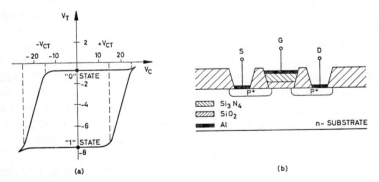

FIG. 3.4.4.6. p-Channel MNOSFET: (a) threshold voltage versus gate charging voltage and (b) device cross-section.

Q

voltage margin $|V_T(\text{"0"}) - V_T(\text{"1"})|$ was greater than 5 V after 100 hours at 125°C and extrapolated to 1 V at 10 000 hours at 125°C on the basis of the activation energy of the silicon nitride current density. It is obvious that discrimination between the "0" and "1" states can be accomplished by interrogating the gate with a voltage lying between the corresponding thresholds.

The Si_3N_4–SiO_2 system is not the only one which has been found to display threshold hysteresis. A similar effect occurs with Al_2O_3–SiO_2 [3.4.39]. In a MAOS system a net negative charge is associated with the insulating layers for both positive and negative gate voltages. Only when a very large negative bias is applied does the charge change to a positive value. Presumably negative charge is associated with traps at the Al_2O_3–SiO_2 interface and under normal circumstances this compensates the positive charge associated with the SiO_2–Si interface. The application of a large negative voltage apparently reduces the negative charge and thus reverses the situation. The positive threshold shift provided by the Al_2O_3–SiO_2 system forms the basis for n-channel enhancement mode devices with low substrate doping. The positive surface charge associated with SiO_2 alone will normally invert this type of substrate causing the device to operate in the depletion mode.

(iv) *Impurity concentration.* Since the last term in the threshold voltage equation for p-channel devices appears with a negative sign, obviously the least negative value of V_T will be obtained when the parameters N_d and $|V_s - V_{substr}|$ are zero. The latter condition can be satisfied by connecting the source directly to the substrate via a metal electrode, which under these conditions eliminates the bias aspect from consideration. Since the device will not operate when there are no donors, the favourable alternative of low doping is generally chosen. For an n-channel enhancement device the plus sign maintains the above relationship between parameters, however, in this case the situation is such that at comparable doping levels and with standard oxide thicknesses (1000 Å thin, 10 000 Å thick) the threshold voltages (device and parasitic) are too low. The solution to this problem is to use the parameters N_a and $|V_s - V_{substr}|$ to increase them. In the former case increasing the substrate doping is not attractive because it increases the depletion layer capacitance of the source and drain regions thereby degrading the speed of the device. The alternative is to selectively increase the doping of the channel region. This can be done conveniently by bombarding the substrate with high energy impurity ions which lodge themselves in the lattice and after subsequent processing become electrically active impurity centres [3.4.40]. This technique can also be used in connection with p-channel devices to compensate for the substrate donor impurities in the channel region, thus further reducing V_T. When the high energy facilities necessary for ion implantation are not available the other alternative in the case of n-channel devices is to use a lightly doped substrate and increase the reverse bias on the source to substrate junction. This method for controlling V_T will be discussed in the next section. Currently there are two techniques which have gained widespread acceptance in connection with planar IC technology which are used to introduce impurities into semiconductors. Epitaxial growth is a process by which a single-crystal film is grown on a substrate of the same or nearly the same lattice structure. For example in planar technology it is common to grow a thin high resistivity silicon layer on top of a thicker low resistivity substrate and use this combination as the starting point for device fabrication. Other noteworthy examples include silicon on sapphire which may also be used in connection with integrated circuits and silicon on quartz which is being investigated as still another alternative. The deposition of a silicon layer on a silicon substrate is commonly effected by the hydrogen reduction of silicon tetrachloride at high temperatures. A gaseous mixture of H_2 and $SiCl_4$ in the neighbourhood of 1200°C is allowed to pass over an exposed surface which serves as the "seed" for the resulting structure. Using this technique epitaxial layers down to $3\mu m$ with $\pm 10\%$ deviation in thickness can be formed. For thinner layers the percent deviation is generally due to the irregular conditions at the start and finish of the process. Impurities may be introduced into the epitaxial layer by adding the required gaseous phase impurity to the H_2–$SiCl_4$ mixture. In this way the doping can be varied between $5 \times 10^{15}\,cm^{-3}$ and $10^8\,cm^{-3}$ with about $\pm 10\%$ accuracy in concentration in the main part of the layer. Because the flow process is continuous the doping profile may easily be controlled as the layer is grown. Rather complicated impurity distributions can be obtained. Generally epitaxial growth is used in connection with MOS ICs only to form a lightly doped layer ($10^{15}\,cm^{-3}$) on a heavily doped substrate ($10^{19}\,cm^{-3}$). As was mentioned, the motivation for building circuits on a high resistivity material is the accompanying reduction in junction capacitance.

Impurities are introduced locally in conventional MOS ICs by solid-state diffusion. Geometrical control is obtained by etching windows in a SiO_2 layer on the silicon surface—the unetched portions of the oxide subsequently act as a mask against diffusion. The impurities are initially introduced into the semiconductor by introducing them into an inert (carrier) gas which flows over the semiconductor sample. The process is generally carried out in a furnace at temperatures in the 800 to 1200°C range and may involve the formation of an oxide layer on the substrate. The reduction of phosphor oxide (P_2O_5) by silicon is commonly used in conventional technology and produces a SiO_2 layer during phosphorous predeposition. When the concentration of impurities at the surface is kept constant the resulting impurity distribution in the semiconductor is described by a complementary error function with characteristic diffusion length $2(Dt_p)^{\frac{1}{2}}$, where D is the diffusivity of the impurity in the host and t_p is the predeposition time. Further high temperature heat treatment in the presence of an inert gas or an oxidizing atmosphere drives the impurities deeper into the semiconductor. Under oxidizing conditions the impurities are sealed into the silicon and the resulting distribution becomes approximately Gaussian with the diffusion length $2(Dt_d)^{\frac{1}{2}}$ being in this case determined by the drive-in diffusion time t_d which is in practice considerable longer than t_p. Using these techniques, doped regions of an few tenths of a micron thick and a few microns wide can be formed, as for example, in the source and drain regions of a MOSFET. Controlling the predeposition conditions (surface concentration), temperature, and time allow a variety of impurity profiles to be obtained. The main limitations stem from the inability to control the surface concentration at low impurity concentrations and anomalous diffusion due to lattice strain at high impurity concentrations.

Recently ion implantation has been receiving more and more attention as an alternative method for introducing impurities into semiconductors [3.4.40]. Interest in this technique stems from three major factors (1) the process can be carried out at temperatures substantially lower than those used for solid state diffusion, (2) the doping profile associated with a monoenergetic beam is considerably different from that obtained by diffusion, (3) almost any dopant may be used in ion implantation—the restrictions associated with undesirable or unwanted chemical reactions are avoided completely. The process involves accelerating ionized particles to energies between 10 and 300 keV and directing a beam of these particles at semiconductor samples. The concentration and penetration depth of the particles can be controlled by varying the beam current and energy respectively. Implantation can be done at room temperature and is generally followed by an anneal at about 600°C which repairs the radiation damage and causes the impurities to take up electrically active sites on the lattice. The physical mechanisms involved to produce these changes are currently being investigated. Figure 3.4.4.7 shows the distribution of electrically active boron impurities in [111] silicon obtained by locating the positions of pn junctions in a series of counterdoped substrates. The maximum penetration depth of about 0.5 μm at 50 keV is typical for boron, arsenic and phosphorus in [111] silicon. The observed distribution lies slightly deeper than that predicted on the basis of the amorphous theory of Lindhard [3.4.41] (solid curve) based upon a gaussian distribution with the maximum located below the surface of the semiconductor (in contrast to the gaussian distribution with the maximum at the surface obtained after a drive-in-diffusion). By varying the energy and dose a number of such distributions can be superimposed to obtain a variety of profiles.

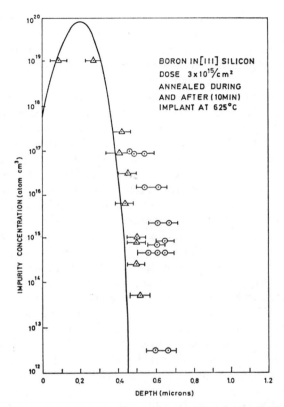

FIG. 3.4.4.7. Distribution of electrically active boron impurities implanted at 60 KeV in (111) silicon [3.4.41].

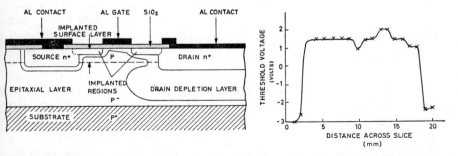

FIG. 3.4.4.8. Ion implanted MOS transistor; (a) cross-section showing channel, source and drain implant regions and (b) device thresholds for MOSFET's constructed on an implanted slice [3.4.46].

Ion implantation is particularly well suited for processing MOS devices because their active regions are very close to the surface which makes them accessible at relatively low voltages (<100 keV). One application which is currently receiving attention is control of MOS threshold voltages by implantation doping of the channel region.

Figure 3.4.4.8(a) shows a cross-section of an n-channel enhancement MOSFET which has been constructed on a high resistivity epitaxial layer. p-Type impurities have been ion implanted in the surface layer to increase the normally low threshold voltage. An added benefit is a reduction in the spreading of the drain depletion layer toward the source with its consequent reduction in output conductance. The source and drain regions of the device shown in Fig. 3.4.4.8(a) have also been implanted in order to reduce gate overlap for reasons which will be discussed in a later section. For this case channel implantation was performed before the gate oxide was grown. 100 keV boron ions were used giving a penetration depth of about 0.6 μm. The resulting concentration of 10^{16} atoms per cubic centimetre produced a threshold voltage of 1.5 V in connection with a 0.12 μm thick gate oxide (grown in wet oxygen at 1100°C) and an aluminium gate. Producing a similar surface layer by diffusion would be extremely difficult due to the low concentration of impurities and shallow depth required. Figure 3.4.4.8(b) shows the variation of device threshold voltages across a slice which has been implanted under the same conditions as the device in Fig. 3.4.4.8(a). Only the central region has been implanted and, as can be seen, the threshold variation is less than ±0.5 V across the slice. While the devices described here were implanted before the gate oxide was formed the order of processing can be reversed because the ions will easily penetrate a thin layer of amorphous material. It is advantageous to arrange the processing so that ion implantation is done after any high temperature treatments because the subsequent low temperature anneal will not alter the previously formed impurity profiles. Low threshold p-channel devices have been constructed after oxide growth by implanting boron through the thin gate oxide using the thick oxide covering other regions as a mask.

(v) *Substrate bias.* Since the depletion region contribution to the threshold voltage arises from bulk impurity charges (fixed) uncovered by the difference between the surface potential at points along the channel and the substrate potential, it can be modified by biasing the substrate. Up to this point it has been implicitly assumed that the substrate is held at the same potential as the source in which case the threshold voltage is determined by eqn (3.4.4.6) with $|V_s - V_{substr}| = 0$. Reverse biasing the substrate relative to the source has the effect of increasing the depletion width at every point along the channel with the result that for a p-channel enhancement device more positive charge is uncovered during inversion thus requiring a corresponding increase in the negative charge on the gate or equivalently an increase in the magnitude of V_T. For an n-channel enhancement device a similar increase in $|V_T|$ occurs due to the increase in uncovered negative fixed charge. These effects are reflected in a contribution:

$$\Delta V_T = \frac{\Delta Q_b}{C_0} = \mp q \frac{N_{a,\,d}}{C_0} \Delta W = \mp \frac{1}{C_0} \left(2\varepsilon_{Si} q N_{a,\,d} |V_s - V_{substr}|\right)^{\frac{1}{2}} \quad (3.4.4.11)$$

ΔW is the increase in width of the depletion region due to the reverse bias and is the same at every point along the channel. This change in depletion width produces a change ΔQ_b in the bulk semiconductor charge which by comparison with the unbiased case produces a shift $\Delta V_T = \Delta Q_b/C_0$ in the threshold voltage.

Figure 3.4.4.9 shows a plot of eqn (3.4.4.11) as a function of the source to substrate voltage for an n-channel transistor for thick and thin oxides [3.4.42].

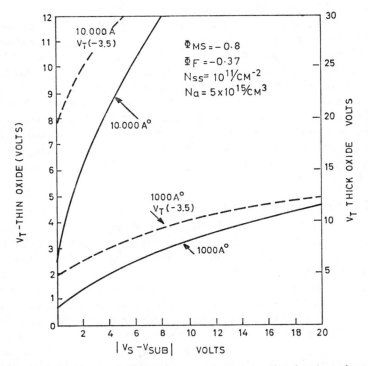

FIG. 3.4.4.9. Calculated threshold voltage V_T for substrate biased n-channel transistor. The dashed curves show the resulting characteristics for a -3.5 V substrate bias [3.4.42].

The curves are computed for a device with a substrate impurity concentration of $N_a = 5 \times 10^{15}$ cm^{-3} and a surface charge density of $N_{ss} = 10^{11}$ cm^{-2}. For this doping level which is desirable from a speed standpoint the threshold voltage of the device is extremely low when $|V_s - V_{substr}| = 0$. A study of the n-channel inverter indicates that the area occupied by the circuit reaches a minimum when the threshold voltage is about 2 V for a 5 V supply. Reducing the supply or threshold voltage much below these values causes a degradation of the noise immunity of the inverter and furthermore requires a non-standard supply; 5 V supplies are used in connection with bipolar TTL. Figure 3.4.4.9 indicates that a -3.5 V substrate bias will produce the desired threshold—the dashed lines show the corresponding characteristics. Using a low substrate doping has a further advantage here (in addition to reducing the junction capacitances) and that is the reduction in sensitivity of the thin oxide threshold voltage to variations in the substrate bias. For a 3.5 V bias the thick oxide threshold voltage is about 20 V which yields a device margin of 10 when $V_T = 2$ V. The threshold curves indicate that this parameter is relatively insensitive to the bias and this allows the more favourable 2 V threshold to be chosen. Since both n- and p-channel devices with this threshold require about the same supply voltage (5–10 V), there will be little difference in their power requirements. There is, however, considerable difference in their switching speed and this makes the speed-power product of n-channel devices about a factor 2.5 lower. The substrate bias makes it possible for n-channel devices to realize their full speed potential and therefore is an important technique. The disadvantages are that it requires an additional power supply and that the substrate can no longer be used as a ground bus. The latter situation forces one to use additional metal interconnections on the surface of the chip thus reducing the useful device area. The light substrate doping also yields a low source to drain breakdown voltage.

3.4.4.3. Speed-power Product

The threshold voltage is probably the most fundamental parameter associated with an inverter because to a large extent it dictates the operating voltage level (V_{DD}) which in turn determines the operating speed and power dissipation. For semiconductor memory devices, however, both of the latter factors are important in their own right from a technological standpoint because there exist a number of different technologies which optimize one or another of these factors alone. It will be convenient to defer the discussion of power dissipation untill the last section of this chapter, where the question of loads is taken up. This allows the comparison of power to be made between what are really different circuit concepts as opposed to different technologies which are discussed in the first three sections.

The basis for the following discussion will initially be the MOS inverter shown in Fig. 3.4.4.1(a). The switching time of this device depends on the type of MOS load used which in this case is assumed to be a saturated enhancement type MOS transistor (*p*- or *n*-channel). Since the conductance of the load is chosen much smaller than that for the "on" driver when resistance-ratio circuitry is employed, the switching time is limited by the process in which C_L is charged through the MOS load. This is illustrated in Fig. 3.4.4.10, where the turn on and turn off transients of a *p*-channel inverter are presented [3.4.43]. The turn-off time is roughly a factor of 10 slower than the turn-on time reflecting the difference in aspect ratios (channel width W/channel length L) of source and driver. The time constant τ governing the turn off time is

$$\tau = \frac{L^2}{\mu_n} \frac{C_L}{C_g} \frac{1}{|V_{DD} - V_T|} = \frac{L^2}{\mu_n} \frac{C_L t_{ox}}{\varepsilon_{ox}} \frac{1}{|V_{DD} - V_T|} \qquad (3.4.4.12)$$

in terms of basic device parameters. Here as in eqns (3.4.4.1) and (3.4.4.2) L is the channel length, μ_n the mobility, ε_{ox} the dielectric constant of the gate oxide, t_{ox} the gate oxide thickness and C_g the gate capacitance. Equation (3.4.4.12) also applies in the case of an unsaturated load. The voltage transient for either case is given, approximately, by

$$\frac{V(t)}{V_{DD} - V_T} = \frac{(2-m)\left[1 - e^{-(1-m)t/\tau}\right]}{(2-m)\left[1 + e^{-(1-m)t/\tau}\right]} \qquad (3.4.4.13)$$

with $m = V_{GG}/V_{DD}$. When the gate voltage on the load transistor V_{GG} equals V_{DD}, the load is saturated ($m = 1$) and for a fixed τ the voltage transient is the

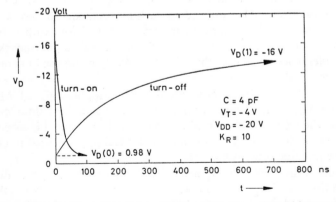

FIG. 3.4.4.10. Turn on and turn off transients of a *p*-channel inverter.

longest. Hence to obtain short switching times it is best to operate the load in the unsaturated mode ($0 \leqslant m < 1$). Since τ is the governing speed parameter in all cases, reducing it through any of the variables L, μ, C_L or C_g will be beneficial in terms of operating speed. Since for conventional silicon processing both t_{ox} and ε_{ox} are fixed, L, μ and C_L are left as possible choices for speed based MOS technologies. The following three sections describe these technologies and the fourth section describes how circuit concepts can lead to speed improvements. Just as going from a saturated to an unsaturated load produces an improvement, so does, for example, replacing an enhancement load by a depletion one. The unsaturated load is inconvenient because it requires a second supply voltage. The alternatives to be discussed in the last section do not suffer from this disadvantage.

(i) *Channel length.* The parameter most effective in controlling the switching speed of a MOSFET inverter is the channel length L because it appears to the second power in eqn (3.4.4.12). For conventional devices a lower limit is set on L by the accuracy of the photomasking techniques used. For contact masking diffraction of light at the pattern edges and at the gap between mask and wafer limits the production of channel lengths to several microns under manufacturing conditions. Using more sophisticated photolithographic techniques such as projection masking the channel length can be reduced to about 1 micron. For typical MOS parameters ($|V_{DD} - V_T| = 10V$ and $\mu_p = 250\,\mathrm{cm^2\,V^{-1}\,s^{-1}}$) an estimate of eqn (3.4.4.12) indicates that when $C_{gate} \approx C_{load}$ the switching time lies in the sub-nano-second range. Note that when $C_{gate}/C_{load} = 1$ the expression for the switching time just corresponds to the transit time required for a hole (p-channel) to pass from the source to the drain. If it were possible to construct MOS transistors with 1 micron channel lengths using conventional photomasking techniques considerable speed improvement over existing digital IC's could be obtained. Recently a two-stage diffusion technique has been announced which has successfully been used to fabricate microwave transistors with sub-micron channel length [3.4.44, 3.4.45]. The technique requires photomasking and diffusion tolerances no stricter than those presently being used in connection with conventional bipolar technology.

Figure 3.4.4.11 shows a cross-section of a double-diffused MOSFET (D/MOS) along with its impurity profile. The terminology double-diffused arises from the technique for forming the channel region and has been taken over the bipolar technology in which a similar technique is used to construct microwave junction transistors.

The process involves forming a narrow channel region by the difference in penetration depth of two consecutive opposite impurity-type diffusions. One method of doing this is to diffuse in a p-region through the source

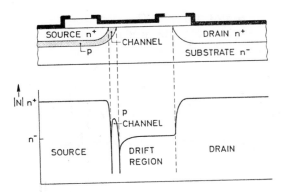

FIG. 3.4.4.11. Double-diffused n-channel MOSFET with doping profile.

window under non-oxidizing conditions. The outer extremities of this diffusion become the channel after the n^+ source is formed. The latter process can be combined with the drain diffusion and therefore can be incorporated into the conventional sequence of steps. Hence only one extra diffusion step is required. The threshold voltage of the device is determined by the doping of the p-channel and values between -4 and $+2$ V have been obtained. The transistor shown in Fig. 3.4.4.11 was constructed for high frequency performance and for this reason is an n-channel device. The high mobility of electrons yields an improvement in speed over a similar p-channel device as will be discussed in the next section.

Discrete transistors of the type shown in Fig. 3.4.4.11 with channel lengths less than a micron have produced gains in the low gigahertz frequency range. A unique feature of the D/MOS transistor is the drift region which overlaps what ordinarily would be the channel region. In a conventional device the resulting source to drain Miller feedback capacitance would seriously hinder its performance. In a D/MOS device this problem is circumvented by reducing the doping of the substrate. As a result a high field drain depletion region forms in the drift region which sweeps the carriers to the drain. Modulation of the carriers occurs only in the channel region, however, so that the effective transit time is determined by the distance L. The length of the drift region may be chosen independently from the channel length and may be used to control the breakdown voltage of the device. Using high-breakdown voltage techniques, values as high as 300 V have been obtained.

(ii) *Capacitance.* The characteristic switching speed of the inverter shown in Fig. 3.4.4.1(a) depends strongly upon the size of the load capacitance

C_L as indicated by eqn (3.4.4.12). The identification of the factors contributing to C_L is complicated by the large number of capacitance parameters associated with the MOSFET. Assuming that the inverter is located at an intermediate point in an integrated circuit for the common source configuration of Fig. 3.4.4.1, with the substrate held at ground potential, C arises from the inverter output capacitance (drain to substrate capacitance) and the input capacitance to the following stage. Assuming the latter to be another inverter, the capacitance C_L is just the sum of the input and output capacitances of two different inverters which becomes essentially (upon neglecting small series substrate resistances)

$$\overset{(1)}{} \qquad \overset{(2)}{}$$
$$C_L = C_{output} + C_{input} \qquad\qquad (3.4.4.14)$$

$$\underbrace{\qquad}_{\text{inverter 1}} \qquad \underbrace{\qquad\qquad\qquad\qquad}_{\text{inverter 2}}$$

$$C_L = \quad \underset{\underset{\text{substrate}}{\underset{\text{to}}{\downarrow}}}{C_{db}} \quad + \quad \underset{\underset{\text{substr.}}{\underset{\text{to}}{\downarrow}}}{C_{gb}} + \underset{\underset{\text{source}}{\underset{\text{to}}{\downarrow}}}{C_{gs}} + \underset{\underset{\text{drain}}{\underset{\text{to}}{\downarrow}}}{C_{gd}} \underset{\underset{\text{effect}}{\underset{\text{Miller}}{\downarrow}}}{(1 + r_{sd}\, g_m)} \quad (3.4.4.15)$$

in which r_{sd} is the drain to source resistance and g_m is the transconductance.

For simplicity it will be assumed that both switching transistors are the same, as this allows a comparison between parameters to be made. The output capacitor $C_{output}^{(1)}$ consists of the drain to substrate depletion region capacitance C_{db} which shunts the output of the inverter and thus adds directly to the input capacitance of the following stage. This input capacitance arises from three contributions. The first of which is the gate to substrate capacitance C_{gb} associated with the conductor running from the output of the first inverter to the input gate of the following stage. This capacitance has both thick and thin oxide contributions; the relationship between the two depending upon cell layout and relative oxide thicknesses. The capacitance C_{gb} along with generally small gate to source overlap capacitor C_{gs} form the storage capacitor used in dynamic MOS circuitry. The third input capacitance C_{gd} is the same as the second for a transistor with symmetrical geometry. It arises from the gate to drain overlap but because it forms a feedback path between the output and input of the second stage it is enhanced by the Miller effect and therefore becomes as important as or even more important than the first input term depending upon device parameters. For a typical source to drain resistance of 10 kΩ and a typical transconductance of 1000 μmhos the enhancement factor is 10 suggesting that the Miller effect will play an important role in determining the switching speed τ. Estimates of the input and output capacitances for a typical low impedance shift register transistor confirm this, yielding values of $C_{gd} = C_{gs} = 0.06\,\mathrm{pF}$, $C_{gb} = 0.22 + 0.28 = 0.5\,\mathrm{pF}$ and $C_{db} = 0.16\,\mathrm{pF}$ for a 2 mil wide channel when the ratio of gate overlap to oxide thickness is about 60. The thin oxide and diffused line contributions are about equal. Hence the principal factors controlling the switching speed τ through the effective load capacitance C are (1) the Miller effect (C_{gd}), (2) the interconnection and gate capacitance (C_{gb}) and (3) the drain depletion region capacitance (C_{db}). If any one or all of these capacitances can be reduced (assuming fixed channel width and oxide thickness) eqn (3.4.4.12) indicates that an improvement in speed will result. A number of different technologies exist (some of which have already been discussed) which accomplish this either as a direct goal or as a fringe benefit.

In conventional MOS technology, mask alignment in connection with gate oxide formation sets the limit on device size and interelectrode overlap. To go beyond this limit it is necessary to eliminate the problem of aligning the gate electrode (or oxide) with the channel. This can be accomplished by performing the source and drain diffusions after the gate oxide is in place. As was mentioned earlier, silicon gate technology provides this self-aligning feature. For fixed impedance levels ($W/L = $ constant) the result is a reduction in device size and source to drain overlap both of which improve the switching times τ through C. The thin oxide contribution to C_{gb} from the gate region can be reduced by as much as 50% (to $0.14\,\mathrm{pF}$) due to the decrease in device size. The interconnection capacitances will also be reduced by the overall size reduction, for a shift register about a 33% decrease in this factor occurs in going from conventional to silicon-gate technology. The overall size decrease is also reflected in the drain junction area resulting in a 30–40% reduction in C_{db} (to $0.064\,\mathrm{pF}$). Finally we come to the most important factor, the Miller capacitance. For conventional technology as much as an 8–10 μm gate overlap above the source occurs. With silicon gate technology this figure is reduced to less than a micron and as a result for the equivalent device size somewhat less than an order of magnitude improvement is possible (to $0.01\,\mathrm{pF}$). Together these figures indicate that for the same impedance level about a 50% reduction in τ occurs in going from conventional to silicon gate technology which corresponds quite well to observed speeds for existing shift registers.

The above speed improvement is primarily due to the reduction in Miller capacitance and device size, both of which are directly or indirectly consequences of the self-aligning diffusion. A number of other techniques can be used to achieve this self-aligning feature, one of which is ion implantation. As was discussed in connection with the threshold voltage, ion implantation can be used to produce a thin high conductivity surface layer upon which a low threshold MOSFET may be formed. It may also be used to extend the source and drain diffusions up to the gate electrode as shown in Fig. 3.4.4.8, thus providing all of the speed advantages associated with a self-aligned structure. In one of the more common approaches the source and drain regions are diffused 15 μm apart instead of the 5–10 μm normally used [3.4.46]. The gate electrode is then formed between the source and drain diffusions on a thin oxide layer which extends over the source and drain regions. Bombarding the structure with 100 keV boron ions (p-channel device) allows the diffused region to extend to the edge of the gate electrode which in this case acts as a radiation shield or impurity mask. Because the process can be done at room-temperature followed by a short low temperature anneal there is virtually no lateral diffusion of impurities as occurs in the case of silicon gate technology. Hence feed-back capacitances as low as 0.002 pF can be obtained for the 2 mil wide structure mentioned previously (compared to 0.06 pF and 0.01 pF for conventional and silicon gate technologies).

Since even at the improved technological level of silicon gate technology the Miller feedback capacitance $C_{gd}(1 + r_{sd} g_m)$ is small relative to the "interconnection capacitance", C_{gb}, not much speed improvement over silicon gate devices should be expected. The principal difference should arise from the interconnection layouts which would appear to give silicon gate technology an advantage due to its two level interconnection capability. From these considerations it is clear that the ultimate speed of MOS devices will be approached only when the interconnection capacitance and drain depletion region capacitance are minimized (presupposing a small Miller feedback capacitance). The device shown in Fig. 3.4.4.8 to a large extent succeeds in achieving this goal because it has low drain to gate feedback and because the drain depletion region is located in a low conductivity epitaxial layer causing the associated capacitance to be small. Unfortunately the high conductivity of the p-layer (assumed to extend over the whole chip) causes the interconnection capacitances to be troublesome. Any portion of the gate conductor (in this discussion the gate conductor extends from the drain of the first inverter to the gate of the second) lying over the p-layer appears as a parasitic capacitor in series with a small resistor connecting the gate to the source. To achieve ultimate MOS speeds it is necessary to break the low resistance path connecting the source to any point below the gate conductor. Since the epitaxial p-layer already has a low conductivity, little change in the speed of the device will occur if it is replaced by an insulator. If, however, the p-layer is removed in regions away from the channel and the gate connector is allowed to lie on the insulator it becomes isolated from the source, thereby eliminating the associated parasitic capacitance. Figure 3.4.4.12(a) shows how silicon on sapphire technology can be used to form isolated silicon islands on an insulating substrate thereby reducing both the interconnection

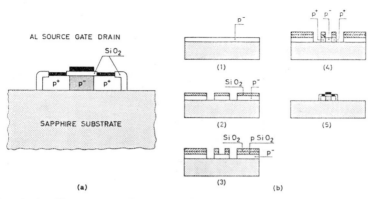

FIG. 3.4.4.12. Silicon on sapphire technology: (a) complete device and (b) processing steps: (1) deposition of p⁻ silicon layer, (2) oxide formation, photomasking, and etching of islands, (3) oxide removal, reformation of phosphorus-doped oxide and undoped oxide layers, etching of gate regions, (4) diffusion of phosphorus into source and drain regions and (5) oxide removal and reformation and deposition of contacts.

and drain depletion region capacitances. [3.4.47]. Figure 3.4.4.12(b) illustrates one process sequence currently being used to form p-channel enhancement devices. Standard oxide masking techniques allow formation of the geometrical patterns and isolation of the transistors. Device parameters are typical for MOS with the semiconductor thickness being 1 μm and channel length being 10 μm. Interconnections between islands are made using 1.5 μm thick aluminium lines, Since conventional processing produces rather large gate to drain overlap the transistor in Fig. 3.4.4.12(a) still suffers from the Miller effect. From the previous estimates it would appear that p-MOS SOS should not be much faster than silicon gate technology. A tremendous improvement in speed would occur, however, if the Miller capacitance could be decreased by employing a self-aligning technique such as ion implantation. Alternatively forming a MOS transistor in an ion implanted layer (just enough to contain the device) located in a low conductivity substrate would achieve essentially the same effect provided ion implantation was used to extend the source and drain regions up to the gate.

(iii) *Mobility.* Equation (3.4.4.12) indicates that mobility plays as important a role in determining the switching speed τ as does the channel length or load capacitance. The number of mobility based MOS technologies is somewhat more limited, however, due to the universal use of silicon in connection with commercially available integrated circuits. Within this restricted range of choices n-channel (silicon) MOS offers a number of features not available with other technologies, the most important of which

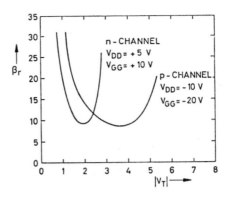

FIG. 3.4.4.13. Relation between β_r and threshold voltage [3.4.48].

are higher speed and bipolar compatibility. The higher speed arises principally because the mobility of electrons in p-type silicon is about a factor of 3 times larger than the mobility of holes based upon values for the (100) substrate. The mobilities for (100), (111) and (110) n-silicon are 450, 200 and 250 cm^2 V^{-1} s^{-1}. The compatibility is a consequence of the low threshold voltages used in connection with n-channel MOS. Figure 3.4.4.13 shows a plot of what amounts to chip area versus threshold voltage for an n- and p-channel inverter [3.4.48]. The ratio β_r is the sum of the W/L ratios for driver and load normalized to the W/L ratio of the load. The curves are based on the requirement that the output of the inverter correctly drives the following stage i.e. $V_{out}(0) = V_T - 0.5$ and $V_{out}(1) = 0.8 V_{DD}$.

The figure indicates that when the n-channel and p-channel thresholds are about 2 and 3.5 V respectively the required chip area is minimum and furthermore that under this condition the areas are about equal. Unfortunately the threshold voltage for an n-channel MOSFET normally lies in the 0.25 to 1 V range, as was mentioned previously. Reducing the supply voltage V_{DD} will shift the n-channel curve toward lower threshold voltages but as eqn (3.4.4.12) indicates it will also degrade the switching speed thus negating the principal motivation for going to n-channel devices. Furthermore the noise immunity of the inverter is poor, when the threshold (and supply) voltage are small. Another alternative is to increase the oxide thickness in order to increase V_T, but here again the switching time is increased through the reduction in gate capacitance. As indicated by the denominator of eqn (3.4.4.12) the speed advantage of n-channel MOS may be realized with no sacrifice in chip area. If substrate bias is used the latter approach allows the use of a low resistivity substrate which is an advantage because it decreases

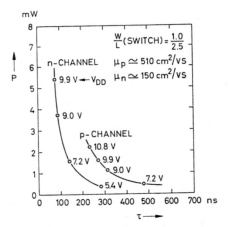

FIG. 3.4.4.14. Calculated speed-power curves for p- and n-channel NOR gates (Fan in = fan out < 3, unsaturated load). Relation between power/NOR gate P and gate delay τ (worst case) [3.4.42].

the depletion region capacitance. The additional bias on the drain to substrate junction has the same effect. Figure 3.4.4.14 compares the calculated speed power curves for both p- and n-channel dc coupled NOR gates (basically inverters with two or more driver transistors (switches) in parallel) and illustrates the trade-off possible between speed and power for the individual devices [3.4.42]. Load dimensions and threshold voltage have been optimized for each supply voltage and the load is operated in the unsaturated (linear) mode, in order to obtain maximum speed. At a fixed supply voltage the factor of 3 improvement in speed is a reflection of the higher mobility of n-channel devices. This same factor in speed can be traded-off for an improvement in power dissipation as may be verified by comparing the power dissipation of n- and p-channel devices at fixed speed. The latter comparison also reflects a 3 : 1 improvement in speed-power product. Thus for inverter based (logic or memory) circuits there is a very big advantage in going to n-channel devices. For example an n-channel two-phase shift register should ultimately be three times faster than its p-channel counterpart at comparable voltage levels. Unfortunately in the latter case the power dissipation also increases by a factor of three. However, at the same power levels the speed improvement is still about two times.

Mobility affects speed in another way and that is through the current level of the devices. Equations (3.4.4.1) and (3.4.4.2) indicate that for a given device geometry and at fixed voltage levels the drain current increases as the mobility. Since (for the same device geometries) the capacitances of p and

R

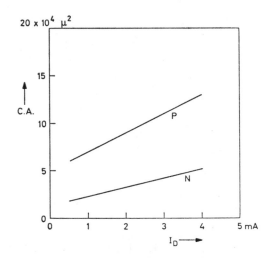

FIG. 3.4.4.15. Digit line current as a function of the cell area C.A. for *n*- and *p*-channel six device MOSFET memory cells [3.4.49].

n-channel circuitry are about the same, the charging time will just reflect this increase in charging current. Hence for device configurations in which a MOS transistor directly drives a load capacitor a factor of three in speed can be gained by using *n*-channel devices. In the six-transistor cell of Fig. 3.4.3.5 the access transistors either drive the flip-flop node capacitances or the digit line capacitances depending upon whether a read or write operation is being performed. Figure 3.4.4.15 compares cell area and digit line read out current for *n*- and *p*-channel six-device cells illustrating how mobility affects the cell area [3.4.49]. For a given cell area and word line voltage amplitude, *n*-channel devices yield considerably higher output currents which is particularly appealing when one thinks in terms of going to the extremely small cell sizes of the future. The lower threshold voltage is also appealing in this respect since it implies less power dissipation.

(iv) *Load.* Just as different MOS technologies can be used to optimize switching speed, so can various circuit concepts. This was suggested in an earlier section in connection with the discussion of dynamic four-phase shift registers. As was mentioned there, the principal limitation on the speed of an inverter is set by the requirement that the relative aspect ratio of load to driver transistor be small. Thus charging the output capacitor through the load becomes the (limiting) factor determining the switching time. In four-phase circuitry the aspect ratio considerations are eliminated by rearranging

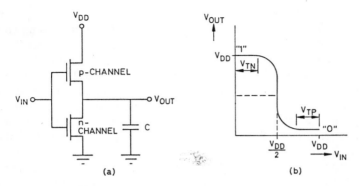

FIG. 3.4.4.16. (a) Complementary MOSFET inverter and (b) static characteristics.

the basic inverter circuit and employing devices with the same aspect throughout, resulting in a net increase in speed. A similar improvement can be
obtained by replacing the load of an inverter by a transistor which is on when
the driver is off and off when the driver is on. This can be accomplished by
interconnecting n- and p-channel transistors in series as shown in the so-
called complementary inverter of Fig. 3.4.4.16(a) [3.4.50]. One transistor
is in a high impedance state when the other is in a low one (considering for
the moment only the "0" and "1" logic states). The output characteristics
of the inverter are similar to those for a ratio logic inverter (compare Fig.
3.4.4.3 and Fig. 3.4.4.16(b)). Furthermore, since the ratio requirements
are relaxed, an improvement in speed can be obtained by decreasing the
impedance of what ordinarily would be called the load. If the threshold
voltages are exactly complementary i.e. $|V_{Tn}| = |V_{Tp}| = V_T$ and if

$$K_p = C_{gp}\,\mu_n\,Z_p/L_p = K_n = C_{gn}\,\mu_p\,Z_n/L_n$$

then the turn on and turn off times of the inverter will be the same with the
characteristic switching time (0–50%) being

$$\tau = \frac{L^2_p}{\mu_n}\,\frac{C_L}{C_{gp}}\,\frac{1}{|V_{DD}-V_T|} \qquad (3.4.4.16)$$

$$= \frac{C_L}{K|V_{DD}-V_T|} \qquad (3.4.4.17)$$

where the subscripts indicate to which transistor the associated parameter
belongs. Note that the required mobility for an n-channel transistor is μ_p
and for an p-channel device it is μ_n. Equation (3.4.4.16) is identical to that

for a p-channel ratio-logic inverter, as can be seen by comparing it to eqn
(3.4.4.12). The speed difference between conventional and complementary
circuitry arises principally from the difference in the parameter K. Since
K for a typical complementary transistor can be made 10 times larger than
for a typical p-channel load transistor, much higher speed would be expected
from complementary circuitry even though in general C_L is larger due to the
requirement that two gates instead of one must be driven. Examination of
the transfer characteristic shown in Fig. 3.4.4.16(b) indicates some other
important features of the complementary inverter. Compared to the conventional inverter the transition from the "0" to "1" state is considerably
more abrupt, suggesting that the noise threshold can be made very high.
Figure 3.4.4.16(b) shows the case when $|V_{Tp}| = |V_{Tn}|$ and $K_n = K_p$ for
which maximum noise immunity occurs with the transition point centred
at $V = V_{DD}/2$. When the threshold voltages differ the transition is located at

$$V = \frac{V_{DD} + V_{Tp} + V_{Tn}(K_n/K_p)^{\frac{1}{2}}}{1 + (K_n/K_p)^{\frac{1}{2}}}. \qquad (3.4.4.18)$$

Since K_n and K_p are related to the aspect ratios of the respective n- and
p-channel transistors, even when the threshold voltages differ, maximum
noise immunity ($V = V_{DD}/2$) can be obtained by adjusting geometries (the
difficulty with the latter approach is that in general the turn-on and turn-off
times will be different—the longer of the two limiting the switching time
much like the load does in an ordinary integrated inverter). Hence one minor
drawback of complementary circuitry is the need to construct transistors on
the same chip with $|V_{Tp}| = |V_{Tn}|$, in order to achieve maximum speed with
maximum noise immunity. The latter requirement places fairly severe
restrictions on the allowable processing technologies. The fact that the noise
margin of the complementary inverter is high ($\sim V_{DD}/2$), however, allows the
use of low threshold technologies (e.g. silicon gate technology) with the
result that complementary circuitry can be made bipolar compatible and the
power requirements can be made extremely small (at the expense of some
speed).

Under static conditions the power requirements of a complementary
inverter are determined by the leakage current I_L of the off device. Since this
current can be made extremely small ($\sim 10^{-9}$ A) the transient power usually
dominates at useful operating frequencies. The transient power is a result
of the current which flows during switching when the transistors conduct
simultaneously. The total power dissipated by a complementary inverter
is given by

$$P = P_s + CV_{DD}^2 f \qquad (3.4.4.19)$$

where the standby power $P_s = I_L V_{DD}$, C is the effective output capacitance

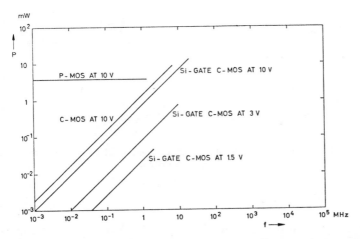

FIG. 3.4.4.17. Relation between power dissipation/gate P and frequency f for different technologies [3.4.51].

and f is the operating frequency. C represents the sum of many capacitances. The gate contribution in this case includes contributions from both p- and n-channel transistors, which are assumed to load the inverter (in the form of another inverter). For minimum power dissipation and maximum speed C should be as small as possible which explains the interest in combining complementary circuitry with capacitance eliminating technologies (such as silicon on sapphire). Reducing the supply voltage can be used to decrease the power requirements but only at the expense of switching speed (see eqn (3.4.4.16)).   Figure 3.4.4.17 summarizes the implications of eqn (3.4.4.19) by comparing conventional p-MOS and C-MOS circuit data with that for silicon gate C-MOS [3.4.51].

As was mentioned before silicon gate technology like SOS is a low capacitance technology but it does not suffer from the processing complications associated with SOS and therefore would appear to be more promising. For comparison purposes the power dissipated by the conventional p-channel inverter is given by

$$P = P_s + C[V_H{}^2 - V_L{}^2]f \qquad (3.4.4.20)$$

where $P_s = \theta\,|V_{DD}I_{Lo}|$ and $V_H = V_{DD} - V_T$. Here θ is the fraction of time spent in the "0" state, I_{Lo} the associated standby current and V_L the associated output "0" state voltage.   In most cases the dc contribution P_s in eqn (3.4.4.20) dominates the transient term up to several megahertz, which explains the flat behaviour of the p-MOS curve in Fig. 3.4.4.17.   It is

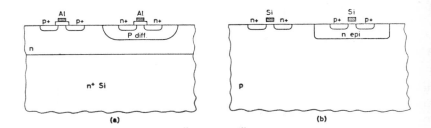

FIG. 3.4.4.18. (a) Cross-section of double diffused C-MOS and (c) cross-section of Si-gate C-MOS.

interesting to note that Si-gate C-MOS at 1.5 V is as fast as conventional p-MOS at 10 V but dissipates two orders of magnitude less power. The difference in speed between conventional C-MOS and Si-gate C-MOS (resulting from a decrease in C) is about a factor of 5 according to Fig. 3.4.4.17. It is fairly clear from Fig. 3.4.4.17 that C-MOS represents an improvement over p-MOS in-so-far as speed and power go. Unfortunately there are a number of other factors which undermine its superiority. Processing has up to this time been a major difficulty. C-MOS only seems desirable when extremely low power dissipation is required.

Conventional C-MOS fabrication involves diffusing a lightly doped p-type well into an n-type substrate. The p-type well becomes an n-channel transistor upon diffusing $n^{\pm}$ source and drain regions into it. A p-channel device can be formed outside the well by diffusing $p^{\pm}$ source and drain regions into the substrate as is illustrated in Fig. 3.4.4.18(a). The difficulty here is in controlling the surface concentration of impurities in the p-region which in turn dictates the threshold voltage of the n-channel device. Other disadvantages include high parasitic capacitance due to the Miller effect and larger than necessary channel length, both being due to photomask alignment and mask tolerances. If desired, doped oxide diffusions (self-aligning) can be used to dope the source and drain regions, thereby greatly reducing the latter problems.

Alternatively silicon gate technology naturally eliminates these problems by virtue of its self-aligned gate. Figure 3.4.4.18(b) shows one approach to Si-gate C-MOS in which epitaxial n-regions are grown in etched holes in a p-type substrate. The control of the n-type concentration is more easily achieved in this way than could be by conventional diffusion techniques. Once the substrate is prepared, the process steps become fairly conventional. The characteristics shown in Fig. 3.4.4.17 are for Si-gate devices prepared in this way.

3.4.5. PHYSICS AND TECHNOLOGY OF CHARGE TRANSFER DEVICES

3.4.5.1. Introduction

Fascinated by the magnetic bubble concept (see Section 3.2.4) where information transfer occurs by the simple shift of magnetic domains in thin magnetic layers or platelets, scientists at Bell Telephone Laboratories working in the semiconductor field searched eagerly for a device mechanism in semiconducting materials similar to the bubble transfer principle. The search was crowned with success in 1969 and a description of the new device called CCD (charge-coupled device) was given by Boyle and Smith [3.4.52] in 1970. The first device consisted of an array of closely spaced metal electrodes on top of an oxidized silicon substrate. Minority carriers can be stored in potential wells beneath the electrodes. These minority carriers move from one electrode to the next when, by means of the application of a voltage, the next potential well is made deeper. Compared to the magnetic bubble concept, the magnetic bubble domain is replaced by a minority carrier charge packet. Information transfer, which in the bubble shift register is realized by magnetic field gradients, occurs in a CCD by drift and diffusion of the minority carriers from one electrode to the next. Figure 3.4.5.1 shows how shift registers based on the CCD concept operate.

The electrodes are connected in groups of three to a three-phase pulse generator. When an n-type silicon substrate is used all the electrodes receive a negative bias (-5 V) voltage such that the surface layer is depleted from majority carriers (electrons). Electrodes 1 receive an extra negative voltage of -5 V causing the formation of potential wells beneath them. By means to be discussed later minority carrier (holes) are injected into this first potential well. When the potentials on electrodes 2 are made more negative (-15 V), these holes will move to electrode 2. Subsequently, the voltages on electrodes 1 and 2 are reduced to -5 V and -10 V respectively keeping the holes in the potential well beneath electrode 2. When electrode 3 now attains a voltage of -15 V the charge packet moves to the first electrode 3. By properly pulsing the electrodes, the charge packet can be moved along the electrode structure. When a positive charge is present a "1" is stored, no charge means a "0". At the end of the CCD register a device is provided which can detect the "charge" or "no charge" condition. Figure 3.4.5.2 shows a drawing of one of the first 8-bit shift registers based on the CCD concept [3.4.53]. Today 16 000 bit shift registers using CCDs are contemplated. Charge-coupled devices present a breakthrough in the field of semiconductor devices. Standard integrated circuits normally consist of a large number of components like transistors, diodes and resistors and the integrated function can also be realized, though much less economically, by building together discrete

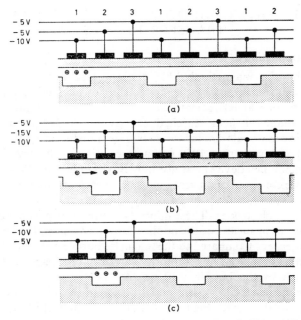

FIG. 3.4.5.1. Operation of a three-phase charge-coupled device shift register.

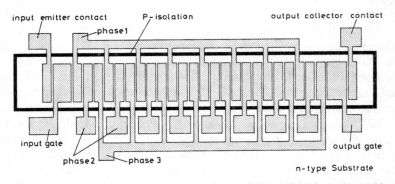

FIG. 3.4.5.2. Drawing of one of the first 8 stage CCD shift registers [3.4.53].

components. However, this is not possible with CCDs. Because information transfer occurs by the shift of minority carriers, a CCD cannot be composed of discrete MOS capacitors connected by copper wires. It is therefore justifiable to state that CCDs belong to a new second IC generation.

An important difference between bubble devices and CCDs must be mentioned. The transfer of information by bubbles occurs without loss. The size of the bubble is determined by the bias field and the properties of the material. At the end of a very long shift register the bubble size is exactly equal to that at the beginning. Loss of information can only occur when due to a defect in the layer, the bubble is not transferred at all. The properties of charge packets are less ideal. In the first place, during an information shift a small amount of the charge is not transferred, with the result that the charge packet at the terminal of the shift register is much smaller than at the first electrode. A second difference originates from the thermal generation of minority carriers in f.i. potential wells where "0's" are stored. In long shift registers it is increasingly difficult to distinguish a "1" from a "0". Refresh amplifiers and pulse shapers have to be used in long CCDs in contrast to bubble registers where the information does not deteriorate. A bubble register can also be operated at very low frequencies; a CCD register is always characterized by a minimum operating frequency. It is a dynamic memory. In the following section the physics of MOS devices and of the transfer process will be discussed. This is followed by Section 3.4.5.4 where more of the device aspects of CCDs are considered.

3.4.5.2. Properties of MOS Devices

The electrodes of a CCD form, with the underlying SiO_2 insulator and semi-conductor, MIS and MOS structures just like the gates in MOSFETS. Many of the physical properties of MOSFETS like threshold voltage, work function of electrode material, surface charge etc. as treated in Section 3.4.4 also apply to CCD structures and will not be repeated again. Only those properties characteristic to surface charge transfer devices will be considered here.

In this section the MOS structure will be analysed, whereas in the next section charge transfer will be discussed.

MOS structure. The understanding of the characteristics of a MOS structure requires an understanding of the non-equilibrium charge distribution produced in a semiconductor upon application of an electric field to its surface. The effect of a negative voltage on the electrode is initially to repel the majority carriers in the semiconductor and as a consequence a surface depletion region is formed (Fig. 3.4.5.3). The width of the depletion region depends on the voltage and the impurity concentration in the semiconductor. The energy band diagram is shown in Fig. 3.4.5.4(a). A part of the voltage is across the insulator and the rest across the depletion region. The energy bands bend upward. In equilibrium the valence band at the surface is closer to the Fermi level than in the bulk, which is equivalent to stating that the concentration of the majority carriers at the surface is much less than in the

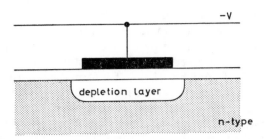

FIG. 3.4.5.3. Formation of a depletion layer in an n-type semiconductor as a result of a negative voltage on the electrode of the MOS structure.

bulk. When the voltage is further increased, the band diagram as indicated in Fig. 3.4.5.4(b) occurs. The depletion layer is now much wider. However, this state is not in equilibrium. Minority carriers (in our case holes) are continually being produced in a semiconductor via the thermal generation of electrons and holes. The holes will accumulate at the surface of the semiconductor under the electrode and the electrons will join the electrons outside the depletion region. Due to the accumulation process the band diagram will change until at equilibrium the state as shown in Fig. 3.4.5.4(c) results. In Fig. 3.4.5.5 the theoretically determined capacitance C_{tot}/C_{ox} and the depletion region width X_d are plotted as a function of the accumulated charge [3.4.53]. Immediately after application of a negative voltage the charge due to the holes is still zero and this is connected with a small capacitance and a large depletion width. As accumulation proceeds with time the charge and the capacitance increase and the width of the depletion region decreases as expected. As can be seen in Fig. 3.4.5.4(c) the Fermi level E_F is the same

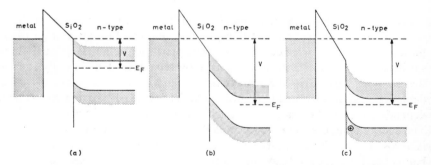

FIG. 3.4.5.4. Energy diagrams for MOS structures: (a) a small negative voltage causes depletion and (b) a large voltage causes strong depletion in non-equilibrium and (c) an inversion layer of holes in equilibrium.

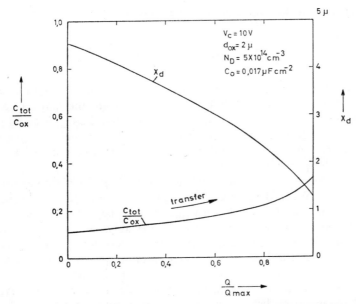

FIG. 3.4.5.5. Theoretically determined depletion region width X_d and capacitance C_{tot}/C_{ox} as a function of the accumulated charge in a MOS structure. (C_{ox} is capacitance due to SiO$_2$ layer, Q_{max} is charge when thermal equilibrium is present.)

at the surface and in the bulk, which indicates that no net current flow exists any longer in the depletion region. The Fermi level is very close to the valence band, therefore one can say that the material at the surface will behave as p-type material. Under the electrode a so called inversion layer is formed. The time required to go from the non-equilibrium state with wide depletion region (Fig. 3.4.5.4(b)) to the equilibrium inverted state (Fig. 3.4.5.4(c)) depends on the rate of minority carriers which in turn depends on such factors as band gap, temperature, illumination and surface preparation. For processed silicon, surface generation controls the rate at which equilibrium is re-established. Relaxation times of the order of 10 ms are often found. In terms of most computer operations this figure represents a relatively long time period which makes the surface depletion region a possible candidate for temporary charge storage. A suitable method for the study of MOS structures is based on the measurement of the total capacitance of the MOS structure as a function of the voltage on the electrode. This measurement is performed for different frequencies, temperatures and illuminations. Such a capacitance voltage curve is shown schematically in Fig. 3.4.5.6.

The total capacitance C_{tot} of the MOS structure is a series combination of the depletion region capacitance C_d and the oxide capacitance C_{ox}

$$C_{tot} = \frac{C_{ox} C_d}{C_{ox} + C_d} \; . \qquad (3.4.5.1)$$

When the voltage is positive we have accumulation of electrons at the surface. This is a fast process because electrons are the majority carriers in the n-type material. As no depletion layer occurs, the C_{tot} is equal to C_{ox}. When the voltage is decreased, depending on the threshold voltage of the device, at a certain magnitude a depletion layer starts to occur with the result that the total capacitance decreases.

When the voltage is made negative the depletion region width increases and C_{tot} decreases. When the frequency is high, so that practically no generation of holes occurs, the C_{tot} reaches a C_{min} for large negative voltages, because the depletion region width does not appreciably increase for increasing voltages on the electrode. However, when a very low frequency is used, thermal generation will cause the formation of an inversion layer of holes at the surface, so that the depletion region width is much narrower. This causes an increase of C_{tot} with increasing negative electrode voltages. At large voltages the inversion layer is strong enough so that again $C_{tot} = C_{ox}$. The low frequency C–V curve can also be obtained by other techniques. For instance, when a pn-junction is placed close to the MOS device, minority carriers can be injected into the non-equilibrium depletion region from an external source. The input device of a CCD is based on this effect. The minority carriers can also be injected from a neighbouring potential well containing minority carriers. Charge transfer in CCDs is due to this effect. A dynamic shift register is obtained when only two signal levels are distinguishable. At the terminal only "1" and "0" threshold detection is then required. However, a CCD structure is also capable of maintaining different signal levels and CCDs therefore can also be readily used as analogue signal delay lines. When the MOS structures are exposed to light, the minority carrier concentration at the surface will be related to the light intensity. CCDs can be used as solid state image converters. A two-dimensional array of a large number of CCD shift registers can convert, as well as store, an image [3.4.54]. Light entering the CCD array through the gaps between the transfer electrodes causes generation of minority carriers. The accumulated charge pattern can be shifted to another part of the array and can be read out by shifting it to the terminal one line at a time. The low frequency C–V curve can also be obtained by increasing the temperature. The thermal generation of minority carriers can keep up with changing voltages on the electrode. For instance, when the C–V curve of a MOS structure is measured at 6 kHz, a temperature increase from 30°C to 170°C converts the high frequency C–V curve into the low frequency one [3.4.55]. It is conceivable that a temperature scan device based on this effect is possible.

In conclusion it appears that a depletion layer below an electrode can function as a potential well in which charge packets can be stored. When the rate of increase of minority carriers due to temperature, illumination or leakage is much too low to fill the potential well during short time intervals determined by the CCD operating frequency, minority carriers injected into these wells from an external source can be used as a measure of stored information. As long as this charge is transferred before thermal equilibrium is reached, no information will be lost.

3.4.5.3. The Charge Transfer Process

Minority charge may be transferred out of an existing well into a new one by producing a deep potential well immediately adjacent to the existing shallow well and by allowing the minority charge to flow from the shallow to the deep well (Fig. 3.4.5.1). In a practical device the complete charge packet will not be transferred. A small fraction ε of it will be left behind at each transfer. This is called the transfer inefficiency per transfer and it may be written as the sum of transfer inefficiencies ε_i caused by different physical effects [3.4.56]. When n transfers occur in a CCD, a transfer inefficiency product $n\varepsilon$ is defined as

$$n\varepsilon = n \sum_0^i \varepsilon_i . \qquad (3.4.5.2)$$

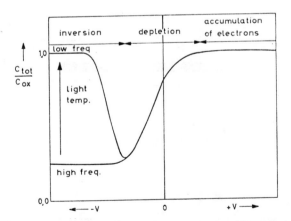

FIG. 3.4.5.6. Capacitance as a function of voltage curves for a MOS (n-type) structure at low and high frequencies. The low frequency behaviour is also obtained when the MOS structure is exposed to light or when the temperature is increased.

The transfer inefficiency is mainly governed by two effects: (1) the non-ideal charge motion from well to well and (2) the presence of surface states at the oxide semiconductor interface.

The first effect involves the dynamics of the minority carriers which are transferred by diffusion due to concentration gradients and by drift caused by electric fields. The solving of the appropriate transport equations is rather difficult. Figure 3.4.5.7 illustrates qualitatively what is expected to occur. When a large negative voltage is applied to the second electrode, the potential distribution of Fig. 3.4.5.7(b) will occur. A few holes will start to move toward the well below the second electrode. When charge is removed from the first electrode, band bending (Fig. 3.4.5.4(c)) under the first electrode will increase and under the second electrode will decrease. This causes an electric field in the desired direction enhancing the transport of holes by drift. For the last fraction of holes only it is assumed that diffusion is again the most important mechanism for charge transfer. The influence of the surface states is even more difficult to analyse. Surface states will trap minority carriers and release them with a characteristic time constant. Only surface states with a time constant which corresponds to the transfer time will be effective. When a charge packet passes along an electrode it fills the surface states. When the charge packet moves on, the surface states empty and will, as shown in Fig. 3.4.5.8 either return to the correct charge packet or move backwards and empty in trailing "zeros" or "ones". The effect of surface states can be reduced by representing zeros not by an absence of charge but by a small background charge sufficient to fill most of the surface states. Such zeros are called "fat zeros". In this case each charge packet would lose

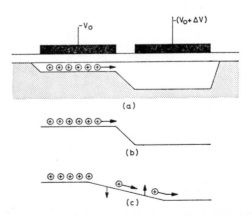

FIG. 3.4.5.7. Schematic representation of drift enhanced hole flow: (a) depletion regions, (b) potential distribution before and (c) after some hole flow.

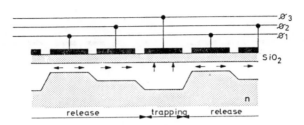

Fɪɢ. 3.4.5.8. Trapping and release of holes during the transfer of a charge packet along a three-phase CCD register.

as much net charge into the surface states as it gained from the previous charge packet. The surface states are mainly due to the oxide-semiconductor interface and therefore CCD structures have been proposed where the charge packets move in the bulk away from the surface. Such structures are called buried channel CCDs [3.4.57] and are obtained by creating a thin surface layer by ion implantation or epitaxy which is of a conductivity type opposite to that of the substrate. An additional advantage of such structures is that the transverse electric fields are higher so that the cycle time of such devices can be much larger than without a buried channel. The first experimental CCDs had a transfer inefficiency of 10^{-2} per gate [3.4.58]. Today transfer inefficiencies of 10^{-4} are realized allowing the construction of 100–300 bit CCD shift registers.

3.4.5.4. Structure of Charge Transfer Devices

CCD dynamic shift register memories consist of an array of separated registers each with input and output devices and, when required, refresh amplifiers. The registers can work as two-, three- or four-phase systems depending on their structures. In this section the different elements of a CCD memory will be briefly presented.

(i) *Input devices*. At the beginning of the CCD structure the information to be stored must be introduced in the CCD by injection of minority carriers in the first potential well. As shown in Fig. 3.4.5.9(a) this can be performed by applying a very large negative voltage pulse (-200 V, 100 ns) to the first electrode causing avalanche breakdown in the semiconductor. The very first CCD was operated in this fashion [3.4.58].

A more convenient means of injection is shown in Fig. 3.4.5.9(b). Here the first electrode forms an inverted region between the forward biased *pn* junction and the potential well of the second electrode. The *pn* junction acts as a source and the second electrode as a "virtual drain" of a MOSFET. Injection of minority carriers can also be realized by shining light on the area beneath one electrode as shown in Fig. 3.4.5.9(c).

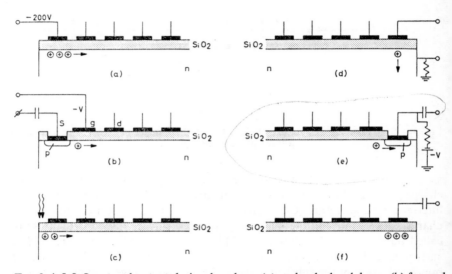

FIG. 3.4.5.9. Input and output devices based on: (a) avalanche breakdown, (b) forward biased emitter p–n junctions, (c) light exposure, (d) hole injection into the substrate, (e) reverse biased collector p–n junctions and (f) sensing of the capacitance.

(ii) *Output devices.* In Fig. 3.4.5.9 some methods of detection are also shown. The holes under the last electrode can be detected by applying a positive voltage to this electrode. This causes the holes to be injected into the substrate. A more common method uses a *pn* diode as an output device (Fig. 3.4.5.9(e)). The diode is reverse biased and will collect the holes causing an output current in the external circuit. The capacitance of the MOS structure is a function of the stored charge as is shown in Fig. 3.4.5.5. This can also be sensed by an external circuit as is shown in Fig. 3.4.5.9(f).

(iii) *Charge transfer devices.* In their simplest form charge transfer registers consist of closely spaced metal electrodes on top of an oxidized semiconductor surface. Pulses are applied to the electrodes in such a way that the charge packet is transferred in a forward direction. When the structures are symmetric a three-phase clock is required. Backwards transfer is also possible when the pulse sequence is reversed. In a symmetric structure one bit position requires three electrodes. Two-phase systems are possible when some asymmetry is built into the structure. Asymmetry can be obtained by changing the oxide thickness, the electrode material or the semiconductor conductivity. Because of the asymmetry the direction of the charge flow is built into the device.

In Fig. 3.4.5.10 three two-phase shift registers are shown [3.4.53]. In

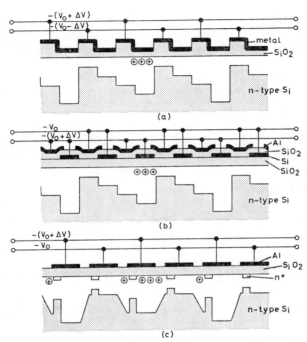

FIG. 3.4.5.10. Two-phase CCD transfer structures based on: (a) different oxide thicknesses, (b) different metals and oxide thicknesses and (c) ion implanted asymmetry.

the first device two oxide thicknesses are used, so that the potential and depletion region widths under one stepped electrode varies. The potential on adjacent electrodes alternates between $V_0 - \Delta V$ and $V_0 + \Delta V$. The holes shift in the direction of the deepest wells and the register cannot be operated backwards.

Si-gate technology can also be applied to CCDs. As shown in Fig. 3.4.5. 10(b) electrodes of aluminium and polycrystalline silicon are used. Because of the different work functions of aluminium and silicon and the different oxide thicknesses, a unidirectional flow of charge occurs. As already shown in Section 3.4.3.3 such a shift register can also be operated bidirectionally, but then a four-phase system is required. In the third example the asymmetry is obtained by introducing small n-type regions by diffusion or ion implantation [3.4.59] beneath the leading edges of the electrodes. The barrier prevents charge from flowing backwards into the potential well beneath the preceding electrode. The charge in the small potential well left of the implanted region is permanently trapped regardless of whether a "1" or a "0" is transferred.

s

(iv) *Signal regeneration.* In practical CCDs charge transfer from under one electrode to the next is not ideal. In long shift registers or recirculated registers regeneration of the signal is required. This can be done simply by connecting the output device of one segment of the CCD register and the input device of the next segment to external electronic amplifying circuits. However, it is also feasible to integrate the amplifiers on the same substrate on which the CCDs are realized. Tompsett [3.4.60] reports about a structure for the regeneration of the signal which can be incorporated in the CCD structure. As shown in Fig. 3.4.5.4 the surface potential of the semiconductor beneath the electrode will depend on the applied voltage and the number of holes in the potential well. When a p-type diffusion is provided under the last electrode, this region will assume the surface potential. When ohmic contact is made to the diffusion, the surface potential can be detected. When the potential is applied to the gate of an input device, as was shown in Fig. 3.4.5.9(b) a charge generator is obtained. The phase of the transfer electrode following the input gate has to be the same as that of the electrode above the p-type diffusion. A "0" at the output device of the first segment causes a large voltage swing at the gate of the input device of the second segment. The gate is turned on and charge representing a "1" from the pn junction flows into the potential well beneath the first transfer electrode. Conversely a "1" generates a "0".

3.4.5.5. Organization of CCD Arrays

As discussed in Chapter 1 modern computers are so organized that they contain a hierarchy of memories in order to use the memory hardware as efficiently as possible. For instance, in a 120×10^6 bit memory about 80×10^6 bits are in slow block-oriented magnetic disk memories and 40×10^6 bits are contained in fast core or semiconductor memories. Although the cost per bit of CCDs is higher than that of magnetic disks, CCD memories might offer an interesting replacement of disks because they have smaller access times, volume, weight and power dissipation. A severe disadvantage of CCDs is, of course, that they are volatile, requiring back-up memories for storing information in a more permanent fashion. Various CCD memory organizations are being considered [3.4.61]. Small CCD memories with rather fast access have a serpentine loop structure as is shown in Fig. 3.4.5.11(a). The charge packet is transferred along a small (100) number of electrodes and is then refreshed before it moves to the next segment. Because the signal is often regenerated the large inefficiency associated with high transfer speed can be tolerated. Bit rates as high as 20 MHz resulting in access times of 10 μs can be achieved. A more efficient, though slower, organization is shown in Fig. 3.4.5.11(b). Here the data is entered in a fast input serial register. It is then slowly shifted in parallel to a fast output serial register.

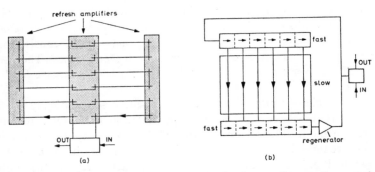

FIG. 3.4.5.11. Organization of CCD memories: (a) fast but small serpentine organizations with many refresh amplifiers and (b) slow but large series-parallel series memory [3.4.61].

Based on this principle CCD memories with densities up to 32 000 bits/chip, access times of about 1 ms and data rates of 1 MHz have been developed. Smallest cell sizes are about 1.8 mil^2, but it is expected that in the future this can be reduced to 0.1 mil^2. This means that potentially a 300 mil by 300 mil chip could contain 4×10^5 bits of CCD memory.

3.4.6. PHYSICS AND TECHNOLOGY OF BIPOLAR MEMORY DEVICES

3.4.6.1. Introduction

Since 1967 semiconductor memories have been used in computers. Because of their high cost, they were only used when no other technologies, like cores or magnetic films, could deliver the desired performance. All these first memories used bipolar memory cells, because MOSFET cells could not be made sufficiently fast and reliable. The first large semiconductor memory, the IBM cache memory [3.4.62] was introduced in 1969. It had an access time of 40 ns and a basic unit size of 150 kilobytes. The first semiconductor main memory introduced in 1970 for the IBM 370/145 also used bipolar circuits, as MOS technology still was not sufficiently advanced. However, since then MOS technology has matured and many semiconductor manufacturers have started to offer rather economic 1024 bit MOS chips which are competitive with core technology.

Generally bipolar cells are large, fast and expensive to produce, whereas MOSFET cells have the opposite characteristics. However, spurred by the success of p-channel and n-channel MOSFET circuits new bipolar technology and circuits were invented, which made it possible to reduce size and power requirements of the bipolar cell considerably. Today it is not at all clear which technology will be the most important in the future. The bipolar memory cell introduced in Section 3.4.3 is based on the well known regenerative multistage switching circuit: the flip-flop. The circuit consists of two inverter stages, cross connected between collector and base. The inverter consists of a driver transistor connected in series with a passive load (Fig. 3.4.6.1(a)).

The I_C–V_{CE} characteristic for an *npn* transistor is schematically shown in Fig. 3.4.6.1(b). Three regions can be distinguished: the OFF region, the active region and the ON region. In the OFF region the emitter and collector junctions are reverse biased. The minority concentration in the base layer is, as shown in Fig. 3.4.6.1(c), very small. In the active region, the emitter is forward-biased and the minority concentration in the base due to injection is very large. In the ON or saturation region the base current is very high which causes the collector voltage V_{CE} to drop so that the collector junction becomes forward biased. The minority concentration in the base is then very high at the collector side also. When a rectangular base current pulse is applied, as shown in Fig. 3.4.6.1(d), a non-rectangular delayed collector pulse will be observed. The time to go from the end of the base pulse to the

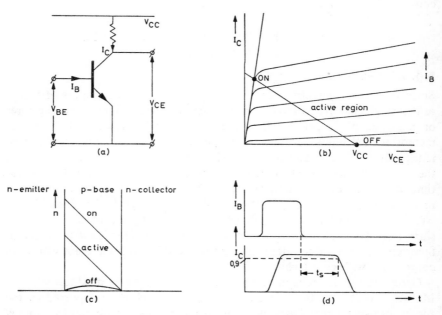

FIG. 3.4.6.1. (a) Inverter circuit, (b) I_C–V_{CE} characteristics for a common emitter *npn* transistor indicating the ON, active and OFF regions, (c) minority carrier concentrations in the base layer for the three operating regions and (d) definition of the storage delay time.

point where the collector current has fallen to 90 per cent of its value is called the storage time t_s. In transistors used in memory cells it is this storage time which mainly determines the switching speed of the transistors and consequently the cycle time of the memory array.

The storage time is a measure of the time required for the minority carrier concentration to return from the saturation level to the level corresponding to the boundary between the saturation and active regions. A reduction of the minority carrier concentration takes place by an electron-hole recombination process. Thus the storage time is a measure of the minority carrier lifetimes. In order to increase the switching speed of memory transistors several methods are in use i.e. (1) avoidance of the saturation region by using emitter coupled logic (ECL), (2) decrease of minority carrier lifetime by gold doping (3) use of Schottky barrier diode clamps and (4) use of majority carrier devices like MESFETs. All methods will be discussed in the next section. In order to lower the price per bit it is necessary to manufacture as many bits as possible on one chip. Early chips contained only 64 bits, later 256 bits, and they now contain 1024 bits, whereas 4096 bit chips are under investigation. This has become possible because new efficient methods have been found to replace the conventional active p-type diffusions between memory cells by more efficient n^+-type diffusions, called collector diffusion isolation (CDI), or by passive-isolation methods using SiO_2 (called LOCOS or ISOPLANAR process) or air (called V-ATE process). The different methods will be discussed in Section 3.4.6.3. Another very important parameter is power dissipation of memory cells. As one side of a flip-flop is always ON, the load resistor must be large to reduce power consumption. However, this increases the switching time. Low power dissipation and high switching speed are incompatible. Therefore in the last section speed-power products of different cells and selection schemes will be discussed. Moreover, a new very small low-power memory cell will be introduced which uses load transistors instead of load resistors. The cell which is known as merged logic (MTL) injection logic (I^2L) promises a significant reduction in the speed-power product.

3.4.6.2. Switching Speed

Methods for decreasing the switching time of memory cell transistors must be directed towards reducing the concentration and the storage time of the minority carriers in the base region. The concentration can be reduced by constructing the flip-flop in such a way that the transistors never are in saturation. This can be achieved by introducing a common emitter resistor. Logic and memory circuits based on the differential amplifier are called "current mode logic" (CML) or "emitter-coupled logic" (ECL), which should not be confused with emitter-coupled memory cells.

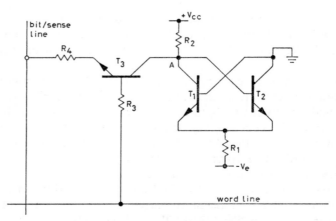

FIG. 3.4.6.2. Memory cell based on the ECL principle [3.4.63].

(i) *Emitter-coupled logic* (*ECL*). A memory cell operating with the ECL principle is shown in Fig. 3.4.6.2 and was first presented by Perkins and Schmidt [3.4.63]. The cell is a typical ECL flip-flop with a common emitter-resistor. Selection of the cell occurs by means of transistor T_3. For reading, a positive pulse is applied to the base of T_3 and turns it on. If node A is positive, that means that T_1 is off, the cell contains a "1". In this case a current will flow through R_2, T_3 and R_4 into the bit/sense line. For writing, positive pulses are applied to the word and bit lines and force the transistor T_2 into conduction and thus the cell is in the "1" state. In order to prevent saturation the collector current of the transistors must be carefully controlled. It is generally impossible to prevent saturation by controlling the base currents because the current gain β varies too much from cell to cell. However, the collector current can be controlled by controlling the emitter current by a current source. In practice this current source takes the form of a common emitter-resistor. As shown in Fig. 3.4.6.3 the "0" and "1" states are set at well defined levels taking care, that the "ON" state is not in the saturation region. Compared to TTL logic based cells, the voltage swing at the collector for ECL cells is smaller for the same current swing. At present ECL memory arrays with 256 or 1024 bits/chip are available with read access times of 25 ns and 45 ns respectively. These arrays are used in fast cache or buffer memories and high speed scratch pad memories.

(ii) *Gold doping*. In the memory cells of Fig. 3.4.3.4 (Section 3.4.3.2) one of the transistors is always in saturation and switching is rather slow due to the charge storage time of the base region. Reduction of the minority carrier lifetime would increase the switching speed. A common method for

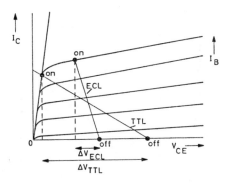

FIG. 3.4.6.3. $I_C - V_{CE}$ characteristics for a *npn* transistor indicating load lines and logic voltage swings for TTL and ECL logic.

achieving this is to introduce gold interstitially in the Si lattice. Gold acts as a recombination centre thereby reducing the time for recombination of holes and electrons. For a recombination centre to be effective, two different charge states must be available. As shown in Fig. 3.4.6.4 gold has one donor and one acceptor level. Recombination occurs when an electron is captured by the donor and a hole is captured by the acceptor state.

It can be expected that the recombination rate increases and thus that the lifetime decreases for increasing gold concentration.

Figure 3.4.6.5 shows the relation between the lifetime of electrons τ_n in p-type material and the gold concentration. One observes that the minority carrier lifetime decreases linearly with the gold concentration over the range of 10^{14} to 10^{17} cm^{-3} from 0.2 μs to 0.2 ns [3.4.64].

Gold is normally introduced in the Si by gold plating or gold vacuum deposition on the back side of the Si wafer. This is followed by a high

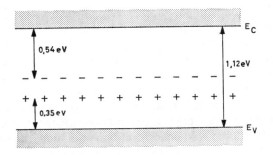

FIG. 3.4.6.4. Energy levels of gold in silicon.

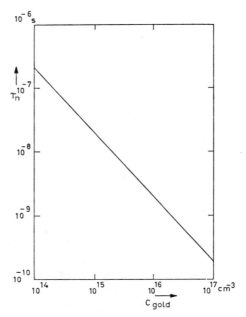

FIG. 3.4.6.5. Relation between the lifetime τ_n of electrons in a p-type material and the gold concentration [3.4.64].

temperature diffusion cycle in which the gold is diffused through the entire wafer. Final gold concentration depends on temperature, diffusion time, wafer thickness and gold layer thickness.

Temperatures of around 1000°C for 30 min. and a gold layer thickness of 800 Å are common. To obtain a maximum gold concentration, the wafer is cooled rapidly, as otherwise gold would start to precipitate and this gold would be inactive as recombination centres.

Memory cells made with gold doping typically show access times of 100 ns for 1024 bits/chip and 50 ns for 256 bits/chip devices.

Unfortunately gold doping has some undesirable side effects. As gold diffusion is very fast, it is almost impossible to produce selected gold doped areas on a wafer. Thus the minority carrier lifetime is reduced throughout the memory array and fast and slow devices cannot exist simultaneously. Moreover, gold doping has a detrimental effect on the current gain of transistors. Because of the high recombination rate the base current must be much higher. When the gold concentration is too high, the proper functioning of the flip-flops is even impaired, leading to increased switching times. Therefore many manufacturers have left the gold doping process and started to increase the switching speed of logic and memory devices by adding Schottky diodes, which will be described in the following section.

(iii) *Schottky diode clamping*. Switching times of memory cells are mainly determined by the charge storage time of the minority carriers in the base. These minority carriers are injected from the collector when the transistor is driven in saturation. When the switching speed of a transistor has to be increased, it is necessary to avoid saturation. A very elegant way to achieve this is the introduction of a Schottky barrier diode parallel with the base-collector junction [3.4.65]. Schottky barrier diodes consist of a metal layer on top of a semiconductor substrate. When a metal and an *n*-type semiconductor having different work functions ϕ_m and ϕ_{n-si} (Fig. 3.4.6.6) are brought together some electrons from the *n*-type semiconductor with the higher Fermi level will flow to the metal. This creates a contact potential within the semiconductor as is shown in Fig. 3.4.6.6(b). This results in the conduction and valence band edges being bent with respect to the Fermi level. Such a shift of the Fermi level means that the equilibrium electron and hole densities are changed. In the case of a metal–*n*-type silicon interface the electron density at the surface is reduced: the surface is depleted.

When an external voltage is applied to the metal semiconductor interface and the current is measured, it appears that such a metal semiconductor junction behaves like a rectifier. When no voltage is applied a number of electrons in the conduction band of the *n*-type Si have sufficient energy to overcome the energy barrier and will move to the left (Fig. 3.4.6.7(a)). Also a number of electrons in the metal will have enough energy to move to the right. At equilibrium these currents are equal in magnitude, so that no

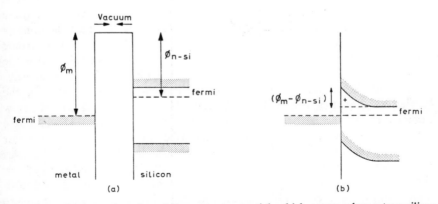

FIG. 3.4.6.6. The explanation of the contact potential, which occurs when *n*-type silicon and a metal with greater work function are brought into contact with each other: (a) before contact and (b) after contact.

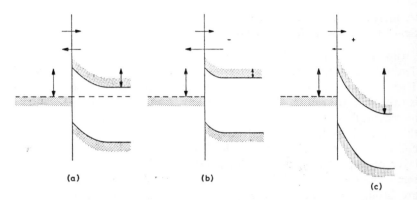

FIG. 3.4.6.7. Metal–semiconductor junction: (a) no voltage, (b) forward bias and (c) reverse bias. The arrows indicate the respective electron flow.

net current results.   When the n-type semiconductor, is made negative (Fig. 3.4.6.7(b)) with respect to the metal, electrons with lower energies can also surmount the energy barrier, whereas the situation for the electrons in the metal does not change. A net electron current results in the metal, and the Schottky barrier diode is forward biased. When the n-type Si is made positive (Fig. 3.4.6.7(c)) the situation for the electrons in the metal does not change and a very small reverse current independent of the reverse voltage is measured.

The characteristics of a Schottky barrier diode should, according to the above explanation, be very dependent on the work function of the metal, the dope concentration and on whether the material is n- or p-type. Indeed differences are observed when different metals are used.   However, these differences are much too small.   This is caused by the fact that the contact potential in the surface region is much more defined by localized electronic states, called surface states, than by the metal work functions.   Also the concentration of the dopant has an important influence on the properties of the interface.   When the doping level is high ($N_D > 10^{18}\,\mathrm{cm}^{-3}$), the barrier, as shown in Fig. 3.4.6.7, is very thin and the electrons can now tunnel through the barrier.   Electrons with much lower energies can move from the semiconductor to the metal and vice versa.   A small positive or negative applied voltage will cause a large current and the interface behaves as an ohmic contact rather than as a diode.   Experimentally, it has been shown that the contact resistance decreases for increasing doping level both on n- and p-type silicon. This effect is widely used in Si technology to ensure good ohmic contacts. Compared to the usual pn Si diode, the Al–Si Schottky diode used in integrated circuits has two important differences. As shown

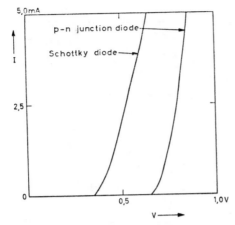

FIG. 3.4.6.8. Forward characteristics of a *p–n* junction diode and a Schottky diode.

in Fig. 3.4.6.8 the voltage at which appreciable current flows in a Schottky diode is about 300 mV lower than in the case of the *pn* junction diode. The second major difference is the storage time. When a Schottky diode is biased in the forward direction, electrons pass from the silicon to the metal, the current is due to transport of majority current carriers. When the diode is reverse biased, the response is very fast, because no slow recombination processes have to occur before equilibrium is reached. The low offset voltage and the fast response time of Schottky diodes make them ideal to use as clamping diodes.

As shown in Fig. 3.4.6.9 the Schottky diode is placed in parallel to the base-collector junction. When the base current is increased, the collector voltage decreases and causes forward biasing of the base-collector junction. When a Schottky diode clamp is used with its much lower offset voltage,

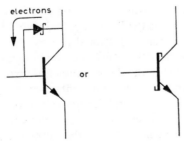

FIG. 3.4.6.9. Schottky clamped *npn* transistor with symbol.

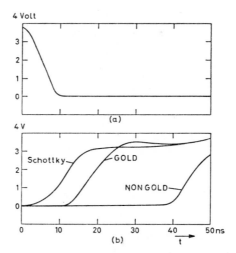

FIG. 3.4.6.10. Response of different transistors: (a) input base signal and (b) output collector signals [3.4.66].

most of the collector-base current is diverted through the Schottky diode. The transistor therefore is not driven into the saturation state. When the clamping diode is a *pn* junction which also shows charge storage, switching time improvement is not very large. However, because a Schottky diode is based on majority carrier transport the switching time of a composite Schottky transistor is very much improved. Figure 3.4.6.10 compares the response of a non-gold-doped, a gold-doped and a Schottky clamped transistor [3.4.66]. The storage time of the Schottky transistor is almost zero compared to 7 ns for a gold doped one and 34 ns for a normal transistor.

Though the suggestion to reduce the storage time of a transistor by using Schottky diodes was proposed in 1967 by Tada and Laraya [3.4.65], the implementation of this idea in integrated circuits had to wait until 1969 [3.4.66]. In memory arrays where cell size is very important, Schottky diode clamping is of no interest, as the Schottky diode would considerably increase the bit size and would require additional processing steps. However in the process used today, the Schottky diode can be integrated very elegantly. As shown in Fig. 3.4.6.11(a) the base contact is extended over the *n*-type collector region by increasing the base-contact opening. An ohmic contact is formed between the aluminum and the *p*-type base region (Fig. 3.4.6.11(b)). Because of the high doping level of the base a tunnelling ohmic contact occurs instead of a Schottky diode. Between the aluminium and the low doped, *n*-type collector region a Schottky diode occurs. When the collector is

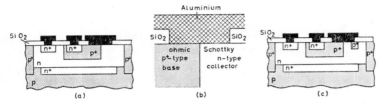

FIG. 3.4.6.11. Schematic presentation of: (a) an integrated Schottky diode, (b) aluminium forms an ohmic contact with the highly doped p-type base and a Schottky contact with the n-type collector and (c) a p^+-type guard ring at the edge prevents leakage currents.

negative with respect to the base contact, the Schottky diode is forward biased and electrons flow from silicon to aluminium.

The integration of Schottky diodes requires more careful processing than in cases where they are not used. In order to obtain reproducible ohmic and Schottky contacts the doping of the base and collector region have to be better controlled. Moreover, a thin SiO_2 film between the aluminium and the silicon will influence the characteristics of the diode. Careful chemical processing and the use of aluminium, which reduces SiO_2, are mandatory.

Another serious problem is leakage current. This is due to the high electric field concentration at the edge of the base contact over the collector region. This field can be reduced by extending the base electrode over the SiO_2 layer or by introducing a so-called guard ring [3.4.67].

This guard ring consists of a diffused p^+ area beneath the edge of the metal (Fig. 3.4.6.11(c)) and also prevents high electric fields. The technology of Schottky clamped memory cells has advanced sufficiently so that today such cells are commercially available. Typical access times of such memory arrays are 35 ns for a 256-bit chip and 60 ns for a 1024-bit chip.

(iv) *Schottky barrier gate field effect transistor (MESFET)*. A Schottky barrier junction can also be used as a gate in a very fast field effect transistor. The device structure is shown in Fig. 3.4.6.12. On a p-type substrate a very thin (1000 Å) n-type epitaxial layer is deposited. The doping concentration N_D is about 10^{17} cm^{-3} leading to 0.1 Ωcm resistivity. Two ohmic contacts form the source and drain and the gate consists of a Schottky contact, which is obtained by directly depositing a metal on top of the silicon substrate. When the gate width is 1 μm and the total source-drain distance is 3 μm, such transistors, known as MESFETs, show maximum frequencies of oscillation of up to 12 GHz [3.4.68].

The small dimensions of the gate require special processing steps like low temperature epitaxy [3.4.69], projection instead of contact masking [3.4.70], and self alignment of the ohmic contacts [3.4.71].

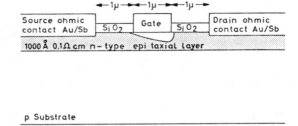

FIG. 3.4.6.12. Cross-section of a Schottky barrier gate transistor or MESFET.

Thin epitaxial layers are obtained by a hydrogen reduction of silicon tetrachloride. Good quality layers of 0.1 μm thickness are obtained with a substrate temperature of 950°C and a deposition rate of 200 Å min^{-1}. The micron structures are obtained by projecting an image of the photomask directly onto the photoresist-covered wafer by means of a very high quality lens. In the first masking step all the critical dimensions of the source-gate-drain structure are defined. The contact areas are metallized with Cr/Ni, Au or Pd, so that three Schottky contacts occur (Fig. 3.4.6.13(a)). In the second step a dot of Au with two percent Sb is deposited in the centre of the source and drain contact (Fig. 3.4.6.13(b)). In a subsequent heat treatment (15 min at 550°C) the Au/Sb alloys with the silicon and covers the complete source and drain areas converting them to ohmic contacts (Fig. 3.4.6.13(c)). Depending on the thickness of the epitaxial layer, MESFETs can be made which are "normally on" or which are "normally off". The pinch-off voltage V_{po} of such a device is given by

$$V_{po} = \frac{e}{2\varepsilon} N_d d^2 \qquad (3.4.6.1)$$

in which e is the electron charge, ε the dielectric constant of the silicon and d the thickness of the epitaxial layer. When the thickness decreases, the pinch off voltage, which is the source-gate voltage at which the depletion region reaches the p substrate, decreases also. As shown in the previous section, a Schottky junction also shows a built-in potential V_{bi} due to the different work functions of the metal and the silicon and the surface states. The threshold voltage V_T of a MESFET is given by

$$V_T = V_{bi} - V_{po}. \qquad (3.4.6.2)$$

When the doping level and thickness are such that $V_{bi} < V_{po}$, the threshold voltage V_T is negative; this means that the MESFET is normally on and that a negative voltage is necessary to pinch-off the channel. On the other hand,

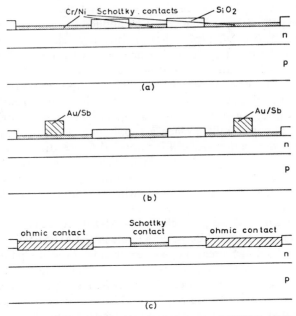

FIG. 3.4.6.13. Processing steps for the fabrication of MESFET's: (a) metallization of the contact holes with Cr/Ni, Au or Pd, (b) deposition of Au/Sb dots and (c) conversion of source and drain Schottky contacts into ohmic contacts by a heat treatment at 550°C. The contacts are self-aligning.

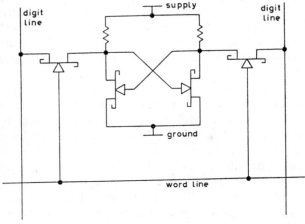

FIG. 3.4.6.14. Memory cell with four MESFET's.

when the thickness d is very small $V_{po} < V_{bi}$ and the channel is normally off, a positive gate-source voltage must be applied to open the channel. As shown by Drangeid et al. [3.4.72] static memory cells using normally off MESFETs can be constructed which are both very fast and very small. Figure 3.4.6.14 shows the basic memory cell. The flip-flop is coupled to the bit and word lines by MESFETs. The components are isolated by Schottky contact strips which deplete the epitaxial layer underneath. The load resistors are formed by surrounding elongated areas by such strips. A test array of 3×3 bits was built. When a supply voltage of $0.6 V$ is used, the stand-by power dissipation per cell is only $5 \mu W$. Reading is accomplished by a positive pulse on the word line which causes a sense current in the digit line of $6 \mu A$. Writing is accomplished by a positive pulse on the word line and a negative one on the bit line. The cell switches from one state to the other in only $4 ns$. The cell size is only $2.6 mil^2$.

When comparing MESFET cells with MOSFET cells, a number of disadvantages are apparent. Because the gate in the MESFET is a Schottky contact, forward voltages create large gate currents. Low dissipation dynamic operation as used in MOSFET memory arrays is therefore not possible with MESFETs. As the switching speed of the MESFET depends strongly on the gate width, $1 \mu m$ structures are required which can only be fabricated with very sophisticated, and thus, expensive process techniques.

3.4.6.3. Size of Bipolar Memory Cell

The price per bit of semiconductor memories is very much related to the number of bits per chip. When this number is increased the yield goes down, which increases the price, but the need for interconnections is reduced, which in turn decreases the price. In the last ten years great improvements have been made with respect to better control of process parameters, smaller memory cell size, better isolation techniques and more efficient cell layout.

As shown in Fig. 3.4.6.15, the number of bits per chip increased from 8 in 1965 to 1024 in 1972 and extrapolating, 4096 bit bipolar memory chips can be expected around 1975.

Until 1972 memory cells were quite large because silicon consuming isolation barriers were needed to separate the memory cells electrically. By forming p-type regions it is possible to separate each element by a reverse biased pn junction. As shown in Fig. 3.4.6.16, one starts by growing an n-type epitaxial layer on top of a p-type substrate. Using photoresist and silicon oxide, a p-type diffusion is carried out everywhere except in the regions in which the components are planned. The p-type regions extend down to the p-type substrate so that the n-type epitaxial islands are completely surrounded by p-type material. When the p-type substrate is connected to a potential more negative than any component of the memory array, all the

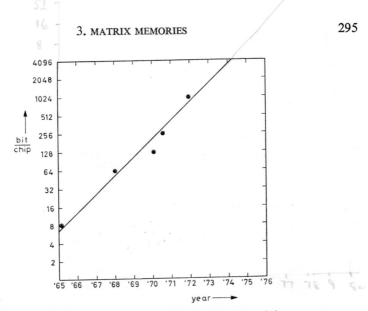

FIG. 3.4.6.15. Number of bits per chip as a function of time.

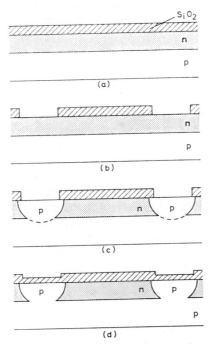

FIG. 3.4.6.16. Isolation with p–n junctions: (a) oxidized n-type epitaxial layer on p-type substrate, (b) SiO_2 removed from holes, (c) p-type diffusion and (d) surface re-oxidized.

T

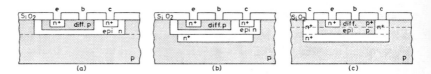

FIG. 3.4.6.17. Cross-sections of: (a) standard double-diffused *npn* transistor, (b) double-diffused *npn* transistor with buried layer and (c) collector diffusion isolated *npn* transistor with epitaxial base layer.

surrounding *pn* junctions are reverse-biased and electrically separate the elements.

However this *pn* junction isolation requires a lot of silicon area. This is because of the area needed for the *p*-type region and because registration problems with the masks require wide tolerances. Moreover the *p*-type dopants tend to diffuse not only straight down but also sideways beneath the mask. In the next sections three alternative isolation methods will be presented.

(i) *Collector diffusion isolation.* In the *n*-type epitaxial islands which occur after the *p*-type isolation regions have been applied, a transistor is fabricated by a double diffusion as indicated in Fig. 3.4.6.17(a). In such a structure the collector current has to traverse a rather long and thin *n*-type collector region. To reduce this collector resistance the majority of bipolar integrated circuits are provided with a so-called buried layer. This is, as shown in Fig. 3.4.6.17(b), an n^+ region which is diffused in the *p* substrate before the *n*-type epitaxial layer is grown. The structure so obtained is known as the standard buried collector (SBC) structure.

Because the transistor is now separated from the *p* substrate by an n^+ layer in the SBC structure, Murphy *et al.* [3.4.73] suggested the use of this buried layer for the electrical isolation of the component. As shown in Fig. 3.4.6.17(c) on top of the n^+-type buried layer an epitaxial *p*-type, instead of the *n*-type as in SBC, is grown over the entire surface. Subsequently *n*-type collector contacts are diffused through this *p*-type epitaxial layer. A *p*-type island is now formed in which the transistor can be made. Because the *n*-type collector regions are used for isolation, this technique is called collector diffusion isolation (CDI). For electrical isolation the *n*-type collector region is biased with respect to the *p*-type substrate and epitaxial layer giving the required reverse-biased *pn* junction isolation. The *p*-type island is used as the base layer. In CDI, epitaxial base layers are used, which is in contrast to the SBC structure, where diffused base layers are employed. Before the emitter diffusion is performed a non-masked shallow *p*-type diffusion is introduced. This is necessary to overcome the disadvantages of *p*-type

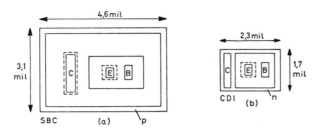

FIG. 3.4.6.18. Comparison of the size of a conventional SBC transistor (13.5 mil²) with a CDI transistor (3.9 mil²).

epitaxial layers. When such layers are oxidized, as is necessary for masking steps, the thermally grown oxide tends to cause an n-type surface to become more n-type, but also to cause a p-type surface to become less p-type. Lightly doped p-type regions eventually can invert to n-type regions causing serious degradation of the component. The shallow p-type diffusion is therefore necessary to prevent this inversion. Moreover, it provides a built-in electric field, which keeps the electrons away from the surface, where recombination is very high. The n^+-type emitter diffusion and the forming of contact holes and aluminium interconnections are accomplished in the conventional way.

The first advantage of the CDI structure is the reduction of the cell size because the p-type isolation regions are no longer necessary. Figure 3.4.6.18 compares the dimensions of an SBC transistor with isolation with one obtained with the CDI techniques [3.4.74]. A reduction of about three is possible. A further advantage of the CDI structure is the fact that fewer masking steps are required. However, the CDI technique also has some drawbacks. Because the p-type epitaxial layer is used as a base, the thickness must be small (1–2 μm) and be very accurately controlled. This is quite difficult, because subsequent oxidations for masking purposes will reduce the p-type epitaxial layer. Another serious drawback is the low collector-base breakdown voltage. Early CDI transistors had breakdown voltages of only three volts. Careful adjusting of doping levels and profiles increased the breakdown voltage to 7.5–8.5 V [3.4.74]. Because a low resistivity collector is used, the collector-base junction capacitance is higher than in the SBC structure. Although the feasibility of the CDI technique for logic and memory cells has been shown, thus far the technique has not been widely applied.

(ii) *LOCOS and Isoplanar isolation.* Instead of isolating components by back biased *pn* junctions as in the SBC and CDI techniques, it has also proven

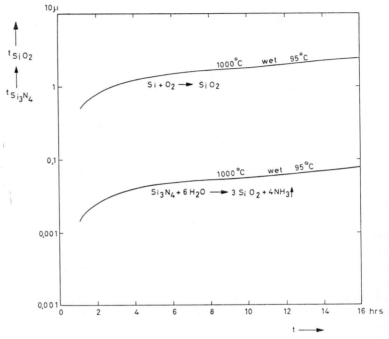

FIG. 3.4.6.19. Comparison of oxidation of Si and Si_3N_4. The upper curve shows the time dependence of the formed SiO_2. The lower curve gives the time dependence of the nitride converted to oxide [3.4.76].

possible to obtain electrical isolation by providing non-conducting (SiO_2 or air) regions between the components. The technique, which is based on the use of SiO_2 isolation, is called the Isoplanar process and at present is used for commercially available logic and memory arrays.

The main problem of using thick SiO_2 regions reaching right through to the p substrate or n^+ buried layer is that one needs a technique of suppressing the oxide growth in the areas where the active components have to be formed. Almost simultaneously such a method based on the masking properties of silicon-nitride (Si_3N_4) was presented by Morandi [3.4.75] and Appels et al. [3.4.76]. The oxidation rate of silicon is much higher than that of silicon nitride. Thick oxide layers can be grown locally on silicon, when silicon nitride is used for masking. In Fig. 3.4.6.19 the oxide thickness formed by thermal oxidation as a function of time is shown for silicon and silicon nitride. From this figure, it is clear that the oxidation rate of Si_3N_4 is considerably lower than that of silicon. A 1000°C wet oxidation of 15 h will produce a 2 μm thick SiO_2 layer on top of unmasked silicon surfaces.

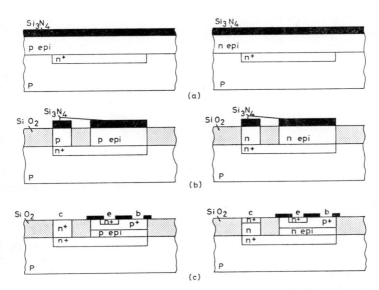

FIG. 3.4.6.20. Isoplanar process: (a) it starts with a p-substrate with n^+ buried layer with either a p- or n-type epitaxial layer covered with a Si_3N_4 layer, (b) subsequently the Si_3N_4 and the Si are etched, the Si holes are oxidized until a flat surface is again obtained and (c) the base and emitter layers are processed, which is followed by the standard contact process.

The masking Si_3N_4 layer should have a thickness of at least 650 Å to prevent oxidation of the silicon beneath the Si_3N_4. The new masking technique was first applied to discrete components and named LOCOS (LOCally Oxide Silicon) by Appels et al. [3.4.76]. Scientists at Fairchild applied the technique to integrated circuits and termed it Isoplanar [3.4.77]. As shown in Fig. 3.4.6.20(a), the Isoplanar process starts with a p-type substrate with n^+-type buried layers. Subsequently a p- or n-type epitaxial layer is grown. An n-type layer is grown when the normal standard double diffused transistors are desired; a p-type layer is provided when p-type epitaxial base layer transistors are wanted. The epitaxial layer is covered by a silicon nitride layer, which is made in a reactor at about 1000°C by the reaction of SiH_4 and NH_3 supplied to the reactor in a hydrogen carrier gas. In a masking step the Si_3N_4 is selectively removed by a phosphoric acid etch. The silicon areas no longer covered by Si_3N_4 are further etched as shown in Fig. 3.4.6.20(b), followed by a long oxidation causing the isolation areas to fill with SiO_2. These areas extend into the p-type substrate or n^+ buried collector regions and ensure good electrical insulation. In the case of a double diffused transistor, the p-type base and n-type emitter are made by

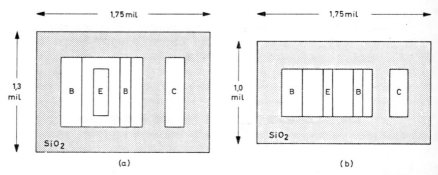

FIG. 3.4.6.21. (a) Self-alignment of base region in Isoplanar I and (b) self-alignment of base and emitter region in Isoplanar II [3.4.77].

applying the standard masking and diffusion steps. When a p-type base epitaxial layer is used, the processing sequence is the same as described for the CDI technique. A separate n^+-type collector sink diffusion is needed to contact the transistor collectors.

An advantage of the Isoplanar technique is that the mask holes for diffusion can often be larger than needed, because the SiO_2 regions can define the collector sink, the base and the emitter regions. The process in which the self alignment of the base region is employed is called the Isoplanar I (Fig. 3.4.6.21(a)) process, whereas in Isoplanar II self alignment of the emitter is also incorporated. (Fig. 3.4.6.21(b)). The use of SiO_2 as isolation saves very much silicon area, which makes it possible to fabricate 1024 bit chips rather easily and to compete with MOSFET arrays. Access times are of the order of 50 ns and in Isoplanar II memory cell sizes of 15 mil^2 are feasible.

(iii) *V-ATE isolation process.* In recent years many other methods have been proposed to reduce the cell size by replacing the *pn* junction isolation by some oxide or air region. An elegant method which uses air as an electrical isolator is the V-ATE (Vertical AnisoTropic Etch) process [3.4.78, 3.4.79]. In this process use is made of the effect that under certain circumstances the etch rate of silicon is different for certain crystallographic directions. The V-ATE process starts with a p-type substrate with an n^+-type buried layer, an *n*-type epitaxial layer and a diffused p-type base layer (Fig. 3.4.6.22(a)). In contrast to conventional bipolar technology where (111) Si wafers are used, the V-ATE process starts with (100) oriented substrates.

The substrate is oxidized and elongated holes are etched in the oxide. Subsequently the wafer is subjected to an etch with diluted hydrazine (100 g N_2H_4–50 ml H_2O) at 100°C. Hydrazine has the interesting property that the etch rate into (111) planes is much slower than into the (100) planes. When

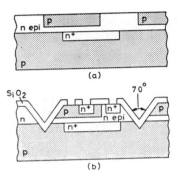

FIG. 3.4.6.22. V-ATE process: (a) it starts with a p-substrate with an n^+ buried layer, an n-type epitaxial layer with a p-type base diffusion and (b) when etched with hydrazine in the silicon V, grooves occur electrically isolating the n-epitaxial islands containing the components.

the elongated isolation holes in the SiO_2 are parallel to the [110] axes, well defined V grooves with a 55° angle to the surface appear reproducibly (Fig. 3.4.6.22(b)).

The bottom V-angle is 70°. The depth D of the groove is 0.7 times the width W of the oxide hole. In the V-ATE process the openings of the oxide holes are chosen such that the V-holes extend into the p-type substrate, electrically isolating the n-type epitaxial islands from each other. In these islands the emitter, the base and the collector contact holes of the transistor can be produced with the conventional masking steps. V-ATE makes it possible to reduce the memory cell size very much. Cell sizes of only 4.3 mil² are reported [3.4.79] leading to 1024 RAMs placed on a chip 91 by 125 mils. Potential problems with the V-ATE process are breaks in the aluminium conductors on the V-grooves and substrate surface channelling on the bottom of the V-grooves between collectors of different transistors. By using proper photoresist techniques, doping concentrations and profiles, these problems can be overcome.

3.4.6.4. Speed-power Product of Bipolar Memory Cells

As discussed in the preceding sections, many possibilities exist to improve memory cells. These improvements can be the result of better cell designs or the use of more sophisticated semiconductor technology. As there exists a tendency for each innovator to believe his contribution is unique and shows improvements over those of others, a simple measure is needed in order to compare different memory cells. Switching time alone is not a satisfactory measure, because larger supply voltages leading to much larger power dissipation will often increase the switching time of many memory cells. Also the measurement of power per bit is not very useful, because a very low dissipation might be obtained with the penalty of large switching delays. Therefore in comparing memory cells, the practice of indicating the speed-power product has been adopted. This product can be calculated for one logic gate or one memory cell, but in comparing memories it is more useful to divide the total power per chip, including peripheral decoding circuits, by the number of bits on the chip and to multiply this by the read access time. For instance when a 256 bit TTL chip consumes a total power of 500 mW and has a read access time of 35 ns the speed power product is 70 pJ (1 pJ = 10^{-12} J = 10^{-12} Ws.).

As discussed in Section 3.4.6.2 the switching speed is very much determined by the charge storage time of minority carriers in the base. Gold doping, Schottky clamping and application of ECL have a favourable effect on the switching time. Also a proper layout of the array metallization will reduce the read access time. Power dissipation occurs mainly in the collector load resistors R_c and is equal to $\Delta V^2/R_c$ where ΔV is the voltage across the resistor. Because in a memory flip-flop only one transistor is on, this ΔV is about equal to the supply voltage. Cells like the MESFET cell which can work with small voltages will have a lower power dissipation. Also ECL circuits, where the transistor is not driven into saturation, show reduced load dissipation as the voltage swing is smaller. A decrease of the power dissipation is also possible by increasing the value of the load resistors. In semiconductor technology the resistors are usually obtained by making long narrow p-type stripes with ohmic contacts in an n-type region. The resistors are usually diffused at the same time as the base region. Typical surface resistivity of a transistor p-type base diffusion is 100 Ω per square. When load resistors of 10 000 Ω are required, a length to width ratio of 100 to 1 is needed. When the stripe width is 1 mil, an area of about 200 mil² would be required for the resistor, which is very large compared to present memory cell sizes. Therefore the optimization of a memory cell requires a subtle choice of the base surface resistivity and the geometry of load resistors. Buried layers and epitaxial layers can also be used for the fabrication of the resistors.

Improvements in cell design made it possible for the power dissipation per bit, which was 60 mW in 1965 for the first bipolar memories, to be reduced to 0.5 mW in 1973 for 1024 bit per chip designs.

In Table 3.4.6.1 a number of old, present and speculative memory arrays are presented. The first rather fast but small bipolar memories had a speed-power product of 220 pJ. This has been reduced to 30 pJ for present day 1024 bit chips and will be reduced further to 5.4 pJ when 4096 bit chips become available. This compares very favourably with the new n-channel MOS memories. A very small projected speed-power product is based on the use of the MESFET cell, though here it is not clear if the technology of 1 μm

TABLE 3.4.6.1. Typical speed power products of memory cells

Type cell	Bits/Chip	Total power/ Chip (mW)	Power/Bit (mW)	Read access time (ns)	Speed-power product pJ
bipolar	64	350	5.5	40	220.0
bipolar	128	750	0.6	125	75.0
bipolar TTL	256	500	2.0	35	70.0
bipolar TTL	1024	500	0.5	60	30.0
bipolar ECL	256	500	2.0	25	50.0
bipolar ECL	1024	500	0.5	45	23.0
bipolar ECL	128	500	4.0	11	44.0
bipolar	4096	400	0.1	54	5.4
p MOS	1024	200	0.2	300	60.0
n MOS	4096	400	0.1	300	30.0
n MOS	1024	250	0.25	100	25.0
C MOS/SOS	256	100	0.4	50	20.0
MESFET	4096	20	0.005	25	0.125
I^2L	1024	6	0.006	300	1.8

gates can become routine. Finally the speed-power product of I^2L or MTL is very attractive. The low speed-power product is mainly due to the low voltage swing possible and the use of load transistors instead of resistors. Because of the importance of this kind of logic and memory device, in the next section the principle of this device will be discussed in more detail.

3.4.6.5. Merged Transistor (MTL) or Injection Logic (I^2 L)

At the 1972 International Solid State Circuits Conference in Philadelphia two papers were presented on a new and exciting bipolar logic or memory concept. In the first paper [3.4.80] it was called merged transistor logic (MTL) because the memory cell described was obtained by extensively merging inverse npn transistors with lateral pnp transistors. In the second paper [3.4.81] it was called injection logic (I^2L) because the operation of the proposed logic cell was based on the direct injection of minority carriers in inverse transistors. The injection was originally realized by shining light on emitter-base junctions and later by adding p-type injection rails. Despite the completely different starting points, the MTL and I^2L concepts appeared to be very similar. The excitement about the concept is due to the fact that it is very versatile, has an extremely low speed-power product, allows very high packing densities and can be manufactured by standard bipolar processes. The MTL memory cell is shown in Fig. 3.4.6.23 [3.4.82]. On top of a p substrate with an n^+ buried layer an n-type epitaxial layer is grown. In this layer p-type base and n^+ layers are diffused in the standard way. The

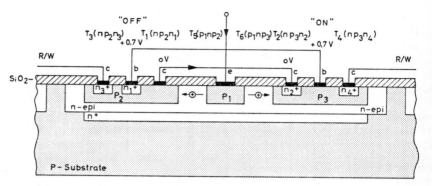

FIG. 3.4.6.23. Cross-section of a merged transistor logic (MTL) memory cell [3.4.82].

memory cell consists of two lateral pnp load transistors (p_1np_2 and p_1np_3) and two npn transistors (n_1p_2n and n_2p_3n) which are inversely operated, which means that n_1 and n_2 are collectors. These two transistors constitute the memory flip-flop. Further, two inverse npn transistors (n_3p_2n and n_4p_3n) are provided for reading or writing operations.

As in a standard transistor flip-flop, the collector of one transistor is connected to the base of the other one and vice versa. Figure 3.4.6.24 shows the equivalent circuit of the six transistor memory cell. A short circuit occurs between the bases of the load pnp transistors and the emitters of the npn flip-flop transistors because the transistors have the n-type epitaxial layer in common.

When a positive voltage is applied to the central injection rail, holes are injected into the surrounding n-type region. A large part of these holes is collected by the adjacent p_2 and p_3 regions, and forward biases the two transistors, when they are not interconnected and the transistors are driven in saturation. However, because the bases and collectors are interconnected, only one transistor can be turned "on", the other will be in the "off" state. When the right transistor is "on" and driven into saturation and the current gain of the inverse transistor is larger than one, the collector-to-emitter voltage is so small that the other transistor stays "off". As shown by Wiedmann and Berger [3.4.82] the inverse current gain β_{inv} is even larger than unity for very small currents. In an experimental memory cell, bistability was even maintained at a current of only 3 nA, corresponding to a power dissipation of about 3 nW. The information state of the flip-flop can be changed when the collectors of the transistors n_3p_2n or n_4p_3n are made negative. This draws away the base current of the "on" transistor and switches it "off".

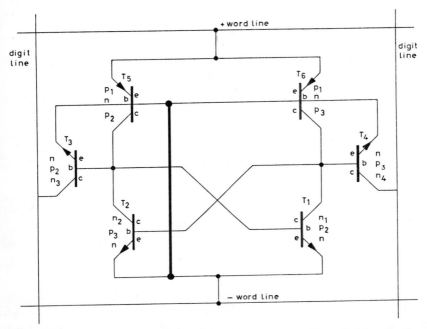

+ word line

digit line

digit line

− word line

FIG. 3.4.6.24. Equivalent circuit of a MTL memory cell. A feature of the structure is that the n-type epitaxial layer is the base region of the T_5 and T_6 pnp transistors and moreover the emitter of the T_1, T_2, T_3 and T_4 npn transistors [3.4.82].

The very small current levels at which the MTL memory cell can operate lead to very small speed-power products. As shown experimentally by De Troye [3.4.83] and theoretically by Berger and Wiedmann [3.4.84] three dissipation levels (1nW–1 μW, 1μ W–1 mW, > 1mW) can be distinguished. Figure 3.4.6.25 shows the measured propagation delay time as a function of the power dissipation per gate for a five-stage closed-loop inverter chain. The propagation delay time of bipolar logic gates generally consists of two terms: (1) the intrinsic delay due to minority carrier storage in the base region and (2) the extrinsic delay due to depletion layer stray and load capacitances [3.4.84]. At low dissipation the extrinsic delay is the most important one. The propagation delay time τ is then proportional to the time necessary to charge and discharge the capacitances. When ΣC_i is the total effective capacitance, ΔV the logic voltage swing, which is constant and about 0.7 V in MTL devices and I the source current, the storage delay time is proportional to $\Sigma C_i \Delta V/I_0$. The power dissipation D is equal to $\Delta V I_0$ so that we find that the speed-power product is proportional to $\Sigma C_i (\Delta V)^2$, which is a constant for a given MTL configuration. Consequently,

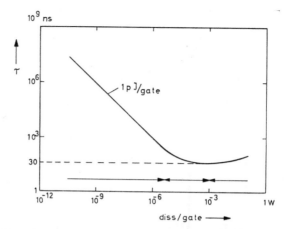

FIG. 3.4.6.25. Experimentally determined propagation delay time as a function of the power dissipation per gate for a five-stage closed-loop inverter chain [3.4.83].

we find in the delay versus dissipation diagram (Fig. 3.4.6.25) a straight line for low dissipation values. The already mentioned five stage inverter chain showed a speed-power product of 1 pJ/gate for dissipation levels between 1 nW/gate and 7 μW/gate. When the dimensions and thus the capacitances are reduced by a factor of two, this value reduces from 1 pJ/gate to 0.25 pJ/gate.

This speed-power product is about 100 times smaller than the best TTL logic gate and compares favourably with the estimated speed-power product of 0.2 pJ of the neurons in the brain [3.4.83].

The picture darkens somewhat when larger dissipation levels are considered. The propagation delay does not further decrease for increasing dissipation, because the delay time is now mainly determined by the storage time of minority carriers. An improvement of the storage time by gold doping is not permitted in MTL cells, because the marginal characteristics of the inverse *npn* transistors would suffer too much. When the dissipation level is further increased, delay time again slightly increases. This effect is due to base series resistance which prevents fast charging and discharging. From Fig. 3.4.6.25 it can be deduced that in the future MTL or I²L cells probably will be used in instances where a small speed-power product is more important than a fast access time.

Figure 3.4.6.26 shows the layout of a word organized array [3.4.82]. The cells belonging to one word are embedded in an *n*-type epitaxial strip which is isolated from the next words by *p*-type isolation barriers. A kind of collector diffusion isolation or oxide isolation is also feasible. The *n*-type

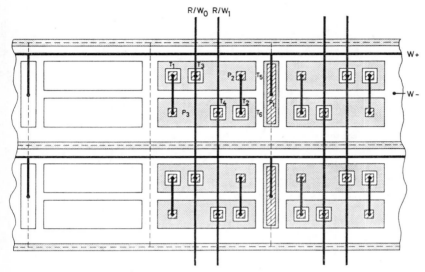

FIG. 3.4.6.26. Word organized array of MTL memory cells. The words are separated by *p*-type isolation regions. The injection *p*-type rail is shared by two memory cells [3.4.82].

epitaxial layer contributes the common emitter regions for all cells of one word. The word line is an aluminium strip, which connects all the *p*-type injection strips. One strip serves two memory cells. The read-write transistors, are connected to "0" and "1" lines. Because of the merging of the transistors, the cell size is only 4 mil². Therefore it seems feasible that memories might be built with 4096 or 8192 bits per chip.

The technology of the MTL or I²L memory cells is rather simple and only requires five masks. When two additional masks are used, injection logic can be combined with other bipolar logic circuits. Injection logic seems to be very well suited for the production of micro-processors and watches.

3.5. SUPERCONDUCTIVE MEMORIES

3.5.1 INTRODUCTION

The application of superconductivity to memory devices promises the construction of computer memories characterized by inexpensive batch fabrication, large packing density, small dissipation, integration of addressing elements on the substrate, no noise and a few other very agreeable properties. The only disadvantage is that the whole memory must be kept in a rather expensive refrigerator at a temperature below 4°K.

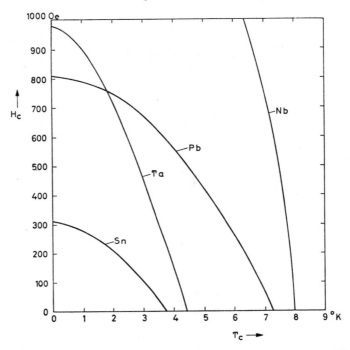

FIG. 3.5.1. Transition temperature as a function of the magnetic field for different materials.

It is no wonder that computer companies like IBM, G.E., Texas Instruments, RCA and Siemens at times had large research groups pursuing the goal of constructing superconductive elements, thus far in vain. And one may even ask oneself the question, if these efforts were successful, would the psychological barrier of working at low temperatures still prevent large scale use of superconductive memories in the future.

Superconductivity was discovered in 1911 by the Dutch scientist H. Kamerlingh Onnes at Leiden University. When he and his co-workers tried to make powerful electromagnets with zero-resistance wires, they discovered, to their disappointment, that the magnetic field due to the wires or an externally applied magnetic field destroyed the superconductive state. A plot of the transition temperature as a function of the magnetic field is shown in Fig. 3.5.1 for different materials.

The first superconducting switch consisting of a wire, which was switched between the normal and the superconducting state by a small coil around it, was first suggested by scientists from Leiden [3.5.1]. In 1956 Buck [3.5.2]

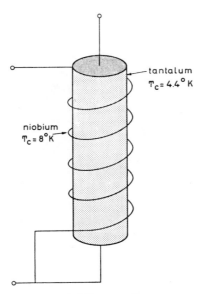

FIG. 3.5.2. Wire wound cryotron.

suggested a similar switch, which he called the cryotron. It consisted of a tantalum wire in a niobium control coil (Fig. 3.5.2). With this wire-wound cryotron he was able to construct flip-flops, OR and AND gates, multi-vibrators and decoding networks. His paper started a large research effort with respect to current switched memory and logic devices, which will be discussed in Section 3.5.2. Because the resistance of a superconductive wire is zero, persistent supercurrents can be started in a superconductive ring. The direction or the presence of the supercurrent can be assigned to a "1" or a "0". Persistent current memory cells will be discussed in Section 3.5.3.

For a long time superconductivity was one of the physical effects physicists had difficulty understanding. This changed when, in 1957, Bardeen, Cooper and Schrieffer [3.5.3] launched their BCS theory, for which they were awarded the Nobel prize in 1972. The essence of the BCS theory is that the electrons in superconductive materials below T_c pair up. In 1962 Josephson [3.5.4] predicted that such electron pairs can tunnel as a pair through extremely thin insulating layers. Based on this effect, Matisoo [3.5.5] showed in 1967 that extremely fast switching elements can be built. This result gave new impetus to the, at that time, dormant field, of super-conductive memories. In Section 3.5.4 computer elements based on the Josephson effect will be discussed. The use of superconductive switching

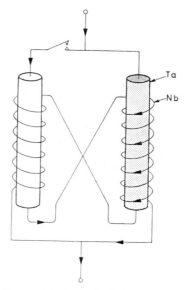

FIG. 3.5.3. Flip-flop with cryotrons.

elements requires a helium liquifier to keep the memory at the proper temperature. In the Section 3.5.5 the refrigeration problem will be briefly discussed.

3.5.2 MEMORY ELEMENTS BASED ON CURRENT STEERING

The first memory element based on cryotrons was constructed by Buck [3.5.2] at MIT. As shown in Fig. 3.5.3 the two wires of the cryotron are each in series with the control winding on the other. When the current flows through one of the sections, that current makes the alternate section resistive due to the magnetic field. This state will remain indefinitely, unless the current is switched off by a switch (preferentially also a cryotron). The current will transfer to the other section and will stay there even when the switch in the other section is again closed. Buck used one-inch tantalum wires with a convenient T_c of 4.4°K which is just above the boiling point of helium (4.2°K) at a pressure of one atmosphere. The control winding consists of a single layer coil with 250 turns per inch. The coil was made of niobium with a transition temperature of 8°K to ensure that on applying a current through the control winding only the tantalum wire transfers to the normal state and the control winding remains superconductive. In a superconductive computer the gate current of one cryotron is the control current of another cryotron.

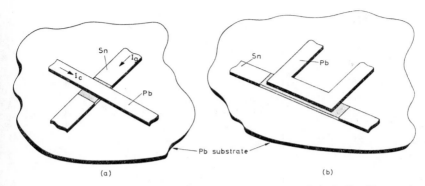

FIG. 3.5.4. Thin film structure of: (a) crossed film cryotron and (b) in-line film cryotron.

For this situation Buck [3.5.2] calculated that the frequency at which the power gain of a cryotron becomes unity is

$$f_{max} = \frac{R}{L} \qquad (3.5.1)$$

in which R is the resistance of the tantalum gate circuit and L is the inductance of the control coil. For fast switching a large R and a small L are required. A practical wire-wound cryotron has such an L and R combination that time constants on the order of milliseconds result, which is much too large to make wire-wound cryotrons of interest to computer designers. Around 1959 it occurred to a number of workers in the field [3.5.6] that better time constants might be obtained by employing thin film technology. As shown in Fig. 3.5.4 two film structures are possible. The gate part is made of tin with a T_c of 3.73°K and the control film is made of lead with a T_c of 7.22°K. It proved to be advantageous to use a superconductive lead substrate. When a current passes through a control conductor, the magnetic flux is not allowed to penetrate the substrate. An "image" current is induced in the substrate such that the field in the substrate remains zero. The favourable result is that the field under the control conductor doubles and is much more homogeneous. In the cryotron the gate section becomes resistive by either a current I_g through the gate or by a control current I_c. The two resulting fields combine vectorially as shown in Fig. 3.5.5 and only the magnitude and not the polarity is important [3.5.7]. This is not true for the in-line cryotron, as here fields can be parallel or antiparallel, which results in an asymmetric characteristic.

The speed of a cryotron can be calculated, when one assumes that one cryotron is used to steer the current of another identical cryotron. The time

U

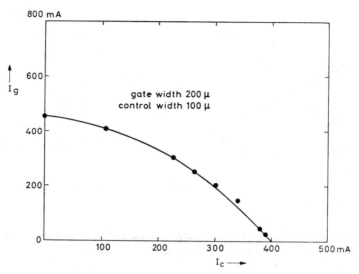

FIG. 3.5.5. Gate current versus control current for a crossed film cryotron at 3.5 °K, gate width 200 μm and control width 100 μm [3.5.7].

constant T is L/R in which R is the resistance of the gate conductor. As shown by Newhouse *et al.* [3.5.6] the inductance L of a control conductor with width w and length W spaced d cm from the superconducting substrate is given by

$$L = 4\pi \frac{Wd}{w} \times 10^{-9} \text{ H.}$$

(3.5.2)

The resistance R of the gate conductor can be expressed by

$$R = \tfrac{1}{2} \frac{\rho w}{W t} \, \Omega$$

(3.5.3)

in which t is the film thickness of the gate and ρ is the resistivity. Combining (3.5.2) and (3.5.3) we obtain

$$\tau = \frac{L}{R} = 8\pi \frac{td}{\rho} \left(\frac{W}{w} \right)^2 \times 10^{-9} \text{ s.}$$

(3.5.4)

Substituting values obtainable with thin film technology, time constants in the range between 0.1 μs and 1 μs are calculated. Thin film cryotrons thus are much faster than wire-wound cryotrons.

Early thin film cryotrons were fabricated by vacuum deposition through mask stencils. These mask stencils consisted of thin metal sheets in which openings were made through which the material was deposited on the substrate. Due to the unavoidable distance between mask and substrate the deposited structures had tapered edges. The high current density at these edges switches the edges to the normal state before the rest of the gate conductor. Therefore slight variations of the edges will lead to indefinite switching fields and currents. A considerable improvement was obtained when Pritchard *et al.* [3.5.8] used photomask-photoresist methods adapted from the semiconductor industry. Memory elements based on current steering require large current sources and connecting striplines continuously carrying currents. Therefore interest changed quite early to persistent current elements.

3.5.3. MEMORY ELEMENTS BASED ON PERSISTENT CURRENTS

In a well known experiment at MIT a current was induced in a superconductive ring. Two years later no decay of this current amplitude could be measured. It showed that currents can persist for a very long time in superconductive materials. When the direction of these currents can be switched from one direction to another at will, computer memory elements can be constructed. Crowe [3.5.9] in 1957 was the first to suggest such a persistent current memory cell. His cell consisted of two holes in a superconducting lead film. The supercurrents representing the "0" state and the "1" state are indicated in Fig. 3.5.6. Also the trapped flux around the holes is shown. Later on in 1961 it was shown by Burns *et al.* [3.5.10] that it is not necessary to have holes to trap flux, but that it is also possible to use small normal conducting regions surrounded by superconductive areas to store information. This kind of device is known as the continuous plane memory cell. Research groups at RCA and Siemens concentrated on this particular device for many years.

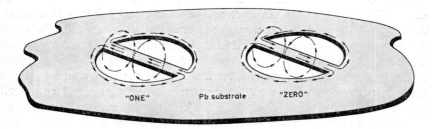

FIG. 3.5.6. Supercurrents and trapped flux in a Crowe cell for the "0" and "1" state.

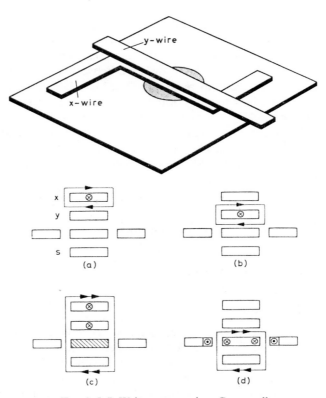

FIG. 3.5.7. Write sequence in a Crowe cell.

The operation of the Crowe cell is as follows. When a current passes through the x wire, the magnetic field is too weak to penetrate the superconducting bridge between the holes (Fig. 3.5.7(a)). A super current is induced in the bridge and around the holes equal and opposite to the drive current. A half select current through the y wire alone will have the same effect (Fig. 3.5.7(b)). When both half select currents coincide at a certain memory cell, the field is large enough to switch the superconducting bridge to the normal state, inducing a signal in the sense wire which is directly underneath the bridge (Fig. 3.5.7(c)). When the field is removed the bridge returns to the superconducting state and the flux around the bridge is trapped. A small decrease of this flux would immediately induce a supercurrent, which increases the flux to the original value. To keep the flux constant, the decrease of the drive current causes a persistent current to flow around the holes (Fig. 3.4.7(d)). The sign of this current is representative of the information

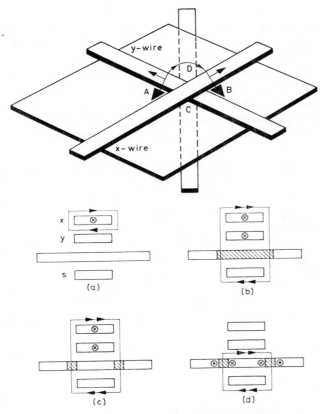

Fig. 3.5.8. Continuous sheet memory cell.

stored.   Because of the edge effect and the accompanying spread in the switching current levels, it proved impossible to make large memory planes based on this cell.   Switching speeds below 1 μs have been reported.   The operation of the continuous film memory cell is rather similar to that of the Crowe cell.

As shown in Fig. 3.5.8 such an element consists of a continuous sheet with x and y lines which are perpendicular.   A sense winding is placed on the other side of the superconducting plane.   When two currents through the x and y-lines are coincident, large fields occur at A and B, whereas the fields cancel at C and D.   The large field exceeds the critical field and causes the area beneath the lines to become normal (Fig. 3.5.8(a)).   Subsequently the centre part becomes superconducting again (Fig. 3.5.8(c)) and two normal dots at A and B exist in the memory plane. When the drive currents are switched off around these normal dots, persistent currents are induced (Fig. 3.5.8(d)). The direction of these currents is again representative of a "0" or a "1". When drive lines with a width of 250 μm are used, calculations and also measurements show that the switching time of continuous sheet memory cells is about one nano second. When half select drive currents are applied no signal is induced on the sense line because the continuous sheet will show no resistive dots. Also no noise signal is induced, because the superconducting plane acts as an ideal shield between the drive lines and the sense line.

Yet, continuous sheet memory cells have not caused the desired breakthrough. In performing disturb sensitivity tests, it appeared that persistent currents representing a "1" were slowly reduced and even disappeared when a large number of half select "0" pulses were applied.

A persistent current cell which does not show this problem uses cryotrons to generate persistent currents of the desired sign in superconductive circuits. As shown in Fig. 3.5.9, the memory cell consists of a lead ground plane into which a hole is etched, a tin sense digit line which contains the loop and two lead drive lines for bit selection [3.5.11]. A "1" is stored in the cell by applying currents in the x and y lines in the presence of a digit current (Fig. 3.5.10). The vertical segments of the loop become resistive and the current is forced into the segment of the loop which is on top of the hole (Fig. 3.5.10(b)). Due to the hole, the inductance of this segment is much higher than that of the other segments. Removal of the x and y select currents causes the vertical segments to return to the superconducting state, but the digit current remains in the high inductance segment because its flux is trapped in the hole (Fig. 3.5.10(c)). When the digit current is switched off, a persistent current results, as is shown in Fig. 3.5.10(d). The information can be read out by

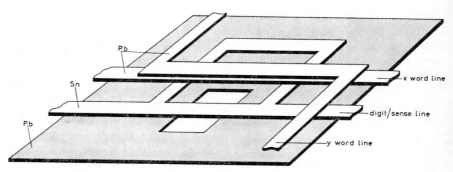

Fig. 3.5.9. Loop cell using persistent currents for data storage.

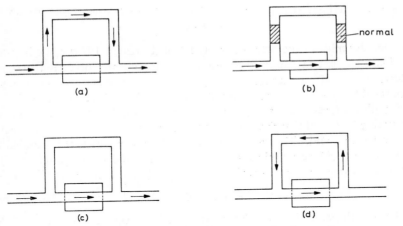

Fig. 3.5.10. Binary "1" writing sequence in a loop cell.

again applying x and y select currents. When a persistent current representative of a "1" is present, a sense voltage is induced on the digit line, which connects all memory cells on one plane. In the absence of a persistent current, which is representative of a "0", no sense signal appears. In order to obtain a large sense signal it is desirable for the persistent current I_L to be as large as possible compared to the write digit current I_0. When L_2 is the inductance of the segment above the hole and L_1 is the inductance of the rest of the loop, the ratio of these currents is given by

$$\frac{I_L}{I_0} = \frac{L_2}{L_1+L_2}. \qquad (3.5.5)$$

For large sense signals, it is necessary that $L_2 \gg L_1$, which is attained by etching a hole in the ground plane beneath the loop segment.

Switching times depend on the speed with which the current switches between the high and low inductance segments of the loop, and for representative memory cells the switching time is on the order of 0.1 μs [3.5.11]. Memory planes based on this principle have been successfully built and tested at RCA [3.5.12]. Sense signals of 200 μV were measured on arrays of 150 cm^2 containing 250 000 bits. Yet no computers have been designed using superconductive memories. This is mainly due to (1) the small yield of the large plane technology necessary to make superconductive memories, (2) the semiconductor memories turning out to be very competitive and (3) the psychological barrier against low temperature techniques of computer system designers.

3.5.4.   MEMORY ELEMENTS BASED ON THE JOSEPHSON EFFECT

In 1962 Josephson, (co-recipient of the Nobel prize in 1973) while he was a graduate student at Cambridge, England, theoretically predicted two very interesting effects occurring in sandwiches of two superconducting layers separated by an extremely thin insulator layer of about 20 Å thickness [3.5.4].

Josephson predicted that super currents would tunnel through the insulating layer and that the magnitude of this current would be very sensitive to a magnetic field. The second prediction he made was that an oscillating supercurrent will occur when a dc voltage is applied to the junction. The frequency f depends on the voltage V (in volt) and is given by

$$f = 483 \times 10^{12} \, V \text{ Hz.} \tag{3.5.6}$$

In 1963 both predictions had been experimentally verified [3.5.13, 3.5.14].

For computer memory elements, the first Josephson effect is of special interest. In Fig. 3.5.11 the dependence of the maximum current due to the tunnelling of electron pairs through a thin insulating layer is shown [3.5.15]. A rather small magnetic field can suppress the super current.

In 1966 Matisoo [3.5.5] made the first superconductive switch based on this effect. Since then interest in superconductive memory and logic devices has revived. Greiner [3.5.16] has shown that a Josephson tunnel junction can be made as follows (Fig. 3.5.12). On a niobium ground plane a Nb_2O_5

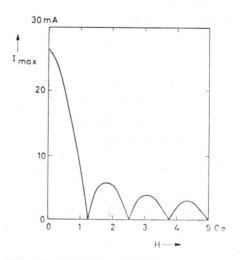

FIG. 3.5.11. Dependence of the maximum current I_{max} due to tunnelling of paired electrons on an external magnetic field.

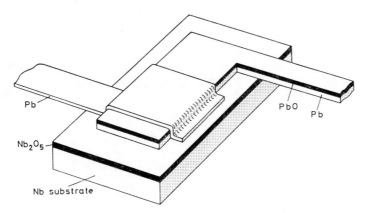

FIG. 3.5.12. Experimental Josephson tunnel junction.

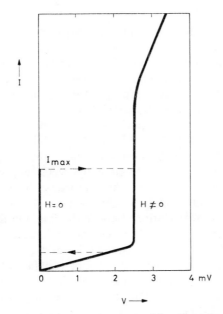

FIG. 3.5.13. I–V characteristic of a Josephson tunnel junction. Section 1 ($V=0$) is due to tunnelling of paired electrons and section 2 is due to single electrons.

insulating film is grown by liquid anodization. On top of this a lead electrode is vacuum evaporated. The lead is oxidized to PbO by an RF oxidation technique such that a very thin ($t < 30$ Å) oxide layer covers the lead

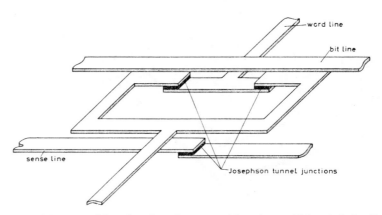

FIG. 3.5.14. Memory cell based on Josephson tunnel junctions, which switch the direction of a persistent current in the loop.

electrode. On top of the thin lead oxide layer a second lead electrode is deposited. The actual junction can be made as small as 10 μm by 10 μm.

The I–V characteristic of a Josephson tunnel junction is shown in Fig. 3.5.13. Because of the tunnelling electron pairs, a zero voltage current appears with a maximum magnitude I_{max}. When a larger current is impressed on the junction, the other characteristic is valid. For these currents a junction voltage appears because now tunnelling of unpaired electrons occurs. The characteristic shows a knee at 2.4 mV at 4°K which is caused by the presence of a forbidden energy gap between the paired and unpaired conducting electrons. When the current is subsequently decreased, at I_{min} the junction returns to the zero voltage I–V characteristic. The I–V characteristic of a Josephson tunnelling junction is hysteretic.

When a control strip is positioned above the junction the junction can be subjected to a magnetic field. The field, when large enough, reduces I_{max} to zero and only the second characteristic is valid.

The switching between the two states can be very fast. Jutzi et al. [3.5.17] have measured switching times smaller than 38 ps (1 ps = 10^{-12} s). Since 38 ps was the resolution limit of their oscilloscope, they believe that the actual switching time was 5–10 ps.

Josephson tunnel junctions can be used to construct logic switches or memory cells. A cell, first proposed by Anacker [3.5.18], is shown in Fig. 3.5.14. The cell is based on the principle of persistent current. The direction of this current is switched by a bit line and two Josephson junctions. On a memory plane a cell is selected by coincident currents along the bit and the word lines. Depending on the direction of the bit and word currents either

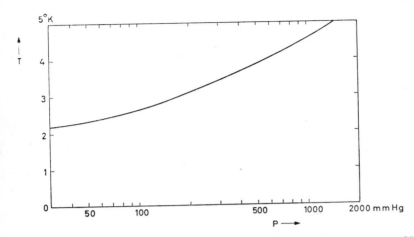

FIG. 3.5.15. Relation between the saturation vapour pressure and the temperature of He.

the left or right junction will switch changing the information state of the cell. Beneath the persistent current loop a sense Josephson junction can distinguish between the two directions the persistent current can have.

The major advantages of memory cells based on Josephson junctions are extremely high speed operation and very low dissipation. The main disadvantage is the fact that the operation of the devices is based on the tunnelling of supercurrents and this requires extremely thin oxide layers. It is not yet certain whether the fabrication of large planes with many thousands of junctions with reproducible properties will ever be feasible.

3.5.5. REFRIGERATION OF SUPERCONDUCTIVE MEMORIES

Most superconductive memory elements are fabricated with tin and lead layers. As the critical temperature of tin is 3.7°K, the cryoelectric memory must be cooled at least to a temperature below 4.2°K. Such temperatures can only be obtained when liquid helium is used. Helium boils at 4.2°K at atmospheric pressure (760 mm Hg). When the pressure above the helium in a closed dewar is lowered, the temperature at which the helium boils also decreases. The saturation vapour pressure of helium has been carefully measured as a function of the temperature (Fig. 3.5.15) and measurement of this pressure is sufficient to know the temperature of the He bath. When a rotary pump is connected to the dewar, the pressure can be lowered. The temperature of the helium will decrease until it reaches the temperature at which the pressure is equal to the saturation vapour pressure. A cryoelectric

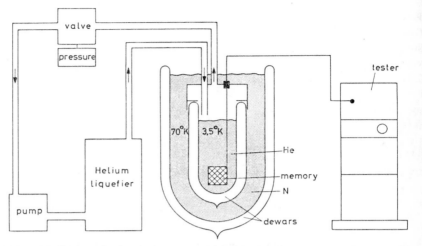

FIG. 3.5.16. Cryostat for keeping a superconductive memory at a temperature of 3.5 °K.

memory containing tin layers will often be operated at 3.5°K, which requires a pressure of about 350 Torr. An apparatus based on this effect and in which low temperature work is generally performed, is called a cryostat.   In Fig. 3.5.16 a schematic representation of such a cryostat is shown.

The dewar containing the liquid helium is immersed in a dewar containing liquid nitrogen (70°K) which reduces heat losses considerably. Via a pressure control gauge a rotary pump removes helium gas from the helium dewar. In a closed system, this helium is again liquefied in a small Collins helium liquefier and pumped back to the dewar. The memory is immersed in the helium bath and connected by coaxial cables to the peripheral electronics. The helium liquefier must be large enough to compensate for the helium loss of the system. The principal sources of helium loss due to heat are [3.5.19]:

(1) Thermal conduction along the coaxial cables,

(2) Power dissipated by electric currents in the coaxial cables,

(3) Power dissipated during operation of the cells, and

(4) Heat leakage through dewar walls and dewar cover.

In a properly constructed cryostat the loss due to the heat leakage can be neglected with respect to the other losses.

In general the losses depend very much on the kind of memory cell and the size of the complete memory. Several authors indicate that a helium liquefier with a cooling capacity between 5 and 10 W would be appropriate; this means a production of between 10 and 20 litres per hour of liquid helium.

Depending on the number of superconductive memories and cryostats made, the price of a cryostat will be somewhere between $10 000 and $50 000. If, as suggested by Newhouse et al. [3.5.20], the helium dewar with a working volume of 9000 cm^3 would hold a memory consisting of 100 plates each with 2×10^5 bits the cryostat costs per bit would be between $0.05 and $0.25. This is too much in order to compete with other technologies. It is generally agreed that cryoelectric memories with capacities larger than 10^8 bits are the only ones of interest, and only then if they offer features like smaller cycle times and NDRO (non-destructive read out) or if cells can be used in associative memories for data retrieval systems. It is generally agreed today that memory cells based on current steering or persistent currents will have no future with respect to memory cells based on Josephson tunnel junctions, it is much too early to venture upon the future of the Josephson devices.

REFERENCES

[3.1.1] J. Reese Brown jr, First and second order ferrite memory core characteristics and their relationship to system performance, *IEEE Trans. Electron. Comp.*, **EC-15**, 485–501, 1966.

[3.1.2] J. A. Rajchman, Computer memories—possible future developments, *RCA Rev.*, **23**, 137–151, 1962.

[3.1.3] R. K. Richards, "Electronic Digital Components and Circuits", D. van Nostrand Company Inc., Princeton, New Jersey, 1967.

[3.1.4] F. P Brooks jr, Mass memory in computer systems, *IEEE Trans. Mag.*, **MAG-5**, 635–639, 1969.

[3.1.5] C. F. Ault, L. E. Gallaher, T. S. Greenwood and D. C. Koehler, No. 1 ESS program store, *Bell Syst. Tech. J.*, **43**, 2097–2146, 1964.

[3.1.6] R. Shahbender, K. Li, C. Wentworth, S. Hotchkiss and J. A. Rajchman, Laminated ferrite memory, *RCA Rev.*, **24**, 705–729, 1963.

[3.2.1] I. S. Jacobs, Role of magnetism in technology, *J. Appl. Phys.*, **40**, 917–928, 1969.

[3.2.2] J. W. Forrester, Digital information storage in three dimensions using magnetic cores, *J. Appl. Phys.*, **22**, 44–48, 1951.

[3.2.3] J. A. Rajchman, Static magnetic matrix memory and switching circuits, *RCA Rev.*, **13**, 183–201, 1952.

[3.2.4] J. M. Carroll, Electronic computers for the businessman, *Electronics*, **28**, 122–131, June 1955.

[3.2.5] L. A. Russell, R. M. Whalen and H. O. Leilich, Ferrite memory systems, *IEEE Trans. Mag.*, **MAG-4**, 134–145, 1968.

[3.2.6] T. J. Gilligan, $2\frac{1}{2}$ High-speed memory systems—past, present and future, *IEEE Trans. Electr. Comp.*, **EC-15**, 475–485, 1966.

[3.2.7] H. Rogge, Vergleich verschiedener Speicherverfahren, *Entw. Ber. Siemens*, **32**, S9–S14, Sept. 1969.

[3.2.8] G. Winkler, Crystallography, chemistry and technology of ferrites, *in* "Magnetic Properties of Materials" (ed. J. Smit), McGraw-Hill Book Co., New York, pp. 20–63, 1971.

[3.2.9] W. Wiechec, New technologies for production of ferrite cores, *IEEE Trans. Mag.*, **MAG-4**, 465–467, 1968.

[3.2.10] A. M. Stoughton, R. J. Merkert, Computer controlled testing for improving ferrite core memory design, *IEEE Trans. Mag.*, **MAG-5**, 651–656, 1969.

[3.2.11] S. Chikazumi, "Physics of Magnetism," John Wiley and Sons Inc., New York, 1964.

[3.2.12] J. Smit and H. P. J. Wijn, "Ferrites", John Wiley and Sons Inc., New York, 1959.

[3.2.13] J. Verweel, Ferrites at radio frequencies, *in* " Magnetic Properties of Materials", (ed. J. Smit), McGraw–Hill Book Co., New York, pp. 64–107, 1971.

[3.2.14] R. S. Weiss, Square-loop ferrites, *in* "Magnetic properties of Materials" (ed. J. Smit), McGraw–Hill Book Co., New York, pp. 205–237, 1971.

[3.2.15] A. P. Greifer, Ferrite memory materials, *IEEE Trans. Mag.*, **MAG-5**, 774–811, 1969.

[3.2.16] E. Schwabe, Uber die Abhängigkeit der Schalteigenschaften von Rechteckferriten von der Korngrösse, *Z. Angew. Phys.*, **17**, 231–235, 1964.

[3.2.17] E. Albers-Schoenberg, Ferrites for microwave circuits and digital computers, *J. Appl. Phys.*, **25**, 152–154, 1954.

[3.2.18] H. J. Williams, R. C. Sherwood, M. Goertz and F. J. Schnettler, Stressed ferrites having rectangular hysteresis loops, *AIEE Trans.* (*Comm. and El.*), **72**, 531–541, 1953.

[3.2.19] H. P. J. Wijn, E. W. Gorter, C. J. Esveldt and P. Geldermans, Conditions for square hysteresis loops in ferrites, *Philips Tech. Rev.*, **16**, 49–58, 1954/55.

[3.2.20] K. Otha and N. Kobayashi, Magneto-striction constants of Mn-Zn-Fe ferrites, *Japan J. Appl. Phys.*, **3**, 576–580, 1964.

[3.2.21] H. Rabl, Ferrit-Ringkerne für Speicher mit hohen Arbeitsgeschwindigkeiten, *Entw. Ber. Siemens-Halske*, **32**, S57–S59, 1969.

[3.2.22] H. van der Heide, H. G. Bruijning and H. P. J. Wijn, Switching time of ferrites with rectangular hysteresis loop, *Philips Tech. Rev.*, **18**, 336–346, 1956/57.

[3.2.23] E. Olson, "Applied Magnetism", Philips Technical Library, Eindhoven, pp. 104–105, 1966.

[3.2.24] H. Stegmeier, Das Keimwachstum als Modell für die Ummagnetisierung von Schalt- und Speicher-Ferritkernen, *Z. Angew. Phys.*, **14**, 157–164, 1962.

[3.2.25] J. E. Knowless, The estimation of domain wall velocity in a "square loop" ferrite and some observations on the reversal process, *Proc. Phys. Soc.*, **78**, 233–238, 1961.

[3.2.26] E. M. Gyorgy, Magnetization reversal in nonmetallic ferromagnets, *in* "Magnetism", Vol. 3 (ed. by G. T. Rado and H. Suhl), Academic Press, New York, pp. 525–552, 1963.

[3.2.27] R. H. Tancrell and R. E. McMahon, Studies in partial switching of ferrite cores, *J. Appl. Phys.*, **31**, 762–771, 1960.

[3.2.28] P. D. Baba, Nonmagnetic inclusions in ferrites for high-speed switching, *J. Am. Ceram. Soc.*, **48**, 305–309, 1965.

[3.2.29] W. Döring, Uber die Trägheit der Wände zwischen Weiszschen Bezirken, *Z. Naturforsch.*, **3A**, 373–379, 1948.

[3.2.30] C. Kittel, Note on the inertia and damping constant of ferromagnetic domain boundaries, *Phys. Rev.*, **80**, 918, 1950.

[3.2.31] W. Metzdorf and H. Rabl, Die wesentlichen Eigenschaften von Ferritringkernen mit rechteckförmiger Hystereseschleife und ihre Wechselbeziehungen, *Elektron. Rechenanl.*, **5**, 168–173, 216–220, 1963.

[3.2.32] E. A. Schwabe and D. A. Campbell, Influence of grain size on square loop properties of lithium ferrites, *J. Appl. Phys.*, **34**, 1251–1253, 1963.

[3.2.33] E. W. Gorter, Saturation magnetization and crystal chemistry of ferrimagnetic oxides, *Philips Res. Rep.*, **9**, 295–365, 403–443, 1954.

[3.2.34] A. Vassiliev and A. Lagrange, Propriétés des ferrites de lithium partiellement substitués par l'aluminium destinés aux dispositifs micro-ondes, *IEEE Trans. Mag.*, MAG–2, 707–710, 1966.

[3.2.35] E. Steinbeiss, Untersuchungen über Ummagnetisierungsprozesse in Rechteckferriten, *Phys. stat. sol.*, **16**, 499–506, 1966.

[3.2.36] E. L. Boyd, Magnetoelastic resonances in ferrite memory cores, *J. Appl. Phys.*, **38**, 2367–2375, 1967.

[3.2.37] G. E. Warner and R. M. Whalen, A 110 nanosecond ferrite memory, *IEEE Trans. Mag.*, MAG–2, 584–588, 1966.

[3.2.38] H. F. Koehler and J. F. Covaleski, Speed capabilities of ferrite cores in NDRO operation, *IEEE Trans. Mag.*, MAG–3, 311–315, 1967.

[3.2.39] L. J. Bosch, R. C. Flaker, H. G. Hottenrott and N. F. Lockhart, An 80 ns NDRO ferrite core memory design, *IEEE Trans. Mag.*, MAG–3, 316–320, 1967.

[3.2.40] E. A. Bartkus, J. M. Brownlow, W. A. Crapo, R. F. Elfant, K. R. Grebe and O. A. Gutwin, An approach towards batch fabricated ferrite memory planes, *IBM J. Res. Dev.*, **8**, 170–176, 1964.

[3.2.41] M. S. Blois Jr., Preparation of thin magnetic films and their properties, *J. Appl. Phys.*, **26**, 975–980, 1955.

[3.2.42] J. I. Raffel, Operating characteristics of a thin film memory, *J. Appl. Phys.*, **30**, 60s–61s, 1959.

[3.2.43] G. A. Fedde and C. F. Chong, Plated wire memory—present and future, *IEEE Trans. Mag.* MAG–4, 313–318, 1968.

[3.2.44] S. Middelhoek, Thin films, *in* "Magnetic Properties of Materials" (ed. J. Smit), McGraw–Hill Book Co., New York, pp. 269–339, 1971.

[3.2.45] J. I. Raffel, Magnetic devices, in "Handbook of Thin Film Technology" (ed. L. I. Maissel and R. Glang), McGraw–Hill Book Co., New York, pp. 21.1–21.30, 1970.

[3.2.46] M. S. Cohen, Ferromagnetism in films, in "Thin Film Phenomena" (ed. K. L. Chopra), McGraw–Hill Book Co., New York, pp. 608–720, 1969.

[3.2.47] M. S. Cohen, Ferromagnetic properties of films, in "Handbook of Thin Film Technology" (ed. L. I. Maissel and R. Glang), McGraw–Hill Book Co., New York, pp. 17.1–17.88, 1970.

[3.2.48] S. Middelhoek, Domain wall velocities in thin magnetic films, *IBM J. Res. Dev.*, **4**, 351–354, 1966.

[3.2.49] T. R. Long, Electrodeposited memory elements for a nondestructive memory, *J. Appl. Phys.*, **31**, 123s–124s, 1960.

[3.2.50] R. M. Richard, J. A. Turner, J. K. Birtwistle and G. R. Hoffman, Thin permalloy films: optimization of properties for computer memories, *Br. J. Appl. Phys.*, **1**, 1685–1696, 1968.

[3.2.51] R. Girard, The electrodeposition of thin magnetic permalloy films, *J. Appl. Phys.*, **38**, 1423–1430, 1967.

[3.2.52] T. F. Longwell, Testing of plated wire for memory use, *Automatic Electr. Tech. J. (USA)*, **11** (no. 5), 214–224, 1969.

[3.2.53] W. S. Carter, F. S. Greene and J. D. Wright, Development of a closed flux magnetic memory element, *J. Appl. Phys.*, **40**, 978–979, 1969.

[3.2.54] K. U. Stein, Limits of speed and capacity of planar magnetic film memories, *Elektron. Rechenanl.*, **11**, 65–73, 1969.

[3.2.55] W. D. Doyle, R. M. Joseph and A. Baltz, Electrodeposited cylindrical magnetic films, *J. Appl. Phys.*, **40**, 1172–1181, 1969.

[3.2.56] H. Hoffmann, Theory of magnetization ripple, *IEEE Trans. Mag.*, MAG-4, 32–38, 1968.

[3.2.57] S. Middelhoek and D. Wild, Review of wall creeping in thin magnetic films, *IBM J. Res. Dev.* **11**, 93–105, 1967.

[3.2.58] W. Kayser, Magnetization creep in magnetic films, *IEEE Trans. Mag.*, MAG-3, 141–157, 1967.

[3.2.59] S. Middelhoek, Domain walls in thin Ni-Fe films, *J. Appl. Phys.*, **34**, 1054–1059, 1963.

[3.2.60] C. Kooy and U. Enz, Experimental and theoretical study of the domain configuration in thin layers of $BaF_{12}O_{19}$, *Philips Res. Rep.*, **15** 7–29, 1960.

[3.2.61] A. H. Bobeck, Properties and device applications of magnetic domains in orthoferrites, *Bell Syst. Tech. J.*, **46**, 1901–1925, 1967.

[3.2.62] P. I. Bonyhard, I. Danylchuck, D. E. Kish and J. L. Smith, Applications of bubble devices, *IEEE Trans. Mag.*, MAG-6, 447–450, 1970.

[3.2.63] P. I. Bonyhard, J. E. Geusic, A. H. Bobeck, Y. S. Chen, P. C. Michaelis and J. L. Smith, Magnetic bubble memory chip design, *IEEE Trans. Mag.*, MAG-9, 433–436, 1973.

[3.2.64] P. C. Michaelis and P. I. Bonyhard, Magnetic bubble mass memory-module design and operation, *IEEE Trans. Mag.*, MAG-9, 436–440, 1973.

[3.2.65] A. H. Bobeck, R. F. Fischer, A. J. Perneski, J. P. Remeika and L. G. Van Uitert, Application of orthoferrites to domain wall devices, *IEEE Trans. Mag.*, MAG-5, 544–553, 1969.

[3.2.66] A. J. Perneski, Propagation of cylindrical magnetic domains in ortho-ferrites, *IEEE Trans. Mag.*, MAG-5, 554–557, 1969.

[3.2.67] T. J. Nelson, Y. S. Chen and J. E. Geusic, Field nucleation of magnetic bubbles, *IEEE Trans. Mag.*, MAG-9, 289–293, 1973.

[3.2.68] I. Danylchuck, Operational characteristics of 10^3 bit garnet Y–BAR shift register, *J. Appl. Phys.*, **42**, 1358–1359, 1971.

[3.2.69] A. H. Bobeck, R. F. Fischer and J. L. Smith, An overview of magnetic bubble domains, *AIP Conf. Proc.*, **5**, 45–55, 1972.

[3.2.70] L. J. Bosch, R. A. Downing, G. E. Keefe, L. L. Rosier and K. D. Terlep, 1024 bit bubble memory chip, *IEEE Trans. Mag.*, MAG-9, 481–484, 1973.

[3.2.71] F. Yamauchi, K. Yoshimi, S. Fujiwara and T. Furuoya, Bubble switch and circuit utilizing YY overlay, *IEEE Trans. Mag.*, MAG-8, 372–374, 1972.

[3.2.72] G. S. Almasi, G. E. Keefe, Y. S. Lin and D. A. Thompson, Magneto-resistive detector for bubble domains, *J. Appl. Phys.*, **42**, 1268–1269, 1971.

[3.2.73] J. L. Archer, L. Tocci, P. K. George and T. T. Chen, Magnetic bubble domain devices, *IEEE Trans. Mag.*, MAG-8, 695–700, 1972.

[3.2.74] A. H. Bobeck and H. E. D. Scovil, Magnetic bubbles, *Sci. Am.*, **227**, 78–90, June 1971.

[3.2.75] J. E. Mee, G. R. Pulliam, J. L. Archer and P. J. Besser, Magnetic oxide films, *IEEE Trans. Mag.*, MAG-5, 717–727, 1969.

[3.2.76] H. J. Levinstein, S. Licht, R. W. Landorf and S. L. Blank, Growth of high quality garnet thin films from supercooled melts, *Appl. Phys. Lett.*, **19**, 486–488, 1971.

[3.2.77] G. A. Keig, GGG substrate growth and fabrication, *AIP Conf. Proc.*, **10**, 237–255, 1973.

[3.2.78] P. Chaudhari, J. J. Cuomo and R. J. Gambino, Amorphous metallic films for bubble domain applications, *IBM J. Res. Dev.*, **17**, 66–68, 1973.

[3.2.79] D. C. Cronemeyer, Perpendicular anisotropy in $Gd_{1-x}Co_x$ amorphous films prepared by rf sputtering, *AIP Conf. Proc.*, **18**, 85–89, 1974.

[3.2.80] J. P. Reekstin, A. G. Lehner, F. Vratny and G. W. Kammlott, Fabrication of 10^4 bit permalloy first magnetic bubble circuits on epitaxial garnet chips, *J. Vac. Sci. Technol.*, **10**, 847–851, 1973.

[3.2.81] A. A. Thiele, Theory of the static stability of cylindrical domains in uniaxial platelets, *J. Appl. Phys.*, **41**, 1139–1145, 1970.

[3.2.82] G. P. Vella-Coleiro, Domain wall mobility in epitaxial garnet films, *AIP Conf. Proc.*, **10**, 424–441, 1973.

[3.2.83] W. J. Tabor, A. H. Bobeck, G. P. Vella-Coleiro and A. Rosencwaig, A new type of cylindrical magnetic domain (hard bubble), *AIP Conf. Proc.*, **10**, 442–457, 1973.

[3.2.84] A. P. Malozemoff, Interacting Bloch lines: a new mechanism for wall energy in bubble domain materials, *Appl. Phys. Lett.*, **21**, 149–150, 1972.

[3.2.85] J. C. Slonczewski, A. P. Malozemoff and O. Voegeli, Statics and dynamics of bubbles containing Bloch lines, *AIP Conf. Proc.*, **10**, 458–477, 1973.

[3.2.86] A. H. Bobeck, S. L. Blank and H. J. Levinstein, Multilayer epitaxial garnet films for magnetic bubble devices—hard bubble suppression, *Bell Syst. Tech. J.*, **51**, 1431–1435, 1972.

[3.2.87] R. Wolfe and J. C. North, Suppression of hard bubbles in magnetic garnet films by ion implantation, *Bell Syst. Tech. J.*, **51**, 1436–1440, 1972.

[3.2.88] A. Rosencwaig, The effect of a second magnetic layer on hard bubbles, *Bell Syst. Tech., J.*, **51**, 1440–1444, 1972.

[3.2.89] U. F. Gianola, D. H. Smith, A. A. Thiele and L. G. Van Uitert, Material requirements for circular magnetic domain devices, *IEEE Trans. Mag.*, **MAG–5**, 558–561, 1969.

[3.2.90] F. Bertaut and R. Pauthenet, Crystalline structure and magnetic properties of ferrites having the general formula $5Fe_2O_3.3M_2O_3$, *Proc. IEEE Suppl.*, **104B**, 261–266, 1957.

[3.2.91] R. A. Laudise, Single crystals for bubble domain memories, *J. Cryst. Growth*, **13/14**, 27–33, 1972.

[3.2.92] F. B. Hagedorn, Domain wall motion in bubble domain materials, *AIP Conf. Proc.*, **5**, 72–90, 1972.

[3.2.93] A. J. Kurtzig, R. C. Le Craw, A. H. Bobeck, E. M. Walters, R. Wolfe, H. J. Levinstein and S. J. Licht, Correlation of domain wall mobility with gallium concentration in bubble garnets, *AIP Conf. Proc.*, **5**, 180–184, 1972.

[3.3.1] J. M. Herbert, L'utilisation des corps ferroélectriques dans les mémoires, *Onde Elec.*, **45**, 1187–1191, 1965.

[3.3.2] E. Fatuzz and W. J. Merz, "Ferroelectricity", North Holland Publ. Co., Amsterdam, 1967.

[3.3.3] A. B. Kaufman, Ferroelectric memories for special applications, *Electronics*, **42**, 116–118, May 12, 1969.

[3.4.1] D. A. Hodges, Large capacity semiconductor memory, *Proc. IEEE*, **56**, 1148–1162, 1968.

[3.4.2] T. W. Hart, D. W. Hillis, J. Marley, R. C. Lutz and C. R. Hoffman, A main frame semiconductor memory for fourth generation computers, *Fall Joint Comp. Conf., AFIPS*, 479–488, 1969.

[3.4.3] L. M. Terman, MOSFET memory circuits, *Proc. IEEE*, **59**, 1044–1058, 1971.

[3.4.4] A. P. Speiser, "Digitale Rechenanlagen", Springer–Verlag, Berlin, p. 46, 1967.

[3.4.5] D. A. Hodges, "Semiconductor Memories", MOS LSI shift registers 1402A, 1403A, 1404A, IEEE Press, New York, pp. 243–249, 1972.

[3.4.6] R. Igarashi and T. Yaita, An integrated MOS transistor associative memory system with 100 ns cycle time *Spring Joint Comp. Conf.*, 499–506, 1967.

[3.4.7] D. H. Gibson and W. L. Shevel, Cache turns up a treasure, *Electronics*, **42**, 105–107, Oct. 13, 1969.

[3.4.8] D. Frohman-Bentchkowsky, ROM can be electrically programed and reprogramed, *Electronics*, **44**, 91–95, May 10, 1971.

[3.4.9] "Scratching the surface", *Electronics*, **43**, 40, 42, Aug. 17, 1970.

[3.4.10] R. G. Neale, D. L. Nelson and G. E. Moore, Nonvolatile and reprogramable the read-mostly memory is here, *Electronics*, **43**, 56–60, Sept. 28, 1970.

[3.4.11] J. Marino and J. Sirota, There's a read-only memory that's sure to fill your needs, *Electronics*, **43**, 112–116, March 16, 1970.

[3.4.12] M. R. McCoy, MOS read only memories, *in* "Semiconductor Memories", (ed. J. Eimbinder), John Wiley and Sons Inc., New York, pp. 47–58, 1971.

[3.4.13] D. Frohman-Bentchkowsky, A fully-decoded 2048 bit electrically programmable MOS-ROM, *ISSCC digest*, 80–81, Feb., 1971.

[3.4.14] Plessey develops MNOS read-mostly memory, *Electronics*, **43**, 21–22, Dec. 7, 1970.

[3.4.15] Adding alumina gives 2048-bit ROM chip, *Electronics*, **43**, 10E–11E, Oct. 26, 1970.

[3.4.16] J. E. Iwerson, J. H. Wuorinen Jr., B. T. Murphy and D. J. D'Stefan, "Beam-lead sealed-junction semiconductor memory with minimal cell complexity", *IEEE J. Solid-State Circ.*, **SC-2**, 196–201, 1967.

[3.4.17] K. E. Drangeid, R. E. Broom, W. Jutzi, Th.O. Mohr, A. Moser and G. Sasso, A fixed address memory cell with normally-off-type Schottky-barrier FET'S *ISSCC digest*, 68–69, 1971.

[3.4.18] E. J. Boleky and J. E. Meyer, High performance low-power CMOS memories using silicon-on-sapphire technology, *IEEE J. Solid-State Circ.*, **SC-7**, 135–145, 1972.

[3.4.19] D. J. Kinniment and M. J. Turner, An 8 bit associative memory IC, *Microelectronics*, **2**, 22–24, Feb., 1969.

[3.4.20] D. N. Leonard, MOS content-addressable memories, *in* "Semiconductor Memories" (ed. J. Eimbinder), John Wiley and Sons Inc., New York, pp. 69–74, 1971.

[3.4.21] R. Dunn and G. Hartsell, At last, a bipolar shift register with the same bit capacity as MOS, *Electronics*, **42**, 84–87, Dec. 8, 1969.

[3.4.22] F. L. J. Sangster and K. Teer, Bucket-brigade electronics: New possibilities for delay, time axis conversion, and scanning, *IEEE J. Solid-State Circ.*, **SC-4**, 131–136, 1969.

[3.4.23] F. L. J. Sangster, Integrated MOS and bipolar analog delay lines using bucket-brigade capacitor storage, *ISSCC digest*, 74–75, 1970.

[3.4.24] W. E. Engeler, J. J. Tiemann, and R. D. Baertsch, A memory system based on surface-charge transport, *IEEE, J. Solid-State Circ.*, SC-6, 306–313, 1971.
[3.4.25] F. M. Smits, Charge storage semiconductor devices, *Solid-State Dev. Conf. Series No. 12, The Institute of Physics, London*, pp. 1–16, 1971.
[3.4.26] H. Z. Bogert, Metal oxide silicon integrated circuits, *SCP Solid-State Techn.*, 9, 30–35, March, 1966.
[3.4.27] L. Boysel and J. Murphy, Multiphase clocking achieves 100nsec MOS memory *EDN.*, 13, 50–55, June 1968.
[3.4.28] L. Boysel, W. Chan and J. Faith, Random-access MOS memory packs more bits to the chip, *Electronics*, 43, 109–115, Feb. 16, 1970.
[3.4.29] L. Cohen, R. Green, K. Smith and J. Leland Seely, Single-transistor cell makes room for more memory on a MOS chip, *Electronics*, 44, 69–75, Aug. 2, 1971.
[3.4.30] R. Gereth and H. M. Rein, Problems related to advanced integrated circuits, *Solid-State Dev. Conf. Series No. 12, The Institute of Physics, London*, pp. 45–65, 1971.
[3.4.31] S. M. Sze, "Physics of Semiconductor Devices", John Wiley and Sons Inc., New York, pp. 515–524, 1969.
[3.4.32] F. Faggin and T. Klein, Silicon gate technology, *Solid-State Electron.*, 13, 1125–1144, 1970.
[3.4.33] L. L. Vadasz, A. S. Grove, T. A. Rowe and G. E. Moore, Silicon gate technology, *IEEE Spectrum*, 6, 28–35, Oct. 1969.
[3.4.34] D. M. Brown, W. E. Engeler, N. Garfinkel and P. V. Gray, Refractory metal silicon device technology, *Solid-State Electron.*, 11, 1105–1112, 1968.
[3.4.35] E. Yon, W. H. Ko and A. B. Kuper, Sodium distribution in thermal oxide on silicon by radiochemical and MOS analysis, *IEEE, Trans. Electron Dev.*, ED–13, 276–280, 1966.
[3.4.36] A. S. Grove, "Physics and Technology of Semiconductor Devices", John Wiley and Sons Inc., New York, pp. 350–351, 1967.
[3.4.37] F. Leuenberger, Dependence of threshold voltage of silicon *p*-channel MOSFET's on chrystal orientation, *Proc. IEEE (Corresp.)*, 54, 1985–1987, Dec. 1966..
[3.4.38] D. Frohman-Bentchkowsky, The metal-nitride-oxide-silicon (MNOS) transistor-characteristics and applications, *Proc. IEEE*, 58, 1207–1219, Aug. 1970
[3.4.39] S. Nakanuma, A read-only memory using MAS transistors, *ISSCC digest*, 68–69, 1970.
[3.4.40] J. F. Gibbons, Ion implantation in semiconductors, Part I, Range distribution theory and experiments, *Proc. IEEE*, 56, 295–319, 1968.
[3.4.41] W. J. Kleinfelder, W. S. Johnson, and J. F. Gibbons, Impurity distribution profiles in ion-implanted silicon, *Can. J. Phys.*, 46, 597–606, 1968.
[3.4.42] G. Cheroff, D. L. Critchlow, D. H. Dennard and L. M. Terman, IGFET circuit performance, n-channel vs p-channel, *ISSCC digest*, 180–181, 1969.
[3.4.43] W. M. Penney and L. Lau. "MOS Integrated Circuits", Van Nostrand Reinhold Co., New York, 1972.
[3.4.44] D/MOS promises speed, easy fabrication, *Electronics*, 44, 24–25, Jan.4, 1971
[3.4.45] T. P. Cauge, J. Kocsis, H. J. Sigg, and G. D. Vendelin, Double-diffused MOS transistor achieves microwave gain, *Electronics*, 44, 99–104, Feb. 15, 1971.
[3.4.46] R. W. Bower, H. G. Dill, K. G. Aubuchon, S. A. Thompson, MOS field effect transistors formed by gate masked ion implantation, *IEEE Trans. Electron Dev.*, ED–15, 757–761, 1968.

[3.4.47] J. E. Meyer, J. R. Burns and J. H. Scott, High speed silicon on sapphire 50-stage shift register, *ISSCC digest*, 200–201, 1970.

[3.4.48] D. Maitland, N- or p-channel MOS: Take your pick, *Electronics*, **43**, 79–82, Aug. 3, 1970.

[3.4.49] Y. Tarui, Y. Hayashi, T. Koyanagi, H. Yamamoto, M. Shiraishi and T. Kurosawa, A 40 ns 144-bit n-channel MOS LSI memory, *IEEE J. Solid-State Circ.*, **SC-4**, 271–279, 1969.

[3.4.50] J. W. Ahrons and R. D. Gardner, The interaction of technology and performance in complementary symmetry MOS integrated circuits, *ISSCC digest*, 154–155, 1969.

[3.4.51] R. R. Burgess and R. G. Daniels, C/MOS unites with silicon gate to yield micro-power technology, *Electronics*, **44**, 38–43, Aug. 30, 1971.

[3.4.52] W. S. Boyle and G. E. Smith, Charge coupled semiconductor devices, *Bell Syst. Tech. J.*, **49**, 587–593, 1970.

[3.4.53] W. S. Boyle and G. E. Smith, Charge coupled devices—A new approach to MOS device structures, *IEEE Spectrum*, **8**, 18–27, July, 1971.

[3.4.55] S. M. Sze, "Physics of Semiconductor Devices", John Wiley and Sons, Inc., New York, pp. 425–504, 1969.

[3.4.54] C. H. Séquin, D. A. Sealer, W. J. Bertrain Jr., M. F. Tompsett, R. R. Buckley, Th.A. Shankoff and W. J. McNamara, A charge coupled area image sensor and frame store, *IEEE Trans, Electron Dev.*, **ED-20**, 244–252, 1973.

[3.4.56] M. F. Tompsett, Charge transfer devices, *J. Vac. Sci. Technol.*, **9**, 1166–1181, 1972.

[3.4.57] R. H. Walden, R. H. Krambeck, R. J. Strain, J. McKenna, N. L. Schryer and G. E. Smith, The buried channel charge coupled device, *Bell Syst. Tech. J.*, **51**, 1635–1640, 1972.

[3.4.58] G. F. Amelio, M. F. Tompsett and G. E. Smith, Experimental verification of the charge coupled device concept, *Bell Syst. Tech. J.*, **49**, 593–600, 1970.

[3.4.59] R. H. Krambeck, R. H. Walden and K. A. Pickar, Implanted barrier two phase charge-coupled device, *Appl. Phys. Lett.*, **19**, 520–522, 1971.

[3.4.60] M. F. Tompsett, A single charge regenerator for use with charge transfer devices and the design of functional logic arrays, *IEEE J. Solid-State Circuits*, **SC-7**, 237–242, 1972.

[3.4.61] L. Altman, Charge coupled devices move in on memories and analog signal processing, *Electronics*. **47**, 91–101, Aug. 8, 1974.

[3.4.62] I. J. K. Ayling, R. D. Moore and G. K. Tu, A high-power performance monolithic store, *ISSCC digest*, 36–37, 1969.

[3.4.63] H. A. Perkins and J. D. Schmidt, Integrated semiconductor memory system, *Proc. Fall Joint Comp. Conf.*, 1053–1064, 1965.

[3.4.64] J. M. Fairfield and B. V. Gokhale, Gold as a recombination centre in silicon, *Solid State Electron.*, **8**, 685–691, 1965.

[3.4.65] K. Tada and J. L. R. Laraya, Reduction of the storage time of a transistor using a Schottky barrier diode, *Proc. IEEE*, **55**, 2064–2065, 1967.

[3.4.66] R. N. Noyce, R. E. Bohn and H. T. Chua, Schottky diodes make IC scene, *Electronics*, **42**, 74–80, July 21, 1969.

[3.4.67] M. P. Lepselter and S. M. Sze, Silicon Schottky barrier diode with near ideal I-V characteristics, *Bell Syst. Tech. J.*, **47**, 195–208, 1968.

[3.4.68] P. Wolf, Microwave properties of Schottky barrier field effect transistors, *IBM J. Res. Dev.*, **14**, 125–141, 1970.

[3.4.69] Th. O. Mohr, Silicon and silicon dioxide processing for high frequency MESFET preparation, *IBM J. Res. Dev.*, **14**, 142–147, 1970.

[3.4.70] S. Middelhoek, Projection masking, thin photoresist layers and interference effects, *IBM J. Res. Dev.*, **14**, 117–124, 1970.

[3.4.71] S. Middelhoek, Metallization processes in fabrication of Schottky barrier FET's, *IBM Res. Dev.*, **14**, 148–151, 1970.

[3.4.72] E. Drangeid, R. F. Broom, W. Jutzi, Th. O. Mohr, A. Moser and G. Sasso, A memory cell array with normally off-type Schottky barrier FET's, *IEEE J. Solid-State Circ.*, SC-7, 277–282, 1972.

[3.4.73] B. T. Murphy, V. J. Glinski, P. A. Gary and R. A. Pedersen, Collector diffusion isolated integrated circuits, *Proc. IEEE*, vol. 57, pp. 1523–1527, 1969.

[3.4.74] D. L. Grundy, J. Bruchez and B. Down, Collector diffusion isolation packs many functions on a chip, *Electronics*, **45**, 96–104, July 3, 1972.

[3.4.75] F. Morandi, The MOS planox process, *IEEE Int. Electron. Devices Meeting, Washington*, 1969.

[3.4.76] J. A. Appels, E. Kooi, M. M. Paffen, J. J. H. Schatorjé and W. H. C. G. Verkuylen, Local oxidation of silicon and its application in semiconductor-device technology, *Philips Res. Rep.*, **25**, 118–132, 1970.

[3.4.77] W. D. Baker, W. H. Herndon, T. A. Longo and D. L. Pelzer, Oxide isolation brings high density to production bipolar memories, *Electronics*, **46**, 65–70, March 29, 1973.

[3.4.78] T. J. Rodgers and J. D. Meindl, Epitaxial V-groove bipolar integrated circuit process, *IEEE Trans. Electron. Dev.*, ED-20, 226–232, 1973.

[3.4.79] J. Mudge and K. Taft, V–ATE memory scores a new high in combining speed and bit density, *Electronics*, **45**, 65–69, July 17, 1972.

[3.4.80] H. H. Berger and S. K. Wiedman, Merged-transistors logic (MTL)—A low cost bipolar logic concept, *IEEE J. Solid-State Circ.*, SC-7, 340–346, 1972.

[3.4.81] K. Hart and A. Slob, Integrated injection logic: A new approach to LSI, *IEEE J. Solid-State Circ.*, SC-7, 346–351, 1972.

[3.4.82] S. K. Wiedmann and H. H. Berger, Superintegrated memory shares functions on diffused islands, *Electronics*, **45**, 83–86, Feb. 14, 1972.

[3.4.83] N. C. de Troye, Integrated injection logic—Present and future, *IEEE J. Solid-State Circ.*, SC-9, 206–211, 1974.

[3.4.84] H. H. Berger and S. K. Wiedmann, Terminal-oriented model for merged transistor logic (MTL), *IEEE J. Solid-State Circ,*. SC-9, 211–217, 1974.

[3.5.1] J. M. Casimir-Jonker and W. J. de Haas, Some experiments on a supra-conductive alloy in a magnetic field, *Physica*, **2**, 935–942, 1935.

[3.5.2] D. A. Buck, The cryotron—A superconductive computer component, *Proc. IRE*, **44**, 482–493, 1956.

[3.5.3] J. Bardeen, L. N. Cooper and J. R. Schrieffer, Theory of super-conductivity, *Phys. Rev.*, **108**, 1175–1204, 1957.

[3.5.4] B. D. Josephson, Possible new effects in superconductive tunnelling, *Phys. Lett.*, **1**, 251–253, 1962.

[3.5.5] J. Matisoo, The tunnelling cryotron—a superconductive logic element based on electron tunnelling, *Proc. IEEE*, **55**, 172–180, 1967.

[3.5.6] V. L. Newhouse, J. W. Bremer and H. H. Edwards, An improved film cryotron and its application to digital computers, *Proc. IRE*, **48**, 1395–1404, 1960.

[3.5.7] J. P. Pritchard Jr., Superconducting thin-film technology and applications, *IEEE Spectrum*, **3**, 46–54, 1966.

[3.5.8] J. P. Pritchard Jr., J. T. Pierce and B. G. Slay, Photomask-photoresist techniques for cryotron fabrication, *Proc. IEEE*, **52**, 1207–1215, 1964.

[3.5.9] J. W. Crowe, Trapped-flux superconducting memory, *IBM J. Res. Dev.*, **1**, 295–303, 1957.

[3.5.10] L. L. Burns, Jr., G. A. Alphonse and G. W. Leck, Coincident-current superconductive memory, *IRE Trans. Electr. Comput.*, **EC–10**, 438–446, 1961.

[3.5.11] R. A. Gange, Cryoelectric hybrid system for very large random access memory, *Proc. IEEE*, **56**, 1679–1690, 1968.

[3.5.12] R. A. Gange, Cryoelectric memories best hope for large and fast storage units, *Electronics*, **42**, 108–112, March 17, 1969.

[3.5.13] P. W. Anderson and J. M. Rowell, Probable observation of the Josephson superconducting tunnelling effect, *Phys. Rev. Lett.*, **10**, 230–232, 1963.

[3.5.14] S. Shapiro, Josephson currents in superconducting tunnelling; the effect of microwaves and other observations, *Phys. Rev. Lett.*, **11**, 80–82, 1963.

[3.5.15] J. Matisoo, Josephson-type superconductive tunnel junctions and applications, *IEEE Trans. Mag.*, **MAG–5**, 848–873, 1969.

[3.5.16] J. H. Greiner, Josephson tunnelling barriers by RF sputter etching in an oxygen plasma, *J. Appl. Phys.*, **42**, 5151–5155, 1971.

[3.5.17] W. Jutzi, Th. O. Mohr, M. Gasser and H. P. Gschwind, Josephson junctions with 1 μm dimensions and with picosecond switching times, *Electronics Lett.*, **8**, 589–591, 1972.

[3.5.18] W. Anacker, Potential of superconductive Josephson tunnelling technology for ultrahigh performance memories and processes, *IEEE Trans. Mag.*, **MAG–5**, 968–975, 1969.

[3.5.19] A. C. Rose-Innes, Refrigeration of a superconducting memory for a computer, *Brit. J. Appl. Phys.*, **10**, 452–454, 1959.

[3.5.20] V. L. Newhouse and H. H. Edwards, Cryotron storage cells for random access memories, *Radio Electronic Engr.*, **33**, 161–170, 1967.

Chapter 4

BEAM ACCESSIBLE MEMORIES

4.1. COMPUTER STORAGE BY OPTICAL TECHNIQUES

Since the invention of the laser, considerable work has been done in the area of optical storage of digital data. Two system approaches to optical storage have been thoroughly investigated. These are bit-by-bit serial storage and holographic page-by-page storage, both methods promise high bit densities (10^4–10^5 bits cm^{-2}) and large total capacity (10^8–10^{10} bits).

In both methods, a laser beam has to be deflected to one of many storage locations. For this purpose, all electronic acousto-optic and electro-optic beam deflectors have been developed. The storage material itself has been receiving much attention and many proposals, varying from photographic films, photochromics and thermoplastics to thermomagnetic/magneto-optic and ferroelectric materials, are encountered in literature. Matrices of fast photodetectors have been constructed and Ga–As injection lasers with extremely small dimensions (order of cubic millimetres) and high efficiency (order of 40%) have been fabricated.

Despite substantial progress in the development of these various components for beam accessible memories, it is still an open question whether optical memories will find their place in the computer memory market. The state of the art is such that optical beam accessible memories couple high density recording and large total capacity to medium access time and data rate. In order to be competitive with mechanically accessible magnetic memories like drums, tapes and disks, it is required that either the total capacity outnumbers the total capacity of tapes by several factors of 10 or the access time and data rate outnumber the access time and data rate of disk files. Both areas are still under development and at the time it seems risky to forecast whether or not beam accessible memories will ever be commercially used.

A beam accessible memory consists of many unconventional components; unconventional with respect to the standard components of existing memories.

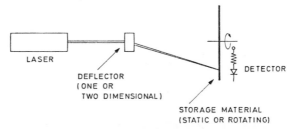

FIG. 4.1.1. Laser beam accessible memory consisting of a laser, a laser deflector and a light or heat sensitive storage material.

As shown in Fig. 4.1.1 a laser is used for the beam source. This laser beam is addressed through an optical beam deflector to any one of the total number of positions in the storage plane. The information is written using some physical light or heat sensitive effect of the material. The information is read through use of the same or another laser beam in conjunction with a photosensitive detector array at the back of the memory plane. As already mentioned there are two kinds of optical beam accessible memories envisioned: bit-wise organized and page-wise organized. The page-wise organized beam accessible memory uses holography for the parallel transfer of pages of information. Since holograms can be stored in thermoplastic [4.1.1] and thin magnetic films [4.1.2, 4.1.3] construction of erasable holographic memories seems feasible.

Basically the use of holography provides just another organization of a beam accessible memory. The system as a whole does not change substantially. A reference beam and a page composer are added to the system as is illustrated in Fig. 4.1.2 [4.1.4]. Holograms of entire pages can be recorded. The information is read by addressing the reference beam to the proper hologram which illuminates the photodetector matrix with the image of the originally recorded page.

Bottlenecks in the system design of laser beam accessible memories are the laser beam deflector, which is responsible for speed limitations, and the storage material, whose physical stability plays a major role in the feasibility of these memories.

In the early days of computer memories, as is shown in Section 1.2 on the history of storage techniques, a memory was employed based on the usage of electron beams to access memory spots on the screen of a cathode ray tube. Poor reliability of these so-called Williams tubes caused this kind of memory to pass into oblivion. Very recently electron beams have again been proposed for use in a MOS electron beam memory [4.1.5].

The purpose of Chapter 4 is to show where the limitations in storage

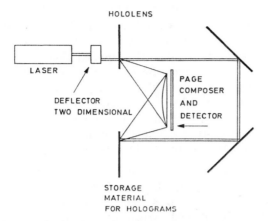

FIG. 4.1.2. Holographic memory. By means of the reference beam the contents of the page composer is stored in the hologram.

capacity, bit density and speed of the various approaches are. The chapter will be divided into three parts. The first part (Section 4.2) will be devoted to a description of performance characteristics of bit-by-bit and holographic methods. Here, ultimate bit density and total capacity will be discussed.

The second part (Section 4.3) gives a description of acousto-optic and electro-optic laser beam deflector techniques. Limitations of optical storage speed will be found to originate from the intrinsic physical properties of acousto-optic and electro-optic deflector materials.

The third part (Section 4.4) presents the physics of the proposed storage materials. Various techniques like thermomagnetic writing, magneto-optic reading, and thermoplastic writing will be reviewed.

4.2. PERFORMANCE LIMITATIONS OF BEAM ACCESSIBLE MEMORIES

The ultimate capacity of a beam accessible memory is determined by the field of view and the optical resolution of the focusing lens. Three types of beam accessible memories will be briefly analysed in this respect: (1) static bit-by-bit memory, (2) moving bit-by-bit memory (optically accessed disk memory) and (3) the page organized holographic memory. An analysis with respect to access time will not be presented here since access time mainly depends on the beam deflector performance, which is the subject of Section 4.3.

4.2.1. BIT-BY-BIT ORGANIZATION

In a bit-wise organized beam accessible memory, bit size is determined by the smallest possible focus diameter of the Gaussian intensity distribution. When the Rayleigh criterion [4.2.1, 4.2.2] is applied, which says that two equal Gaussian intensity distributions are distinguishable if the intensity in the region between them is less than 80% of the peak intensities of the separate beams, the focus diameter d_F is given in terms of the D/f number of the lens which is used to focus the beam on the memory plane and is given by $d_F = 2.54 \lambda f/D$ where λ is the wavelength of the coherent beam and f and D are the focal length and aperture of the lens respectively.

(a) Static bit-by-bit memory: The bit density n is found as the reciprocal of d_F^2, so $n = 1/d_F^2$. Using $\lambda = 0.5 \times 10^{-6}$ m (approximately green line of Argon laser) and a lens of $D = 50$ mm and $f = 250$ mm, a density of $n = 2.5 \times 10^4$ mm^{-2} is obtained. When the laser beam is deflected over wide angles, the focused spot will deteriorate. According to Räth [4.2.3], an upper limit of $\pm 10°$ for deflection angles can be tolerable. The total field of view of the above presented lens will then be π ($f \tan 10°)^2$ or approximately 75 cm which leads to a total capacity of about 1.8×10^8 bits.

(b) Optically accessed disk memory: When the same optical equipment as above is used for track addressing in a revolving beam accessible memory, the total area of the disk filled with tracks will be $\pi (R^2 - r^2) = 2\pi (2f \tan 10°)$ $(R+r)/2$, where R is the radius of the outer track and r is the radius of the inner track. Since bit density is the same as above, i.e. 2.5×10^4 mm^{-2}, the total capacity as limited by the optical parts for a disk with $r = 1$ cm and $R = r + 2f \tan 10°$ is about 9.5×10^8 bits.

This simple analysis does not, of course, give the ultimate capacity as obtainable in bit-wise beam accessible memories, but it gives a fairly good impression of the limits as put forth by optical parts of the system. A further limiting factor arises due to beam deflection. Nowadays optical beam deflectors are capable of resolving 1000 positions in one dimension, which means that a total capacity in two dimensions of 10^8 bits can only be achieved by cascading beam deflectors. (Section 4.3.)

4.2.2. ORGANIZATION OF A HOLOGRAPHIC BEAM ACCESSIBLE MEMORY

The organization of a holographic memory plate is schematically illustrated in Fig. 4.2.1. In an analysis of the system Kiemle [4.2.4] shows that the capacity of such a holographic memory can be expressed as

$$C \approx \frac{0.2}{(\lambda k_1 k_2)} \cdot \left(\frac{l \delta H}{l \delta + H} \right)^2 \tag{4.2.1}$$

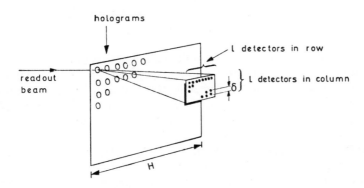

FIG. 4.2.1. Organization of a holographic memory plate.

where $l\delta$ is the side of the square detector array and H the side of the square hologram array; k_1 and k_2 are constants determined by geometry. Their values are around 1.5.

Assuming chips of 32×32 detectors, spaced by $\delta = 200\ \mu m$, fabricated by integrated circuit techniques and assembling four of these chips to a matrix of 64×64 detector elements, the dimension $l\delta$ is approximately $13\ mm$. Equation (4.2.1) shows that the capacity reaches its maximum value for $H \gg l\delta$. With $k_1 = k_2 = 1.5$ and $\lambda = 0.5 \times 10^{-6}\ m$, $C_{max} = 2.8 \times 10^7$ bits.

Assuming that $l\delta$ can be increased to $100\ mm$ and H to $350\ mm$ (which is set by the limits of optical components as necessary for guidance of the read-out beam), this value will increase to $C_{max} \approx 7 \times 10^8$ bits.

Equation (4.2.1) shows that with a detector matrix much smaller than the hologram plate the area of the detector matrix determines the capacity limit. If, on the contrary, the area of the detector matrix is made larger than the hologram plate, the plate dimension H, rather than the detector dimension $l\delta$, determines the capacity. The analysis of Kiemle shows that the number of detector elements is irrelevant. The matrix can thus be built with discrete components.

Assuming again H to be made as large as optical components allow, i.e. $H = 350\ mm$, the maximum capacity goes up to 10^{10} bits. In this case, access with two single x and y beam deflectors becomes impossible. If the detector matrix consists—as in the above configuration—of 4096 elements, the deflectors should resolve 2.5×10^7 positions, requiring 5×10^3 positions to be resolved per deflector. This means that, as with the bit-by-bit organized beam accessible memories, cascading of deflectors is necessary.

4.3. OPTICAL BEAM DEFLECTION

4.3.1. MECHANICAL DEVICES

In its simplest form an optical beam deflector consists of a mirror which by some means can be rotated about an axis perpendicular to the plane which is formed by the incident and reflected light beams or which can be translated normal to its surface. Both ideas have been elaborated, the translating mirror by, among others, Rabedeau [4.3.1] and the rotating mirror (galvanometer) by Zook [4.3.2].

Rabedeau's approach is shown in Fig. 4.3.1. His deflector is based on total internal reflection at the surface of a rectangular prism. A piezoelectric platelet cemented to a tiny slab of glass is mounted on this surface. When a signal is applied to the piezoelectric crystal, the piece of glass is pressed against the surface of the prism, thus extending the transmission of the incident light beam to the outer surface of the glass slab and displacing the reflected beam. In addition to the lateral displacement an unwanted longitudinal focus shift is produced. A multistage deflector can be composed of a series of parallelogram prisms. The thickness of the glass plates of each stage is given by $t_k = 2^{k-1} t_1$ where k is the stage number and t_1 is the thickness of the glass plate of the first stage. Operating speed is limited by the inertia of the glass plates. Individual stages have been constructed and tested with plate diameters ranging from 1 to 5 cm and with plate thicknesses ranging from 0.06 to 0.51 cm. Using potential differences of 200 to 300 V across the piezoelectric plate, switching times ranging from 7 μs to 35 μs were achieved. In order to limit the temperature increase of the piezoelectric plate to a few degrees centigrade, deflection rates of these devices are low (2000 s^{-1} when uncooled, approximately 50 000 s^{-1} when circulating water is used for cooling).

Zook's approach consists of driving a critically damped galvanometer coil by analogue electrical signals. The resolution is defined as the maximum deflection angle Φ_m divided by the diffraction limited angle, i.e. $N_R = \Phi_m W/e\lambda$ where W is the aperture of the mirror, λ is the light wavelength and e is a

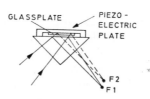

FIG. 4.3.1. Mechanical laser deflector [4.3.1].

constant of order unity that depends on the beam intensity profile, and the resolution criterion.

Random access time is defined as $\tau_a = 1/2f_0$ where f_0 is the resonant frequency of the galvanometer. When the mirror is mounted on a string which allows a maximum angular displacement $\theta = \Phi_m/4$, then the torsion constant is expressed by $K = T/\theta$, where T is the maximum torque. The resonant frequency is given by $\omega^2 = K/J$, where J is the moment of inertia of the mirror and simultaneously moving armature. A square mirror rotating about its centre of gravity has a moment of inertia

$$J = (\tfrac{1}{12})\rho t W^4, \tag{4.3.1}$$

where ρ and t are the density and thickness of the mirror, respectively. Hence, the access time is found to equal

$$\tau_a = \pi W^2 \{(\rho t \Phi_m/48\,T)\}^{\frac{1}{4}}, \tag{4.3.2}$$

which shows that access time is proportional to the mirror area W^2. Since the resolution N_R is proportional to the width W of the mirror, a trade off has to be made as to which one of the quantities τ_a and N_R is most important relative to the application. Zook gives the approach to maximize ω with respect to all geometrical variables of a galvanometer for a given N_R. A sample calculation, based on the characteristics of the Honeywell 301 servo, shows that a 10 000 position galvanometer deflector should have an access time of 1 ms.

4.3.2. ACOUSTO-OPTIC DEFLECTORS

When a longitudinal acoustic wave travels in a liquid or solid, the material is alternately compressed and diluted, which gives rise to an alternating perturbation of the refractive index (Fig. 4.3.2). An incident optical wave

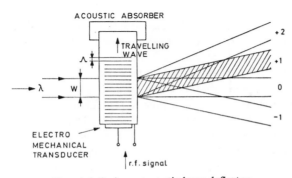

FIG. 4.3.2. Acousto-optic laser deflector.

is diffracted by this acoustic wave in many directions. Constructive interference will only occur in those directions where the difference in optical path between rays, which are scattered at corresponding phases in the acoustic wave pattern, is a whole number of optical wavelengths [4.3.3].

When Λ is the acoustical wavelength, α and θ are the angles of incidence and diffraction respectively and λ is the optical wavelength, the following relation is obtained

$$\Lambda(\sin\alpha + \sin\theta) = n\lambda, \tag{4.3.3}$$

where n is an integer.

For reasons to be discussed later in this section, the optimum efficiency of an acousto-optical deflector is obtained when α equals θ. In that case eqn (4.3.3) reduces to (in small angle approximation)

$$2\theta = \frac{\lambda}{\Lambda} = n\lambda\frac{f}{V}, \tag{4.3.4}$$

where f is the frequency of the acoustic wave and V is the propagation velocity of sound defined by $V = f\Lambda$.

Using numerical values for these quantities based on the use of water ($V = 1.5 \times 10^3 \, \text{m s}^{-1}$) and green light ($\lambda = 500 \, \text{nm}$) and assuming a frequency of 15 MHz, the first-order diffracted beam makes an angle of $2\theta = 5 \times 10^{-3}$ rad with the incident beam. It is not, however, the total angle that is important, but the resolving power of the deflector.

If the aperture of the optical beam is W, then the minimum angular separation is approximately $\theta_{\min} = \lambda/W$. Using an acoustic bandwidth Δf, the total number of positions which can be resolved within this bandwidth is

$$N_R = \frac{\Delta\theta}{\theta_{\min}} = \frac{W}{V}\Delta f = \tau_a\,\Delta f, \tag{4.3.5}$$

where τ_a is the time taken by the acoustic wave front to pass the optical aperture W. Since this is the time to completely bring the light beam under the influence of an acoustic wave of different frequency, τ_a is the random access time. Inserting reasonable values: $\Delta f = 10 \, \text{MHz}$, $W = 1 \, \text{cm}$ and $V = 1.5 \times 10^3 \, \text{m s}^{-1}$ one obtains $N_R = 60$ and $\tau_a = 6 \, \mu\text{s}$. For use in beam accessible memories, the number of positions is far too small. Therefore it is useful to investigate how N_R can be increased and τ_a can be decreased.

An increase of N_R can be achieved in two ways, either by increasing Δf or by increasing τ_a; the latter possibility is undesirable. So it follows that the resolution of an acousto-optic deflector is determined by the acoustic bandwidth, once τ_a has been chosen.

The only material constant which has influence in this respect on the deflector performance is the sound velocity V. For most materials (liquids and solids), V is in the range between $1.2 \times 10^3 \, m \, s^{-1}$ and $10 \times 10^3 \, m \, s^{-1}$ as can be seen in Table 4.3.1 in which some important material constants relative to application as acousto-optic deflection medium are given [4.3.4, 4.3.5].

TABLE 4.3.1. Material constants of several acousto-optic materials.

material	refractive index n	density ρ (g/cm³)	sound velocity V (10^3 cm/s)	figure of merit $M(\times 10^{18})$
fused quartz	1.46	2.2	5.95	1.51
TiO_2	2.58	4.6	7.86	3.93
αAl_2O_3	1.76	4.0	11.15	0.34
ADP	1.58	1.8	6.15	2.78
CdS	2.44	4.82	4.17	12.1
H_2O (lig.)	1.33	1.0	1.5	160.0
As_2S_3	2.46	3.2	2.6	433.0
αHIO_3	1.91	4.63	2.44	83.7
$PbMoO_4$	2.32	6.95	3.75	35.8

When a material with a large sound velocity (normally a solid) is used for the construction of a beam deflector, the total number of positions can be kept high when the geometric quantity W is increased in the same order of magnitude as V. So when using solid state acousto-optic deflectors, larger apertures are required than when using liquids. Furthermore, due to the low absorption of acoustical energy in solids at high frequencies, the bandwidth can be larger, thus enabling the construction of deflectors with a larger number of total positions.

When power consumption is considered, the deflection efficiency comes into the discussion. Deflection efficiency is defined as the ratio of the intensity of the first-order deflected beam I_1 to the intensity of the incident beam I_0.

A first approach to increase the ratio I_1/I_0 is to suppress the generation of diffraction orders other than the positive first order. The occurrence of higher orders is due to angular spread in the sound beam. This angular spread $\Delta\Psi$ is given by $\Delta\Psi = \Lambda/Z$, where Z is the width of the sound column. In terms of wave vectors, angular spread means that the beam can be thought to consist of plane waves whose wave vectors make a maximum angle $\Delta\Psi$ with each other (Fig. 4.3.3(a)). If only one plane wave exists and the angle of incidence of the light beam equals the angle of first-order deflection, the so-called Bragg diffraction would occur (only first order) since momentum

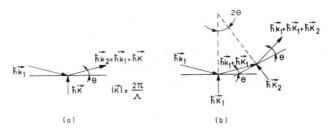

FIG. 4.3.3. Bragg diffraction at: (a) one single plane acoustic wave and (b) second generation due to angular spread in the acoustic wavefront.

would not be conserved otherwise [4.3.6]. Then:

$$2\Lambda \sin \theta = \lambda \quad \text{or} \quad \sin \theta = \frac{\lambda}{2\Lambda} \qquad (4.3.6)$$

and in the small angle approximation $\theta \approx \lambda/2\Lambda$. Since angular spread exists, a second Bragg diffraction may occur when there is a sound wavefront which travels at the angle 2θ with respect to the propagation direction of the first diffracting acoustical plane wave (Fig. 4.3.3(b)). Thus in order to prevent second-order deflection, the angular spread in the sound beam should be smaller than 2θ or:

$$2\frac{\Lambda}{Z} < \frac{\lambda}{2\Lambda} \quad \text{or} \quad Z > \frac{\Lambda^2}{\lambda} . \qquad (4.3.7)$$

This equation implies that second- and higher-order deflection will not occur when the width of the sound column is chosen large enough. If, again, water is used as a deflector material at a frequency of 10 MHz, a sound column width of $Z > 90$ mm is required in order to fulfill the condition of first-order deflection only. This width is reduced by a factor of 9 when a frequency of 30 MHz is used.

Diffraction efficiency I_1/I_0 is, according to propagation theory of electromagnetic waves, proportional to the square of the variation in refractive index Δn which is induced by the action of the acoustic wave. The refractive index variation is related to the density variations $\Delta\rho$ by [4.3.7]

$$\Delta\left(\frac{1}{n^2}\right) = p\,\frac{\Delta\rho}{\rho} \qquad (4.3.8)$$

in which p is a constant called the elasto-optic constant (Table 4.3.1) and ρ

is the density. Considering an isotropic homogeneous medium in a one-dimensional case, Δn is deduced from this relation and can be expressed in terms of the acoustic intensity

$$I_{ac} = \tfrac{1}{2}\rho V^3 \left(\frac{\Delta \rho}{\rho} \right)^2. \qquad (4.3.9)$$

Then, a relation between I_1 and I_{ac} is found.

$$I_1 \propto \frac{n^6 p^2}{\rho V^3} \times I_{ac}. \qquad (4.3.10)$$

This formula defines a figure of merit,

$$M = \frac{n^6 p^2}{\rho V^3}. \qquad (4.3.11)$$

Materials with a high figure of merit are suitable for application in an optical beam deflector. Looking at eqn (4.3.11), it can be observed that for a high efficiency, V should be low. On the contrary, the criterion that the access time τ_a should be small favours a high sound velocity. The total number of resolvable positions cannot be increased without limit by increasing the acoustic bandwidth. If, for instance, the sound frequency is increased by Δf, the Bragg angle changes by

$$\Delta \theta = (\lambda/2V)\Delta f. \qquad (4.3.12)$$

The angle of incidence, however, will remain constant with respect to the sound wavefront and thus the interaction efficiency decreases. As the sound wave originates from a transducer of finite width, angular spread is responsible for reaching the limit of efficient interaction when second-order generation becomes possible, or when

$$\Delta \theta = \Lambda/Z \quad \text{or} \quad (\Delta f/f) = \frac{2\Lambda^2}{\lambda L}, \qquad (4.3.13)$$

which means that Δf is limited by the width of the transducer.

In order to overcome this limitation a device was developed which is able to tilt the acoustic wavefront as the sound frequency is changed [4.3.8]. An array of four transducers of definite width and spacing (Fig. 4.3.4) is mounted on a stair step type glass block. The height of the steps is chosen to equalize one-half the sound wavelength at the centre frequency. Moreover, when the transducers are energized in an alternating phase mode, the sound wave is caused to travel normal to the transducers at the centre frequency.

w

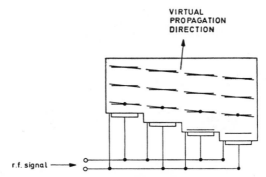

FIG. 4.3.4. Adjustment of the Bragg angle by tilting the acoustic wave front with frequency.

At other frequencies, the wavefront will be tilted due to small phase differences. With the aid of this phased array transducer, bandwidth is increased by a factor of two.

Summarizing the above presented considerations, materials for acousto-optic deflectors are to be selected on the basis of the following parameters.

(1) The refractive index, which determines to a great extent the figure of merit M; n should be large.

(2) The elasto-optic constant p, which should be large for the same reason.

(3) The density ρ, which should be small.

(4) The sound velocity V, which not only plays an important role for the efficiency, but also for the access time, the acoustic bandwidth and the resolution. The requirements on V from the access time point of view and from the efficiency point of view are in opposition to each other.

(5) Acoustic damping. Losses due to acoustic damping should be avoided. For instance, when water (one of the best acousto-optic media according to the figure of merit M) is used, frequency is limited to only 50 MHz.

Commercially available acousto-optic deflectors have been constructed by Korpel [4.3.8], who uses very dense flint glass as the acousto-optic material. Working at a bandwidth of 70 MHz, a resolution of better than 500 points with a random access time of 5 μs has been achieved. Since this does not approach real physical limits, progress can still be expected in this field.

4.3.3. ELECTRO-OPTIC DEFLECTORS

Materials showing the electro-optical effect, i.e. variation of the refractive

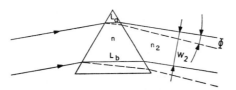

Fɪɢ. 4.3.5. Influence of an electric field on the light path in an electro-optic prism.

index under the influence of an applied electric field, can be used for optical beam deflection.

This is conveniently illustrated using a prism of an electro-optical material as shown in Fig. 4.3.5. When a light beam traverses the prism it is deflected due to the difference between the refractive indices of air and the prism material. When the prism's refractive index is further changed by an electrical bias field, the deflection angle is changed as a result of this action. Lee and Zook [4.3.9] showed that the deflection angle variation for a deflector based on this principle is given by

$$\phi = \frac{\Delta n (L_a - L_b)}{n_2 W_2} \qquad (4.3.14)$$

where Δn is the electro-optically induced change in refractive index and $\Delta n(L_a - L_b)$ is the induced optical path difference.

The resolution of such a deflector is given by $N_R = \phi/\theta_{min}$ where θ_{min} is the diffraction limited angle $e\lambda/n_2 W_2$ with $e = 1.6$ for Gaussian beams and with λ being the wavelength, so that

$$N_R = \frac{\Delta n (L_a - L_b)}{e\lambda} . \qquad (4.3.15)$$

Cascading several prisms results in a larger induced optical path difference which makes N_R increase. Since Δn is directly proportional to the applied field (Pockels effect) or to the square of the applied field (Kerr effect) the deflector can be operated in an analogous mode. Materials for this type of deflector are KD_2PO_4(KDP) and $LiNbO_3$, $LiTaO_3$ and isomorphs.

Quite another type of electro-optic deflector is obtained when induced birefringence is used for polarization switching (Fig. 4.3.6). In polar liquids, an external electric field E_z will orient the dipoles and thus cause a difference in refractive indices for light which is polarized along the bias field and for light which is polarized normal to that direction. Then a linearly polarized light beam with E-vector in the $x-z$ plane under 45° with the z axis and travelling

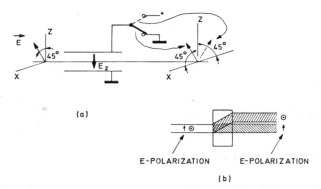

Fig. 4.3.6. Operation of a polarization switch using a birefringent crystal.

in the y direction will be split into two components travelling at different propagation velocities in the liquid. The phase difference which is induced in this way can equal 180° when either the applied field intensity is large enough or the path length inside the liquid is sufficiently long.

Upon emerging from the birefringent medium the light beam will be linearly polarized at an angle of 90° with respect to the polarization of the incident beam. A binary polarization switch is thus obtained. When the light which emerges from the polarization switch again enters a crystal which shows natural birefringence, the light will travel either as an ordinary ray or as an extraordinary ray, i.e. emerge either undeflected or laterally deflected. This type of electro-optic deflector is digitally operated. The magnitude of the lateral deflection is determined by the thickness of the birefringent crystal. This thickness will generally increase or decrease by a factor of two for each additional stage. So $t_N = (1/2^N)t_1$ where t_1 is the thickness of the first stage and t_N is the thickness of the Nth stage. In a practical device, capable of randomly deflecting a laser beam to either one of 1024×1024 positions, Meyer et al. [4.3.10] used birefringent prisms instead of birefringent plates. In this deflector, the prism top angles increase by a factor of two for each additional stage. The physical principle of the deflection methods described here is based on the use of the electro-optical effect.

Generally, the refractive index of a crystal is given by the indicatrix

$$B_{ij} x_i x_j = 1, \qquad (4.3.16)$$

where $B_{ij} = \varepsilon_0 \, \partial E_i / \partial D_j$ are the components of the impermeability tensor at optical frequencies. When the standard reduced index notation $(ij \rightarrow m)$ is used, the linear electro-optic effect can be expressed as [4.3.11]

$$\Delta B_m = r_{mk} E_k, \qquad (4.3.17)$$

where E_k are the electric field components and r_{mk} are the linear electro-optic coefficients. The quadratic electro-optic effect can be described as

$$\Delta B_m = g_{mkl}\, P_k\, P_l, \tag{4.3.18}$$

where P_k are the dielectric polarization components and g_{mkl} are the quadratic electro-optic coefficients.

In liquids and isotropic solids, the linear effect does not occur since any change in the sign of E would not change the physical situation.

The digital electro-optic deflector of Schmidt and Thust [4.3.12] takes advantage of the Kerr (quadratic) effect in nitrobenzene. Nitrobenzene, when not under the influence of an electric field, is an isotropic liquid with polar molecules oriented at random. In the presence of an electric field, orientation of the molecules along the bias field causes the difference in propagation velocities for optical waves polarized along the bias field and polarized perpendicularly to the bias field. This in turn is responsible for an induced phase difference between the two components

$$\Phi = \frac{2\pi L}{\lambda}\,(n_{\mathrm p}-n_{\mathrm s}) \stackrel{\text{def}}{=} 2\pi BLE^2 \tag{4.3.19}$$

where $n_{\mathrm p}$ and $n_{\mathrm s}$ are the components of the refractive index parallel to and perpendicular to the bias field, respectively, and B is the Kerr constant. Kerr constants of nitrobenzene and other polar liquids are tabulated by Krüger et al. [4.3.13].

Under the most favourable circumstances, and using nitrobenzene, switching fields causing a phase difference of $180°$ are of the order of $3.5\ \mathrm{MV\,m^{-1}}$ for a Kerr cell length of $L = 10^{-2}\ \mathrm{cm}$.

The quadratic nature of the Kerr effect can be used to reduce the switching field. The Kerr cell can be biased with a static field $E_{p\pi}$ which induces a phase difference of $\Phi = p\pi$ between the two linearly, mutually, orthogonally, polarized beam components (p is assumed to be an integer here). Polarization switching is now obtained by applying a switching field $E_{\mathrm s}$ which induces an additional phase difference of π radians. Then, using eqn (4.3.19)

$$E_{\mathrm s}(p) = \frac{\{(p+1)^{\frac12}-p^{\frac12}\}}{(2BL)^{\frac12}}. \tag{4.3.20}$$

This expression shows that $E_{\mathrm s}(p)$ decreases with increasing p, or consequently with increasing bias field $E_{p\pi}$.

A decrease in switching fields is advantageous since dielectric losses which are responsible for power dissipation will decrease. Power dissipation is given by

$$p = E_{\mathrm s}^2(\mathrm{eff})\omega\varepsilon' \tan\delta.$$

Here $\tan \delta$ is the dielectric loss factor, ω the switching frequency and ε' the real part of the dielectric permeability at the frequency ω. The frequency limit for a nitrobenzene polarization switch is of the order of 10^9 Hz. Meyer *et al.* [4.3.10] report switching times of 300–900 ns for a 20-stage two-dimensional digital light deflector with nitrobenzene polarization switches. At 5×10^5 switching operations per second, power consumption is 400 W. Switching fields are of the order of 1.3 MV m^{-1} at a bias field of 3.3 MV m^{-1} which means, with an electrode separation of 1.6 mm, that the applied switching voltage and bias voltage are 2.1 kV and 5.3 kV, respectively.

Solid state polarization switches can be operated in a longitudinal mode, i.e. with the switching field parallel to the light propagation direction, and in a transverse mode, with light path and switching field perpendicular to each other. The orientation of the electro-optic crystal, the most prominent of which are KDP (KD_2PO_4) and isomorphs, $LiNbO_3$ and isomorphs, KTN and CuCl, with respect to the applied field and the light path determines the appropriate electro-optic coefficient r_{mk} [4.3.9, 4.3.11]. The electro-optic effect employed in these solids is the Pockels effect.

In a longitudinally operated KDP polarization switch, the induced modulation of the refractive index is

$$\Delta n = \tfrac{1}{2} n_0^3 \, r_{63} \, E_3. \qquad (4.3.21)$$

Due to natural birefringence, the effect of this modulation is superimposed on a stationary phase difference

$$\Phi_s = \frac{2\pi L}{\lambda} \, (n_e - n_o) \qquad (4.3.22)$$

where n_e is the refractive index for the extraordinary ray and n_o is the refractive index for the ordinary ray. This stationary phase difference, however, can be compensated for with the use of a second KDP crystal.

A severe limitation in speed of longitudinally operated polarization switches lies in the use of transparent conducting electrodes. These electrodes form, together with the deflector crystal, an RC network whose power dissipation is

$$P = \tfrac{1}{2} \omega^2 \, C^2 \, V^2 \, R, \qquad (4.3.23)$$

where R represents the resistance of the transparent electrodes, C the capacitance of the deflector crystal, V the switching voltage and ω the frequency. For a given power dissipation the maximum tolerable frequency is

$$f_M = \frac{1}{2\pi CV} \left(\frac{2P}{R} \right)^{\frac{1}{2}}. \qquad (4.3.24)$$

Device characteristics, reported by Kulcke *et al.* [4.3.14] are $C = 85\,pF$, $V = 2\,kV$ and $R = 100\,\Omega$. At a dissipation level of 1 W, a maximum frequency of 150 kHz is found. This results in an access time of 7 μs.

4.4. STORAGE MATERIALS

4.4.1. INTRODUCTION

Storage materials for optical beam accessible memories should essentially have two basic properties. In the first place the material must show a physical effect whereby photons are able to change the material's optical properties and in the second place the difference between unaccessed and accessed sites in the material must be optically detectable. If, in addition to these requirements, the optical induced effect is erasable, a random access optical memory is feasible. When, on the other hand, the memory effect is non-erasable, the material is suited for use in a read only memory. Examples of materials showing reversible effects are magneto-optic materials, ferroelectric materials, thermoplastics and photochromics. Materials showing irreversible effects are photographic emulsions and photoresists.

Magneto-optic materials have been investigated thoroughly on their application in optical memories. Three main areas can be distinguished: the MnBi approach, where thin MnBi films are proposed as the storage material, the Europium chalcogenides approach where EuO and EuSe films are the most promising materials and the magnetic garnet approach with gadolinium iron garnet (GdIG) slabs as promising exponent.

These three groups of magneto-optic materials differ in quite a number of respects and each of them has its features and disadvantages, which will be discussed in the following sections. They have in common the utilization of the magneto-optic effect for readout. For this reason this type of memory is usually referred to as the magneto-optic memory. Writing is achieved by a thermomagnetic effect. The energy of a laser beam is converted into heat, which in turn affects the magnetic state of the medium. The magneto-optic materials will be discussed in Section 4.4.2.

Ferroelectric materials have also been under continuous investigation. The remanent polarization can be switched by external means in one of a few directions of crystalline preference. The optical indicatrix is influenced by the orientation of the remanent polarization and thus optical readout by means of linearly polarized light will be possible.

Writing of information in ferroelectric materials can be performed by either locally heating the material to the Curie temperature or switching at room temperature by an applied electric field. Also electro-optic materials can be used for storage purposes. By means of a laser beam electrons can be forced to diffuse through a material like $LiNbO_3$. Electro-optic materials are discussed in Section 4.4.3.

Thermoplastics have been proposed as a storage medium for holograms. Their properties will be discussed in Section 4.4.4.

4.4.2. MAGNETO-OPTIC MATERIALS

4.4.2.1. The Readout Process

The reading of information from a magneto-optic material is accomplished by using one of the magneto-optic effects: Faraday effect for transmitted light and Kerr effect for reflected light. Phenomenologically these effects can be regarded as a rotation of the plane of polarization of a linearly polarized light beam upon transmission through (Faraday rotation) or upon reflection at (Kerr rotation) the material. For a detailed physical description the reader is referred to Suits [4.4.1].

When the propagation direction of the light beam and magnetization of the medium are parallel, the plane of polarization, after the beam has travelled a distance h in the medium, will be rotated over an angle $\theta_F = Fh$ where F is the specific Faraday rotation. When magnetization and propagation direction of the light are antiparallel, this angle will be negative, i.e. $\theta_F = -Fh$. In general the beam will become elliptically polarized. Then the Faraday rotation angle is defined as the angle between the major axis of the ellipse and the plane of polarization of the incident linearly polarized beam. The difference in sense of the Faraday rotation angle can be detected by an analyser–photodetector set. The intensity of the linearly polarized beam, after traversing the analyser is:

$$I = I_0 \exp(-\alpha h) \cos^2(\phi + \theta_F), \qquad (4.4.1)$$

where α is the optical absorption coefficient of the medium and ϕ is the analyser–polarizer angle. The difference in photodetector signal levels from regions of positive and negative magnetization direction is [4.4.2]

$$\Delta i = S_d I_0 \exp(-\alpha h) \sin 2\phi \sin 2\theta_F, \qquad (4.4.2)$$

where S_d is the photodetector response.

Optimum signal difference is obtained when $h = 1/\alpha$ and $\phi = \pi/4$ and

$$\Delta i = S_d I_0 e^{-1}(2F/\alpha), \qquad (4.4.3)$$

where the approximation $\sin 2\theta_F = 2F/\alpha$ is made under the assumption that $Fh \ll \pi$.

A similar relation can be derived for the Kerr effect. Depending on the angle of incidence and orientation of magnetization with respect to the surface plane, polar, transverse and longitudinal Kerr effects are distinguishable. The largest effect is the polar Kerr effect for normal incidence and perpendicular magnetization. Then [4.4.2]

$$\Delta i = S_d I_0 R\Phi_K, \tag{4.4.4}$$

where R is the surface reflectivity and Φ_K the Kerr rotation angle, which is sensitive to the orientation of the magnetization. The analysis shows that the readout signal is linearly proportional to the figure of merit $2F/\alpha$ or $R\Phi_K$ of the medium used.

The polar Kerr effect and the Faraday effect can only be used in media with magnetization perpendicular to the surface. Since—in regard to the writing process—the thickness of magneto-optic media must be less than a few micrometres, the shape anisotropy field is $4\pi M_s$ in favour of having the easy direction parallel to the surface. However, perpendicular magnetization is obtained when a uniaxial anisotropy $K_u \gg 2\pi M_s^2$ normal to the surface exists. K_u can be growth induced, stress induced or crystalline anisotropy.

Noise in the readout signal may be due to scattering at domain walls, grain boundaries, birefringence induced by strain and fluctuations in magnetization or crystalline homogeneity of the material. It will present itself as a peak-to-peak variation $\Delta\theta$ in the Faraday or Kerr rotation. When this type of noise dominates all other sources of noise, a signal-to-noise ratio is obtained as [4.4.2]

$$\text{SNR}_{medium} = \frac{\Delta i}{(d(\Delta i)/d\theta)\Delta\theta} = \frac{2\sin 2\theta}{(2\cos 2\theta)\Delta\theta} \approx \frac{\theta}{\Delta\theta} \tag{4.4.5}$$

where θ is the magneto-optic rotation and $\theta \ll \pi$ is assumed. When SNR = 10 is allowed, $\Delta\theta$ may be only 10% of the average value of magneto-optic rotation θ.

4.4.2.2. The Writing Process

The writing of information in magnetic materials by means of an optical (laser) beam is accomplished using thermomagnetic effects. The laser beam is focused on the material (spot size is on the order of a micron) and through absorption of the optical energy, the material is heated.

Before discussing the different types of thermomagnetic effects proposed for recording, it is useful to examine two general aspects of this technique. The first aspect is the speed of the thermomagnetic writing process which determines the access time and the second is the energy and power required to record the information.

The first obvious observation relevant to thermomagnetic writing is that the volume of the bit has to be kept as small as possible in order to obtain fast heating (high speed) and low power requirements. Thin films of materials with a low heat capacity are in favour of these requirements. The access time is determined by the cooling cycle of a heated spot, provided that the duration of the laser pulse which heats the material to the temperature at which the thermomagnetic effect works is small compared to the heat decay constant [4.4.3]. When the diameter of a written bit is d, this decay time constant is approximately $d^2/4K$ where K is the thermal diffusivity. Normal values for K are of the order of $10^{-7}-10^{-6} \, \text{m}^2 \, \text{s}^{-1}$, which, for bits of $1 \, \mu\text{m}^2$ area results in thermal decay times of about $0.1-1 \, \mu\text{s}$. The temperature rise time is given by

$$\tau = \rho c_\text{p} V \Delta T / I \qquad (4.4.6)$$

where ρ is the specific density, c_p the specific heat, V the bit volume, ΔT the temperature excursion and I the laser power. For thin film materials with $\rho = 10 \, \text{g cm}^{-3}$, $c_\text{p} = 4 \, \text{J g}^{-1}\text{K}^{-1}$, $\Delta T = 100 \, \text{K}$, a thickness of 1000 Å and working with bit areas of $1 \, \mu\text{m}^2$, heated with a laser of 10 mW power, this rise time is $0.04 \, \mu\text{s}$, which is well below the thermal decay time. Laser pulses of $0.04 \, \mu\text{s}$ are easily obtained by electro-optic switches. Temperature rise time can be reduced by using more powerful lasers.

Summarizing, it can be concluded that access times will be of the order of several tenths of a microsecond, enabling bit rates of 1–10 MHz and that thermomagnetic writing can be performed by use of lasers with power above 10 mW, which means that common HeNe lasers and Argon lasers are suited.

4.4.2.3. Curie Point Writing

This method uses the temperature dependence of the magnetization of ferromagnetic materials. Above the Curie temperature T_c, the magnetization M_s is zero and at temperatures well below T_c, M_s reaches its saturation value. An important material showing this behaviour is MnBi with $T_\text{c} = 360°\text{C}$ (Fig. 4.4.1). MnBi films can be fabricated with the easy axis perpendicular to the film substrate. Both Faraday effect and polar Kerr effect can be used for readout. Another material which has been intensively investigated for use in a magneto-optic beam accessible storage is EuO with $T_\text{c} \approx 77°\text{K}$ [4.4.4].

The Curie point writing technique is as follows. The memory film is held at an operating temperature well below the Curie temperature. A focused laser beam locally heats a bit spot on the film to above the Curie temperature. Subsequently the bit is allowed to cool to the operating temperature in the presence of a net magnetic field whose direction is such as to determine the sense of magnetization in the bit when it becomes ferromagnetic again.

Figure 4.4.2 illustrates how, for an MnBi film, the net magnetic field is composed of two components, the demagnetizing field H_d, which arises due to the magnetic dipole distribution in the surrounding ferromagnetic film,

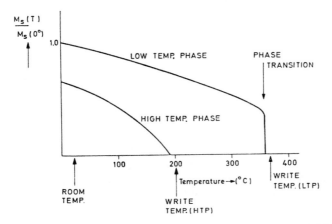

FIG. 4.4.1. Temperature dependence of the saturation-magnetization of MnBi for the high and low temperature phase.

and the externally applied field H_a. When the magnetization of the bit to be written has to be reversed with respect to the surrounding material (say this defines a "1"), the external field H_a must be smaller than H_d. When the bit magnetization has to be parallel to the magnetization of the surrounding material ("0"), the external field should exceed H_d, but not exceed the coercive force H_c of the film, since otherwise, bits already written as a "1" would unintentionally become reversed.

When the easy direction of magnetization is in the plane of the film, which is the case in EuO films, demagnetizing fields are smaller.

4.4.2.4. Compensation Point Writing

In ferrimagnetic substances, the magnetic sublattices which oppose each other may have different temperature dependences (Fig. 4.4.3(a)). At a certain temperature then, called the compensation temperature T_{comp}, the net magnetization may become zero and consequently coercivity will increase

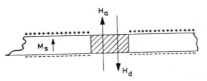

FIG. 4.4.2. The total magnetic field in a bit area is composed of the demagnetizing field H_d and the externally applied field H_a.

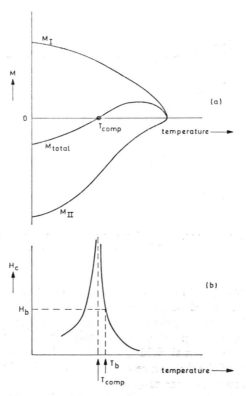

FIG. 4.4.3. (a) Temperature dependence of the magnetization of a ferrimagnetic garnet and its sublattices and (b) temperature dependence of the coercive force.

dramatically since an external field cannot exert a torque on $M = 0$ (Fig. 4.4.3(b)). A few degrees above the compensation point, coercivity drops rapidly and switching at moderate fields becomes possible.

The operating temperature is chosen at $T_0 = T_{comp}$. The bit spot to be written is heated by means of the laser to $T = T_b > T_{comp}$ and H_c drops to H_b. With an external field $H_a > H_b$, the bit magnetization is switched in the direction of H_a. No demagnetizing field exists since the magnetization of the surrounding material is zero. When $H_a = 0$, the bit remains in its original state. After cooling to the operating temperature, the magnetization becomes zero in the bit, but the magnetic sublattices will have changed polarity when H_a was larger than H_b.

Readout by magneto-optic techniques is possible only when one of the sublattices gives a larger contribution to the magneto-optic effect than the other.

A material in which this is the case is gadolinium iron garnet $(Gd_3Fe_5O_{12})$ where the magneto-optic effect is due to the octahedral Fe^{3+}-lattice only.

4.4.2.5. Temperature Dependence of Coercivity

Besides the materials which have a compensation point, there are other materials whose coercivity varies strongly with temperature. One of these is phosphorus-doped cobalt Co(P) [4.4.5]. Coercivity decreases by a factor of three when the material is heated from room temperature to 150°C. Switching can occur by applying a laser pulse sufficient to raise the temperature to 150°C and a suitable applied field. A permalloy film on top of the Co(P) film provides a means for magneto-optic readout.

Another class of devices showing temperature dependence of the coercivity consists of coupled films with different magnetizations, coercivities and Curie points [4.4.6]. The coercivity of such a coupled film is given by

$$H_c = (H_{c_1} M_1 h_1 + H_{c_2} M_2 h_2)/(M_1 h_1 + M_2 h_2), \qquad (4.4.7)$$

where the subscripts 1 and 2 indicate upper and lower film respectively. H_{c_1} and H_{c_2} are the coercivities, M_1 and M_2 are the magnetizations and h stands for film thickness.

The system investigated by de Bouard [4.4.6] consisted of a lower NiFe film and an upper Pd–Co/Co film. By proper choice of the Co concentration in the Pd–Co film, its Curie point is tailored between 60°C and 80°C. Above this temperature, the Pd–Co film becomes paramagnetic and the Ni–Fe film behaves as if it were alone. Then, coercivity is given by H_{c_2}. Below 60°C the magnetization of the Pd–Co film differs from zero and the coercivity will increase to the value as given by the above expression.

In practice, the room temperature coercivity of the coupled film is approximately 10 Oe and the coercivity above the Pd–Co Curie temperature is 4 Oe. The writing process is as follows. The film is held at an operating temperature well below T_{c_1}. When a focused laser pulse is applied, the heated area can be switched by a field H_a which is bigger than H_{c_2}, but smaller than H_c of the coupled film in order to avoid unwanted erasures.

4.4.2.6. Review of Materials

(i) *Materials for Curie point writing*

(a) *MnBi films.* MnBi films are fabricated on glass or mica substrates with the easy axis of magnetization normal to the film plane. The coercive force decreases with increasing film thickness which enables tailoring of required properties. The Curie temperature of MnBi is not exactly known since at 360°C, the material transforms from the so-called low temperature phase to the high temperature phase, thereby losing the spontaneous magnetization of the low temperature phase. The phase transition therefore can

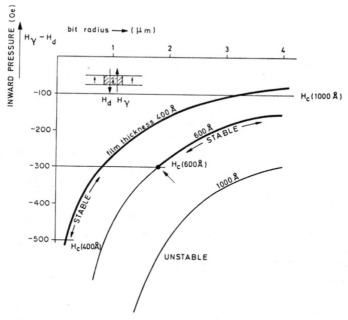

FIG. 4.4.4. Diagram showing stability regions for different film thicknesses.

be regarded as a quasi-Curie point. Stability of Curie point written reversed cylindrical domains was calculated by Schuldt and Chen [4.4.7] and by Esho *et al.* [4.4.8].

The wall of a reversed cylindrical domain experiences three pressures: an inward pressure H_y due to the domain wall energy, an outward pressure due to the distribution of magnetic dipoles inside and outside the domain (H_d) and a pressure which may be either outward or inward due to an externally applied field H_a. The total pressure is given by

$$H_t = H_y - H_d \pm H_a. \qquad (4.4.8)$$

When reversed bits are written in the absence of an applied field, the first two terms in the right-hand side of eqn (4.4.8) should cancel each other out in order to have no pressure on the domain wall. Calculations of $H_y - H_d$ for films with thicknesses between 400 Å and 1000 Å as a function of domain radius show that above a radius of 0.5 μm, $H_y - H_d$ behaves like $-c(h)/r$ (Fig. 4.4.4), where r is the domain radius and $c(h)$ is a positive function which depends on film thickness only and increases monotonically with film thickness. This means that the outward pressure is always larger than the inward pressure. So in the absence of a bias field which provides an inward

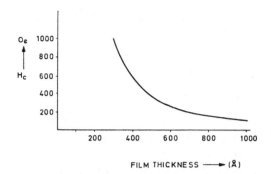

FILM THICKNESS ⟶ (Å)

FIG. 4.4.5. Thickness dependence of the coercive force H_c of thin MnBi films.

pressure (anti parallel to the domain magnetization), the domain will expand and form stripe domains. Fortunately, MnBi films possess large coercive forces, which act as a friction with respect to domain wall displacement and therefore more or less replace the external bias field. Since coercivity increases with decreasing film thickness (Fig. 4.4.5), thinner films are more favourable than thicker films. This is also an advantage when laser power has to be kept as low as possible.

Readout efficiency is optimized when $h = 1/\alpha$. Since $\alpha = 4 \times 10^5 \, \text{cm}^{-1}$, a thickness of 250 Å would be optimum in this respect. The decisive point in MnBi films, however, is a practical one. The film has to be free of pinhole inclusions and coercivity has to be fairly uniform throughout the film. In films with thicknesses smaller than 400 Å, coercivity may vary by 500 Oe for films of one thickness prepared under the same conditions. These films usually show pinholes. Thicker films are more reproducible [4.4.9] ($\Delta H_c(800 \, \text{Å})$ 100 Oe). Readout by means of the Kerr effect is preferred then, since at $h = 800 \, \text{Å}$, $R\Phi_K \approx 0.4$ whereas $(2F/\alpha) \exp(-\alpha h)$ is of the order of 0.1. Complete memory test setups have been built [4.4.10]. There is experimental proof that MnBi films of 800 Å thickness, prepared on glass substrates, written by the Curie point technique and read by employing the Kerr effect are capable of storing 25×10^6 bits cm^{-2}.

MnBi films have a serious disadvantage in that the Curie point writing technique which is usually referred to is in fact a method of heating a bit area to above the phase transition temperature. The phase transition which takes place then brings the film to another ferromagnetic state with a Curie point at 190°C, which means that this phase is paramagnetic at 360°C (Fig. 4.4.1). The high temperature phase thus obtained is stable above 360°C only, but can be quasi stable below this temperature by quickly cooling to room temperature (quenching). It will relax very slowly to the low temperature phase. Since the quenched high temperature phase has a lower Curie point than the low temperature phase, there is no direct effect on the writing process when the laser pulses are chosen such as to assure writing above 360°C. Both phases will then be written. On the other hand, the reading process is affected in a less favourable manner since the saturation magnetization of the quenched high temperature phase has a 30% lower value than the saturation magnetization of the low temperature phase [4.4.11]. This means that the magneto-optic readout signal will also be reduced by 30%. The decrease of M_s is due to a shift of 15% of the octahedral Mn^{3+} ions to bipyramidal and tetrahedral sites, where an antiferromagnetic coupling to the remaining Mn^{3+} lattice is observed.

A further disadvantage of MnBi is the low decomposition temperature at 446°C. When laser write pulses contain an amount of energy which is 20% larger than the amount which is necessary to reach the 360°C limit, the material will decompose, which leads to serious signal degradation. Therefore, it seems advantageous to find a method to stabilize the quenched high temperature phase at room temperature. Unger [4.4.12] partially succeeded in such an approach by replacing octahedral Mn^{3+} ions by Ti^{3+} ions, thereby forcing the surplus of Mn^{3+} ions to move to interstitial positions in the Bi lattice. In this manner an artificial quenched high temperature phase is obtained which is more stable than the normal quenched high temperature phase. The relaxation to the low temperature phase was reduced by a factor of 20, i.e. the relaxation time was increased by this factor.

(b) *Europous chalcogenides.* The europous chalcogenides are compounds consisting of europium with one of the elements of the oxygen group. The

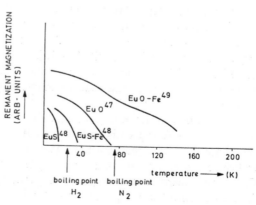

FIG. 4.4.6. Temperature dependence of pure and doped europous chalcogenides.

two exponents in this class of materials which have been most intensively investigated are EuO and EuS [4.4.13, 4.4.14]. Thin films of both EuO and EuS are easily obtained by electron beam evaporation from a source of the materials themselves or by evaporating Eu_2O_3 and Eu separately.

EuO has a Curie temperature of 70°K (Fig. 4.4.6) and a coercive force of 120 Oe at 4.2°K which monotonically decreases with temperature. The material possesses a large specific Faraday rotation of $5 \times 10^5 \deg cm^{-1}$ normal to the film surface when saturated in this direction. In contrast to MnBi, however, EuO (as well as EuS) has no strong easy axis of magnetization normal to the film surface. Therefore, the magnetization is constrained to the film plane, which means that magneto-optic readout has to be accomplished by obliquely incident light. This results in a 10 times smaller Faraday effect. EuO has a very small heat capacity of $0.03 Jg^{-1}°C^{-1}$, which, together with a low required temperature excursion, leads to a low-energy Curie point writing process. On the other hand, the material has to be operated at liquid hydrogen temperatures (20°K) which requires powerful refrigerators.

The squareness of the hysteresis loop M_r/M_s is on the order of 0.8. Operating margins are enlarged by doping with Fe [4.4.15]. EuO doped with 8 wt% Fe has a Curie point of 180°K which enables a shift to the operating temperature of liquid nitrogen temperatures (77°K). The saturation magnetization is slightly reduced to 0.8 of the value for pure EuO films. The loop squareness, on the other hand, is improved to 0.92 [4.4.16].

The mechanisms which raise the Curie temperature by Fe doping are not fully understood. Mössbauer and other experiments reveal that the iron is present predominantly as Fe^0 and to a few percent as Fe^{3+} and Fe^{2+}. It is believed that the presence of Fe^0 around grain boundaries causes a strong interaction with Eu^{2+} ions thereby increasing exchange forces.

EuS behaves in very much the same manner as EuO [4.4.14]. Magnetization is constrained to the film plane also. Pure EuS has a Curie temperature of 16.5°K and should be operated at liquid helium temperatures (4.2°K). Iron doping again increases the Curie point in this material to 45°K at 16 wt% dope. This enables operation at liquid hydrogen (20°K) temperatures. The squareness of EuS hysteresis loops is 0.9. Though EuS has a lower specific Faraday rotation than EuO, and though it has to be operated at lower temperatures than EuO, it is more stable than the latter compound, which is a great advantage. However, methods have been developed to protect EuO films against corrosion. For instance Eu_2O_3 which is a chemically stable compound is used. Finally, EuO–Fe seems an attractive medium when used in conjunction with GaAs injection lasers which have to be operated at the same low temperature of 77°K.

(ii) *Materials for compensation point writing*. Besides GdIG whose

x

characteristics relative to the writing process were illustrated in Fig. 4.4.3, other compensation point materials suitable for magneto-optic memory applications are known. These are the amorphous metallic films of the rare earth transition metal compounds such as Gd–Co [4.4.17].

One of the features of Gd–Co is the ability to tailor the compensation temperature by changing the Gd to Co ratio of the films. T_{comp} can be varied over a wide range from 50°K to 500°K. However, the slope of the coercivity versus temperature curve near the compensation point is steepest when T_{comp} is near room temperature. Since the temperature excursion for writing is directly related to this slope, it is clear that use of a film with T_{comp} near room temperature will cost less energy than when T_{comp} is far below this temperature.

The figure of merit for magneto-optic readout $2F/\alpha$ lies between 0.3 and 0.5 degrees, which is second best to MnBi. Magnetization is normal to the film surface.

One problem with compensation point materials is bit stability. Operation at T_{comp} means that the magnetization is zero, i.e. there is no demagnetizing field which provides an outward pressure to stabilize the reversed bit against collapse due to the domain wall energy minimization. This complication can be overcome by grooving a scratch pattern in the film or crystal platelet. Domain walls preferentially locate at surface defects, where scratches are.

4.4.3. ELECTRO-OPTIC MATERIALS

Whereas the magneto-optic thin film materials described in the previous section are well suited for storage and erasure of separate bits, thereby offering the possibility of a read and write random access memory, ferro-electric, electro-optic and photochromic materials are best suited for recording and erasure of holographic pages.

Examples of electro-optic materials with this property are SbSe, $BaTiO_3$, SBN (strontium barium niobate) and $LiNbO_3$. The most sensitive material for this class of devices is $LiNbO_3$, which is eventually doped with iron.

The principle of recording in $LiNbO_3$ is illustrated in Fig. 4.4.7 [4.4.18]. Two coherent light beams are incident on the material. An interference pattern inside the material is set up by the incident beams. Electrons, trapped deep within the forbidden band (~ 3.3 eV) of $LiNbO_3$ are excited at the regions of constructive interference. These electrons will drift or diffuse through the crystal and become trapped preferentially in regions of low-intensity light. The result is a net space-charge pattern that is positive in the high intensity regions and negative in the low intensity regions. This space charge generates a field that—via the electro-optic effect—modulates the refractive index and gives rise to a phase hologram.

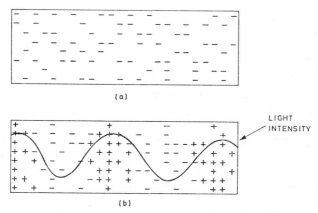

FIG. 4.4.7. Electro-optic medium: (a) before exposure showing uniform trap distribution and (b) after exposure showing space charge distribution.

When reading the stored information from an $LiNbO_3$ hologram, special care has to be taken to prevent erasure of the stored interference pattern. Illuminating the hologram with uniform light will result in de-trapping and redistribution of the electrons.

One means of overcoming this problem is to use a light source of smaller energy quantums. Another way is to take advantage of the extremely low electronic conductivity of the material.

Heating $LiNbO_3$ to 150°C will cause ionic conduction. The ions will diffuse in the local electric field as set forth by the trapped electronic space charge until they nearly compensate the trapped electronic charge. When cooling to room temperature, the ionic charge pattern is frozen in. Exposure to uniform light will result in redistribution of the electronic charges leaving an electric field pattern that mirrors that of the original hologram. This ionic field pattern is optically stable. The hologram is fixed. Diffraction efficiency of $LiNbO_3$ holograms can be 100%. The relation between the refractive index variation n_1 and the diffraction efficiency η is

$$\eta = \sin^2\left(\frac{\pi n_1 d}{\lambda \cos \theta/2}\right)$$

where d is the thickness of the medium. The refractive index variation in $LiNbO_3$ due to an electric field E is given by $n_1 = 1.8 \times 10^{-8}$ under the most favourable conditions with respect to crystal orientation and electric field polarization. For a 1 cm thick crystal, using light of 0.5 μm wavelength and for small angles θ between the interfering beams, the refractive index variation required for 100% diffraction efficiency is $\sim 2.5 \times 10^{-5}$ which corresponds to local fields of about 1400 V cm^{-1}. Fields of this magnitude can easily be achieved through drift or diffusion.

The minimum absorbed energy that would be required to generate a refractive index variation pattern with 100% diffraction efficiency is found by calculating the peak charge density p_m from the local field requirement $E \sim 1400$ V cm^{-1}. This results, for a grating period of 1 μm, in $p_m = 2.5 \times 10^{-4}$ coul cm^{-3}. Assuming a sinusoidal varying space charge, the average displaced charge is p_m/π. The total number of displaced electrons is then $N = p_m/\pi e \approx 0.5 \times 10^{15}$ electrons cm^{-3} where e is the elementary electronic charge. Further, when the diffusion length of excited electrons is large compared to the fringe spacing, unity quantum efficiency can be expected. Since light of 0.5 μm wavelength has an energy per photon of $\hbar\omega = 4 \times 15^{-19}$ J, the minimum energy required for 100% diffraction efficiency of holograms recorded in LiNbO$_3$ is

$$W_{min} = \hbar\omega . N \approx 2 . 10^{-3} \text{ J cm}^{-2}.$$

In practice, however, this energy is much larger.

The sensitivity of the material can be improved by doping with impurity ions thereby increasing the concentration of lattice defects available to act as electron trips [4.4.19]. The best improvement in this respect was obtained by Fe-doping. Whereas undoped LiNbO$_3$ had to be exposed to an incident optical power density of 400 mW cm^{-2} for 100 s in order to obtain a 1% diffraction efficiency, an Fe-doped sample showed a 60% diffraction efficiency after 10 s of exposure to the same power density (Fig. 4.4.8).

In brief, pure or doped LiNbO$_3$ offers a sensitive means for recording holograms. The information can be erased by either light or a temperature treatment. The long exposure times make the material unsuitable for a random access read and write memory but it has useful properties for archival read only memories.

4.4.4. THERMOPLASTIC RECORDING

Thermoplastic films form a class of devices in which holograms can be stored as a spatial ripple in the film thickness. An important property of thermoplastics is the erasability of the stored information, which makes them suitable for read-write memory applications.

Thermoplastic films for holographic recording are usually used in a sandwich structure with a photoconductor layer (Fig. 4.4.9). The writing procedure is as follows. The thermoplastic photoconductor sandwich is charged by a corona charging device. The voltage is capacitively divided between the photoconductive and thermoplastic layers. Then, the sandwich

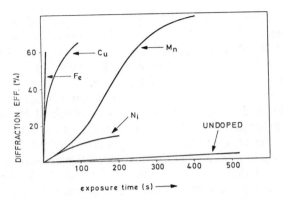

FIG. 4.4.8. Diffraction efficiency as a function of the exposure time for undoped and several doped LiNbO₃ crystals [4.4.19].

is exposed to illumination by the optical pattern to be recorded. The photoconductor acts as conductor in the illuminated areas and discharges the voltage (typically several hundred volts) across these areas. When the light is turned off, the sandwich is recharged such as to re-establish a uniform

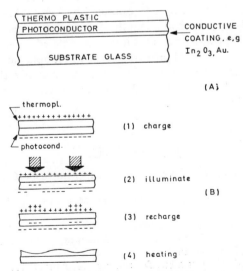

FIG. 4.4.9. (a) Structure of sandwich for thermoplastic recording and (b) thermoplastic writing process.

potential at the surface. A surface charge which is a copy of the optical pattern is thus obtained. Finally, the thermoplastic is heated to its softening temperature (50–100°C) and the electrostatic forces will deform the structure, as shown in Fig. 4.4.9(b). When the thermoplastic cools, the information will become frozen in as a ripple in the film surface.

Holograms recorded in this way have diffraction efficiences of 10–30% [4.1.1]. Gain in diffraction efficiency can be obtained by recharging the surface after deformation [4.4.20], which results in a nonuniform surface charge with higher charge in the valleys than on top of the hills. Heating the thermoplastic again gives an additional co-operative deformation of the film. Erasure of information is obtained when the thermoplastic film is heated so that surface tension smooths out the thickness variation. Residual charge patterns will not occur because of the increased electrical conductivity of the photoconductor and thermoplastic.

The write energy for thermoplastic photoconductor sandwiches is as low as $1 \mu J \, mm^{-2}$ due to the high light sensitivity of the photoductor. Development time of the ripple hologram (determining the write time) is on the order of 10–100 ms. Heating of the thermoplastic is accomplished by applying an audio frequency pulse to the conductive coating (Fig. 4.4.9). The number of write-erase cycles is limited. It has been shown for instance that the diffraction efficiency drops after a thousand cycles and reaches zero at two thousand cycles. The major cause for this phenomenon is the corona charging method which damages the thermoplastic by pitting its surface.

The shortest development time as obtained by Lee [4.1.1] was 7 ms. The audio frequency heat pulse had a length of 4 ms; 1 ms after switching off the head pulse, development started and it was completed 2 ms later. The delay of 1 ms is an intrinsic material property of the thermoplastic since the thermal diffusion time in the material was only 20 μs. So probably, the thermoplastic recording time is limited to about 7 ms due to inertia in relocation of the molecules in the thermoplastic.

REFERENCES

[4.1.1] T. C. Lee, Holographic recording on thermoplastic films, *Appl. Opt.*, **13**, 888–895, 1974.

[4.1.2] G. Fan, K. Pennington, J. H. Greiner, Magneto-optic hologram, *J. Appl. Phys.*, **40**, 974–975, 1969.

[4.1.3] R. S. Mezrich, Magnetic holography, *Appl. Opt.*, **9**, 2275–2279, 1970.

[4.1.4] L. K. Anderson, Holographic optical memory for bulk data storage, *Bell Lab. Records*, **46**, 318–325, 1968.

[4.1.5] Memory at 0.04 cents a bit, *Datamation*, 17, April 1975.

[4.2.1] J. D. Zook and T. C. Lee, Geometrical interpretation of Gaussian beam optics, *Appl. Opt.*, **11**, 2140–2145, 1972.

[4.2.2] H. Kogelnik, Imaging of optical modes—Resonators with internal lenses, *Bell Syst. Tech. J.*, **44**, 455–494, 1965.

[4.2.3] R. Räth, Storage capacity and density of bitwise operating nonholographic magneto optic storage devices, *Intermag Conf.*, *Washington D.C.*, Paper 19.2, 1973.

[4.2.4] H. Kiemle, Considerations on holographic memories in the gigabyte region, *Appl. Opt.*, **13**, 803–807, 1974.

[4.3.1] M. E. Rabedeau, Switchable total internal reflection light deflector, *IBM J. Res. Dev.*, **13**, 179–183, 1969.

[4.3.2] J. D. Zook, Light beam deflector performance: a comparative analysis, *Appl. Opt.*, **13**, 875–887, 1974.

[4.3.3] M. Born and E. Wolf, "Principles of Optics", Pergamon Press, London, pp. 593–610, 1965.

[4.3.4] R. W. Dixon, Photoelastic properties of selected materials and their relevance for applications to acoustic light modulators and scanners, *J. Appl. Phys.*, **38**, 5149–5153, 1967.

[4.3.5] D. A. Pinnow, Guide lines for the selection of acoustooptic materials, *IEEE J. Quant. El.*, **QE–6**, 223–238, 1970.

[4.3.6] R. W. Damon, W. T. Maloney and D. H. McMahon, Interaction of light with ultrasound, *in* "Physical Acoustics", Vol. VII (eds W. P. Mason and R. N. Thurston), Academic Press, New York, pp. 273–366, 1970.

[4.3.7] A. Korpel, Acoustooptics, *in* "Applied Solid State Science", Vol. 3 (ed. R. Wolfe), Academic Press, New York, pp. 111–114, 1972.

[4.3.8] A. Korpel, R. Adler, P. Desmares and W. Watson, A television display using acoustic deflection and modulation of coherent light, *Proc. IEEE*, **54**, 1429–1437, 1966.

[4.3.9] T. C. Lee and J. D. Zook, Light beam deflection with electro-optic prisms, *IEEE J. Quant. El.*, **QE–4**, 442–454, 1968.

[4.3.10] H. Meyer, D. Riekman, K. P. Schmidt, U. J. Schmidt, M. Rahlff, E. Schröder and W. Thust, Design and performance of a 20-stage digital light beam deflector, *Appl. Opt.*, **11**, 1732–1736, 1972.

[4.3.11] J. F. Nye, "Physical Properties of Crystals", Oxford University Press, London, 1969.

[4.3.12] U. Schmidt and W. Thust, A 10 stage digital light beam deflector, *Opt. Electr.*, **1**, 21–23, 1969.

[4.3.13] U. Krüger, R. Pepperl and U. J. Schmidt, Electrooptic materials for digital light beam deflectors, *Proc. IEEE*, **61**, 992–1007, 1973.

[4.3.14] W. Kulcke, K. Kosanke, E. Max, M. A. Habegger, T. J. Harris and H. Fleisher, Digital light deflectors, *Appl. Opt.*, **5**, 1657–1667, 1966.

[4.4.1] J. C. Suits, Faraday and Kerr effects in magnetic compounds, *IEEE Trans. Mag.*, **MAG–8**, 95–105, 1972.

[4.4.2] D. Chen, Magnetic materials for optical recording, *Appl. Opt.*, **13**, 767–778, 1974.

[4.4.3] D. Chen, G. N. Otto and F. M. Schmit, MnBi films for magnetooptic recording, *IEEE Trans. Mag.*, **MAG–9**, 66–83, 1973.

[4.4.4] G. Y. Fan and J. H. Greiner, Low temperature beam addressable memory, *J. Appl. Phys.*, **39**, 1216–1218, 1968.

[4.4.5] D. Treves, R. P. Hunt, B. Dickey, Laser beam recording on a magnetic film, *J. Appl. Phys.*, **40**, 972–973, 1969.

[4.4.6] D. de Bouard, Feasibility study of a large capacity magnetic film optical memory, *IEEE J. Quant. El.*, **QE–4**, 378, 1968.

[4.4.7] S. Schuldt and D. Chen, Wall stability of cylindrical (bubble) domains in thin films and platelets, *J. Appl. Phys.*, **42**, 1970–1976, 1971.

[4.4.8] S. Esho, S. Noguchi, Y. Ono and M. Nagao, Optimum thickness of MnBi films for magnetooptical memory, *Appl. Opt.*, **13**, 779–783, 1974.

[4.4.9] R. L. Aagard, D. Chen, R. W. Honebrink, G. N. Otto and F. M. Schmit, Optical mass memory experiments on thin films of MnBi, *IEEE Trans. Mag.*, **MAG–4**, 412–416, 1968.

[4.4.10] R. L. Aagard, T. C. Lee and D. Chen, Advanced optical storage techniques for computers, *Appl. Opt.*, **11**, 2133–2139, 1972.

[4.4.11] K. Kempter, A new method of magnetization measurement applied to thin MnBi films, *Int. J. Mag.*, **5**, 91–94, 1973.

[4.4.12] W. K. Unger, Experiments on Curie-temperature writing in $Mn_{0.8}Ti_{0.2}Bi$ films, *Int. J. Mag.*, **3**, 43–46, 1972.

[4.4.13] K. Y. Ahn and J. C. Suits, Preparation and properties of EuO-films, *IEEE Trans. Mag.*, **MAG–3**, 453–455, 1967.

[4.4.14] K. Y. Ahn and M. W. Shafer, Preparation and properties of EuS films and effects of Fe doping, *IEEE Trans. Mag.*, **MAG–7**, 394–396, 1971.

[4.4.15] T. R. McGuire, G. F. Petrich, B. L. Olson, V. L. Moruzzi and K. Y. Ahn, Magnetic and magneto-optical properties of Fe-doped EuO films, *J. Appl. Phys.*, **42**, 1775–1777, 1971.

[4.4.16] K. Lee and J. C. Suits, Preparation of doped EuO films on rotating disks, *IEEE Trans. Mag.*, **MAG–7**, 391, 1971.

[4.4.17] B. R. Brown, Optical data storage potential of six materials, *Appl. Opt.*, **13**, 761–766, 1974.

[4.4.18] J. J. Amodei and D. L. Staebler, Holographic recording in lithium niobate, *RCA Review*, **33**, 71–93, 1972.

[4.4.19] W. Phillips, J. J. Amnodei and D. L. Staebler, Optical and holographic storage properties of transition metal doped lithium niobate, *RCA Review*, **33**, 94–109, 1972.

[4.4.20] T. L. Credelle and F. W. Spong, Thermoplastic media for holographic recording, *RCA Review*, **33**, 206–226, 1972.

Chapter 5

ELECTROMECHANICALLY ACCESSIBLE MAGNETIC SURFACE MEMORIES

5.1. INTRODUCTION

As shown in Chapter 3, matrix memories permit rather fast access times, but are expensive to produce. These memories are therefore used as main memories, where speed is very important as the shift of information between logic circuits and memory cells may not be restricted by the memory cell. A user of a computer system normally possesses a huge amount of data and instructions which have to be processed or searched regularly. It would be exorbitantly expensive to store this data in ferrite cores and, therefore, other storage devices have been developed. Today magnetic disks and magnetic tapes are mainly used for storing input and output information. These devices consist of a magnetic surface which is rotated to bring it into position and which is written in and read out by a magnetic head. The head can also be electromechanically moved as in the case of the magnetic disk or the head is fixed as is the case in a magnetic tape memory. Besides disks and tapes, magnetic drums, strips, cartridges and cards have been used for information storage, but much less frequently.

Access by electromechanical means is very slow and in modern computers the longer access times of these storage devices make expensive core buffer stores necessary. The computer industry is spending a large effort in investigating new means of storage, hoping to find devices which are as inexpensive and reliable as magnetic surface storage devices but with a much faster access time. The laser beam accessible memories which are discussed in Chapter 4 might eventually fulfil these requirements in the future.

The first usage of magnetic surface storage was not for storing input data but was for main memory. In the early history of electronic computers, when system designers started realizing the need for a memory for storing data and instructions, not many useful devices were around. As discussed in Chapter 1, the first storage devices were relays, unreliable electrostatic storage tubes and bulky mercury delay lines. Since the ferrite core was not

367

yet invented, designers turned to the magnetic drum for main memory. The first computers containing a magnetic drum were built around 1950. The first commercially successful computer with a magnetic drum was the IBM-650 which appeared on the market in the beginning of 1955. Many hundreds of these machines were built. In the next years the drum, with its long access time was replaced by the successful ferrite core and since then surface stores have not been used as main memories. The suitability of magnetic tape for the storage of input and output data was recognized quite early also. The Univac machine built by the Eckert–Mauchly Computer Corp. around 1950 seems to have been the first machine using magnetic tape. Magnetic tape has the disadvantage of having very large average access times but it is very inexpensive compared to other media. For a long time magnetic tape has been the most important input and output medium. Large computers were surrounded by vast numbers of tape memories. Magnetic drums were too expensive and have the disadvantage of not being exchangeable as are tape reels. In order to combine the relatively short access time of the drum and the large capacity of the tape, around 1960 a storage system was developed which consisted of many disks covered on both sides with a magnetic layer. Access to the desired information is realized by moving an arm with a magnetic head to the desired disk and then radially to the track. The first disk memory did not permit the exchange of disks, but later disk memories had this feature and made it the most popular input and output storage medium.

Another technique of using surface storage is by means of strips, cartridges or cards which are electromechanically moved toward the magnetic head. The storage capacity of such devices is enormous, but due to the long access time, the strip and card memories have not been used on a large scale. In the next sections we will describe the principle of the recording process (Section 5.2). This is followed by short descriptions of the devices based on magnetic surface storage (Section 5.3). The main part will be devoted to the physics of the different materials used, such as the well known γFe_2O_3 and new materials like Co and CrO_2 (Section 5.4). Finally the physics of the magnetic head transducer will be presented in Section 5.5.

5.2. PRINCIPLE OF THE RECORDING AND REPRODUCING PROCESS

In a magnetic surface recording system, a thin layer of magnetic material deposited on tape, drum, disk, card, cartridge or strip, is moved relative to a small zone of high magnetic field intensity, which is commonly produced by a split ring type transducer. Except in the case of video recording, the field zone is fixed, whereas the magnetic surface is moved (Fig. 5.2.1). The magnetic field magnitude is such that the direction of the magnetization of the

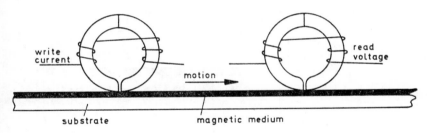

FIG. 5.2.1. Sketch of basic tape recording and reproducing system.

magnetic surface can be changed, and this change is partly permanent even when the magnetic surface moves away from the field zone. To reproduce the information, the magnetic surface is brought close to a read transducer. This transducer consists of a piece of magnetic material, around which a coil is wound. The most common form is again the split ring head. The magnetic stray field of the differently magnetized zones of the magnetic surface will change the magnetization distribution in the reproducing transducer so that a voltage is induced in the coil.

Although at first sight the recording and reproducing processes seem to be very simple, in reality they constitute very complicated occurrences, which still await rigorous analytical treatment. In the first place the direction and magnitude of the field due to the recording transducer varies with distance, consequently the magnetic surface is not subjected to a well defined magnetic field, but experiences a complicated field variation with time. Moreover, the magnetic surface has a finite thickness, so that different parts of the surface undergo different field variations. When the surface moves out of the transducer field zone the magnetized areas tend to demagnetize.

Depending on the magnetic properties of the surface and the geometry of the recorded areas, the demagnetization will be more or less severe. When the magnetic surface is on tape which is wound on a reel, it even becomes possible for the stray field of one layer to produce a change of magnetization in the adjacent layers. Also the reproducing process is far from simple. The output signal is not proportional to the recorded signal but is proportional to the first time derivative of it. Further, due to the finite thickness of the surface, not all layers contribute in the same way to the signal.

Because of the non-ideal behaviour of magnetic surfaces, successful audio or analogue recording can only be realized by adding a high frequency magnetic bias field to the signal. In the case of digital recording the situation is more favourable because during recording the magnetization of the surface is brought to saturation by the head field. In the course of time different methods of representing binary information by magnetized areas have been

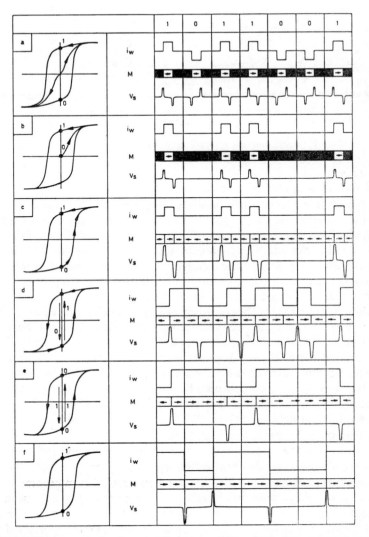

FIG. 5.2.2. Different methods of representing binary information. For explanation see text.

studied. In Fig. 5.2.2 these different methods are illustrated. Two main groups are distinguished namely Return-to-zero (RZ) and Non-return-to-zero (NRZ) recording. In the first case the current through the writing head coil is reduced to zero after recording a "one" or a "zero", whereas in NRZ recording a positive or negative current always flows through the coil.

Another difference between the methods is the way in which the magnetization of the tape represents a bit. In RZ recording the magnetization direction itself is an indication of the bit information, whereas in NRZ recording a change of magnetization direction is related to a bit. Each main group in turn consists of three methods as illustrated in Fig. 5.2.2. Figure 5.2.2(a) shows RZ recording, where a "one" is recorded by sending a positive pulse through the coil and a "zero" by a negative pulse. Between the pulses the coil current is zero and the magnetic medium is not affected. In order to avoid spurious signals the magnetic medium has to be demagnetized before recording. This is quite impractical because an erase head consumes a large amount of power. Method (b) is similar to (a) except that the "0" is represented by the absence of an output signal. In method (c) the need for ac demagnetization is avoided. The magnetic medium is magnetized before writing in one direction by a dc head or a permanent magnet. A "1" is recorded by sending a pulse through the writing head. Another advantage of this method is the increased signal. Because the magnetization changes from negative to positive instead of from zero to positive, the output signal amplitude is twice as large. A "0" is recorded by the absence of a drive current and produces no output signal. A clock pulse is necessary to indicate the time of sampling of the read head signal.

The three NRZ methods are indicated in Fig. 5.2.2(d), (e) and (f). Method (d), usually called phase encoding, is characterized by the fact that a change of the magnetization direction from negative to positive represents a "1" and a change from positive to negative a "0". An elegant feature of this method is that a "1" produces a positive pulse and a "0" a negative pulse in the read head coil. A disadvantage of the method is that when two "0s" or two "1s" have to be recorded the magnetization direction has to be reversed between the bits, which requires additional electronic circuitry and reduces the maximum bit density along a track. Thanks to the easy discrimination between positive and negative sense signals which ease error detection, phase encoding is still preferably used in high density recording systems.

The second NRZ system is often called NRZI recording, which stands for Non-return-to-zero-ones. The difference with phase encoding is that each change of magnetization direction indicates a "1", whereas a "0" is represented by no change and subsequently no read signal. This again requires a clock pulse. NRZI recording is the most commonly used method.

Finally method (f) represents the most consistent NRZ encoding system. A positive current passes the write head as long as a "1" is to be recorded and a negative current, passes when a "0" is wanted. The magnetization direction in the tape is a true image of the information to be recorded. However, because a signal is only induced in the read head coil when the magnetization direction in the medium changes, a whole series of "ones" leads to only one

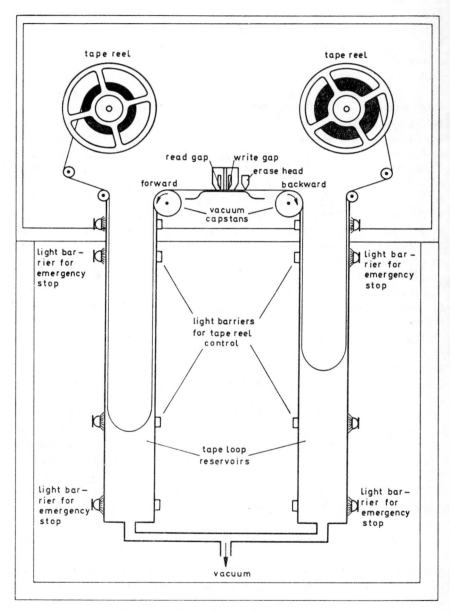

FIG. 5.3.1. Magnetic tape computer memory.

output pulse and since this occurs when the first "one" passes the read head gap electronic circuitry is needed to restore the original train of bits. A disadvantage of this recording method is that one dust particle can cause a large number of bits along a track to be in error.

5.3. MAGNETIC SURFACE STORAGE DEVICES

In the course of time several magnetic storage devices have been developed. In the early days of the computer, magnetic drum and tapes were employed, whereas today the changeable magnetic disk memory is very popular because it shows a very favourable combination of access time, capacity and cost. Magnetic card, strip or loop memories did not become popular and are found in special storage applications. In the following sections the different devices will be presented briefly.

5.3.1. MAGNETIC TAPE STORES

In principle a magnetic tape store is no different from the well known home sound recorder; its construction is only adapted to its special use.

The storage medium consists of a thin mylar tape on which a γFe_2O_3 layer is deposited. A typical reel contains 750 m of tape with a mylar thickness of 35 μm (1.4 mil) and an oxide thickness of 12 μm (0.5 mil). The tape width is standardized to 12.8 mm ($\frac{1}{2}$ in). Figure 5.3.1 shows schematically the main components of a typical tape transport mechanism.

A reel of tape is mounted on the right spindle. Automatically or by hand the tape is threaded along the heads to an empty reel at the left. To achieve fast starts and stops of the magnetic tape, which is important with respect to fast access time and economic use of the tape, the influence of the inertia of the reels has to be reduced. This is realized by pulling the tape into two storage pockets. Light barriers control the length of the tape loops in the storage pockets. On activating the forward or backward capstan only the tape has to be accelerated. In order to reduce wear of the tape an elegant solution was found for the capstans. Both capstans rotate permanently in opposite directions as shown in Fig. 5.3.1. The capstans have slots in their outer surface. The interior of the capstan can be connected by a magnetic valve to a vacuum pump, so that the tape is sucked down onto the capstan surface. When the vacuum is disconnected the friction is such that the tape is not moved by the capstan.

By actuating only the vacuum valves one can easily switch from forward to backward motion. Another advantage of this capstan construction is that the oxide covered side of the tape is not touched at all by the drive mechanism.

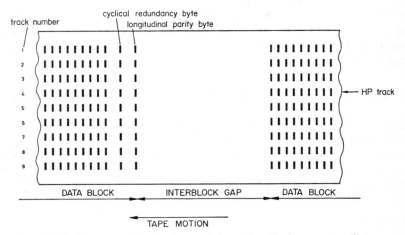

FIG. 5.3.2. Arrangement of tracks and information blocks on magnetic tape.

The head array consists of an erase head and a head which contains both a write and a read gap. An erase head is not really necessary when NRZ recording is employed. However, in most tape units such an erase head is mounted in front of the write gap to avoid the results of an eventual misalignment between the write gap and an old track written perhaps on another tape unit. The gap width of the erase head is a little bit wider than the tape, so that the whole tape is erased simultaneously. The gap width of the write and read gap is about 1 mm, whereas the gap lengths range between 2 μm and 20 μm. Today nine tracks (Fig. 5.3.2) are written simultaneously on the $\frac{1}{2}$ in tape, whereas formerly seven tracks was the industry standard. This simultaneous writing requires a write/read head with nine write and nine read gaps and such a head has to be constructed with very tight mechanical tolerances. The nine tracks form a byte. The data is recorded in blocks which might vary from 18 to 2048 bytes. The blocks are separated by block gaps, which are 0.6 in wide.

During writing the tape passes the read gap immediately after the write gap and it is possible to check the written data instantly. To reduce the influence of dust particles or permanent tape defects, ingenious error detecting methods have been developed. Data is recorded in eight of the nine tracks and the ninth track is occupied by the vertical parity (VP) bit (Fig. 5.3.2). Usually the fourth track is used for this VP bit. The VP bit is inserted during writing in such a way that the sum of the bits of each byte is odd. An additional bit is added to a track at the end of a block. These nine horizontal parity (HP) bits form the longitudinal check or LC byte. The bit is chosen such that the sum of the track is even.   Still another check, the so-called cyclical redundancy check (CRC), is performed. The data of one block is subjected to some calculations and the resulting byte is written between the block and the LC byte as shown in Fig. 5.3.2. The CRC byte enables the detection of multiple errors which might not show up with the parity checks. When errors are detected during writing, a standard routine repeats the writing process on a part of the tape which is shifted with respect to the original data block location. When errors are detected during reading, the reading process is repeated several times. When the error cannot be overcome (for example a dust particle remains in its position) action of the operator becomes necessary.

Another way to increase the reliability of magnetic tape stores is used by a manufacturer of small and relatively inexpensive computer systems. Each bit of a byte is recorded in two separate tracks, which requires broader 0.75 in tape, but eliminates the need for parity checking. An error rate of 1 part in 2.5×10^{10} is claimed, which is comparable to the error rates of other systems with parity check.

Tape speeds vary from 30 to 200 in s^{-1}, whereas the recording density is 800 bytes per in (bpi) when NRZI encoding is used with VP, HP and CR checks. A density of 1600 bpi is used with phase encoding. Due to the better error detection of this system, it is sufficient to perform only the VP check.

The highest data rate of 320 000 bytes/s is obtained with a tape speed of 200 ips and a recording density of 1600 bpi. At a recording density of 1600 bpi, 1600×9 bits are recorded on a piece of tape 1 in long and $\frac{1}{2}$ in wide, which gives a bit density of about 46 bits/mm^2 and a bit size of about 20 000 μm^2. It has been experimentally found that in thin layers of certain materials stable magnetic domains can be generated which are as small as 1 μm^2. This shows that there is still ample room for improvement with respect to the recording density in magnetic surface recording in general.

5.3.2. MAGNETIC DISK STORES

Commercial data processing requires storage of a large volume of records. In the early days of computers, magnetic tape was used for this purpose, but tape has the disadvantage that the average access time to an arbitrary record is very long. The desirability of random access to any record stimulated the development of the so-called disk file. The first disk file (1956) which was produced in some quantity was called RAMAC and consisted of 50 disks with a diameter of 24 in on one rotating shaft. Both sides of each disk were covered with iron oxide and had 200 concentric tracks each storing 400 bits. Access to a record was realized by moving an arm vertically to the selected disk and then horizontally to the selected track. In such a device the access

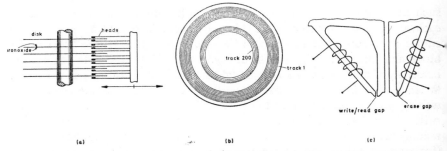

(a)   (b)   (c)

FIG. 5.3.3. (a) Disk store, (b) arrangement of tracks and (c) head with write/read and erase gap.

time to a bit consists of three terms: (1) the time necessary for the vertical motion of the head, (2) the time necessary for the horizontal motion of the head, and (3) the time between the moment the proper track is selected and the moment the bit passes beneath the head. The RAMAC could contain 80×10^6 bits and had an average access time of 0.15 s. In order to reduce the access time, the vertical motion of the head was soon abandoned and as many heads were mounted as there were recording surfaces.

Early disk stores however had a disadvantage not shown by tape stores since the disks with the records were fixed to a shaft and could not be removed, whereas a tape reel can be stored outside the tape storage unit. To remove this disadvantage, disk stores were constructed with exchangeable disk packs. Today the exchangeable disk store incorporating six or 11 disks has become the most popular peripheral storage device. Figure 5.3.3(a) is a schematic representation of a disk store. Each disk is covered on both sides with an iron oxide layer. The diameter of a disk is 14 in. The upper and lower surfaces of a disk pack are not used, so that six disks and 11 disks respectively provide 10 and 20 usable surfaces. The rotating speed is 2400 rpm, so that the maximum access time to a bit, when the head is already positioned on the track, is equal to 25 ms. The average access time is 12.5 ms. One disk surface (Fig. 5.3.3(c)) contains 200 tracks of which the total width is 2 in. The track width is only 125 μm wide. The bytes are stored in series along a track and not in parallel as on tape. Due to timing problems, it is not possible to store the eight bits of one byte on eight different magnetic surfaces. The information on a disk is grouped in sectors which can be addressed. NRZI recording is commonly used, although in newer disk stores phase encoding is employed to enable higher bit densities. Average track densities of about 2000 bpi are used. The disadvantage of disks is that the track density and therefore the output signal is a function of the track radius and needs electronic correction.

The magnetic heads are in close proximity (a few microns) to the magnetic surface. This is realized by having the head float on a thin layer of air. To ensure that the timing of an access to a bit location is the same for writing and reading the heads have only one gap for both purposes (Fig. 5.3.3(c)). In addition an erase gap is placed in the head. When a large number of tracks per inch is desired, it is best to have an erase head which erases the intertrack spaces after writing.

The horizontal motion of the head to find the proper track takes on the average about 60 ms. To reduce the access time, it makes more sense to improve the track access than to increase the rotation speed of the disk. To eliminate the horizontal motion of the head, heads are in development which contain 200 gaps, for each track one. Access would be performed by electronically switching from one gap to the other. However, such a head would require extremely flat surfaces. It appears that the disk pack store is firmly established in today's memory technology and that there is still room for technological improvement.

5.3.3. MAGNETIC DRUM, CARD OR STRIP STORES

Magnetic material can be deposited not only on tapes or disks, but on any kind of geometric shape, such as drums, cards, cartridges, strips etc.

The magnetic drum store is very old, in fact it was used as main memory in one of the first commercially successful machines, the IBM-650. A drum store consists of a metallic cylinder covered with a thin magnetic layer which typically rotates at 3000 rpm. Higher rotational speeds are not possible since too large stresses develop in the drum due to its rotation. The drum is divided (Fig. 5.3.4) into tracks and each track is served by one head. Some drum stores contain 800 heads. A combined write/read gap is common. To increase the recording density the heads have a suitable shape enabling them

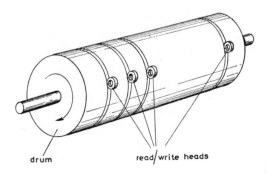

drum   read/write heads

FIG. 5.3.4. Magnetic drum with one magnetic head for each track.

to float on an air film a few microns above the drum surface. An advantage of such a structure is that small variations of the drum surface have no influence on the recording process.

The tracks are selected by electronically switching from head to head, thus the average access time is determined by the rotation speed of the drum and is equal to half the revolution time (10 ms.) Access-time of drum stores are, therefore, shorter than those of disk stores. A disadvantage of drum stores is that the drum is not easily exchangeable. It is for this reason that the drum store is on its way out, and is being replaced by the disk pack store.

Another kind of memory, the magnetic card store, has not gained wide acceptance either. A card store consists of a mechanism with which one card can be extracted from a card magazine. Such a card has a magnetic surface with, for instance, 100 tracks each containing 16 000 bits. With another mechanism the card is mounted on a rotating drum, where the card is read or written by a row of magnetic heads. Access times are rather long, about 500 ms and are mainly determined by the time necessary to bring the magnetic card from the magazine to the rotating drum. Mass stores with a capacity of 4×10^8 bytes have been constructed based on the above principle.

In a recently announced external memory a cartridge is used, which also can be transported to a write/read head.

5.4. MAGNETIC RECORDING MATERIALS

As already indicated in Section 5.2 the magnetic recording and reproducing process is very complicated and various theories have been presented to explain the many results found experimentally. Two approaches are possible. In the first, one tries to find analytical expressions for the head field components, the magnetic behaviour of the recording material and write and read transfer characteristics [5.4.1, 5.4.2]. Due to the many approximations, agreement between theory and experiment is only moderate. In the other approach [5.4.3], which will be followed here, the recording process is presented graphically and this provides a means of easily understanding how the different parameters affect the recording process. In the next sections we will discuss first the recording and reproducing process and investigate those material parameters which are most important. In the second section we will present the domain theory of recording surfaces and in the third section we will provide a review of the magnetic recording materials which are presently employed.

5.4.1. DIGITAL RECORDING THEORY

The recording process is rather difficult to visualize because the magnetic

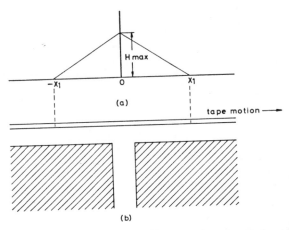

FIG. 5.4.1. Simple linear approximation of the magnetic head field.

surface is subject to a place and time dependent magnetic field. The magnetization state of a certain location on the magnetic surface is determined by the magnetic field as a function of time at this location. In most cases the maximum field determines the magnetization state, which simplifies the situation. Figure 5.4.1 shows a very simple approximation of the head field at a distance from the head surface. When the magnetic surface, for instance in the form of magnetic tape, passes the head, the tape is subjected to a linearly increasing field followed by a linearly decreasing field. Each piece of tape is subjected at a certain instant to the maximum field H_{max} and therefore this field will determine the final magnetization state.

When the field is abruptly switched on during tape motion, each part of the tape between 0 and x_1 will experience a maximum field, which is given by the linearly decreasing part of the field distribution and which is smaller than H_{max}, whereas the tape between $-x_1$ and 0 will always experience the maximum field H_{max}. The linear field distribution between $-x_1$ and 0 thus has no influence on the final magnetization state of the tape and therefore can be disregarded in the following discussions. Figure 5.4.2(a) shows the maximum field distribution along the tape, when the head current polarity is reversed a number of times as occurs in NRZI recording, when writing "ones". Figure 5.4.2(b) shows the magnetization distribution along the tape. When we assume the tape to be originally in the "0" direction at x_1, the field starts to reverse the magnetization. At x_2 the maximum field reaches the value H_1, so that the magnetization is fully in the "1" direction. When location x_6 of the tape is just above the centre of the headgap the current is reversed, so

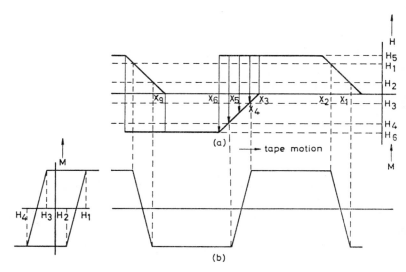

FIG. 5.4.2. (a) Maximum field distribution and (b) magnetization distribution along the tape.

that the part of the tape between x_6 and x_3 that experienced the maximum field H_5 in the past is now subjected to a linearly decreasing field between H_6 and 0 in the opposite direction. These field changes lead to the magnetization changes as shown in Fig. 5.4.2(b).

The tape areas x_2-x_1 and x_5-x_4 contain the "ones", whereas the intermediate areas x_4-x_2 and x_9-x_5 contain no information and should be reduced for large information density. The assumption is made, that the magnetization distribution is stable and does not change after leaving the head zone. With the help of the graphical representation of the recording process just discussed, some important relations between recording performance and physical material and head parameters can be illustrated.

Field gradient of recording head. As shown in Fig. 5.4.2 the width of the area x_2-x_1 for a given tape material depends on the head field gradient. If the gradient is very large, then the area x_2-x_1 will be very small. The bit density is not dependent on the gap length of the recording head but only on the field gradient at one of the edges of the head. Further, the field gradient must only be large for the field range between H_2 and H_1. An obvious way to increase the field gradient is to increase the head current. Yet this does not lead to the desired result. In reality the head field does not change linearly with distance as proposed above, but it changes in a more complicated way. This leads to the disagreeable fact, that the field gradient in the range H_2-H_1

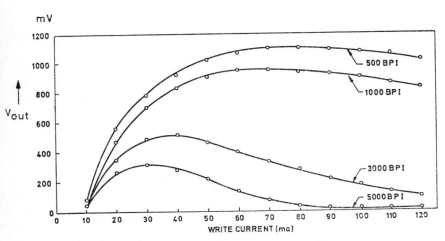

FIG. 5.4.3. Output signal of "ones" in NRZI recording as a function of write current and bit density [5.4.4].

decreases for increasing write current. The transition region x_2-x_1 becomes wider and the maximum possible bit density becomes smaller.

The effect of large write currents was measured by Morrison and Speliotis [5.4.4] on iron oxide tape. They measured the output signal of "ones" in NRZI recording as a function of write current and bit density. For large bit densities the output signal goes to zero for large write currents as is shown in Fig. 5.4.3.

Anisotropy of magnetic layer. Until now only the total field gradient was considered. However, a magnetic surface has a large demagnetization factor perpendicular to the surface, so that the magnetization is confined to the plane. Therefore, it can be expected that only the horizontal component of the head field is active. This is favourable since the horizontal field gradient of a conventional head is always larger than the total field gradient. To reinforce this effect it is advantageous to use very thin tape or to align the particles in the tape material such that the magnetization is oriented in the tape parallel to the direction of tape motion.

Thick magnetic layers. The influence of the head field gradient is also noticeable when thick magnetic layers are used or when "not in contact" recording, as in disk stores, is employed.

The field gradient decreases for increasing head distance. This can lead to a horizontal shift of the transition zone representing the "one" and to a broadening of the zone, both of which have a detrimental effect on the

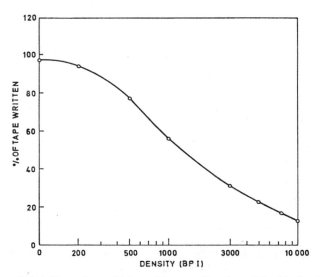

FIG. 5.4.4. Percentage of tape written as a function of the bit density.

recording density. It is therefore desirable to use layers as thin as possible, which require a large saturation magnetization to keep the output signal on a reasonable level. Due to the deterioration of the field gradient in thick layers at high bit densities, only the surface of the layer is recorded. This is illustrated in Fig. 5.4.4, where the percentage of tape written is plotted as a function of the bit density as measured by Morrison and Speliotis [5.4.4].

Rectangularity of the hysteresis loop. As shown in Fig. 5.4.2 the transition zone $x_2–x_1$ not only depends on the field gradient but also on the slope of the hysteresis loop. When the difference between H_2 and H_1 decreases, the transition zone in which the magnetization reverses sign also decreases. Indeed materials like CrO_2 with rather square hysteresis loops allow higher bit densities than Fe_2O_3.

Minimum head field and maximum bit density. With the graphic construction of the magnetization distribution as shown in Fig. 5.4.2 it is possible to determine the conditions for maximum bit density. As shown, at x_2 the field reaches H_1 so that the magnetization is in saturation beyond x_2. A further increase of the field has no influence on the transition regions representing the "ones". The head construction must be such that a large field gradient is obtained with the maximum field equal to H_1.

To increase the bit density, the next current reversal will follow the first as soon as possible. In Fig. 5.4.2(a) the zone $x_5–x_4$ is shifted to the right with

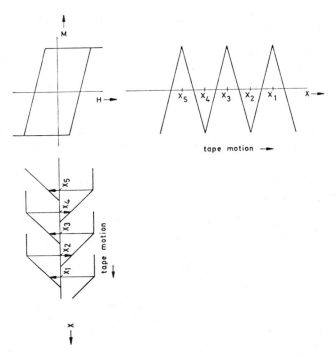

FIG. 5.4.5. Maximum bit density is obtained by reducing $x_4 - x_2$ in Fig. 5.4.2 to zero.

respect to zone x_2-x_1. Maximum bit density is reached when x_4 coincides with x_2. A further shift leads to the overlapping of the transition zones and a decrease of output signal. In Fig. 5.4.5 the situation of maximum bit density is constructed. Here the magnetization as a function of the co-ordinate is on the horizontal axis, whereas the field is drawn vertically.

In the above discussion we have assumed that the magnetization is stable and does not change when the tape leaves the head surroundings. In reality this proves to be a too rough an approximation. A magnetic layer written with a large bit density contains a large number of small areas in which the magnetization alternates. At the boundaries free magnetic poles occur which cause in these areas demagnetization fields which tend to reverse the magnetization. The greater the coercive force of the layer, the less the areas will be de-magnetized.

For stable recordings a large H_c, a small thickness and a low saturation magnetization are necessary. Since the read signal is proportional to both the magnetization and the thickness obviously a compromise must be sought.

With respect to the material properties, the following parameters prove to be important for the recording and reproducing process.

(1) Particle alignment. This increases the output signal and bit density, as only the horizontal field component is active.

(2) Thickness. Greater thickness leads to a lower bit density but also to larger signals.

(3) Saturation magnetization. A high saturation magnetization is favourable since a large signal can be combined with high bit density when thin layers are used.

(4) Coercive force. The coercive force must be large enough to prevent self demagnetization of recorded areas.

(5) Hysteresis loop form. Since the transition region is smaller in good rectangular loop materials, higher bit densities are obtained.

5.4.2. THEORY OF FINE MAGNETIC PARTICLES

Usually γFe_2O_3 tapes consist of a plastic tape coated with γFe_2O_3 powder embedded in a binder material. The packing factor is about one-third, which means that only one-third of the volume consists of magnetic material. When the iron oxide particles are relatively large, they consist of a number of domains in each of which the magnetization is in saturation (Fig. 5.4.6). The magnetization in the different domains need not be parallel, consequently the particle as a whole has a magnetic moment considerably smaller than the saturation magnetization value. When such a particle is subjected to a magnetic field, it appears that a relatively small field is sufficient to change the magnetic moment. This has the advantage that during writing only small head fields are required. However, a serious disadvantage is that due to self demagnetization the resulting magnetic moment is very low, which leads to small read signals. Therefore much research was focused on methods to increase the H_c of Fe_2O_3 particles. The low H_c results from the fact that the particles are divided into domains by domain walls and only small fields are necessary to displace these walls.

When particles can be made in which no domain walls exist, it can be expected that other magnetization reversal mechanisms will take place at probably higher coercive forces. It appears that this indeed occurs in very small particles. The theory describing the influence of the particle size on the reversal process is usually referred to as the single domain theory.

(i) *Critical particle size.* Several calculations of the critical particle size have been proposed in literature; the one by Kittel [5.4.5] illustrates the problem most clearly. In his model Kittel compares the energy of a single domain

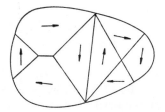

FIG. 5.4.6. Large Fe_2O_3 particles consist of many domains.

needle of square cross-section with the energy of one subdivided into domains as shown in Fig. 5.4.7. The width of the domain walls is assumed to be infinitely small. This assumption is not correct as Néel [5.4.6] has shown because the real wall width might be even larger than the particle size. Yet the results of Kittel's calculation have been shown to be reasonably valid.

The demagnetizing energy of the uniformly magnetized single domain needle is equal to

$$E_{dem} = \tfrac{1}{2} N M_s^2 D^2 L \qquad (5.4.1)$$

in which N is the demagnetizing factor in the long direction. D is the width, L is the length of the needle and M_s the saturation magnetization.

The wall energy is equal to

$$E_{wall} = \gamma DL \qquad (5.4.2)$$

when we neglect the small triangular closure domains. The critical size, below which the single domain is the most stable configuration, is calculated from

$$\tfrac{1}{2} N M_s^2 D^2 L = \gamma DL \qquad (5.4.3)$$

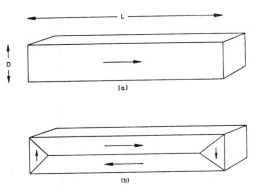

FIG. 5.4.7. Needle shaped particle: (a) in single domain state and (b) subdivided into domains.

giving a critical diameter of

$$D = \frac{2\gamma}{NM_s^2} \qquad (5.4.4)$$

A large length to diameter ratio giving a small N leads to a large critical diameter. The normally used Fe_2O_3 particles have a length to diameter ratio of five which gives a critical diameter of about $0.1 \ \mu m$.

(ii) *Coercive force of small particles.* When one assumes that the magnetization direction is uniform not only at zero external field but also during the switching process, it is rather easy to calculate the coercive force. Two different cases are usually considered.

(a) First, one assumes that the particle is spherical, so that the demagnetization field is independent of the direction. The material shows uniaxial anisotropy. When the magnetization makes an angle θ with the easy axis, the anisotropy energy is

$$E_k = K \sin^2 \theta. \qquad (5.4.5)$$

When the external field is applied parallel to the easy axis and antiparallel to the magnetization the field energy is

$$E_H = -M_s H \cos \theta. \qquad (5.4.6)$$

The total energy per volume is

$$E_{tot} = -M_s H \cos \theta + K \sin^2 \theta. \qquad (5.4.7)$$

For a given H, the angle θ is stable, for which E_{tot} is a minimum

$$\frac{\partial E_{tot}}{\partial \theta} = M_s H \sin \theta + 2K \sin \theta \cos \theta = 0. \qquad (5.4.8)$$

The solutions are $M_s H = -2K \cos \theta$ and $\sin \theta = 0$.

When $\partial^2 E/\partial \theta^2 > 0$ the solution of the above equation represents a minimum and θ is stable, whereas for $\partial^2 E/\partial \theta^2 < 0$ the solution represents a maximum. Transition from a stable to an unstable state will occur when $\partial^2 E/\partial \theta^2 = 0$.

$$\frac{\partial^2 E}{\partial \theta^2} = M_s H \cos \theta + 2K(\cos^2 \theta - \sin^2 \theta) = 0 \qquad (5.4.9)$$

These equations lead to the result that the field at which the magnetization will abruptly rotate from $\theta = 0$ to $\theta = \pi$ is given by

$$H_c = \frac{2K}{M_s}. \qquad (5.4.10)$$

When the material shows cubic anisotropy instead of uniaxial anisotropy, the expression is slightly different. In a practical tape the easy axes of the particles will be randomly oriented, which leads to an H_c which is about four times smaller than in the case of well aligned particles.

If one substitutes the right values for γFe_2O_3 [5.4.7], one obtains $H_c = 77$ Oe. This value is much smaller than the experimentally found ones. It appears that the model of spherical single domain particles with cubic anisotropy does not give a satisfactory explanation of the reversal in γFe_2O_3 tape.

(b) The second model represents a tape particle by an ellipsoid, without any magnetocrystalline anisotropy.

When no field is applied, the magnetization will be parallel to the long axis reducing the demagnetizing energy to a minimum.

When the magnetization makes an angle θ with the long axis, the total energy is expressed by

$$E_{tot} = \tfrac{1}{2}M_s^2(N_{//}\cos^2\theta + N_\perp \sin^2\theta) - M_s H \cos\theta. \qquad (5.4.11)$$

This leads to a coercive force:

$$H_c = (N_\perp - N_{//})M_s \qquad (5.4.12)$$

in which $N_{//}$ is the demagnetizing factor parallel and $N_\perp$ perpendicular to the long axis of the ellipsoid.

When we assume very long particles with $N_{//} = 0$ and $N_\perp = 2\pi$, we find, for γFe_2O_3, $H_c \approx 2500$ Oe [5.4.7] which is much larger than the experimentally found values.

The discrepancy between the experimental and the theoretical values has been the subject of many investigations, especially because similar problems showed up in the study of permanent magnetic materials. Some approaches to the problem started by assuming that the reversal process is not uniform and that during reversal the magnetization need not be parallel throughout the sample [5.4.8]. This indeed leads to lower coercive forces. Others [5.4.9] assumed that the particles form chains (Fig. 5.4.8). When a field is applied, the magnetization in adjacent particles rotates in opposite directions. This process, which is called "fanning", indeed leads to lower coercive forces. Even though discussion is still going on, there is a tendency to believe that the particle chain theory describes the reversal behaviour of γFe_2O_3 particles most satisfactorily.

(iii) *Remanence and particle alignment.* When no external field is applied and the interaction between particles is very weak, the magnetizations in all particles will be in the easy directions. Without any alignment during fabrication the easy axes and thus the magnetizations are then randomly

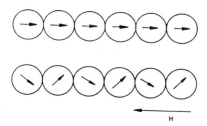

FIG. 5.4.8. Reversal of magnetic tape particles by "fanning".

oriented. After the application of a magnetic field, the resulting remanent magnetization is only half the saturation magnetization for uniaxial particles. To increase the output signal it is important to align the particles. This is done by passing the tape through a strong magnetic field while the coating is not yet hardened. The remanent magnetization then increases to about $0.8\,M_s$. Particle alignment is also important to increase the bit density, as we have seen in a preceding chapter.

(iv) *Superparamagnetism.* Large particles contain domain walls and have low coercive forces. Therefore it seems advisable to make the particles much smaller than the critical size for single domain behaviour. However, in such small particles other unwanted reversal processes occur, which are known as superparamagnetic reversal processes. When the volume V of a particle is decreased a stage is reached where the energy to reverse the magnetization $2VH_c\,M_s$ becomes of the same order as kT. In the absence of an external field the resulting remanent magnetization will decrease with time due to thermal activation [5.4.10]. The critical diameter below which superparamagnetism occurs is about 300 Å for γFe_2O_3 particles.

The remanent magnetization of superparamagnetic particles will slowly increase in small external fields. Such fields can exist due to neighbouring bits in a reel of tape. The effect is then called the "print through" effect.

To avoid this very disagreeable effect, it is necessary to produce tape in which the particle size is very well controlled and the size shows only a narrow distribution. A small percentage of very small particles will cause print through, especially when the working temperature is increased due to extended use or sunlight.

5.4.3. REVIEW OF MATERIALS

As discussed in the preceding sections, materials suited for recording media should show anisotropy, large saturation magnetization and rectangular hysteresis loops with coercive forces of the order of some 100 Oe. Similar requirements apply to the construction of permanent magnets. All materials used for permanent magnets could also be used for recording purposes. A large number of different recording materials could be the result. But because of tradition, economic considerations, ease of fabrication this has not occurred. Only one magnetic material has predominated the recording market, namely γFe_2O_3. Almost 99% of tapes, drums and disks are coated with a layer consisting of a dispersion of acicular γFe_2O_3 particles immersed in an organic binder.

A few other materials have also been investigated and used. Instead of the γFe_2O_3, another iron oxide has been proposed, namely Fe_3O_4. Also oxides in which Co or other divalent metal ions are substituted for the iron ions have been considered. At present the ferromagnetic oxide CrO_2 is getting attention because it promises a higher bit density, although at slightly higher cost. The volume packing fraction of oxide particles is below 40%. Since the bit density strongly depends on the layer thickness and the magnetization, the use of continuous metallic films can be fortuitous. In the following section the fabrication and the magnetic and recording properties of the different materials will be discussed with, of course, the main emphasis on γFe_2O_3.

(i) *Iron oxides*

(a) *Preparation.* The preparation of γFe_2O_3 consists of many steps (Fig. 5.4.9). The process starts with the formation of small nuclei of hydrated ferric oxide $\alpha FeO.OH$ by bringing together NaOH and $FeSO_4$ under agitation. These nuclei are used to produce light yellow acicular crystals in a mixture of $FeSO_4$, H_2O and Fe at 60°C through which air is bubbled [5.4.7]. The $\alpha FeO.OH$ crystals already have the size and shape of the final γFe_2O_3 particles and therefore careful adjustment of the process parameters is necessary.

After filtering, washing and drying, the $\alpha FeO.OH$ crystals are dehydrated, resulting in red crystals of αFe_2O_3

$$6\alpha FeO.OH = 3\alpha Fe_2O_3 + 3H_2O.$$

In the next step the αFe_2O_3 crystals are reduced by heating them in hydrogen at 300–400°C to black crystals of magnetite (Fe_3O_4).

$$3\alpha Fe_2O_3 + H_2 = 2Fe_3O_4 + H_2O.$$

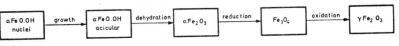

FIG. 5.4.9. Scheme of production process of γFe_2O_3 particles.

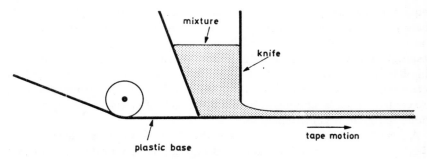

FIG. 5.4.10. Sketch of a knife tape coater.

Finally the magnetite crystals are reoxidized at 200–250°C in the presence of water vapour, to reddish-brown γFe_2O_3 particles

$$2Fe_3O_4 + \tfrac{1}{2}O_2 = 3\gamma Fe_2O_3.$$

To obtain magnetic layers of γFe_2O_3 on the surfaces of tapes, drums and disks a number of production steps have to be performed.

First the oxide must be carefully mixed with resins, additives and solvents [5.4.11]. The small γFe_2O_3 particles have a tendency to agglomerate and therefore the mixture must be thoroughly dispersed in a rotating ball mill to ensure that the oxide particles are uniformly distributed throughout the resin. The prepared mixture is, in the case of magnetic tape, applied to the plastic base material by a knife coater as shown in Fig. 5.4.10. The thickness of the layer depends on the distance between the bottom of the knife and the base film, the viscosity of the mixture and the coating speed. To orient the acicular particles, a magnetic field in the range of 1000–5000 Oe is applied in the direction of the tape motion. The alignment is not complete; instead of the expected $M_r/M_s = 1$, one finds values between 0.7–0.8 for commercial tapes. A completely random assembly of uniaxial particles would have 0.5. After orienting, the solvents are evaporated with the aid of heat resulting in a tape coating which contains 38–40% γFe_2O_3 by volume. This percentage cannot be increased, because the adhesion of the γFe_2O_3 particles to each other and to the plastic film cannot be ensured. Finally the broad tape is slit to its appropriate width by circular rotating knives and wound onto a reel. In the case of computer tape, the reel is completely tested. Actual recordings are made on all tracks to be sure that the tape is completely error free.

Similar techniques as were just described are used for the production of magnetic drums, disks and cards.

(b) *Structural and magnetic properties.* Gamma ferric oxide (γFe_2O_3) is a metastable phase of αFe_2O_3; when γFe_2O_3 is heated in air above 400°C it will transform into αFe_2O_3. To obtain γFe_2O_3 from Fe_3O_4 by oxidation it is important that the temperature be much lower than 400°C. Magnetite (Fe_3O_4) is the simplest example of a ferrimagnetic material with an inverse spinel structure (see also Section 3.2.2.5). The structure of Fe_3O_4 can be represented by

$$Fe^{3+}(Fe^{2+}.Fe^{3+})O_4,$$

where the brackets indicate so-called octahedral B sites, where the Fe ions are located on tetrahedral A sites, surrounded by four oxygen atoms. Due to the antiferromagnetic coupling between A and B site ions the magnetic moment per molecule is equal to four $(5+4-5 = 4)$ Bohr magnetons. A unit cell of the magnetite crystal contains eight molecules. On oxidation to γFe_2O_3 the oxygen lattice remains practically unchanged, only the lattice constant decreases slightly. However, the number of Fe-ions decreases from 24 to $21\frac{1}{3}$ per unit cell, causing $2\frac{2}{3}$ lattice vacancies per original unit cell:

$$Fe_8^{3+}(Fe_8^{2+}.Fe_8^{3+})O_{32} \rightarrow Fe_8^{3+}(Fe_{13\frac{1}{3}}.X_{2\frac{2}{3}})O_{32}.$$

The lattice vacancies are indicated by X. As the magnetic moment of a Fe^{3+} ion is five Bohr magnetons the original Fe_3O_4 unit cell has a resultant moment of $(13\frac{1}{3}-8)5 = 26\frac{2}{3}$ Bohr magnetons or $\frac{3}{32} \times 26\frac{2}{3} = 2.5$ Bohr magnetons per γFe_2O_3 molecule. The magnetic moment per unit volume is found with the relation

$$M_s = M_{mol}\, \rho\, \frac{\text{Avogadro's number}}{\text{molecular weight}}$$

in which M_{mol} is the moment per molecule and ρ the density. The theoretical value of M_s at 20°C is 413 G cm^{-3}, which is slightly larger than the experimentally found value.

When γFe_2O_3 is heated above 400°C it transforms into αFe_2O_3. In this oxide the lattice vacancies are no longer present and the spins of both Fe^{3+} ions are antiparallel so that the resulting magnetic moment is zero. Therefore this oxide is useless for recording purposes and its formation must be prevented during the fabrication of the desired γFe_2O_3 by keeping the temperature as low as possible.

In order to decide whether the coercive force of γFe_2O_3 particles is due to crystalline or shape anisotropy the crystalline anisotropy and the shape of the γFe_2O_3 particles must be known. Takei and Chiba [5.4.12] found from resonance experiments that $K_1 = -4.64 \times 10^4$ erg cm^{-3} and that the easy directions are parallel to the [110] crystal axes. As shown in Section 5.4.2

z

the coercive force H_c is equal to $2K/M_s$ in the case of uniaxial anisotropy. Since in γFe_2O_3 the anisotropy is not uniaxial and the particles are not well aligned the coercive force H_c will be smaller than $2K/M_s$ (230 Oe). Observed coercive forces are higher than this, so crystalline anisotropy cannot be the origin of H_c. This is confirmed by measurements of the temperature dependence of H_c. Although the crystalline anisotropy constant is highly temperature sensitive, H_c is constant over a large temperature range.

The γFe_2O_3 acicular particles used for magnetic tape, when observed by electron microscopy, have a length between 0.5 and 1.0 μm and a length-to-width ratio of 5 : 1. The coercive force H_c due to the shape anisotropy is equal to $2\pi M_s$, which is about 2500 Oe for γFe_2O_3, much larger than the observed values. Therefore, it is certain that in γFe_2O_3 particles no coherent rotation occurs but that reversal takes place by the fanning process.

The final stage in the γFe_2O_3 production process is oxidation of Fe_3O_4 to γFe_2O_3. Since Fe_3O_4 is also magnetic and the magnetic moment per volume (480 G cm^{-3}) is even larger than that of γFe_2O_3, the question is justified as to why this material is not used instead of γFe_2O_3. When γFe_2O_3 particles are reduced to Fe_3O_4 particles without changing the size and shape, observations show that H_c is also larger. The lack of popularity of Fe_3O_4 is due to a number of reasons of which the most important are the tendency of Fe_3O_4 to oxidize, the temperature dependence of H_c and disaccommodation effects, i.e. changes of the magnetization state with time.

The so-called cobalt substituted iron oxides are not very popular either. These oxides are obtained by substituting Co ions for iron ions in Fe_3O_4. From 2 to 10% Co substitution has been investigated. The coercive force increases very strongly and, it appears that an increased crystalline anisotropy is responsible for this. As a consequence, the coercive force is, just as in Fe_3O_4, very temperature dependent and disaccommodation effects have also been observed.

The thickness of γFe_2O_3 layers on tapes is usually between 5 and 12 μm and on disks between 1 and 5 μm. The properties of γFe_2O_3 layers have been adequate with respect to output signal and bit density. As shown in Fig. 5.4.11 a 12.5 μm γFe_2O_3 layer allows bit densities of up to 2000 bpi and a thinner layer even up to 5000 bpi [5.4.13]. In view of the standard 800 or 1600 bpi used in tape stores this performance is satisfactory.

(ii) *Chromium dioxide.* Recently chromium dioxide has become of interest since its recording properties are superior to those of γFe_2O_3 (5.4.14).

Acicular CrO_2 particles are prepared by hydrothermal decomposition of CrO_3 at high pressures (50–3000 atm) in the presence of such metal oxide catalysts as RuO_2 and Sb_2O_3 at temperatures between 300°C and 525°C. When 2% Sb_2O_3 is added, very acicular particles with lengths in the range

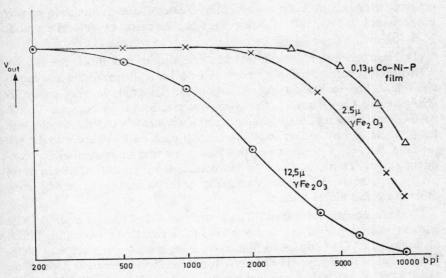

FIG. 5.4.11. Normalized output signal, employing "in contact" recording, as a function of bit density for a 2.5 μm and a 12.5 μm γFe_2O_3 layer ($H_c = 300$ Oe, write gap 4 μm, read gap 1 μm) and a 0.13 μm Co–Ni–P layer [5.4.13].

of 0.2–1.5 μm and axial ratios of 20 : 1 are obtained. The coercive force is between 350–650 Oe and due to shape anisotropy. The saturation magnetization is 490 G cm^{-3} and thus higher than that of γFe_2O_3. A disadvantage of CrO_2 is its low Curie temperature of 119°C, which makes its use at elevated temperatures risky. The higher production cost and the marginal improvement of recording behaviour with respect to γFe_2O_3 make it doubtful that CrO_2 will replace γFe_2O_3 as a computer recording material. Moreover, the high coercive force of CrO_2 tapes makes it difficult to use them on stores designed to work with lower H_c γFe_2O_3 tapes.

(iii) *Metallic films.* Thin metallic films of Co–Ni show high resolution capability without sacrificing the sense signal. Yet these films did not replace γFe_2O_3 because of other disadvantageous properties. Thin metallic films are rather soft and the adhesion to the plastic substrate is poor. This makes them unsuitable for contact recording.

For out-of-contact recording such as is applied in drum and disk stores, metallic films are sometimes used.

In contrast to γFe_2O_3 it is quite easy to change the remanent magnetization and the coercive force by changing the deposition parameters of metallic films and it is of interest to study the relation between magnetic and recording

Z*

properties. The literature on metallic films is extensive and remains in no way proportional to their use. Metallic films can be made by several methods [5.4.13].

(1) Electrochemical deposition: Metallic drums and disks are electroplated using a bath containing among many other additives nickel and cobalt chlorides. The saturation magnetization can be adjusted very easily by changing the Co–Ni ratio. The coercivity can be varied between 50 and 1500 Oe by changing the deposition parameters such as current density and temperature and by adding small amounts of chemicals. In order to deposit metallic films on a plastic base, this base must first be coated with a conducting film. Thin non-magnetic but conducting layers of Ni–P can autocatalytically be deposited from an aqueous solution containing among many other chemicals nickel chloride.

(2) Autocatalytic deposition: The above method of coating a plastic base with a conducting layer can be altered in such a way that the resulting film is also magnetic. Co and Co–Ni films containing a small percentage of phosphorus can be deposited. The coercive force and loop squareness depends on the P content and other parameters such as crystallite size, thickness and Co/Ni ratio.

(3) Vacuum deposition and sputtering: High coercive force magnetic films can be obtained by evaporating these films in a vacuum at a high angle of incidence. The high coercive force is attributed to the formation of somewhat elongated particles in the plane of incidence. It appears that the coercive force is due to shape and not to crystalline anisotropy. The composition of multicomponent layers is difficult to adjust when the elements have different vapour pressures. Therefore, multicomponent layers can also be obtained by the sputtering process. The coercive force of sputtered films is lower than that of high angle of incidence evaporated films.

The attraction of metallic film is its high saturation magnetization compared to that of an oxide film.

As discussed in Section 5.4.1 the resolution is determined by the head field gradient. This field gradient decreases for increasing head to tape distance. For high resolution, therefore, it is necessary to use very thin films. Using magnetic oxides with low saturation magnetizations and packing densities this would lead to too weak output signals. Metallic films do not have these disadvantages and can be made sufficiently thin for high resolution, keeping the sense signal at an acceptable level.

In Fig. 5.4.11 the resolution of metallic films is compared to that of γFe_2O_3 layers. As can be seen, the resolution is much better, whereas the output signal of the 0.13 μm Co–Ni–P film is about the same as that of the 2.5 μm γFe_2O_3 layer.

5.5. MAGNETIC RECORDING AND REPRODUCING HEADS

In the preceding sections the magnetic and recording materials have been discussed. It is self evident that an efficient use of the tape material can be made only when the head transducers are also well designed. The recording head converts an electrical signal into a magnetized area on a tape, whereas the reproducing head converts this magnetized area into a signal which should be a faithful copy of the original electrical signal, even at high bit densities.

5.5.1. RECORDING HEAD

As discussed in Section 5.4.1 the recording head should create a field parallel to the tape motion direction and in order to obtain a high bit density the longitudinal field gradient should be as large as possible. A recording head consists of a ring of soft magnetic material, such as laminated Mumetal or nickel–zinc ferrite, with a small non-magnetic gap. The leakage flux from the gap provides the recording field, which magnetizes the magnetic layer. The ring is magnetized by two symmetrically mounted coils (Fig. 5.5.1) and is usually divided into two sections for ease of fabrication and for reducing the influence of external stray fields. The field in the gaps is found from

$$\oint H dl = 2NI = 2H_m l_m + 2H_g l_g \qquad (5.5.1)$$

in which N is the number of windings of one coil, I is the current, H_m is the magnetic field in the magnetic material, H_g is the field in the air gaps, l_m is the magnetic path in one section half and l_g is the gap length.

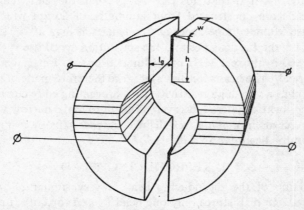

FIG. 5.5.1. Schematic diagram of a split-ring type magnetic head transducer.

Further we find in the gap

$$B_g = B_m = \mu_0 \mu_r H_m = \mu_0 H_g \qquad (5.5.2)$$

in which B_g and B_m are the magnetic flux densities at the head-gap interface and μ_r is the permeability of the head material. For the field in the gap we find

$$H_g = \frac{NI}{\dfrac{l_m}{\mu_r} + l_g} \cdot \qquad (5.5.3)$$

Since μ_r is large (for Mumetal $\approx 20\,000$) this expression reduces to

$$H_g = \frac{NI}{l_g} \cdot \qquad (5.5.4)$$

At a distance z above the centre of the head, the longitudinal field is [5.5.1].

$$H_{long} = \frac{NI}{l_g} \frac{2}{\pi} \arctan \frac{l_g}{2z} \qquad (5.5.5)$$

The field decreases to about 30% of the field in the gap at a distance equal to the gap length. When thick recording tape is used, the gap width should not be too small, as otherwise a part of the tape will not contribute to the recording process. In tape stores multitrack heads are used. A nine-track system has nine write heads side by side. The width of each track is 1.1 mm. The heads are separated from each other by Mumetal screens to prevent inductive crosstalk. At high bit densities and tape speeds, the permeability of the head is much lower than in the dc case. This is caused by eddy currents and, to a smaller degree by hysteretic losses. To prevent the eddy currents, the Mumetal heads are constructed from laminates of 25 μm which make it possible to use Mumetal tape heads at frequencies as high as 200 kHz.

In disk stores the bit densities and the revolution speed are such, that the operation speed is above 1 MHz and Mumetal can no longer be employed. Single track read/write heads for disk stores are therefore made of nickel–zinc ferrite, which has a very high resistivity, thus preventing eddy currents. Since ferrite is a very brittle material, it is very difficult to make narrow well defined gaps. One succeeds in making well defined narrow gaps by using very thin glass layers in the head gap [5.5.2].

5.5.2. REPRODUCING HEAD

The construction of the reproducing head is very similar to that of the recording head. In disk stores only one head is used for both functions. In the reproduction process the magnetized areas in the tape pass the magnetic head and induce a voltage proportional to the change of magnetization with time in the head coil. The gap and head should be constructed in such a way that a strong signal is obtained even at high bit rates. In contrast to the recording process, where the high frequency behaviour of the head depends on the material used for its construction and not on the gap width in the reproducing process, the gap width determines the maximum bit density. When the gap width is equal to two times the distance between two flux-reversals the signal will be very small. Therefore, it is necessary for the gap width to be much smaller than the bit density. In a tape store with 800 bpi the distance between bits is about 30 μm. In such a system, the read gap is 6 μm.

REFERENCES

[5.4.1] J. G. J. Fan, A study of the playback process of a magnetic ring head *IBM J.Res.Dev.*, **5**, 321–325, 1961.

[5.4.2] P. I. Bonyard, A. V. Davies and B. K. Middleton, A theory of digital magnetic recording on metallic films, *IEEE Trans. Mag.*, **MAG–2**, 1–5, 1966.

[5.4.3] J. Greiner, Der Aufzeichnungsvorgang auf Speicherband mit und ohne Vormagnetisierung bei kleinen Wellenlängen, *Frequenz*, **23**, 240–248, 1969.

[5.4.4] J. R. Morrison and D. J. Speliotis, The optimum write current for digital recording on particulate oxide and metallic recording surfaces, *Proc. Intermag.*, 12.4.1–12.4.8, 1965.

[5.4.5] C. Kittel and J. K. Galt, Ferromagnetic domain theory, *in* "Solid State Physics", Vol. 3, (eds. F. Seitz and D. Turnbull), Academic Press Inc., New York, pp. 437–564, 1956.

[5.4.6] L. Néel, Propriétés d'un ferromagnétique cubique en grains fins, *Compt. Rend. Acad. Sci. Paris*, **224**, 1488–1490, 1947.

[5.4.7] G. Bate and J. K. Alstad, A critical review of magnetic recording materials, *IEE Trans. Mag.*, **MAG–5**, 821–839, 1969.

[5.4.8] S. Shtrikman and D. Treeves, The coercive force and rotational hysteresis of elongated ferromagnetic particles, *J. Phys. Radium*, **20**, 286–289, 1959.

[5.4.9] I. S. Jacobs and C. P. Bean, An approach to elongated fine-particle magnets, *Phys. Rev.*, **100**, 1060–1067, 1955.

[5.4.10] C. P. Bean and D. J. Livington, Superparamagnetism, *J. Appl. Phys.*, **30**, 120s–129s, 1959.

[5.4.11] D. F. Eldridge, Magnetic tape production and coating techniques, *Memorex monograph* 4, 1965.

[5.4.12] H. Takei and S. Chiba, Vacancy ordering in epitaxially grown single crystals of γFe_2O_3, *Jap. J. Phys.*, **21**, 1255–1263, 1966.

[5.4.13] D. E. Speliotis, Magnetic recording materials, *J. Appl. Phys.*, **38**, 1207–1214, 1967.

[5.4.14] D. E. Speliotis, A digital recording study of CrO_2 particulate media, *IEEE Trans. Mag.*, **MAG–4**, 553–557, 1968.

[5.5.1] E. D. Daniel, The influence of some head and tape constants on the signal recorded on a magnetic tape, *Proc. IEE.*, **100**, 168–175, 1953.

[5.5.2] S. Duinker, Durable high resolution ferrite transducer heads employing bonding glass spacers, *Philips Res. Rep.*, **15**, 342–367, 1960.

SUBJECT INDEX

A

Access time, 77
Accumulation, 272
Acoustic gain, 37
Acousto-optic deflector, 339–344
Acousto-optic materials, 341
Akhieser attenuation, 33–35
Aluminium oxide, 246
Amorphous films, 173–175, 360
"Angel fish" bubble mover, 162
Anisotropy energy, 150, 176, 386
Associative
   bipolar cell, 219–221
   matrix memory, 202–203
   MOSFET cell, 221–223

B

Babbage, Charles, 4
Bandwidth-delay product, 19
Barium titanate, 191
BCS theory, 309
Beam accessible memories, 333–364
Bipolar flip-flop, 282
Bipolar memory devices, 281–307
Bloch walls, 182
Bragg diffraction, 341
Bubble
   detection devices, 167–169
   diameter, 178
   generator, 160–161
   logic devices, 169
   memory substrates, 173
   propagation circuits, 162
   transfer circuits, 165–167
Bucket-brigade delay line, 224–226
Bulk wave
   delay lines, 43–52
   transducers, 49–52
Burgers vector, 38

Byte, 374

C

"Cache" memory, 3
CCD memory
   charge transfer, 278
   input devices, 277
   organization, 280
   output devices, 278
   signal regeneration, 280
Central processing unit (CPU), 2
Charge coupled devices (CCD), 269–281
Charge coupled shift register, 226–229
Charge transfer process, 275–277
Chemical vapour deposition (CVD), 170–172
Chevron, 164
Chevron bubble stretcher, 169
"Chinese letter" detector, 169
Chromium dioxide, 392
Coincident current selection, 83
Collector diffusion isolation, 296–297
Compensation point writing, 353
Complementary MOSFET inverter (CMOS), 265–268
Computer architecture, 1–4
Conductor access method, 158
Critical particle size, 384–386
Crossed film cryotron, 312
Crowe cell, 314
Cryostat, 322
Cryotron, 309–313
Curie point, 191, 356
Curie point writing, 352
Current mode logic (CML), 283
Current steering, 310–313
Cycle time, 77
Cyclical redundancy check (CRC), 375